5

SMP**interact**

Higher

1

for **AQA, Edexcel** and **OCR two-tier GCSE mathematics**

CAMBRIDGE
UNIVERSITY PRESS

The School Mathematics Project

Writing and editing for this edition   John Ling, Paul Scruton, Susan Shilton, Heather West
SMP design and administration   Melanie Bull, Pam Keetch, Nicky Lake, Cathy Syred, Ann White

The following people contributed to the original edition of SMP Interact for GCSE.

Benjamin Alldred	David Cassell	Spencer Instone	Susan Shilton
Juliette Baldwin	Ian Edney	Pamela Leon	Caroline Starkey
Simon Baxter	Stephen Feller	John Ling	Liz Stewart
Gill Beeney	Rosemary Flower	Carole Martin	Biff Vernon
Roger Beeney	John Gardiner	Lorna Mulhern	Jo Waddingham
Roger Bentote	Colin Goldsmith	Mary Pardoe	Nigel Webb
Sue Briggs	Bob Hartman	Paul Scruton	Heather West

CAMBRIDGE UNIVERSITY PRESS
Cambridge, New York, Melbourne, Madrid, Cape Town, Singapore, São Paulo, Delhi, Mexico City

Cambridge University Press
The Edinburgh Building, Cambridge CB2 8RU, UK

www.cambridge.org
Information on this title: www.cambridge.org/9780521689915

© The School Mathematics Project 2006

First published 2006
3rd printing 2013

Printed in India by Replika Press Pvt. Ltd

A catalogue record for this publication is available from the British Library

ISBN 978-0-521-68991-5 paperback

Typesetting by The School Mathematics Project
Technical illustrations by The School Mathematics Project and Jeff Edwards
Illustration on page 24 by Matthew Soley; other illustrations by Robert Calow and Steve Lach at Eikon Illustration
Cover design by Angela Ashton
Cover image by Jim Wehtje/Photodisc Green/Getty Images

The authors and publisher thank the following for supplying photographs: page 206 Astrid and Hanns-Frieder
Michler/Science photo library (amoeba), Manfred Kage/SPL (diatom, radiolarium), Custom Medical Stock Photo/SPL
(red blood cells), Biophoto Associate/SPL (chromosomes), CNRI/SPL (basophil), Barry Dowsett/SPL (ebola virus),
EM Unit, VLA/SPL (scrapie virus), Dr Kari Lounatmaa/SPL (influenza virus); all other photographs by Graham Portlock

The authors and publisher are grateful to the following examination boards for permission to reproduce questions
from past examination papers, identified in the text as follows.

AQA	Assessment and Qualifications Alliance
Edexcel	Edexcel Limited
OCR	Oxford, Cambridge and RSA Examinations
WJEC	Welsh Joint Education Committee

The authors, and not the examination boards, are responsible for the method and accuracy of the answers to
examination questions given; these may not necessarily constitute the only possible solutions. The AQA questions
reproduced on pages 35 and 52, and as T3, T4 and T8 on page 184 are not from the live examinations for the
specification current at the date of publication of this book; new specifications were introduced in 2003.

Using this book

This book, *Higher 1*, is the first of two main books for Higher tier GCSE and is suitable as the year 10 text for students who have followed any 'extension' course in key stage 3. It is also designed to follow on from *Higher transition*, a preparatory key stage 4 text for students who have followed a 'core' key stage 3 course.

The 'check-up' on pages 8–10 is designed to help identify topics assumed in this book, but which may have been missed earlier or need to be revised.

To help users identify material that can be omitted by some students – or just dipped into for revision or to check competence – chapter sections estimated to be at national curriculum level 6 are marked as such. These levels are also given in the detailed contents list on the next few pages.

At the end of the contents list is a precedence diagram to help those who want to use chapters selectively or in a different order from that of the book.

Each chapter begins with a summary of what it covers and ends with a self-assessment section ('Test yourself').

 Topics that can be used as the basis of teacher-led activity or discussion – with the whole class or smaller groups – are marked with this symbol.

There are clear worked examples – and past exam questions, labelled by board, to give the student an idea of the style and standard that may be expected, and to build confidence.

Questions to be done without a calculator are marked with this symbol.

Questions marked with a star are more challenging.

 Suggestions for work on a spreadsheet, web searches and use of a graph plotter are marked with these symbols.

After every few chapters there is a review section containing a mixture of questions on previous work.

The small number of resource sheets linked to this book can be downloaded in PDF format from www.smpmaths.org.uk and may be printed out for use within the institution purchasing this book.

Practice booklets

There is a practice booklet for each students' book. The practice booklet follows the structure of the students' book, making it easy to organise extra practice, homework and revision. Unlike the students' books, the practice booklets do not contain answers; these can be downloaded in PDF format from www.smpmaths.org.uk

Contents

continues >

The precedence diagram below, showing all the chapters, is designed to help with planning, especially where the teacher wishes to select from the material to meet the needs of particular students or to use chapters in a different order from that of the book. A blue line connecting two chapters indicates that, to a significant extent, working on the later chapter requires competence with topics dealt with in the earlier one.

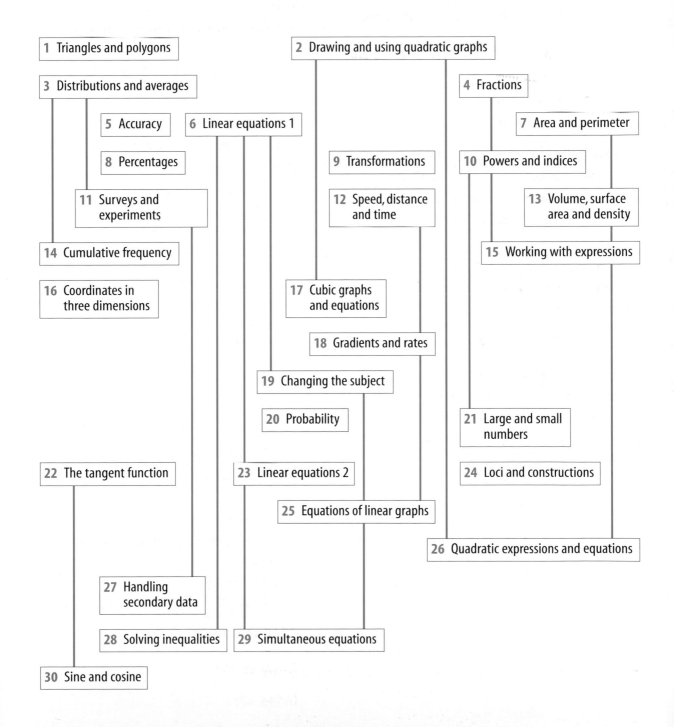

Check-up: what you should already know

This is designed to provide guidance on whether topics assumed in this book have been covered and understood.

Each question is labelled in blue with the number of a chapter in *Higher transition*, the optional preparatory book for this GCSE tier: if you have difficulty with a question, it may help to work through part of the corresponding *Higher transition* chapter.

In red, to the right of each question, is the number of the chapter in this book, *Higher 1*, that first depends on the assumed ideas.

It is best if a few questions are tried at a time and the reasons for any difficulties are considered carefully. The check-up is not intended as a formal test to be worked through in one go at the start of the course.

Ch 1 **(a)** Write down   **Ch 3**

    (i) 20 853 to the nearest hundred   **(ii)** 4.6072 to 2 decimal places

    (iii) 13 642.6 to 3 significant figures   **(iv)** 0.005 351 to 2 significant figures

  (b) A bar of chocolate weighing 155 grams is shared out equally among 6 people. How much should each person receive? Give your answer to a sensible degree of accuracy.

Ch 3 **(a)** Simplify by cancelling, then evaluate   **(i)** $\dfrac{21 \times 45}{30}$ **(ii)** $\dfrac{14}{16} \times 24$ **Ch 4**

  (b) 220 g of Stilton cheese contains 78 g of fat. To the nearest gram, how much fat does 160 g of this cheese contain?

  (c) 1 mile is equivalent to 1.609 34 km. A lunar probe is 220 470 km from Earth. Give this distance in miles, to the nearest 10 miles.

Ch 4 **(a)** Work these out, simplifying each answer where possible.   **Ch 4**

    (i) $\frac{1}{4} + \frac{1}{3}$ **(ii)** $\frac{3}{5} - \frac{1}{6}$ **(iii)** $\frac{2}{3} \div 4$ **(iv)** $1\frac{1}{4} \times \frac{2}{5}$

  (b) Give as a decimal   **(i)** $\frac{2}{5}$ **(ii)** $\frac{3}{8}$ **(iii)** $\frac{1}{25}$

Ch 6 **(a)** In a sale, a DVD is reduced by 20% from its previous price of £16.00. What is its sale price?   **Ch 8**

  (b) Val's council tax goes up from £1356 to £1421. What percentage increase is this?

  (c) The price of a holiday is cut from £895 to £695. What is the percentage reduction?

Ch 7 This table gives the numbers of different types of season ticket holder at a swimming pool.   **Ch 11**

Females aged 30 or above	205
Females under 30	103
Males aged 30 or above	194
Males under 30	164

  (a) Draw a pie chart for the data.

  (b) Approximately what fraction of all the season ticket holders are males under 30?

  (c) Briefly compare the data for the different age groups.

Ch 8 **(a)** The hypotenuse of a right-angled triangle is 9.7 m long and one of the other sides is 7.2 m long. Find the length of the third side. **Ch 7**

(b) Find, to 1 d.p., the length of the line segment joining the points $(^-2, ^-4)$ and $(5, 2)$ on a coordinate grid of centimetre squares.

Ch 9 **(a)** What is the value of $4(8 - 3x)$ when $x = 2$? **Ch 6**

(b) Write each of these in its simplest form without brackets.

(i) $6 + 3h - 5 - 5h$ **(ii)** $4(3k - 1)$ **(iii)** $\dfrac{16n - 24}{8}$

(c) Carol has 4 bags of sweets, each containing x sweets. She eats 10 sweets herself. She shares the remainder equally with her sister. Write an expression for the number of sweets each person now has.

Ch 10 Draw a possible net of a cuboid that measures 3 cm by 4 cm by 5 cm. **Ch 13**

Ch 11 **(a)** Solve each of these equations. **Ch 6**

(i) $2x + 15 = 9x + 1$ **(ii)** $5(4 - n) = n + 2$ **(iii)** $3(2y + 5) = 8(y - 4)$

(b) Solve this problem using algebra.

> I think of a number.
> I subtract 8.
> I multiply by 3.
> My answer is the same as the number I started with.
> What was my number?

Ch 12 **(a)** List all the powers of three between 5 and 500. **Ch 8**

(b) What is the value of 'two to the power five'?

(c) For each of these, write the value of k that makes it true.

(i) $6^4 = k$ **(ii)** $2^k = 16$ **(iii)** $k^3 = 125$ **(iv)** $10^k = 10$

Ch 13 **(a)** What is the value of each of these when $x = ^-5$? **Ch 2**

(i) $2x + 1$ **(ii)** $6(3 - x)$ **(iii)** $x^2 - 3$ **(iv)** $1 - 2x^2$

(b) Solve each of these equations. Check that each solution works.

(i) $6 - 5x = 21$ **(ii)** $3n + 5 = 2(5n + 6)$ **(iii)** $1 - 9k = 9 - 5k$

Ch 14 **(a)** On the same set of axes, draw the graphs of $x + 3y = 6$ and $y = x - 1$. **Ch 2**

(b) Estimate, to 1 d.p., the coordinates of the point where the graphs cross.

Ch 15 Use a calculator to evaluate these, correct to 1 decimal place. **Ch 7**

(a) 4×2.6^2 **(b)** $\dfrac{4.3 + 2.6}{2} \times 3.8$ **(c)** $\sqrt{\frac{2}{3}}$

Ch 16 Make the bold letter the subject of each of these formulas. **Ch 19**

(a) $h = 3\boldsymbol{k}$ **(b)** $y = 2\boldsymbol{x} + 5$ **(c)** $m = 7 + 4\boldsymbol{n}$ **(d)** $a = 5\boldsymbol{b} - 3$

Ch 19 **(a)** Evaluate the following expressions, given that $a = 3$, $b = {}^-1$ and $c = 6$.   **Ch 7**

        (i) $\dfrac{ac}{9}$ **(ii)** $\frac{1}{2}bc$ **(iii)** $\dfrac{c(a+b)}{4}$

     (b) Given that $p = 2.6$, $q = 5.3$ and $r = {}^-4.7$, evaluate the following expressions to 1 d.p.

        (i) $3r^2 - q$ **(ii)** pq^2 **(iii)** $\dfrac{2p^2 - q^2}{4r}$

     (c) Find the area of a triangle with base 120 cm and height 2.4 m, stating the units of your answer clearly.

Ch 20 The rectangular design on a certain postage stamp is 25 mm wide by 30 mm high.   **Ch 9**

     (a) A scaled-up copy of the stamp is made. The design is now 40 mm wide by 48 mm high. By what scale factor has it been enlarged?

     (b) The designer of the stamp originally produced a rectangular design 125 mm wide by 150 mm high. This was then scaled down to the dimensions given at the start of this question. What scale factor, as a decimal, was used?

Ch 21 **(a)** **(i)** List all the integers that satisfy the inequality ${}^-2 < x < 5$.   **Ch 3**

        (ii) State three different numbers that satisfy the inequality $2 < x \leq 3$.

     (b) Using w to represent weight in kilograms, use inequality symbols to write the statement: 'The weight must be at least 22 kg but no more than 31 kg.'

Ch 22 **(a)** The first five terms of a linear sequence are 5, 8, 11, 14, 17, …   **Ch 25**
        Write an expression for the nth term and use it to evaluate the 100th term.

     (b) An expression for the nth term of a sequence is $3n^2 - 2$.
        Write down the first five terms of this sequence.

Ch 23 This table shows how some 15-year-olds spent their leisure time one week.   **Ch 11**

Hours watching TV	26	18	27	11	27	1	24	30	8	22	34	17	10
Hours doing exercise	6	9	8	9	3	12	5	7	14	8	2	12	19

Draw a scatter diagram with hours watching TV on the horizontal axis and hours doing exercise on the vertical axis.

Comment on any correlation between the two quantities.
If there is strong enough correlation, draw a line of best fit.

Ch 24 Point A has coordinates $({}^-2, 4)$ and point B has coordinates $(3, {}^-6)$.   **Ch 9**

     (a) Give the equation of the line through A that is parallel to the y-axis.

     (b) Give the coordinates of the mid-point of the line segment AB.

Ch 25 Simplify these expressions.   **Ch 6**

     (a) $(5n - 7) - (5 - 2n)$ **(b)** $2(3 - 5k) + 3(2k - 1)$ **(c)** $4(1 - x) - 3(x - 5)$

Ch 26 Evaluate these, giving your answers to 2 d.p where necessary.   **Ch 19**

     (a) 1.7^3 **(b)** $({}^-4)^2$ **(c)** $\sqrt[3]{-343}$ **(d)** $\sqrt{9.6^3}$ **(e)** $\sqrt[3]{\dfrac{2.6^2}{2.1}}$

1 Triangles and polygons

You will revise the names and properties of special triangles and quadrilaterals.

This work will help you

- use the sum of the interior angles of a triangle and of a quadrilateral
- use the interior and exterior angles of a polygon, including a regular polygon

A Special triangles and quadrilaterals

A1 This regular hexagon has been split into two trapeziums.

Draw sketches to show how a regular hexagon can be split into each of the following. Use triangular dotty paper if you like.

- **(a)** Three rhombuses
- **(b)** Six equilateral triangles
- **(c)** Four trapeziums
- **(d)** A kite and two isosceles triangles
- **(e)** A rectangle and two isosceles triangles
- **(f)** An equilateral triangle and three isosceles triangles
- **(g)** An isosceles triangle and two trapeziums

A2 This square has been divided into two right-angled triangles and a parallelogram.

Draw sketches to show how a square can be split into each of the following. Use square dotty paper if you like.

- **(a)** Two right-angled triangles
- **(b)** Three right-angled triangles
- **(c)** Two isosceles triangles and two trapeziums
- **(d)** A kite and two right-angled triangles
- **(e)** An isosceles triangle and two right-angled triangles
- **(f)** Two trapeziums
- **(g)** A square and four right-angled triangles

A3 A quadrilateral has rotation symmetry of order 4.
- **(a)** What is the name of the quadrilateral?
- **(b)** Describe some other special properties that it has.

B Angles of a triangle

The sum of the angles of a triangle is 180°.

B1 Work out the missing angles.

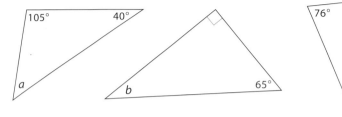

B2 Work out the missing angles in these isosceles triangles.

 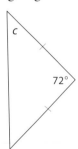 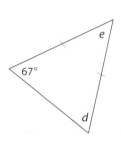 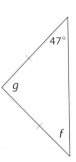

B3 Work out the angles marked with small letters.
Explain how you worked out each angle.

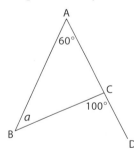 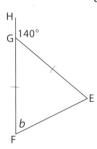 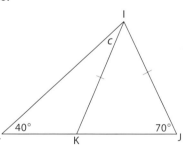 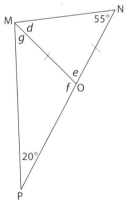

B4 Find the values of x and y.

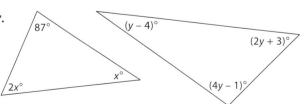

12   1 Triangles and polygons

C1 You can split a quadrilateral into two triangles like this.

(a) What is the sum of the 'black' angles?

(b) What is the sum of the 'white' angles?

(c) What is the sum of the interior angles of a quadrilateral?

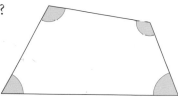

C2 Find the angles marked with letters.
Explain how you worked out each angle.

(a)
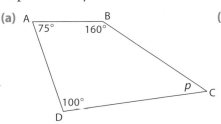

(b)
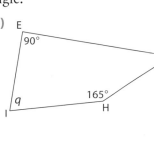

(c)

C3 (a) Draw any polygon and record how many sides it has.

Choose a vertex. Draw straight lines from it to all the other vertices.

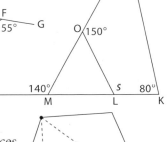

(b) How many triangles have you made?

(c) What is the total of all the angles in the triangles?

(d) From your answer to (c) write the total of
all the interior angles of your polygon.

(e) Do (a) to (d) again, for a polygon with a different number of sides.

(f) Suppose the polygon you start with has n sides.
Go through (a) to (d) again to find a formula for the total of the interior angles.

The method of reasoning in C3 (f) is an example of mathematical deduction.
We assumed it's true that the angles of a triangle add up to 180°.
We then used this assumption in a sequence of steps leading to a statement
about any polygon that can be split into triangles as in the diagram:

The sum of the interior angles of a polygon with n sides is $180(n-2)°$.

C4 What is the sum of the interior angles of an 11-sided polygon?

C5 For each of these polygons,

    (i) record the number of sides

    (ii) work out the sum of the interior angles

    (iii) work out the missing angle

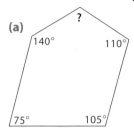

(a)

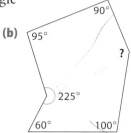

(b)

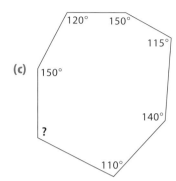

(c)

C6 Each of these polygons has one line of reflection symmetry. Work out the missing angles.

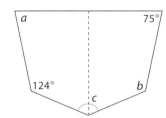

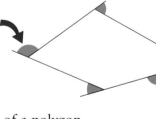

C7 The sum of the interior angles of a certain polygon is 2160°. How many sides does it have?

A **regular** polygon has all its sides equal and all its angles equal.

C8 Find the size of each interior angle of

    (a) a regular hexagon   **(b)** a regular nonagon (nine sides)

If you extend a side of a polygon, the angle made is called an **exterior angle**.

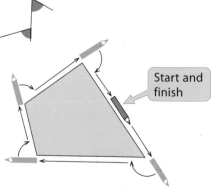

C9 If a pencil is moved around the sides of a polygon, at each vertex it turns through the exterior angle.

    (a) When the pencil gets back to where it started from, it will be pointing in the same direction as before. What angle has it turned through?

    (b) What is the sum of the exterior angles of a polygon?

Start and finish

The sum of the exterior angles of a polygon is 360°.
This is true however many sides it has.

C10 For each of these polygons,

  (i) find the missing exterior angle or angles

  (ii) work out the interior angle at each vertex

  (iii) work out the total of the interior angles.
  Use the formula from C3 to check whether
  this total agrees with the number of sides of the polygon.

(a)

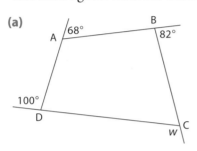

(b)

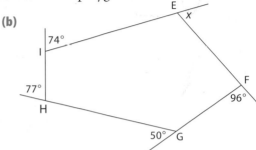

(c)

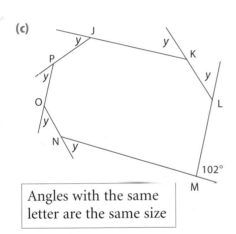

Angles with the same
letter are the same size

(d)

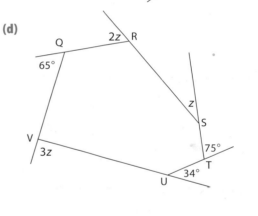

C11 This is a regular 12-sided polygon (a dodecagon).
Each exterior angle is marked e.

Calculate the size of e.

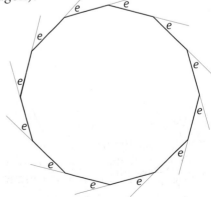

C12 Calculate the size of each exterior angle of a regular polygon with

(a) 5 sides (b) 24 sides (c) 30 sides (d) 45 sides

C13 This is a close-up a vertex of the dodecagon in C11.
What is the size of the interior angle, i?

C14 Calculate the interior angle for each regular polygon in C12.

C15 This is part of a regular decagon (a 10-sided shape).
Calculate the size of the interior angle of
the regular decagon.

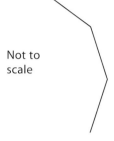

Not to
scale

OCR

C16 Each exterior angle of a certain regular polygon is 40°.
How many sides must this polygon have?

C17 How many sides does a regular polygon have if each exterior angle is

(a) 9° (b) 24° (c) 10° (d) 18°

C18 How many sides does a regular polygon have if each interior angle is

(a) 135° (b) 160° (c) 175° (d) 174°

C19 A regular polygon has n sides. Write an expression in n for

(a) the size of an exterior angle (b) the size of an interior angle

D Mixed questions

D1 PQRST is a regular pentagon.
Giving reasons for your answers, calculate

(a) angle a (b) angle b

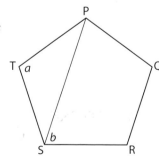

D2 Two interior angles of a kite are 70° and 100°.
What could be the other two angles?
(Draw sketches and give reasons.)

D3 ABCD is a rhombus and ABCE is a kite.
Work out the value of x.

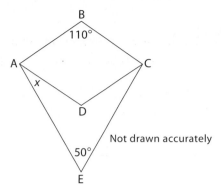

Not drawn accurately

AQA

*D4 A polygon like this cannot be divided into triangles by drawing lines
from one vertex as was done in question C3.

Does the formula $180(n-2)°$ for the sum of the interior angles of
a polygon still apply? Give your reasons.

Test yourself

T1 Calculate the lettered angles.

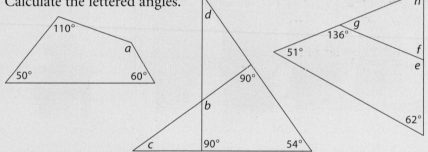

T2 The diagram shows part of a regular polygon.
Each interior angle is 162°.
Calculate the number of sides of the polygon.

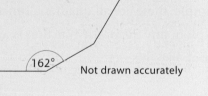

Not drawn accurately   AQA

T3 ABCDEFGHI is a regular nonagon.

Giving reasons, calculate angles x, y and z.

2 Drawing and using quadratic graphs

This work will help you

- substitute positive and negative numbers into quadratic expressions such as $2x^2 + x - 4$
- draw the graphs of quadratic functions and use them to solve equations and problems

A Parabolas and quadratic functions

Any object thrown, hit or fired into the air follows a path in the shape of a **parabola**.

A rule such as $y = 2x + 1$ is called a **function** as it links each value of x with one value of y.

A **quadratic** function has an equation of the form $y = ax^2 + bx + c$.
For example, these are all quadratic functions: $y = 2x^2 - 3$, $y = {}^-5x^2 + 2x - 7$, $y = 8 - x^2$.

The graph of any quadratic function is a parabola that has a vertical axis of symmetry.

It will look like this  or like this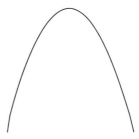

 Use a graph plotter to plot graphs of the form $y = ax^2 + bx + c$ for various values of a, b and c.
Include some negative values for a, b and c.

How can you predict which way up the graph will be?

To draw the graph of a quadratic function, first draw up a table of values.
Include a range of positive and negative values for x.

This is a table of values for $y = x^2$, the simplest quadratic function.

x	-2	-1.5	-1	-0.5	0	0.5	1	1.5	2
x^2	4	2.25	1	0.25	0	0.25	1	2.25	4

Plot the points shown by your table and join them with a **smooth** curve.

Label your graph with its equation.

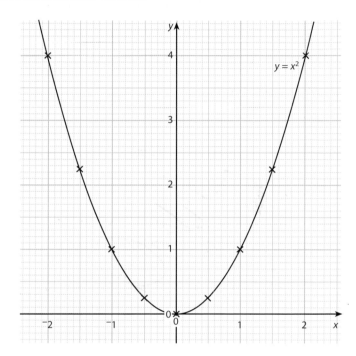

T Each of the graphs below is an attempt to draw $y = x^2$.
What is wrong with each one?

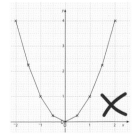 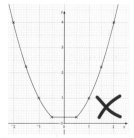 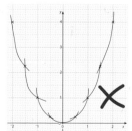 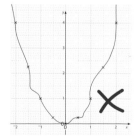

A1 Use the graph of $y = x^2$ above to answer these.

    (a) Find the approximate value of

        (i) 1.2^2 **(ii)** $(-1.9)^2$

    (b) Find the two solutions of the equation $x^2 = 2.5$, correct to 1 d.p.

    (c) What is the value of the positive square root of 2, correct to 1 d.p.?

    (d) What is the equation of the line of symmetry of the graph?

A2 (a) Copy and complete this table of values for $y = x^2 - 2$.

x	-2	-1	0	1	2
x^2	4	1			
$y = x^2 - 2$	2	-1			

(b) On graph paper draw a pair of axes with x from $^-2$ to 2, and y from $^-2$ to 2. Draw the graph of $y = x^2 - 2$.

(c) Use your graph to find the two solutions to the equation $x^2 - 2 = 0$, correct to 1 d.p.

(d) What value of x makes y smallest (a **minimum**)?

A3 (a) Copy and complete this table of values for $y = 2x^2 + 1$.

x	-2	-1	0	1	2
x^2	4			1	
$2x^2$	8			2	
$y = 2x^2 + 1$	9			3	

(b) Draw the graph of $y = 2x^2 + 1$ for values of x from $^-2$ to 2.

(c) What is the minimum value of y for this graph? How can you be sure your answer is right without plotting more points?

(d) Use the graph to solve the equation $2x^2 + 1 = 4$, correct to 1 d.p.

(e) Explain why there is no solution to the equation $2x^2 + 1 = 0$.

A4 (a) Copy and complete this table of values for $y = x^2 + x$.

x	-2	-1	0	1	2
x^2	4				
$x^2 + x$	2				

(b) Draw the graph of $y = x^2 + x$ for values of x from $^-2$ to 2.

(c) Use your graph to find the two solutions to $x^2 + x = 1$, correct to 1 d.p.

(d) On your graph draw the line of symmetry of $y = x^2 + x$. Write down the equation of the line of symmetry.

(e) (i) What value of x makes y a minimum?

(ii) Substitute this value of x into the equation and thus calculate the minimum value of y.

(iii) Compare this value with the minimum value given by your graph. How accurate was your graph?

A5 **(a)** Copy and complete this table of values for $y = x^2 + 2x - 4$.

x	$^-4$	$^-3$	$^-2$	$^-1$	0	1	2	3
x^2				1				
$2x$	$^-8$			$^-2$				
-4	$^-4$	$^-4$	$^-4$	$^-4$	$^-4$	$^-4$	$^-4$	$^-4$
$y = x^2 + 2x - 4$				$^-5$				

(b) Draw the graph of $y = x^2 + 2x - 4$ for values of x from $^-4$ to 3.

(c) What is the minimum value of $x^2 + 2x - 4$?

(d) Use your graph to solve the equation $x^2 + 2x - 4 = 0$, correct to 1 d.p.

(e) Solve the equation $x^2 + 2x - 4 = 1$, correct to 1 d.p.

A6 **(a)** Copy and complete this table for $y = 6 - x^2$.

x	$^-3$	$^-2$	$^-1$	0	1	2	3
x^2		4					9
$y = 6 - x^2$		2					$^-3$

(b) Draw the graph of $y = 6 - x^2$ for values of x from $^-3$ to 3.

(c) Use your graph to solve the equation $6 - x^2 = 3$, correct to 1 d.p.

(d) What value of x makes y a **maximum**?

A7 **(a)** Copy and complete this table for $y = 6x - x^2$.

x	$^-1$	0	1	2	3	4	5	6
$6x$						24		
x^2						16		
$y = 6x - x^2$						8		

(b) Draw the graph of $y = 6x - x^2$ for values of x from $^-1$ to 6.

(c) What is the maximum value of $6x - x^2$?

(d) Use your graph to solve the equation $6x - x^2 = 6$, correct to 1 d.p.

(e) Can you solve the equation $6x - x^2 = 10$?
Explain your answer.

A8 **(a)** Copy and complete this
table for $y = 2x^2 - 6x$.

(b) Draw the graph of $y = 2x^2 - 6x$
for values of x from $^-1$ to 4.

x	$^-1$	0	1	2	3	4
$2x^2$	2			8	18	
$6x$	$^-6$			12		
$y = 2x^2 - 6x$				$^-4$		

(c) Use your graph to solve the equation $2x^2 - 6x = ^-1$, correct to 1 d.p.

(d) **(i)** Calculate the minimum value of $2x^2 - 6x$.

(ii) Compare this value with the minimum value given by your graph.

A9 **(a)** Copy and complete this table for $y = x^2 - 4x + 4$.
(Add extra rows if you find it helpful.)

x	-2	-1	0	1	2	3	4	5
y								9

(b) Draw the graph of $y = x^2 - 4x + 4$ for values of x from -2 to 5.

(c) What is the minimum value of $x^2 - 4x + 4$?

(d) Solve the equation $x^2 - 4x + 4 = 5$, correct to 1 d.p.

A10 **(a)** Copy and complete this table for $y = 4 - \frac{1}{2}x^2$.

x	-4	-3	-2	-1	0	1	2	3	4
y									-4

(b) Draw the graph of $y = 4 - \frac{1}{2}x^2$ for values of x from -4 to 4.

(c) What is the maximum value of y?

(d) Solve the equation $4 - \frac{1}{2}x^2 = 0$.

A11 **(a)** Copy and complete the table of values for $y = 2x^2 - 4x - 1$.

x	-2	-1	0	1	2	3
y	15		-1		-1	5

(b) Draw the graph of $y = 2x^2 - 4x - 1$ for values of x from -2 to +3.
Use axes as shown here.

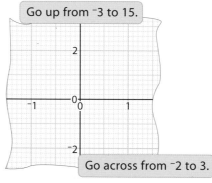

Go up from -3 to 15.

Go across from -2 to 3.

(c) An approximate solution of the equation $2x^2 - 4x - 1 = 0$ is $x = 2.2$.

(i) Explain how you can find this from the graph.

(ii) Use your graph to write down another solution of this equation.

AQA

B Using graphs to solve problems

B1 Julia throws a stone from the top of a cliff, as shown.

The equation of the path of the stone is $y = 60 - \frac{1}{2}x^2$.
(x and y are measured in metres.)

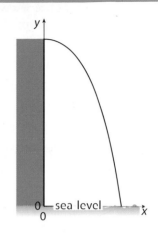

(a) Copy and complete this table for $y = 60 - \frac{1}{2}x^2$.

x	0	2	4	6	8	10	12
x^2	0	4	16	36			
$\frac{1}{2}x^2$	0	2	8	18			
$y = 60 - \frac{1}{2}x^2$	60	58	52	42			

(b) On graph paper, draw axes for x from 0 to 12 and for y from $^-20$ to 60.
Plot the graph.

(c) What is the height of the cliff?

(d) How far from the bottom of the cliff does the stone hit the sea?

(e) Use the equation to work out the value of y when x is 16.
Why is this information meaningless in this case?

B2 A ball is kicked so that it clears a fence. The diagram shows the path of the ball.

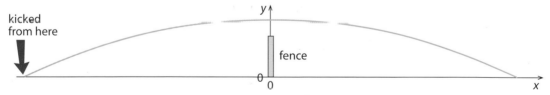

The equation of the path of the ball is $y = 4 - \frac{x^2}{144}$
(x and y are measured in metres).

(a) (i) Find the value of y when $x = 0$.

(ii) The fence is 2.5 metres high.
By how much does the ball clear the fence?

(b) (i) Find the value of y when $x = 24$.

(ii) How far from the fence is the ball kicked?

B3 A stone is dropped from a block of flats.
The height of the stone above the ground is given by $s = 125 - 5t^2$.
s is the height of the stone in metres.
t is the time in seconds from the release of the stone.

(a) Make a table using suitable values of t from 0 to 5.

(b) Draw the graph of $s = 125 - 5t^2$ for these values of t.

(c) Use your graph to estimate the height of the stone after 2.5 seconds.
Check your answer by calculation.

(d) (i) Use your graph to solve the equation $125 - 5t^2 = 75$.

(ii) What is the meaning of your answer?

B4 A children's toy is designed to project a small teddy bear
vertically into the air when a button is pressed.

The vertical height, h metres, of the bear above the firing point
t seconds after firing is given by the equation $h = 6t - 5t^2$.

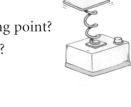

(a) Work out the values of h for $t = 0, 0.25, 0.5, \ldots$ up to $t = 1.5$.

(b) Plot the graph of $h = 6t - 5t^2$ for your values.

(c) What is the maximum height of the teddy bear above the firing point?

(d) How long after firing does it take the bear to reach this height?

(e) The bear is fired from a table 1 metre above the floor.
How long does it take to hit the floor?

*B5 A farmer has 20 metres of fencing.
He wishes to use it to form a rectangular enclosure
in the corner of a field, as in the plan view.

(a) Write down an expression for the area, $A\,m^2$,
enclosed by the fencing.

(b) Plot the graph of A for values of x
between 0 and 20.

(c) For what values of x is the area $40\,m^2$?

(d) What values of x give an enclosed area
greater than $90\,m^2$?

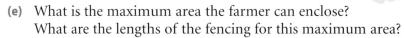

(e) What is the maximum area the farmer can enclose?
What are the lengths of the fencing for this maximum area?

*B6

Suppose that the farmer wishes to use $20\,m$ of
fencing to form a rectangular enclosure against
one side of a field, as in the plan view.

Investigate the area that can be enclosed.

Test yourself

T1 (a) Copy and complete this table for $y = x^2 - 3x$.

x	$^-1$	0	1	2	3	4
x^2	1	0		4	9	
^-3x	3	0		$^-6$	$^-9$	
$x^2 - 3x$	4	0		$^-2$		

(b) On graph paper draw a pair of axes with x from $^-1$ to 4 and y from $^-3$ to 5.
Draw the graph of $y = x^2 - 3x$.

(c) Use your graph to solve these equations correct to 1 d.p.

(i) $x^2 - 3x = 0$ (ii) $x^2 - 3x = 1$

(d) What value of x makes y a minimum?

T2 (a) Copy and complete the table of values for $y = 8x - x^2$.

x	0	1	2	3	4	5	6	7	8
y	-	7	12			15	12	7	0

(b) On axes like these draw the graph of $y = 8x - x^2$.

(c) Use your graph to solve the equation $8x - x^2 = 6$.

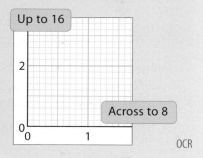

OCR

T3 A cannonball is fired from a cannon.

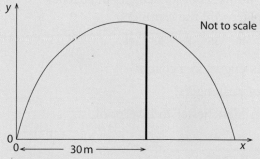

Not to scale

The equation of its path is $y = \dfrac{x}{2} - \dfrac{x^2}{80}$.

The cannonball just clears a wall which is 30 metres horizontally from the cannon, and lands on the ground on the other side.

(a) How high is the wall?

(b) Find the value of y when

(i) $x = 10$ (ii) $x = 40$ (iii) $x = 20$

(c) How far from the wall does the cannonball land?

3 Distributions and averages

You will revise how to

- find the mean, median, range and mode of a set of data
- use a stem-and-leaf table

This work will help you

- use a grouped frequency table
- estimate the mean from a grouped frequency table
- draw a frequency polygon

A Review: mean, median, range and mode   level 6

For a set of data,

- the **mean** is $\dfrac{\text{the sum of the values}}{\text{the number of values}}$

- the **median** is   the middle value or the mean of the two middle values when the values are put in order of size

- the **range** is   the highest value minus the lowest value

- the **mode** is   the value that occurs most often

A1 A coach company kept a record of the numbers of passengers in coaches from Manchester to Sheffield one day. Here are the numbers.

| 34 | 27 | 41 | 48 | 30 | 33 | 29 | 44 | 40 | 36 | 28 | 33 | 45 |

(a) What is the median number of passengers in a coach?

(b) What is the range of the number of passengers?

Here are the numbers for coaches from Manchester to Liverpool.

| 26 | 29 | 38 | 42 | 27 | 29 | 25 | 37 | 38 | 41 | 33 | 32 |

(c) What are the median and range of this set of data?

(d) Write a couple of sentences comparing the two sets of data.

(e) Calculate the mean number of passengers in each of the two sets of coaches.

(f) If you compare using the means, do you come to the same conclusion as with the medians?

Stem-and-leaf tables

Here are the ages of the members of a club.

45	22	19	26	18	30	48	55	27	38
33	61	47	33	28	40	41	37	56	20
47	53	22	54	27	31	25	24	58	39

To make a stem-and-leaf table of the ages, use the tens digit as the 'stem' and the units digit as the 'leaf'.

<table>
<tr><td>Here the first two numbers, 45 and 22, have been entered.</td><td>Now all the numbers have been entered.</td><td>Finally the 'leaves' are put in order of size.</td></tr>
<tr><td>

```
1 |
2 | 2
3 |
4 | 5
5 |
6 |
```

</td><td>

```
1 | 9 8
2 | 2 6 7 8 0 2 7 5 4
3 | 0 8 3 3 7 1 9
4 | 5 8 7 0 1 7
5 | 5 6 3 4 8
6 | 1
```

</td><td>

```
1 | 8 9
2 | 0 2 2 4 5 6 7 7 8
3 | 0 1 3 3 7 8 9
4 | 0 1 5 7 7 8
5 | 3 4 5 6 8
6 | 1
```

</td></tr>
</table>

A2 From the stem-and-leaf table above, find

(a) the median age   (b) the range of the ages   (c) the modal age group

A3 (a) Make a stem-and-leaf table for this set of examination marks.

(b) Find the median mark and the range of the marks.

Marks out of 80

56	39	47	28	66	72	24	35	47	58
63	70	30	49	56	44	68	41	55	47
69	31	71	63	55	39	28	44	51	70

A4 (a) Make a stem-and-leaf table for this set of data. Use the units digit as the stem and the tenths digit as the leaf.

(b) Find the median weight and the range of the weights.

Weights, in kg, of 30 newborn babies

2.5	3.2	1.7	2.6	3.8	4.2	3.6	2.8	1.9	0.8
4.0	2.7	3.1	3.0	3.3	2.8	1.8	2.6	1.7	2.7
3.5	3.5	2.9	3.3	2.2	3.6	1.5	1.7	2.8	3.7

A5 Write a couple of sentences comparing the boys' and girls' test marks shown in this double stem-and-leaf table.

Boys		Girls
5 5 4 3 3 2	4	1 3 6
8 6 6 4 2 2 1 0	5	2 5 5 7 8
7 7 4 2 2 1	6	1 3 3 5 7 8 9 9
5 4 2	7	0 2 4 4 6 7 8

stem = 10 marks

A6 This stem-and-leaf table shows the weights, in kg, of the members of a rugby team.

(a) Find the median weight.

(b) Find the mean weight.

```
6 | 5 8
7 | 0 2 3 3 7 8 9 9
8 | 2 3 4 4 5
```

stem = 10 kg

Frequency tables and charts

A7 This frequency chart comes from a survey of the number of people in cars travelling past a checkpoint.

(a) How many cars were there in the survey?

(b) How many people were there altogether in the cars?

(c) Calculate the mean number of people per car.

(d) What is the median number in a car?

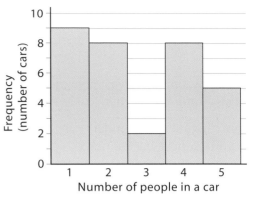

A8 A survey of the number of people in each household in a street resulted in the data shown on the right.

(a) How many households are there in the street?

(b) How many people altogether live in the street?

(c) Calculate the mean number of people per household.

Number of people	Frequency
1	5
2	8
3	12
4	18
5	9
6	4
7	2

A9

Number of children	Frequency
0	13
1	7
2	20
3	9
4	1

This data comes from a survey of the number of children (under 16) in the families in another street.

Calculate the mean number of children per family.

A10 A survey asked people to estimate how many eggs they had eaten in the previous week.

(a) What is the modal number of eggs?

(b) Work out the mean number of eggs eaten per person.

(c) What is the median number of eggs?

Number of eggs	Number of people
0	3
1	16
2	28
3	25
4	18
5	11
6	4
7	2

Two friends are playing 'Shove coin'.

The idea is to tap with the palm of their hand to get the coin as close to the target line as possible.

If the coin goes over the line, the player goes again. Each player records their shove by making a small mark on the next grid line between the front edge of the coin and the target line.

Each player has 50 shoves.

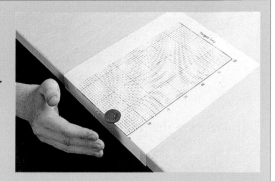

Amy's results are shown here.

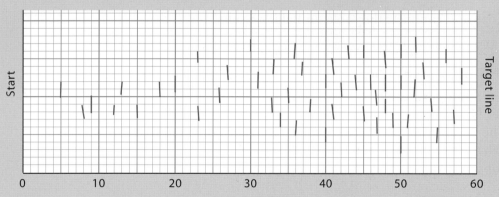

One way to record Amy's results is in a grouped frequency table.

Distance from start (units)	Frequency
0–10	3
10–20	4
20–30	5
30–40	10
40–50	16
50–60	12
Total	50

- Which group did the 20 mark go into?
- Which group did the three 50 marks go into?
- How can you make it clear which group marks at the ends of groups go into?

It does not matter whether marks on a boundary go in the group above or below provided the same rule is used with every group.
To make it clear which rule has been used here one way the **intervals** can be described is:

$0 \leq d < 10$
$10 \leq d < 20$
$20 \leq d < 30$ ← So 20 goes in this group.
....

... where d is the distance from the start. The $\leq$ sign shows that all the numbers in that group are greater than or equal to the first number.

B1 Here are the results for Amy's friend Baljit.

44	5	30	44	49	29	56	21	12	56	24	57	14	54	7	48	17	18
47	32	53	54	19	54	54	39	26	12	10	22	41	52	58	49	23	40
58	46	18	45	38	50	52	39	37	28	39	43	51	36				

(a) Copy and complete this table for Baljit's results.

Distance (d units)	Tally	Frequency
$0 \leq d < 10$		
$10 \leq d < 20$		
$20 \leq d < 30$		

(b) The group with the greatest frequency is called the **modal group** or **class**. What is the modal group for Baljit's shoves?

(c) What was the modal group for Amy's shoves?

B2 A class recorded their weights in kilograms.

Weight (kg)	46	45	52	61	57	47	61	52	47	47	42	59	51	35	48
	62	62	47	52	39	72	69	57	43	50	38	61	47	54	40

The teacher asks the students to record this data in a grouped frequency table with these groupings.

(a) Which group will the weight 50 kg go into?

(b) Which group will the weight 40 kg go into?

(c) Copy and complete the table showing these students' weights using these groupings. Check that you have recorded the correct number of weights.

(d) Write down the modal group of weights.

(e) Use your table to copy and complete this frequency diagram for the weights of the students.

Weight (w kg)	Frequency
$30 < w \leq 40$	
$40 < w \leq 50$	
$50 < w \leq 60$	
$60 < w \leq 70$	
$70 < w \leq 80$	
Total	

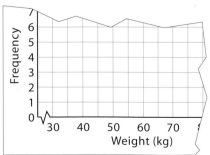

B3 The following is a record of the heights, in centimetres, of 40 guinea pigs.

21	22	11	16	22	13	11	25	9	17	21	24	27	25	12	14	8	12	6	17
23	7	12	26	14	8	12	26	17	19	23	29	21	19	26	26	18	21	13	9

(a) Copy and complete this frequency table.

Height (h cm)	Tally	Frequency
$5 \leq h < 10$		
$10 \leq h < 15$		
$15 \leq h < 20$		
$20 \leq h < 25$		
$25 \leq h < 30$		

(b) Draw a frequency diagram for this information on squared paper.

(c) How many guinea pigs were under 15 cm in height?

(d) Write down the modal class interval of the heights.   Edexcel

B4 The maximum daily temperature for the month of October was recorded at a Sussex weather station.

Max. temp. (°C)	16.7	13.9	15.4	14.6	14.1	14.2	12.5	14.6	12.2	12.9	12.2	13.1	14.7
	12.7	13.9	12.7	13.9	14.4	13.9	14.5	14.7	14.1	14.7	12.9	14.4	13.1
	13.6	14.6	12.8	13.3	12.4								

(a) Copy and complete this grouped frequency table to record the temperatures.

Max. temp. (°C)	Frequency
$12.0 \leq t < 13.0$	
$13.0 \leq t < 14.0$	
$14.0 \leq t < 15.0$	
$15.0 \leq t < 16.0$	
$16.0 \leq t < 17.0$	
Total	

(b) What is the modal group of temperatures in Sussex during October?

(c) On how many days in October did the temperature not reach 14 °C?

This data shows the heights in cm of 44 male African elephants.

272 273 287   84   95 153 165 161 168 257 262 293 194 193 204 218 218
227 186 181 182 224 231 236 237 256 260 238 235 247 200 207 201 215
245 290 317 108 124 270 287 121 135 142

These frequency tables and diagrams show this data grouped in different intervals.

Height (h cm)	Frequency
$80 \leq h < 100$	2
$100 \leq h < 120$	1
$120 \leq h < 140$	3
$140 \leq h < 160$	2
$160 \leq h < 180$	3
$180 \leq h < 200$	5
$200 \leq h < 220$	7
$220 \leq h < 240$	7
$240 \leq h < 260$	4
$260 \leq h < 280$	5
$280 \leq h < 300$	4
$300 \leq h < 320$	1
Total	44

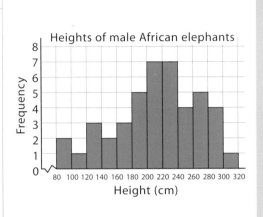

Height (h cm)	Frequency
$50 \leq h < 100$	2
$100 \leq h < 150$	5
$150 \leq h < 200$	9
$200 \leq h < 250$	16
$250 \leq h < 300$	11
$300 \leq h < 350$	1
Total	44

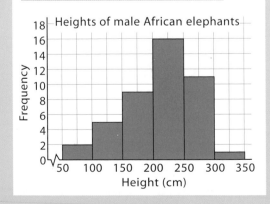

Height (h cm)	Frequency
$0 \leq h < 100$	2
$100 \leq h < 200$	14
$200 \leq h < 300$	27
$300 \leq h < 400$	1
Total	44

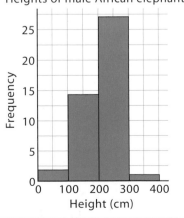

- Which way of grouping gives the clearest picture of the pattern of the data?
- Which way gives the most useful value for a modal class?
- Would using intervals of 5 cm give a clearer picture?
  Would intervals of 200 cm give you more information?
- Would using intervals of 35 cm be a useful grouping?

C1 This data shows the foot length (f) in centimetres of the 44 male African elephants.

49 49 51 17 18 28 30 30 31 46 47 52 35 35 37 40 40 41 34 33 33 41
42 43 43 46 47 43 42 45 36 38 37 39 44 52 57 21 23 48 51 23 25 26

(a) Record this data in a frequency table with intervals
$15 \le f < 20$, $20 \le f < 25$, $25 \le f < 30$, ...
What is the modal group?

(b) Write out another table with intervals $10 \le f < 20$, $20 \le f < 30$, $30 \le f < 40$, ...
What is the modal group now?

(c) Which of these two sets of intervals gives the clearer picture of the data?

C2 For each of these sets of data decide on a suitable set of intervals.
Put the data into a frequency table using these intervals.
Draw a frequency diagram from your table.

(a)
Reaction times (thousandths of a second)
20 18 18 13 18 15 16 17 17 18 22 27 17 15 11 12 12 12 13 17 18
21 19 15 16 10 11 16 15 20 16 22 15 14 14

(b)
Weights (kg)
62.5 63.1 62.9 63.8 62.4 65.7 65.3 66.9 64.7 66.1 65.0 65.2 67.6 66.3 67.3 68.1
69.0 68.4 69.6 68.9 68.5 69.2 70.5 71.3 70.4 71.8 70.0 70.8 70.3 70.7 71.2 70.1
72.4 73.6 72.7 72.9 74.5 75.1

Open-ended groups

This data records the time in seconds between eruptions at
the Kiama Blowhole near Sydney, Australia.

83 51 87 60 28 95   8 27 15 10 18 16 29 54 91   8 17 55 10 35 47 77 36
17 21 36 18 40 10   7 34 27 28 56   8 25 68 146 89 18 73 69   9 37 10 82
29   8 60 61 61 18 169 25   8 26 11 83 11 42 17 14   9 12

- What would be a suitable set of intervals to record this data?

When there are just a few 'extreme' pieces of data,
an open-ended top group is often used.
The data above could be recorded in the groups shown here.

Time (s seconds)
$0 \le s < 20$
$20 \le s < 40$
$40 \le s < 60$
$60 \le s < 80$
$80 \le s < 100$
$100 \le s$

This group includes any times greater than 100 seconds.

This frequency diagram and table summarise the amount collected in a day for a charity.

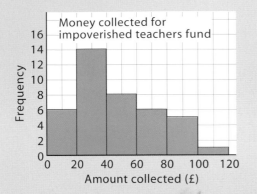

Money (£ m)	Frequency
$0 \leq m < 20$	6
$20 \leq m < 40$	14
$40 \leq m < 60$	8
$60 \leq m < 80$	6
$80 \leq m < 100$	5
$100 \leq m < 120$	1
Total	40

To find the mean amount collected per person we need the total amount collected.

The 6 people in the $0 \leq m < 20$ interval all collected between £0 and £20.
We do not know exactly what each of these people collected.
So we take the value halfway along the interval (£10) as an estimate of
what each person collected. This is called the **mid-interval value**.

So an estimate of the amount collected by these six people is $6 \times £10 = £60$.

The mid-interval for the interval $20 \leq m < 40$ is 30, and so on.

A reasonable estimate of the total amount collected would be

$$(6 \times 10) + (14 \times 30) + (8 \times 50) + (6 \times 70) + (5 \times 90) + (1 \times 110) = £1860$$

So an estimate of the mean amount collected per person is $1860 \div 40 = £46.50$.

D1 A local police force wants to estimate the mean speed of cars along
a particular stretch of road which has a 40 m.p.h. speed limit.
This table shows the speeds recorded one morning and some
unfinished working to estimate the mean speed.

Speed (s m.p.h.)	Frequency	Mid-interval value	Group total estimate
$20 < s \leq 30$	7	25	$7 \times 25 = 175$
$30 < s \leq 40$	21	35	$21 \times 35 = 735$
$40 < s \leq 50$	8		
$50 < s \leq 60$	3		
$60 < s \leq 70$	1		
Total	40		

(a) How many people were breaking the speed limit?

(b) Copy and complete the table above.

(c) Use your table to estimate the mean speed of the cars.

D2 This bar chart gives information about the temperatures of some patients with a particular illness.

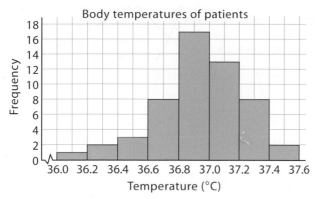

Body temperatures of patients

(a) How many patients were involved altogether?

(b) Use the chart to write out a frequency table with groups $36.0 < t \le 36.2$, …

(c) Use your table to find an estimate of the mean temperature of these patients.

D3 On holiday Val records the length of time people stay in the pool. The results are shown in the table.

Calculate an estimate of the mean time spent in the pool. Give your answer to an appropriate degree of accuracy.

Time (t mins)	Number of people
$0 < t \le 10$	4
$10 < t \le 20$	7
$20 < t \le 30$	3
$30 < t \le 40$	2
	16

AQA

D4 This grouped frequency table shows the marks in a test.

Mark	Frequency
1–5	2
6–10	5
11–15	19
16–20	4
21–25	3

(a) Meg says that the mid-interval value for the first group is 2.5.
Noel says that it must be 3.
Which answer is correct and why?

(b) Copy the table and add appropriate columns to find an estimate of the mean mark in the test.

This dot plot shows the weights of a group of newborn babies.

Weight in kg

If the data is grouped using the class intervals $0 < w \leq 1$, $1 < w \leq 2$, …
(where w is weight in kg) we get this frequency table:

Weight (w kg)	$0 < w \leq 1$	$1 < w \leq 2$	$2 < w \leq 3$	$3 < w \leq 4$	$4 < w \leq 5$
Frequency	2	4	7	6	3

In a **frequency polygon**, each frequency is plotted at the mid-interval value and the points are joined by straight lines.

This is the frequency polygon for the babies' weights.

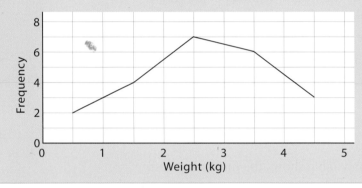

E1 This dot plot shows the times, in seconds, for which a group of people could hold their breath.

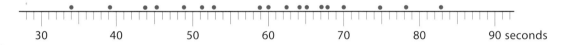

30   40   50   60   70   80   90 seconds

(a) Copy and complete this frequency table for the data.

(b) Which is the modal interval?

(c) Draw a frequency polygon for the data.

Time (t seconds)	Frequency
$30 < t \leq 40$	2
$40 < t \leq 50$	
$50 < t \leq 60$	
$60 < t \leq 70$	
$70 < t \leq 80$	
$80 < t \leq 90$	

E2 Here are the heights in metres of two groups of students.
Each set of data is given in height order.

Girls	1.51	1.53	1.54	1.55	1.56	1.58	1.58	1.60	1.62	1.63
	1.63	1.66	1.67	1.67	1.69	1.70	1.70	1.71	1.73	1.75
Boys	1.57	1.57	1.60	1.62	1.66	1.68	1.70	1.70	1.70	1.70
	1.72	1.74	1.75	1.77	1.79	1.82	1.82	1.83	1.83	1.86

(a) Find the median height of the girls and the median height of the boys.

(b) Find the range of the girls' heights and the range of the boys' heights.

(c) Copy and complete this table.

(d) Draw, on the same axes, a frequency polygon for the girls and for the boys.

(e) Write a couple of sentences comparing the girls' and boys' heights.

Height (h m)	Frequency (girls)	Frequency (boys)
$1.5 < h \le 1.6$	8	
$1.6 < h \le 1.7$		
$1.7 < h \le 1.8$		
$1.8 < h \le 1.9$		

Height (h cm)	Frequency
$120 < h \le 130$	3
$130 < h \le 140$	5
$140 < h \le 150$	8
$150 < h \le 160$	7
$160 < h \le 170$	4

E3 This table shows the distribution of the heights of a group of women.

(a) Draw a frequency polygon for this data.

(b) Calculate an estimate of the mean height of the women.

E4 This frequency polygon shows the distribution of the weights in kg of a group of students.

Calculate an estimate of the mean weight of the students.

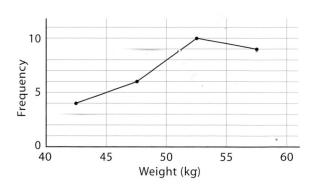

E5 This table shows the distribution of the lengths of some snakes.

Calculate an estimate of the mean length of the snakes.

Length (L cm)	Frequency
$0 < L \le 50$	4
$50 < L \le 100$	10
$100 < L \le 150$	17
$150 < L \le 200$	9

Test yourself

T1 This data shows the pulse rates of a group of university students who smoked.

Pulse (b.p.m.)	70 92 75 68 88 86 65 80 90 76 69 83 70 76 88

(a) Record this data in a stem-and-leaf table with a stem of 10 b.p.m.

(b) Use the table to find the median and range of the pulse rates of these students who smoked.

(c) These are the pulse rates of some students at the same university who were non-smokers.

Find the median and range of the pulse rates of the non-smokers.

(d) Make two statements about the difference in pulse rates between the students who smoked and those who were non-smokers.

Non-smokers' pulse rates

```
 5 | 0 8 9
 6 | 0 4 4 5 6 6 6 8 8
 7 | 0 1 1 8
 8 | 0 1 6 8 8
 9 |
10 | 4
```

Stem = 10 b.p.m.

T2 A set of 25 times in seconds is recorded.

12.9	10.0	4.2	16.0	5.6	18.1	8.3	14.0	11.5	21.7	22.2	6.0	13.6
3.1	11.5	10.8	15.7	3.7	9.4	8.0	6.4	17.0	7.3	12.8	13.5	

(a) Copy and complete the table below, using intervals of 5 seconds.

Time (t seconds)	Tally	Frequency
$0 \leq t < 5$		

(b) Write down the modal class interval.

Edexcel

T3 This table shows the distribution of the weights of the apples picked from a tree.

Weight w in grams	Frequency
$0 < w \leq 20$	7
$20 < w \leq 40$	10
$40 < w \leq 60$	14
$60 < w \leq 80$	20
$80 < w \leq 100$	18
$100 < w \leq 120$	4

(a) How many apples have weights in the interval $40 < w \leq 100$?

(b) Draw a frequency polygon to show the distribution.

(c) Calculate an estimate of the mean weight of the apples.

4 Fractions

You will revise adding, subtracting and multiplying fractions.

This work will help you

- understand what a reciprocal is
- divide by a fraction

A Review: adding, subtracting and multiplying

Examples

$$1\frac{1}{2} + 1\frac{5}{7} = \frac{3}{2} + \frac{12}{7}$$

Change mixed numbers to improper fractions

$$= \frac{21}{14} + \frac{24}{14}$$

Use a common denominator

$$= \frac{45}{14} = 3\frac{3}{14}$$

$$1\frac{1}{4} \times 2\frac{2}{3} = \frac{5}{4} \times \frac{8}{3}$$

$$= \frac{5}{1\cancel{4}} \times \frac{\cancel{8}^2}{3}$$

Cancel common factors before multiplying

$$= \frac{10}{3} = 3\frac{1}{3}$$

A1 Work these out.

(a) $\frac{1}{2} + \frac{1}{3}$ (b) $\frac{2}{3} + \frac{1}{5}$ (c) $\frac{1}{3} + \frac{1}{10}$ (d) $\frac{3}{8} + \frac{2}{3}$ (e) $\frac{4}{5} + \frac{5}{8}$

(f) $1\frac{1}{4} + 1\frac{1}{6}$ (g) $1\frac{3}{4} + 2\frac{1}{5}$ (h) $1\frac{2}{3} + \frac{4}{5}$ (i) $3\frac{2}{3} + \frac{3}{4}$ (j) $2\frac{3}{5} + 1\frac{1}{6}$

A2 Work these out.

(a) $\frac{2}{3} - \frac{1}{2}$ (b) $\frac{4}{5} - \frac{1}{4}$ (c) $\frac{7}{8} - \frac{2}{3}$ (d) $\frac{7}{10} - \frac{2}{3}$ (e) $\frac{5}{8} - \frac{2}{5}$

(f) $1\frac{1}{2} - \frac{5}{6}$ (g) $2\frac{1}{4} - \frac{5}{8}$ (h) $2\frac{1}{8} - 1\frac{1}{3}$ (i) $3\frac{3}{8} - 1\frac{1}{3}$ (j) $4\frac{1}{4} - 1\frac{5}{6}$

A3 Work these out.

(a) $\frac{1}{8} + \frac{5}{6}$ (b) $\frac{5}{6} - \frac{1}{8}$ (c) $1\frac{1}{4} - \frac{2}{5}$ (d) $1\frac{1}{4} + \frac{2}{5}$ (e) $2\frac{1}{2} + \frac{2}{3}$

(f) $3 - 1\frac{3}{5}$ (g) $1\frac{5}{12} + \frac{3}{8}$ (h) $1\frac{5}{12} - \frac{3}{8}$ (i) $1\frac{2}{7} + 2\frac{1}{5}$ (j) $2\frac{1}{5} - 1\frac{2}{7}$

A4 Work these out.

(a) $\frac{2}{3} \times \frac{3}{4}$ (b) $\frac{4}{5} \times \frac{3}{8}$ (c) $\frac{5}{6} \times \frac{3}{4}$ (d) $\frac{1}{3} \times \frac{4}{5}$ (e) $\frac{4}{5} \times \frac{3}{10}$

A5 Work these out.

(a) $1\frac{1}{2} \times \frac{3}{4}$ (b) $\frac{2}{3} \times 1\frac{1}{3}$ (c) $1\frac{1}{2} \times 1\frac{1}{3}$ (d) $\frac{3}{4} \times 2\frac{1}{2}$ (e) $2\frac{1}{2} \times 1\frac{1}{2}$

A6 Work these out.

(a) $2 \times \frac{1}{2}$ (b) $\frac{1}{3} \times 3$ (c) $5 \times \frac{1}{5}$ (d) $\frac{2}{3} \times \frac{3}{2}$ (e) $\frac{3}{4} \times \frac{4}{3}$

B Reciprocals

If two numbers multiply together to give 1, each is called the **reciprocal** of the other.

$$2 \times \tfrac{1}{2} = 1$$

$\tfrac{1}{2}$ is the reciprocal of 2

2 is the reciprocal of $\tfrac{1}{2}$

$$\tfrac{3}{4} \times \tfrac{4}{3} = 1$$

$\tfrac{4}{3}$ is the reciprocal of $\tfrac{3}{4}$

$\tfrac{3}{4}$ is the reciprocal of $\tfrac{4}{3}$

B1 Write down the reciprocal of each of these.

(a) 3   (b) $\tfrac{1}{3}$ (c) 5   (d) $\tfrac{2}{5}$ (e) $\tfrac{5}{6}$

(f) $\tfrac{1}{8}$ (g) $\tfrac{5}{7}$ (h) $\tfrac{5}{4}$ (i) 8   (j) 1

B2 (a) Write $1\tfrac{1}{2}$ as an improper fraction.

     (b) Hence write down the reciprocal of $1\tfrac{1}{2}$.

B3 What is the reciprocal of each of these?

(a) $3\tfrac{1}{2}$ (b) $1\tfrac{1}{3}$ (c) $2\tfrac{1}{4}$ (d) $1\tfrac{2}{5}$ (e) $2\tfrac{2}{3}$

B4 (a) As a decimal, $\tfrac{5}{8} = 0.625$.

     Without using a calculator, work out, as a decimal, the reciprocal of 0.625.

     (b) Find the reciprocal of each of these.

       (i) 0.1   (ii) 0.4   (iii) 0.125   (iv) 1.25   (v) 2.5

B5 (a) If A stands for a number, what is the reciprocal of the reciprocal of A?

     (b) Which number has no reciprocal?

C Dividing by a fraction

$4 \div \tfrac{1}{3}$ can mean 'how many $\tfrac{1}{3}$s make 4 whole ones?'

The answer is 12.

Notice that $4 \div \tfrac{1}{3} = 4 \times 3$

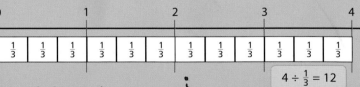

$4 \div \tfrac{1}{3} = 12$

$4 \div \tfrac{2}{3}$ can mean 'how many $\tfrac{2}{3}$s make 4 whole ones?'

The answer is 6 (half of 12).

So $\boxed{4 \div \tfrac{2}{3}}$ is the same as $\boxed{4 \times \tfrac{3}{2}}$

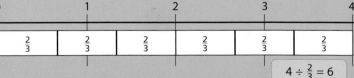

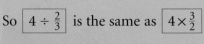

$4 \div \tfrac{2}{3} = 6$

Dividing by a fraction is the same as multiplying by its reciprocal.

C1 Work these out. Imagine a diagram like those on the opposite page if it helps.

(a) $4 \div \frac{1}{2}$ (b) $3 \div \frac{1}{5}$ (c) $2 \div \frac{1}{8}$ (d) $5 \div \frac{1}{4}$ (e) $6 \div \frac{1}{3}$

C2 Work these out.

(a) $6 \div \frac{1}{4}$ (b) $6 \div \frac{3}{4}$ (c) $6 \div \frac{1}{3}$ (d) $6 \div \frac{2}{3}$ (e) $4 \div \frac{2}{5}$

C3 Work these out.

(a) $5 \div \frac{2}{3}$ (b) $2 \div \frac{3}{4}$ (c) $4 \div \frac{3}{5}$ (d) $1 \div \frac{3}{4}$ (e) $8 \div \frac{3}{5}$

C4 (a) Ashish's kitten eats $\frac{1}{3}$ of a tin of cat food each day.
Find how many days 8 tins will last the kitten, by dividing 8 by $\frac{1}{3}$.

(b) The kitten's mother eats $\frac{2}{3}$ of a tin each day.
Find how many days 8 tins will last the mother, by dividing 8 by $\frac{2}{3}$.

C5 Max's ox pulls a heavy cart at $\frac{3}{4}$ m.p.h.
How long will it take the cart to travel 6 miles?

C6 Only $\frac{4}{5}$ of the weight of apples is usable for making puddings,
because the peel and core are thrown away.
What weight do you need to start with in order to have 20 kg usable?

Here is another way to see why dividing is the same as multiplying by the reciprocal.

to multiply by $\frac{3}{4}$, multiply by 3 and divide by 4

Division is the **inverse** operation, so

to divide by $\frac{3}{4}$, multiply by 4 and divide by 3

Example of dividing a fraction by a fraction

Work out $\frac{3}{4} \div \frac{5}{8}$.

To divide by $\frac{5}{8}$, multiply by its reciprocal, $\frac{8}{5}$.

$$\frac{3}{4} \div \frac{5}{8} = \frac{3}{4} \times \frac{8}{5} = \frac{3}{{}_1 4} \times \frac{8^2}{5}$$

First cancel common factors

$$= \frac{6}{5}$$

You can leave your answer as an improper fraction

C7 Work these out.

(a) $\frac{5}{6} \div \frac{3}{4}$ (b) $\frac{5}{6} \div \frac{1}{4}$ (c) $\frac{2}{3} \div \frac{3}{4}$ (d) $\frac{1}{2} \div \frac{2}{3}$ (e) $\frac{3}{4} \div \frac{5}{8}$

C8 Work these out.

(a) $\frac{5}{8} \div \frac{3}{4}$ (b) $\frac{1}{6} \div \frac{3}{4}$ (c) $\frac{2}{5} \div \frac{3}{4}$ (d) $\frac{2}{3} \div \frac{3}{5}$ (e) $\frac{3}{8} \div \frac{1}{3}$

*C9 Work these out.

(a) $1\frac{1}{3} \div \frac{2}{9}$ (b) $2\frac{1}{4} \div \frac{3}{5}$ (c) $\frac{3}{4} \div 1\frac{1}{2}$ (d) $1\frac{7}{8} \div 1\frac{1}{4}$

D Mixed questions

D1 If $a = \frac{1}{2}$ and $b = \frac{1}{3}$, find the value of each of these.

(a) $4a$ (b) $9b$ (c) $3a + 1$ (d) $6b - 2$ (e) $7 - 5a$

(f) ab (g) $6 \div a$ (h) $4 \div b$ (i) $a \div b$ (j) $b \div a$

D2 If $s = \frac{2}{3}$ and $t = \frac{3}{4}$, find the value of each of these.

(a) $6s$ (b) $8t$ (c) $3s - 1$ (d) $6t - 2$ (e) $2 - 2s$

(f) st (g) $1 \div s$ (h) $1 \div t$ (i) $s \div t$ (j) $t \div s$

D3 If $x = \frac{4}{5}$ and $y = \frac{1}{2}$, find the value of each of these.

(a) $x + y$ (b) $x - y$ (c) xy (d) $\frac{x}{y} (= x \div y)$ (e) $\frac{y}{x}$

D4 To solve the equation $4x = 36$, you divide both sides by 4.
This is the same as multiplying both sides by the reciprocal of 4, or $\frac{1}{4}$.

Solve the equation $\frac{3}{4}x = \frac{2}{5}$, by multiplying both sides by the reciprocal of $\frac{3}{4}$.

D5 Solve   (a) $\frac{2}{3}x = \frac{1}{5}$ (b) $\frac{3}{5}x = \frac{2}{3}$ (c) $\frac{3}{8}x = \frac{1}{2}$ (d) $\frac{2}{5}x = \frac{5}{6}$

D6 20 pizzas are shared between a group of children so that each gets $\frac{2}{3}$ of a pizza. How many children are in the group?

D7 People went one by one into a kitchen where there was a jug of water.
The first person drank half of the water.
The second drank half of what was left.
The next drank half of what was left, and so on.

What fraction of the water was left after the fifth person had had a drink?

D8 Re-do question D7, but this time the first person drinks $\frac{1}{3}$ of the water and the others each drink $\frac{1}{3}$ of what is left.

Test yourself

T1 Write down the reciprocal of each of these.

(a) 4 (b) $\frac{1}{5}$ (c) $\frac{4}{7}$ (d) $4\frac{1}{2}$ (e) 0.02

T2 Work these out.

(a) $3 \div \frac{1}{6}$ (b) $3 \div \frac{5}{6}$ (c) $\frac{2}{3} \div \frac{1}{6}$ (d) $\frac{2}{3} \div \frac{5}{6}$ (e) $\frac{3}{8} \div \frac{2}{5}$

T3 Solve these.

(a) $\frac{1}{5}x = \frac{3}{4}$ (b) $\frac{3}{4}x = \frac{1}{6}$ (c) $\frac{2}{3}x = \frac{3}{8}$ (d) $\frac{5}{6}x = \frac{4}{5}$

5 Accuracy

This work will help you find the lower and upper bounds for a rounded quantity.

A Lower and upper bounds

- What is the height of each person, to the nearest 10 centimetres?

| 178 cm | 181 cm | 177 cm | 180 cm | 183 cm | 176 cm |

- What other heights give the same result when rounded to the nearest 10 cm?

- What is the length of each pencil, to the nearest centimetre?

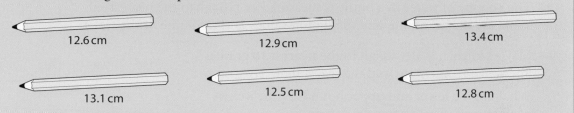

12.6 cm   12.9 cm   13.4 cm

13.1 cm   12.5 cm   12.8 cm

- What other lengths give the result 13 cm when rounded to the nearest centimetre?

If you are rounding to the **nearest whole number**,

- which of these numbers will be rounded to 18?

    18.63   17.842   17.486   18.33
        17.752   17.497   18.761   18.2794
    17.741   18.523   18.464   17.503

- What is the **lowest** number you can think of that will be rounded to 18?
- What is the **highest** number you can think of that will be rounded to 18?

(This number line may help.)

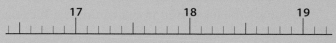

17   18   19

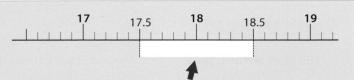

All the numbers for which 18 is the nearest whole number lie in this **interval**.

The **lower bound**, or minimum, of the interval is **17.5**.
The **upper bound**, or maximum, is **18.5**.

(Strictly speaking, if we round up, 18.5 itself should not be in the interval, because 18.5 becomes 19. But usually this does not matter.)

A1 You are told that the temperature of some water is 13 °C, to the nearest degree.

   (a) What is the lowest possible temperature of the water?

   (b) What is the highest possible temperature?

A2 The volume of water in a glass is measured as 347 ml, to the nearest ml.
What are the lower and upper bounds of the volume of the water?

A3 A man's weight is recorded as 78 kg, correct to the nearest kg.
What are the lower and upper bounds of his weight?

A4 The volume of water in a bottle is measured as 170 ml, to the nearest ml.
What are the minimum and maximum values of the volume of the water?

A5 Marie's kitchen scales weigh to the **nearest 10 grams**.
She weighs some flour and the scales show 270 g.

What are the lower and upper bounds of the weight
of the flour? (The diagram may help.)

A6 The speed of an aircraft is 420 km/h, correct to the nearest 10 km/h.
What are the minimum and maximum possible values of the speed?

A7 The length of a river is given as 3800 km, correct to the **nearest 100 km**.
What are the lower and upper bounds of the length of the river?

Test yourself

T1 The scales in an airport weigh luggage to the nearest kilogram.
What are the greatest and least possible weights of a case
showing 25 kg on the scale?   AQA

T2 The length of a bed is displayed as 202 cm, to the nearest cm.
What are the lower and upper bounds of the length of the bed?

6 Linear equations 1

This work will help you

- solve a variety of linear equations, including those that involve algebraic fractions
- form equations to solve problems

A Solving equations

Examples

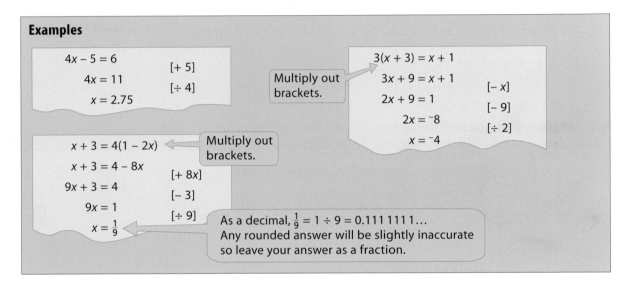

$4x - 5 = 6$
$4x = 11$ [+ 5]
$x = 2.75$ [÷ 4]

Multiply out brackets.

$3(x + 3) = x + 1$
$3x + 9 = x + 1$
$2x + 9 = 1$ [– x]
$2x = {}^-8$ [– 9]
$x = {}^-4$ [÷ 2]

Multiply out brackets.

$x + 3 = 4(1 - 2x)$
$x + 3 = 4 - 8x$
$9x + 3 = 4$ [+ 8x]
$9x = 1$ [– 3]
$x = \frac{1}{9}$ [÷ 9]

As a decimal, $\frac{1}{9} = 1 \div 9 = 0.111\,111\,1\ldots$
Any rounded answer will be slightly inaccurate so leave your answer as a fraction.

A1 Solve these equations.

(a) $2x - 8 = 1$ (b) $5x + 11 = 1$ (c) $5x - 2 = 19$

(d) $8 - 5x = 3$ (e) $13 = 10 - 3x$ (f) $1.5x + 8 = 2$

A2 Solve these equations.

(a) $2n + 1 = n + 4$ (b) $5n + 6 = 3n + 4$ (c) $2n + 7 = 7n - 3$

(d) $5 - n = n + 9$ (e) $1 + 2n = 10 - 2n$ (f) $2.5n - 5 = 0.5n + 3$

(g) $5n - 12 = 6n - 15$ (h) $21 - n = 26 - 5n$ (i) $10 - 3n = 7 - 5n$

A3 Solve these equations.

(a) $2(x + 3) = 4$ (b) $2(x - 3) = x$ (c) $3(2x + 3) = 17 - 2x$

(d) $2(x + 7) = 5(3x + 8)$ (e) $3(x + 2) = 6(1 - x)$ (f) $8(x + 4) = 2(1 - x)$

(g) $4(x + 2) = 2x - 7$ (h) $11(2x - 5) = 0$ (i) $4(2x + 1) = 3(3x + 5)$

A4 Solve these equations, giving each answer as a fraction.

(a) $5k = 1$ (b) $3k + 5 = 6$ (c) $4(k + 1) = 5$

(d) $3(1 + 2k) = 4(2 - k)$ (e) $2(1 + k) = 5k$ (f) $4(2 + k) = 5 - 2k$

A5 Copy and complete this working to solve $3(x - 4) + 2(3x + 2) = 19$.

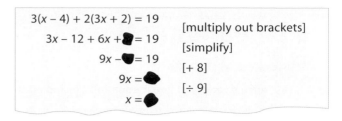

$3(x - 4) + 2(3x + 2) = 19$
$3x - 12 + 6x + \blacksquare = 19$ [multiply out brackets]
$9x - \blacksquare = 19$ [simplify]
$9x = \blacksquare$ [+ 8]
$x = \blacksquare$ [÷ 9]

A6 Solve each of these equations.

(a) $2(2n + 2) + 3(n - 1) = 15$ (b) $3(4m - 10) + 5(2m - 12) = 20$

(c) $4(3k + 7) + 3(5 - 2k) = 25$ (d) $3(2h - 1) + 4(3h - 4) = 5(3h - 1)$

A7 Copy and complete this working to solve $2(3x + 2) - 2(2x - 1) = 8$.

$2(3x + 2) - 2(2x - 1) = 8$
$(6x + 4) - (4x - 2) = 8$ [multiply out brackets]

A8 Solve these equations.

(a) $5(x + 7) - 3(2x + 1) = 35$ (b) $6(5 - x) - 2(3x - 1) = 2$

B Forming equations

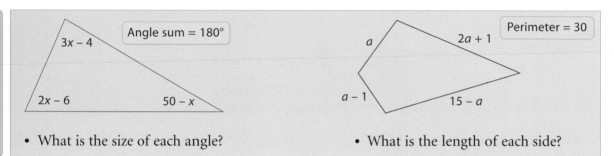

Angle sum = 180°

$3x - 4$

$2x - 6$ $50 - x$

• What is the size of each angle?

Perimeter = 30

a $2a + 1$

$a - 1$ $15 - a$

• What is the length of each side?

B1 Find the size of each angle in these shapes. The expressions are in degrees.

(a)

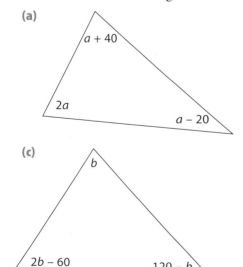

$a + 40$

$2a$

$a - 20$

(b)

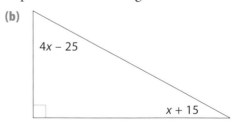

$4x - 25$

$x + 15$

(c)

b

$2b - 60$ $120 - b$

(d)

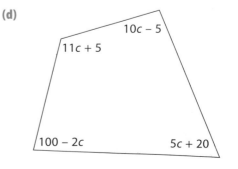

$10c - 5$

$11c + 5$

$100 - 2c$ $5c + 20$

B2 The perimeter of each of these shapes is 100.
Find the length of each side.

(a)

5h – 5

4h – 5

70 – 6h

3h + 4

(b)

5x – 10

x + 12

B3 I think of a number.
I multiply by 4 and add 9.
My answer is 3.
What was my number?

B4 (a) Find an expression for the perimeter of this kite.

(b) What value of x gives a perimeter of 68?

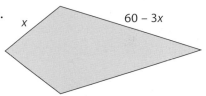

x   60 – 3x

B5 Work out the starting number in each of these 'think of a number' puzzles.

(a)
I think of a number.
I add 5 and then multiply by 2.
My answer is 6.
What was my number?

(b)
I think of a number.
I multiply by 3 and then add 7.
My answer is 11 more than the
number I started with.
What was my number?

(c)
I think of a number.
I multiply by 6 and then subtract 1.
My answer is double the number
I started with.
What was my number?

(d)
I think of a number.
I subtract 2 and then multiply by 3.
My answer is 8 less than the number
I started with.
What was my number?

B6 Ria and Julia both think of the same number.
Ria takes 6 off the number and then multiplies her result by 3.

Julia adds 1 to the number and then doubles her result.

They both end up with the same answer.
What number did they both think of at the start?

B7 The shapes below are rectangles.

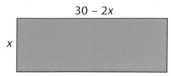

30 – 2x

42 – 3x

x

x

(a) Find the length and width of each rectangle when $x = 13$.

(b) Explain why it is not possible to sketch an orange rectangle for $x = 14$.

(c) For the blue rectangle, what value of x gives a perimeter of 44?

(d) For the orange rectangle, what value of x gives a perimeter of 60?

(e) What value of x gives both rectangles the same perimeter?

(f) What value of x gives a blue square?

(g) What value of x gives an orange square?

(h) Explain why it is not possible to sketch a blue rectangle with a perimeter of 100.

B8 Find the size of the smallest angle in this quadrilateral.

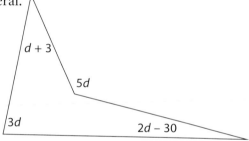

$d + 3$

$5d$

$3d$

$2d – 30$

B9 Work out the starting number in each of these 'think of a number' puzzles.

(a)
| I think of a number. |
| I multiply it by 3. |
| I take the result off 10. |
| My answer is 4. |

(b)
| I think of a number. |
| I double it. |
| I take the result off 100. |
| My answer is 1 more than the number I thought of. |

(c)
| I think of a number. |
| I subtract it from 4. |
| My answer is 6 more than the number I thought of. |

B10 Find the size of the largest angle in the pentagon.

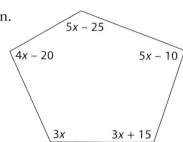

$5x – 25$

$4x – 20$

$5x – 10$

$3x$

$3x + 15$

Edexcel

C Equations that involve a fraction

Examples

$\frac{x}{3} + 5 = 9$

$\quad$ [− 5]

$\frac{x}{3} = 4$

$\quad$ [× 3]

$x = 12$

$\frac{1}{2}x − 9 = 3$

$\quad$ [+ 9]

$\frac{1}{2}x = 12$

$\quad$ [×2]

$x = 24$

$\frac{3x + 5}{4} = 2$

$\quad$ [× 4]

$3x + 5 = 8$

$\quad$ [− 5]

$3x = 3$

$\quad$ [÷ 3]

$x = 1$

C1 Solve these equations.

(a) $\frac{y}{3} = 5$

(b) $\frac{k}{4} + 8 = 10$

(c) $\frac{1}{2}m − 1 = 4$

(d) $\frac{x}{5} − 1 = 3$

(e) $3 + \frac{p}{2} = 1$

(f) $\frac{1}{4}q + 3 = 5$

(g) $\frac{4v}{3} = 8$

(h) $\frac{2w}{5} + 5 = 1$

(i) $\frac{3n}{2} − 1 = 1$

C2 Solve these equations.

(a) $\frac{x + 1}{3} = 4$

(b) $\frac{x − 3}{2} = 5$

(c) $\frac{1 + x}{2} = 1.5$

(d) $\frac{2x + 17}{7} = 1$

(e) $\frac{3x − 1}{5} = 2$

(f) $\frac{5x + 7}{4} = 2$

C3 Solve these equations.

(a) $\frac{1}{3}n + 4 = 7$

(b) $\frac{n}{2} + 5 = 2$

(c) $\frac{n + 5}{6} = 11$

(d) $\frac{3n}{7} + 1 = 3$

(e) $\frac{5 + n}{2} = 1$

(f) $\frac{4n + 1}{3} = 7$

C4 (a) Which of the equations on the right corresponds to this number puzzle?

I think of a number.
I add 5.
I divide by 3.
My answer is 6.
What was my number?

$\frac{n}{3} + 5 = 6$

$\frac{n + 5}{3} = 6$

(b) Use the correct equation to solve the number puzzle.

C5 Work out the starting number in each of these 'think of a number' puzzles.

(a)
I think of a number.
I divide by 3.
I subtract 4.
My answer is 1.

(b)
I think of a number.
I add 4.
I divide by 5.
My answer is 5.

(c)
I think of a number.
I multiply by 2.
I add 12.
I divide by 4.
My answer is ⁻2.

Examples of equations with the unknown on each side

$$\frac{x + 10}{3} = x$$
$$x + 10 = 3x \qquad [\times 3]$$
$$10 = 2x \qquad [- x]$$
$$5 = x \qquad [\div 2]$$
$$\text{or} \quad x = 5$$

$$\frac{2x - 3}{5} = x - 6 \qquad [\times 5]$$
$$2x - 3 = 5(x - 6) \qquad [\text{multiply out brackets}]$$
$$2x - 3 = 5x - 30 \qquad [+ 30]$$
$$2x + 27 = 5x \qquad [- 2x]$$
$$27 = 3x \qquad [\div 3]$$
$$9 = x$$
$$\text{or} \quad x = 9$$

C6 Solve these equations.

(a) $\dfrac{h + 8}{2} = h$

(b) $\dfrac{k + 15}{4} = k$

(c) $\dfrac{14j - 3}{3} = j$

(d) $\dfrac{11f + 3}{5} = 2f$

(e) $\dfrac{12 - g}{2} = g$

(f) $2d = \dfrac{27 - d}{4}$

C7 Solve these.

(a) $\dfrac{a + 1}{2} = a - 2$

(b) $\dfrac{b + 2}{3} = b + 4$

(c) $\dfrac{2c + 3}{4} = c - 3$

(d) $\dfrac{d - 4}{2} = 2d - 5$

(e) $\dfrac{3e + 4}{2} = 3e + 1$

(f) $\dfrac{2 - 3f}{2} = 2 - 2f$

C8 I think of a number.
I multiply by 3, add 5 and then divide by 4.
My answer is the same as my starting number.
What was my number?

C9 Work out the starting number in each of these 'think of a number' puzzles.

(a)
I think of a number.
I add 22 and then divide by 6.
The answer is double the number I first thought of.

(b)
I think of a number.
I add 1 and then divide by 3.
My answer is 5 more than the number I first thought of.

(c)
I think of a number.
I multiply by 2.
I subtract 1.
I divide by 3.
The answer is 2 less than the number I first thought of.

(d)
I think of a number.
I multiply by 5.
I add 2.
I divide by 2.
The answer is double the number I first thought of.

D More than one fraction

It is often useful to multiply to get rid of any fractions as soon as you can.

Examples

$$\frac{6x - 3}{4} = \frac{3}{2}$$

$$\frac{4(6x - 3)}{4} = \frac{4 \times 3}{2} \quad [\times 4]$$

$$6x - 3 = 6 \quad \text{[cancel fractions]}$$
$$6x = 9 \quad [+ 3]$$
$$x = 1\tfrac{1}{2} \quad [\div 6]$$

$$\frac{4x - 1}{2} = \frac{5x + 1}{3}$$

> 6 is a multiple of 2 and 3, so multiply by 6.

$$\frac{6(4x - 1)}{2} = \frac{6(5x + 1)}{3} \quad [\times 6]$$

$$\qquad \text{[cancel fractions]}$$
$$3(4x - 1) = 2(5x + 1) \quad \text{[multiply out brackets]}$$
$$12x - 3 = 10x + 2 \quad [- 10x]$$
$$2x - 3 = 2 \quad [+ 3]$$
$$2x = 5 \quad [\div 2]$$
$$x = 2\tfrac{1}{2}$$

D1 Solve each of these equations.

(a) $\dfrac{x + 1}{3} = \dfrac{x - 1}{2}$

(b) $\dfrac{2x + 1}{3} = \dfrac{1}{2}$

(c) $\dfrac{3x + 5}{4} = \dfrac{x}{2}$

(d) $\dfrac{3x}{4} = \dfrac{4x - 1}{5}$

(e) $\tfrac{1}{2}(3x + 1) = \tfrac{1}{3}(5x + 3)$

(f) $\dfrac{4x + 1}{5} = \dfrac{7x - 2}{8}$

D2 Work out the starting number in each of these 'think of a number' puzzles.

(a)
> Carla and Sue both think of the same number.
>
> Carla doubles her number, adds 1 and then divides by 5.
>
> Sue subtracts 1 and then halves her result.
>
> They both end up with the same answer.

(b)
> Martin and Joe both think of the same number.
>
> Martin trebles his number, subtracts 1 and then divides by 4.
>
> Joe subtracts 3 and then halves his result.
>
> They both end up with the same answer.

Example

> 12 is a multiple of 4, 3 and 6, so multiply by 12.

$$\frac{2x - 1}{3} - \frac{x + 3}{4} = \frac{1}{6}$$

$$\frac{12(2x - 1)}{3} - \frac{12(x + 3)}{4} = \frac{12}{6} \quad [\times 12]$$

> Be careful with signs.

$$\qquad \text{[cancel fractions]}$$
$$4(2x - 1) - 3(x + 3) = 2 \quad \text{[multiply out brackets]}$$
$$8x - 4 - 3x - 9 = 2 \quad \text{[simplify]}$$
$$5x - 13 = 2 \quad [+ 13]$$
$$5x = 15 \quad [\div 5]$$
$$x = 3$$

D3 Solve these equations.

(a) $\dfrac{x+1}{2} + \dfrac{x-1}{4} = 4$ (b) $\dfrac{2x+1}{3} + \dfrac{x-4}{2} = \dfrac{2}{3}$ (c) $\dfrac{2x-7}{3} + \dfrac{x-2}{4} = \dfrac{5}{6}$

D4 Solve the equation $\dfrac{2x-3}{6} + \dfrac{x+2}{3} = \dfrac{5}{2}$.

WJEC

D5 Solve the equation $\dfrac{3x-5}{4} + \dfrac{12-11x}{6} = 4$.

OCR

D6 Solve these equations.

(a) $\dfrac{x-1}{2} - \dfrac{x+9}{10} = 3$ (b) $\dfrac{x+16}{3} - \dfrac{2x+11}{5} = 3$ (c) $\dfrac{2x+1}{4} - \dfrac{4x-7}{6} = \dfrac{1}{4}$

D7 Solve these.

(a) $\dfrac{5x+2}{3} - \dfrac{3x+1}{4} = x$ (b) $\dfrac{3x+7}{4} - \dfrac{x}{3} = \dfrac{x}{6}$

(c) $\dfrac{1-2x}{5} - \dfrac{5-2x}{3} = 2(x+1)$ (d) $\dfrac{3x}{4} - 2(x-1) = \dfrac{1}{3}$

(e) $\frac{1}{4}(3x+7) - 2(1+x) = {}^{-}x$ (f) $\frac{1}{4}(3x-1) + \frac{1}{5}(8x+3) = \frac{1}{3}(7x+1)$

E Mixed questions

E1 Solve the equation $5(2x+7) = 11 + 4x$.

OCR

E2 Solve these equations.

(a) $0.8x - 9 = 3$ (b) $\frac{1}{2}y + 5 = 8$ (c) $0.1z + 3 = 5 - 0.4z$

(d) $1.4 + f = 2.6 - 2f$ (e) $\frac{1}{2}g + 4 = 1 - \frac{1}{2}g$ (f) $10 + h = \frac{1}{3}h + 12$

(g) $\dfrac{2p-1}{5} = 5$ (h) $\dfrac{3q}{4} + 5 = 2$ (i) $\dfrac{20-3r}{2} = r + 5$

E3 Find the size of each angle in this triangle.

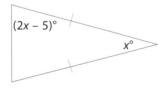

E4 Solve these equations.

(a) $3a - 2 = 10$ (b) $5(2x-1) + 6x = 7 - 8x$

OCR

E5 Solve these equations.

(a) $\dfrac{x-7}{5} = 2$ (b) $5x + 6 = 24 - 10x$

AQA

E6 Solve these equations.

(a) $2(3x-1) + 3(2x-3) = 73$ (b) $3(2x+7) - 2(2x-1) = 17$

E7 Work out the starting number in each of these 'think of a number' puzzles.

(a)
| I think of a number. |
| I add 3. |
| I multiply by 5. |
| My answer is double the number I started with. |

(b)
| I think of a number. |
| I multiply by 2. |
| I subtract 19. |
| I divide by 3. |
| My answer is 5. |

(c)
| I think of a number. |
| I multiply by 4. |
| I subtract 3. |
| I divide by 5. |
| My answer is 2 less than the number I started with. |

E8 Solve these equations.

(a) $\dfrac{4x-3}{5} = \dfrac{x}{2}$

(b) $\dfrac{x+5}{2} = \dfrac{x-1}{3}$

(c) $\dfrac{2x+1}{4} = \dfrac{1-3x}{2}$

(d) $\dfrac{x+5}{3} + \dfrac{x-2}{5} = 5$

(e) $\dfrac{x-1}{4} + \dfrac{5x+2}{3} = 10$

(f) $\dfrac{2x+11}{3} - \dfrac{x+10}{6} = \dfrac{3}{2}$

E9 Solve these equations.

(a) $\frac{1}{4}c - 2 = 1 + \frac{1}{5}c$

(b) $\dfrac{e}{5} - 7 = 19 - \dfrac{e}{8}$

Test yourself

T1 Solve the equation $3x - 14 = 5(6 - x)$.   WJEC

T2 Solve these equations.

(a) $6a - 2 = 7$

(b) $3b + 10 = b + 4$

(c) $5(3 - c) = 5c + 3$

T3 The perimeter of the parallelogram and the perimeter of the square are equal. Find this perimeter.

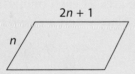

T4 Solve these.

(a) $3(x - 6) = 10 - 2x$

(b) $\dfrac{y+1}{3} = \dfrac{1-y}{2}$ Edexcel

T5 Solve the equation $4 - \dfrac{2x}{3} = 3(x + 3)$.   Edexcel

T6 Solve these equations.

(a) $\dfrac{12-y}{3} = 5$

(b) $\dfrac{2x+1}{4} + \dfrac{4x+1}{6} = 1$ AQA

T7 (a) Solve the equation $9(x - 1) = 5(x - 2)$.

(b) Solve the equation $\dfrac{x+1}{2} + \dfrac{x-3}{4} = 2$.   AQA

7 Area and perimeter

You will revise

- finding the area of a parallelogram, triangle and trapezium
- finding the area and circumference of a circle

This work will help you

- deal with composite shapes (shapes that are made up of simpler shapes)
- solve area and perimeter problems, including some that use Pythagoras's theorem

A Parallelogram

The area of a parallelogram is **base × height**.

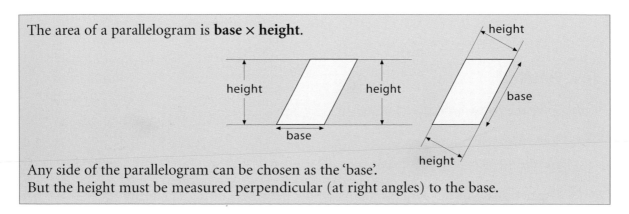

Any side of the parallelogram can be chosen as the 'base'.
But the height must be measured perpendicular (at right angles) to the base.

A1 These parallelograms are not drawn to scale. Find the area of each one, using the correct units. Round your answer to one decimal place where necessary.

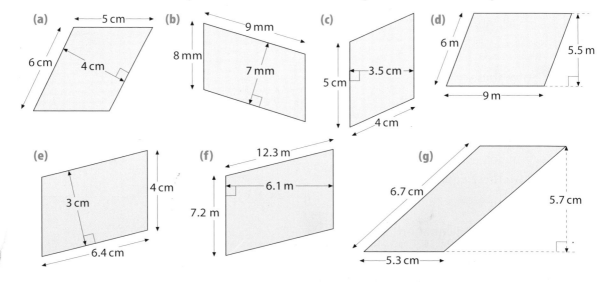

A2 Find the perimeter of each parallelogram in A1.

A3 Write, as simply as possible, an expression for the area of each parallelogram.

(a)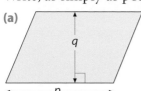

(b)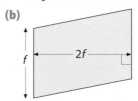

(c)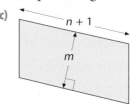

A4 Calculate the missing length in each parallelogram.

(a) Area = 26 cm²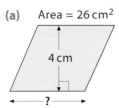

(b) Area = 10.5 cm²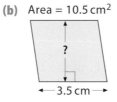

(c) Area = 16.5 cm²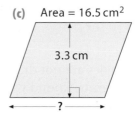

A5 A parallelogram has an area of 12 cm². One of its sides is 3 cm long.
Is it possible to calculate its perimeter? Give a reason.

A6 Calculate the missing length in each parallelogram.

(a)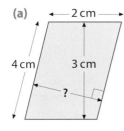

(b)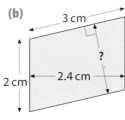

(c)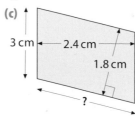

(d)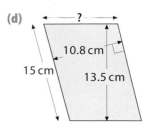

A7 For each of these parallelograms,
work in centimetres to get its area in cm²,
then work in metres to get its area in m².
Give all answers to two significant figures.

(a)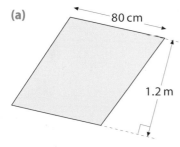

(b)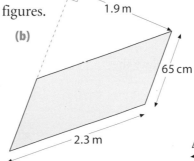

(c)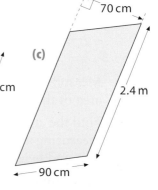

A8 This is a parallelogram.
The lengths marked are in centimetres.

(a) Work out the area of the parallelogram.
State the units of your answer.

(b) Work out the perimeter of the parallelogram.
State the units of your answer.

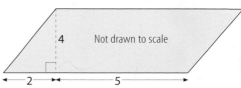

OCR

B Triangle

B Triangle — level 6

The area of a triangle is (**base × height**) ÷ 2.

This is usually written as $\frac{1}{2}bh$ or $\frac{bh}{2}$.

Any side of the triangle can be chosen as the base.
But the height must be measured perpendicular to the base.

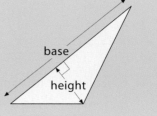

B1 These triangles are not drawn to scale. Find the area of each one, using the correct units. Round your answer to one decimal place where necessary.

(a) 13 cm, 11 cm, 19 cm

(b) 12 mm, 20 mm, 18 mm

(c) 10 cm, 23 cm, 21 cm

(d) 11 m, 9 m, 17 m

(e) 8.4 cm, 7.6 cm

(f) 6.9 m, 9.4 m

(g) 8.1 cm, 6.2 cm, 7.5 cm

(h) 10.2 cm, 7.8 cm, 8.9 cm

B2
- Measure, then calculate the area of this triangle.
- Find the area again, measuring a different base and height.
- Compare your results and comment on any difference.

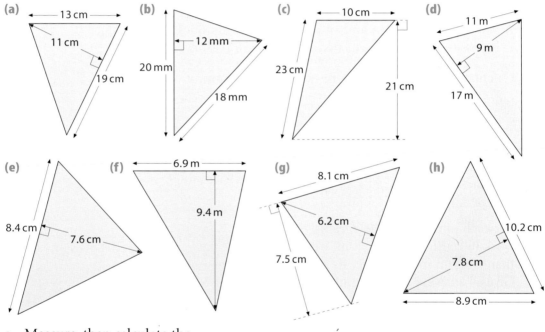

B3 Write, as simply as possible, an expression for the area of each triangle.

(a)

(b)

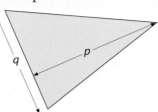

(c)

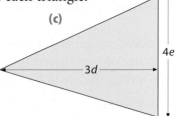

B4 For each of these triangles, work in centimetres to get its area in cm^2, then work in metres to get its area in m^2.
Give all answers to two significant figures.

(a)

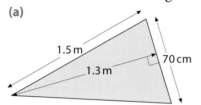

(b)

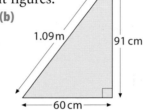

(c)

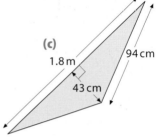

B5 (a) Substitute the values given in this diagram into the formula $A = \frac{1}{2}bh$.

(b) Solve the equation you get to find the height.

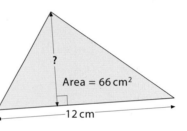

B6 Find the missing length in each of these.

(a)

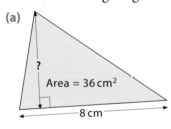

(b)

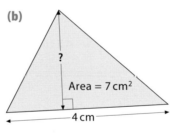

(c)

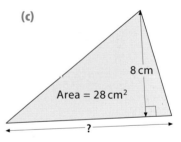

B7 Find the missing length in each of these.

(a)

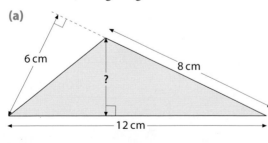

(b)

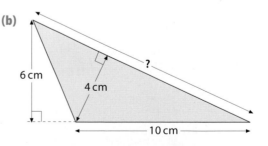

B8 Two identical triangles have been placed together.

(a) What shape is made from these two triangles?

(b) What is the area of the shape that is made?

(c) Explain how this proves the formula for the area of a triangle.

C Composite shapes and algebra

A **composite** shape is one made by putting together simpler shapes (or subtracting one shape from another).
When finding the area of a composite shape,

- sketch the diagram with its dimensions, showing the simpler parts whose area you intend to find
- label the parts A, B, … so you can refer to them in your working
- work out any extra dimensions you will need for your calculations and add them to your diagram
- show all your working
- use the same units throughout and give the correct units in your answer

By doing these things you can avoid errors and make it easy to check your work.

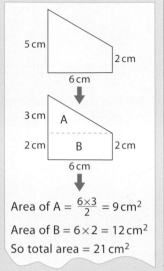

Area of A = $\frac{6 \times 3}{2}$ = 9 cm²

Area of B = 6 × 2 = 12 cm²

So total area = 21 cm²

C1 Calculate the area of each of these shapes. Round to 2 s.f. where necessary.

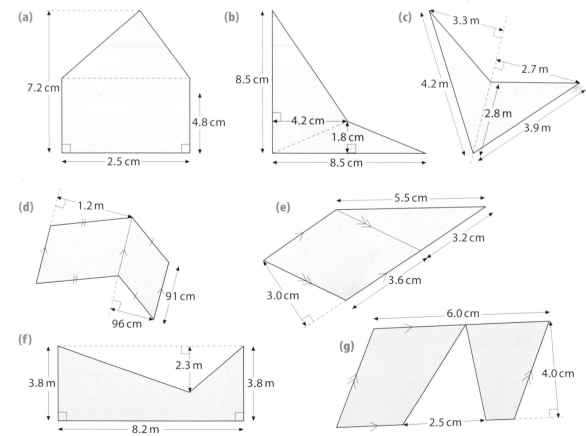

C2 Write, as simply as possible, an expression for the area of each shape.

(a)

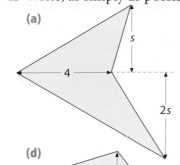

(b)

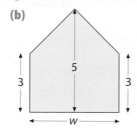

(c)

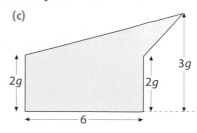

(d)

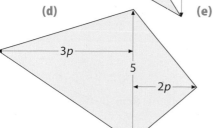

(e)

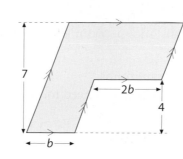

(f)

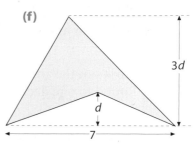

C3 (a) Find and simplify an expression for the area of each of these shapes.

(b) Find the value of *a* that gives both shapes the same area.

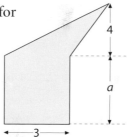

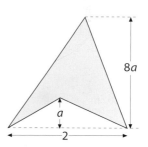

*C4 (a) Find and simplify an expression for the area of each of these shapes.

(b) Find the value of *x* that gives both shapes the same area.

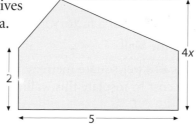

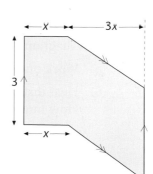

C5 Write a formula for the area of this shape, in terms of *a*, *b* and *h*.

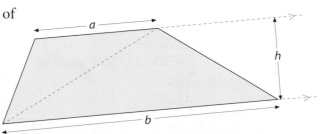

The shape in C5, a quadrilateral with a pair of parallel sides, is called a **trapezium**.

You perhaps wrote $\frac{1}{2}ah + \frac{1}{2}bh$ as your formula.

This is correct, but the more usual ways of writing it are

$$\frac{(a+b)h}{2} \quad \text{and} \quad \frac{1}{2}(a+b)h$$

You can think of them as saying 'Add the lengths of the parallel sides, multiply by the perpendicular distance between them, then halve.'

D1 Work out the area of these trapeziums.
Round to one decimal place where you need to.

(a)

(b)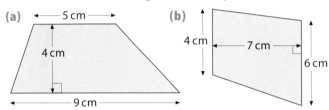

(c)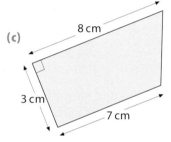

(d)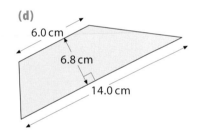

(e)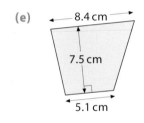

(f)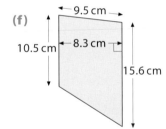

D2 This diagram shows the end wall of a factory.

(a) Work out the area of the wall.

(b) Heat insulation costs £18 per square metre.
How much would it cost to insulate this wall?

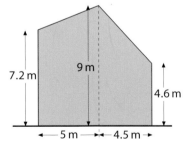

D3 The green area under the curve can be found approximately by calculating the area of each of the trapeziums A to E and adding them together.

Carry out this calculation.

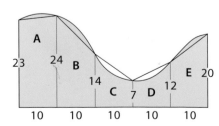

D4 For each of these trapeziums,
work in millimetres to get its area in mm², **(b)**
then work in centimetres to get its area in cm².

(a)

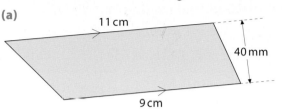

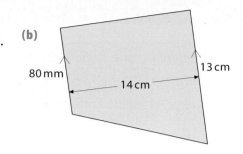

D5 The parallelogram has the
same area as the trapezium.
Find h.

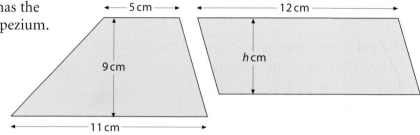

D6 (a) Find and simplify an expression for the area of each of these trapeziums.

(b) Find the value of a that gives both trapeziums the same area.

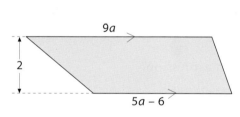

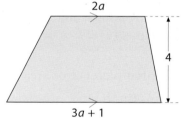

D7 (a) This shape is a trapezium.
Substitute the values given in the diagram
into the formula $A = \frac{1}{2}h(a + b)$.

(b) Solve the equation you get to find the height.

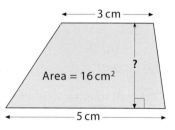

D8 Find the missing length in each of these.

(a)

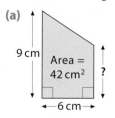

(b)

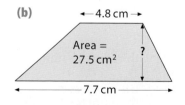

(c)

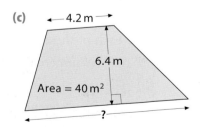

E Circle

The circumference of a circle is the diameter (twice the radius) times π. $C = \pi d = 2\pi r$

The area of a circle is the radius squared times π. $A = \pi r^2 = \pi \times r \times r$

π is a number whose decimal value goes on forever: $\pi = 3.141\,592\,654\ldots$

E1 Using the π key on your calculator find **(i)** the circumference and **(ii)** the area of circles that have the following radii. (Give your answers to 1 d.p.)

    (a) 3 cm   **(b)** 3.2 m   **(c)** 8 mm   **(d)** 7.5 cm   **(e)** 20 m

E2 Find **(i)** the circumference and **(ii)** the area of circles with these diameters.

    (a) 8 m   **(b)** 4.8 cm   **(c)** 5 cm   **(d)** 7 mm   **(e)** 100 m

Exact values involving π

The area or circumference of a circle can be left as an expression with the symbol π in it.

For example a circle with radius 2 units has area $\pi \times 2^2$, which we can leave as 4π.

We call this an **exact** value of the area.

The area given as a decimal would be **inexact**, because π cannot be written out exactly, however many decimal places we use.

E3 Match each circumference or area to an exact expression.

A The circumference of a circle with radius 3 units

B The area of a circle with radius 2 units

C The circumference of a circle with radius 4 units

D The area of a circle with radius 5 units

E The circumference of a circle with radius 8 units

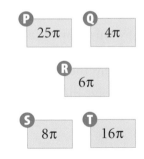

P 25π **Q** 4π

R 6π

S 8π **T** 16π

E4 Give each of these as an exact value.

    (a) The circumference of a circle with radius 15 units

    (b) The area of a circle with radius 6 units

    (c) The circumference of a circle with **diameter** 10 units

    (d) The area of a circle with diameter 7 units

    (e) The area of a **semicircle** with diameter 6 units

Finding the radius

Circumference $= 2\pi r$

radius $\longrightarrow$ $\times\, 2$ $\longrightarrow$ $\times\, \pi$ $\longrightarrow$ circumference

radius $\longleftarrow$ $\div\, 2$ $\longleftarrow$ $\div\, \pi$ $\longleftarrow$ circumference

Area $= \pi r^2$

radius $\longrightarrow$ square $\longrightarrow$ $\times\, \pi$ $\longrightarrow$ area

radius $\longleftarrow$ square root $\longleftarrow$ $\div\, \pi$ $\longleftarrow$ area

Give all your answers in this section to one decimal place.

E5 A bicycle wheel has a circumference of 200 cm.
What is the radius of the wheel?

E6 A rectangular piece of metal
is curved to make a tube.

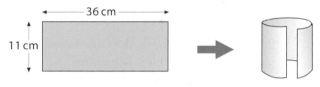

36 cm

11 cm

(a) What is the radius of the tube?

(b) What is the diameter of the tube?

E7 What would be the radius of circles with these areas?

(a) 50 cm^2 (b) 100 cm^2 (c) 25 m^2

E8 The roughly circular crater Copernicus on the Moon has an area of 3200 km^2.
What is the diameter of the crater to the nearest kilometre?

E9 (a) A farmer wants to make a circular pen which contains an area of 200 m^2.
What would be the radius of the circle needed?

(b) How long a piece of fencing would she need to go round this circle?

E10 A piece of land is a square of side length 50 m.

(a) What radius would a circular piece of land need in order to cover the same area?

(b) How much fence would the square and circular fields need around the edge?
Which shape needs more fencing?

E11 Which of these circles has the greatest radius?

Circle A: diameter 12.5 cm
Circle B: circumference 40 cm
Circle C: area 105 cm^2

E12 Find the radius of each of these.

(a) A circle with area π units   (b) A circle with circumference 12π units

F Population density

- In which countries are people crowded together?
- In which countries are people most spread out?
- Why must you be careful when using area to make comparisons of this kind?

Working out the number of people per square kilometre is called calculating the **population density**.

$$\text{population density} = \frac{\text{population}}{\text{area}}$$

By making an estimate of area from a map and finding out about the local population, you could calculate the population density for your town or village, county or region.

Country	Population	Area (km²)
Australia	20 155 000	7 687 000
Bangladesh	141 822 000	144 000
Canada	32 268 000	9 985 000
India	1 103 371 000	3 288 000
Japan	128 085 000	378 000
Kenya	34 256 000	583 000
Libya	5 853 000	1 760 000
Netherlands	16 100 000	42 000
Russia	143 202 000	17 075 000
Saudi Arabia	24 573 000	2 150 000
South Africa	45 000 000	1 221 000
United Kingdom	59 300 000	243 000
United States	298 213 000	9 631 000

F1 **(a)** Calculate the population density for the United Kingdom.

(b) Which country in the table has the closest population density to that of the United Kingdom?

F2 Rwanda has an area of 26 000 km² and is estimated to have a population density of 260 people per square kilometre. Estimate the population of Rwanda.

F3 Mr Jones keeps a herd of 82 beef cattle on 160 000 m² of pasture. His neighbour keeps 48 beef cattle on 70 000 m² of pasture.

How many more cattle could Mr Jones keep on his pasture if he used the same stocking density as his neighbour?

F4 Farm animals can only be described as 'free-range' if they are given enough space. The table shows the limits.

Bird	Maximum live weight per m²
Chicken	27.5 kg
Duck, guinea fowl or turkey	25.0 kg
Goose	15.0 kg

(a) Assuming that the live weight of an adult chicken is about 4 kg, how many chickens could you keep in a yard with area 7.8 m²?

*(b) A farmer has 18 m² available for free-range birds. These are the birds she wants to keep, with their typical live weights.

Duck 3 kg   Turkey 12 kg   Goose 9 kg

She wants to keep an equal number of each type of bird. What is the most she can keep?

You might like to calculate the area of your back garden or a suitable place in the school grounds, and work out numbers of birds for your own free-range farm!

G Converting units of area

G1 (a) Calculate the area of this rectangle in cm².

(b) Change the length and width into metres and calculate the area in m².

(c) How many cm² are there in 1 m²?

(To check your answer makes sense, imagine filling a metre square with centimetre squares.)

50 cm

400 cm

G2 Change these areas in cm² into m².

(a) 6 500 000 cm² **(b)** 480 000 cm² **(c)** 50 000 cm² **(d)** 500 cm²

G3 How many mm² are there in 1 cm²?

1 cm

1 cm

G4 How many m² are there in 1 km²? Explain how you worked it out.

G5 Convert

(a) 3 m² to cm² **(b)** 7.2 m² to cm² **(c)** 50 cm² to m² **(d)** 1040 cm² to m²

(e) 0.7 m² to cm² **(f)** 302 cm² to m² **(g)** 11 km² to m² **(h)** 8000 m² to km²

(i) 0.09 km² to m² **(j)** 720 m² to km² **(k)** 6 000 000 m² to km²

Area can also be measured in **hectares**.　　1 hectare (ha) = 10 000 m²

G6 (a) A city centre square is an exact square, and has area 1 hectare. How long is each side of the square?

(b) How many hectares are there in 1 km²?

G7 A ranch has 4.8 km² of grazing land which is stocked at 8 cattle per hectare. How many cattle are there?

H Mixed questions

H1 A farmer has a length of fence 240 m long.
How big an area would this surround if it was set out as

(a) a square

(b) a rectangle which is twice as long as it is wide

(c) a circle

(d) a right-angled triangle with sides 60 m, 80 m and 100 m long?

H2 Calculate each of the blue areas.

(a)

(b)

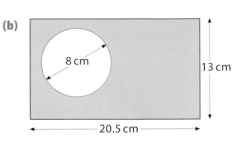

H3 The circle in this pattern has radius 2.3 cm. Find the area of

   (a) one of the blue triangles

   (b) the square

   (c) one of the black segments

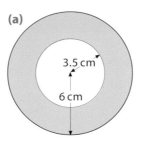

H4 (a) Calculate the area of the kite PQRS.

   (b) Calculate the length of the diagonal PR.

   (c) Calculate the length of the kite's other diagonal SQ.

H5 This running track has semicircles at each end.

   (a) How much further would someone running around the outside of the track run compared with someone running around the inside? (Give your answer to the nearest metre)

   (b) What is the area of the track (coloured)? (Give your answer to the nearest square metre.)

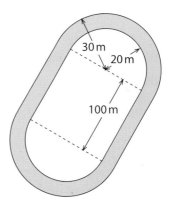

H6 These shapes are on a grid of unit squares. Give the area of each shape as an exact value.

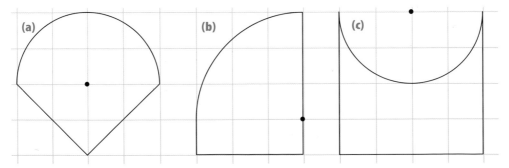

(a)   (b)   (c)

Test yourself

T1 (a) Find the area of this parallelogram.

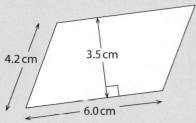

(b) Find the area of this trapezium to 1 d.p.

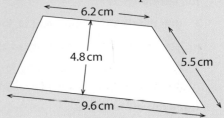

T2 Calculate the areas of these shapes, in cm² to three significant figures.
Each is either a semicircle, a quarter circle or three-quarters of a circle.

(a)

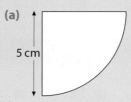

5 cm

(b)

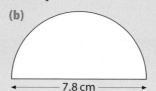

7.8 cm

(c)

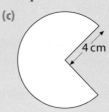

4 cm

(d)

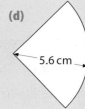

5.6 cm

T3 Give your answers to T2 in mm².

T4 The diagram shows the plan of a room.
The plan consists of a rectangle and a semicircle.
Calculate the total area of the floor.

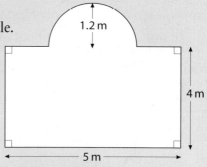

1.2 m

4 m

5 m

OCR

T5 A piece of stiff wire 2 m long is bent and the ends joined to make a circle.
What is the diameter of the circle?

T6 A gardener harvests 8320 kg of potatoes from a plot of area 1600 m².

(a) Calculate the yield in kg/m².

(b) What weight of potatoes could he expect to obtain from
a plot of area 2150 m² if the conditions were the same?

8 Percentages

You should know

- that the decimal equivalent of, for example, 43% is 0.43
- how to express one quantity as a percentage of another
- how to increase a quantity by, for example, 8% by multiplying by 1.08, and how to decrease it by 8% by multiplying by 0.92

This work will help you

- calculate the overall percentage change given two successive percentage changes
- calculate the final amount when money is invested at a given rate of interest
- calculate the original value given a percentage change and the final value

A Review: percentage change

A1 Write down the decimal equivalent of   (a) 72%   (b) 6%   (c) 14.5%   (d) 3.5%

A2 In a class of 31 children, 13 are absent with flu.
What percentage of the class (to the nearest 1%) are absent with flu?

A3 Express each of these as a percentage, to the nearest 0.1%.
   (a) 26 out of 85   (b) 49 out of 65   (c) 64 out of 818   (d) 21.3 out of 34.7

A4 What is missing in each of these statements?
   (a) To increase a quantity by 4%, multiply it by ……
   (b) To decrease a quantity by 7%, multiply it by ……
   (c) To decrease a quantity by ……%, multiply it by 0.88.
   (d) To increase a quantity by ……%, multiply it by 1.125.

A5 (a) Increase £43 by 13%.   (b) Increase £74 by 7%.   (c) Decrease £38 by 16%.

A6 (a) What do you have to multiply £58 by to get £66.70?
   (b) What is the percentage increase when a price of £58 is increased to £66.70?

A7 What is the percentage increase
   (a) from £26 to £33.28   (b) from £48 to £50.40   (c) from £140 to £178.50

A8 (a) What do you have to multiply £64 by to get £60.16?
   (b) What is the percentage decrease when a price of £64 is decreased to £60.16?

A9 What is the percentage decrease
   (a) from £36 to £30.60   (b) from £120 to £86.40   (c) from £320 to £264

A10 The prices on a computer supplies website are displayed excluding VAT. Calculate the prices including VAT at $17\frac{1}{2}$% for

- (a) a laptop advertised at £599
- (b) a DVD writer advertised at £72.55

A11 In a sale, the price of a dress is reduced from £80 to £70.

- (a) Calculate the percentage reduction in the price of the dress.
- (b) On the final day of the sale, prices are reduced by a further 20%. Calculate the final price of the dress.

A12 In June, 2640 people paid £1.20 each to ride on a miniature railway. In July the fare went up to £1.50 and 2250 people rode on the railway. Calculate, to the nearest 0.1%,

- (a) the percentage increase in the fare
- (b) the percentage decrease in the number of people riding on the railway
- (c) the percentage change in the total amount of money paid, stating whether it was an increase or a decrease

A13 Instone's Olde Fashioned Ginger Beer used to be sold in 1.5 litre bottles costing £1.85. It is now sold in 2 litre bottles costing £2.65. Calculate, to the nearest 0.1%,

- (a) the percentage increase in the quantity in a bottle
- (b) the percentage increase in the price of a bottle
- (c) the percentage change in the price per litre

*A14 A photo measures 10 cm by 8 cm. It is enlarged to fit a frame 15 cm by 12 cm. Calculate the percentage increase in the area of the photo.

B Successive percentage changes

A hardware shop increases all its prices by 15% in April, …

Buy now!
Prices up 15% from 1st April!

… and increases them again by 20% in September.

Buy now!
Prices up 20% from 1st September!

What is the overall percentage change?

Example

The population of a town grows by 12% in one year and by 15% in the next year.
What is the overall percentage increase?

This diagram shows the two increases.

original population — ×1.12 → ×1.15 → final population

Multiplying by 1.12 and then by 1.15 is equivalent to multiplying by 1.12 × 1.15, or **1.288**.

original population ——— ×1.288 ———→ final population

This is equivalent to a **28.8% increase**.

B1 Calculate the overall percentage change for each of these.

   (a) A 25% increase then a 20% increase   (b) A 16.5% increase then a 13.5% increase

B2 Calculate the overall percentage change for each of these.

   (a) A 25% decrease then a 20% decrease   (b) A 6% decrease then a 40% decrease

B3 Calculate the overall percentage change for each of these, stating whether
it is an increase or a decrease.

   (a) A 30% increase then a 20% decrease   (b) A 20% decrease then a 30% increase

   (c) A 12% decrease then a 12% increase   (d) A 14.5% decrease then a 20.5% increase

B4 A car dealer increases his prices by 4% in September.
In the following January, prices go up by 6%.

A car cost £7645 before the first price increase.
What does it cost after the second increase, to the nearest pound?

B5 The population of a town is expected to rise by 7% during the next twelve months.
During the following twelve months a fall of 7% is expected.
If the present population is 28 570, what is it expected to be after 24 months?

B6 Over the last three years, the wren population in a wood increased by 20% in the first
year, increased by 15% in the second year and decreased by 25% in the third year.
Calculate the overall percentage change.

B7 The edges of a cube are each increased in length by 10%.
Calculate the percentage increase in

   (a) the volume of the cube   (b) the surface area of the cube

*B8 Between 1998 and 2000, the lapwing population on an island went up by 51.2%.
It increased by 35% between 1999 and 2000.
What was the percentage increase between 1998 and 1999?

C Compound interest

Aunt Ethel wanted to save some money to give to her favourite niece in 10 years time. She considered three ways of saving the money.

  A Put £1000 in a jar on the mantelpiece and at the end of each year put in an extra £100.

  B Put £1000 into a bank account earning 8% interest every year.

  C Put £1000 in a safe, and add £1 after one year, £2 after two years, £4 after three years, £8 after four years, … doubling the amount each year.

What would Aunt Ethel's niece like her to do?

C1 Rajesh puts £500 into a building society account which pays 5% interest p.a. (per annum, i.e. per year).

Copy and complete this table, which shows the amount in the account at the end of each year for 4 years. (Keep all decimals on your calculator but write each amount in the table to the nearest penny.)

Number of years	Amount
0	£ 500.00
1	£ 525.00
2	
3	
4	

C2 Calculate the final amount when

  (a) £800 is invested at 7% p.a. for 3 years   (b) £650 is invested at 4% p.a. for 5 years

  (c) £1200 is invested at 2.5% p.a. for 4 years   (d) £800 is invested at 3.75% p.a. for 3 years

---

Using the power key on a calculator

If £400 is invested at 6% p.a. for 5 years, the final amount can be calculated like this.

$$400 \times 1.06 \times 1.06 \times 1.06 \times 1.06 \times 1.06 = 400 \times 1.06^5$$

Do 1.06 $\boxed{x^y}$ 5 or 1.06 $\boxed{\wedge}$ 5

C3 Calculate the final amount when

  (a) £400 is invested at 3% p.a. for 8 years   (b) £750 is invested at 8% p.a. for 9 years

  (c) £1500 is invested at 4.5% p.a. for 10 years (d) £300 is invested at 5.5% p.a. for 7 years

C4 Jacqui invests £2000 in an account which pays interest at 4% p.a. Find how many complete years she will have to leave the money in the account for it to become at least £2500.

C5 £5000 is invested in an account paying 6% p.a. interest. For how many complete years will it have to be left to become at least

  (a) £5500   (b) £6000   (c) £10 000

C6 Rachael opens a building society account on 1 January 2006.
She puts £1000 into the account to start with, and adds an extra £500 at
the end of each year.

The building society pays interest at the
rate of 4% p.a.

Continue the calculation and find
the amount on 1 January 2010.

Amount on 01/01/06		£1000.00
Interest for year 2006	+	40.00
Investment, 31/12/06	+	500.00
Amount on 01/01/07		1540.00
Interest for year 2007	+	61.60
Investment, 31/12/07	+	500.00
Amount on 01/01/08		2101.60

C7 Sean borrows £2000 from a bank on 1 January.
He agrees to pay back £500 at the end of each
month.

The bank charges interest at 2% per month on
the outstanding amount of the loan.

(a) Continue the calculation until the loan is
fully repaid. (The final repayment will be
less than £500.) When is it finally repaid?

(b) How much is the last repayment?

Amount on 1 January		£2000.00
Interest, January	+	40.00
Repayment, 31 Jan	–	500.00
Amount on 1 February		1540.00
Interest, February	+	30.80
Repayment, 28 Feb	–	500.00
Amount on 1 March		1070.80

C8 A hospital physiotherapy department gives ultraviolet treatment.
Every patient having the treatment receives a dose of 1 minute 9 seconds on day 1.
Each day the dose is increased by a percentage which depends on the
patient's skin type, as shown in the table below.

Skin type	Percentage increase per day
1 Always burns	10%
2 Tans with care but burns easily	15%
3 Tans easily and rarely burns	20%
4 Always tans, never burns	25%

(The dose is increased until it reaches a maximum of 46 minutes 18 seconds,
and it is kept constant from then on.)

(a) Janine has skin of type 3. Calculate her dose on day 3.

(b) Karl has skin type 4. On which day will his dose first go above 3 minutes?

(c) Rita has skin type 2. On day 14 her dose is 4 minutes 0 seconds.
What is her dose on day 16?

C9 The population of newts in a pond is decreasing by 7% a year.
There are 428 newts in the pond now. How many will there be in 5 years time?

C10 The value of a secondhand Ford Gerbil decreases by 18% every year.
What is the percentage decrease in its value over a period of 3 years?

C11 A credit card company charges interest at a rate of 2% per month.
Calculate the overall percentage rate of interest for 12 months, to the nearest 0.1%.

C12 Another credit card company's monthly interest rate is 1.5%.
Calculate the annual interest rate, to the nearest 0.1%.

*C13 A loan company charges interest at the rate of 60% per half year.
What is the annual interest rate?

*C14 The Sharks Loans Company is considering different ways of charging interest.

Option A	Charge 78% per year
Option B	78% ÷ 2 = 39%, so charge 39% per six months
Option C	78% ÷ 4 = 19.5%, so charge 19.5% per three months
Option D	78% ÷ 12 is 6.5%, so charge 6.5% per month
Option E	78% ÷ 52 is 1.5%, so charge 1.5% per week

(a) Calculate the equivalent yearly interest rate for each option.

(b) Sharks also considers the option of a daily rate of 78% ÷ 365.
Calculate the equivalent yearly rate for this option.
You could also investigate the option of an hourly rate of 78% ÷ (365×24).

D Percentage change in reverse

Problem 1

Jackie bought a printer for £149.95 from a computer shop.
This price included VAT at 17.5%.

What was the cost of the printer excluding VAT?

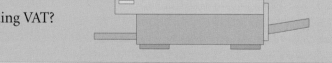

Problem 2

A shop reduces the price of a jacket by 15% in a sale.
The sale price is £39.95.

How much did the jacket cost before the sale?

Example

A rail fare goes up by 8%. The new fare is £37.80.
What was the old fare?

The old fare is multiplied by 1.08 to get the new fare.

So the new fare has to be divided by 1.08 to get the old fare.

Old fare = £37.80 ÷ 1.08 = **£35**

$$? \xrightarrow{\times 1.08} 37.80$$

$$35 \xleftarrow{\div 1.08} 37.80$$

D1 The price of a theatre ticket goes up by 6% to £13.25. What was it before the increase?

D2 The cost of hiring a digger goes up by 15% to £96.60. What was it before?

D3 Given that the rate of VAT is 17.5%, calculate these.

    (a) The price, including VAT, of a camera whose price is '£280 plus VAT'

    (b) The price, excluding VAT, of an amplifier whose price is '£423 including VAT'

D4 Given that the rate of VAT is 17.5%,
copy and complete this table.

Price excluding VAT	Price including VAT
£1430	
	£564
£740	
	£2996.25

D5 A restaurant adds a 12.5% service charge to customers' bills.
The total cost of a meal, including the service charge, is £18.90.
What did the meal cost before the service charge was added?

D6 The price of a coat goes down by 14% to £27.95. What was it before?

D7 Calculate the original price of an article which costs

    (a) £29.50 after an 18% increase   **(b)** £39.60 after a 12% reduction

    (c) £88.80 after a 7.5% reduction   **(d)** £50.50 after a 37.5% reduction

E Mixed questions

E1 The population of a town is decreasing by 2% each year.
At present the population is 80 654.

    (a) What was the population one year ago?

    (b) What is the population expected to be in four years' time?

E2 Calculate, to the nearest penny, the compound interest earned when
£800 is invested for 3 years at 6% per annum.

WJEC

E3 The graph shows the profits of a small business. (10k = 10 000)

Calculate the percentage increase in the profits between

(a) 2001 and 2002

(b) 2002 and 2003

(c) 2003 and 2004

(d) 2004 and 2005

(e) 2002 and 2004

(f) 2002 and 2005

(g) 2001 and 2004

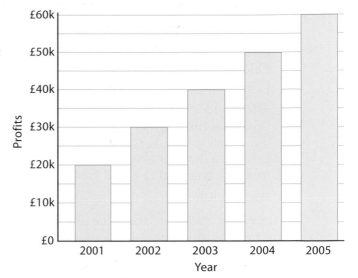

E4 Calculate the missing entries in this table.

Old price	£26.50	£30.50	(c)	(d)	£48.40	£31.50
Percentage change	up 24%	down 18%	up 16%	down 26%	(e)	(f)
New price	(a)	(b)	£16.82	£13.69	£65.34	£28.98

E5 Each year that Jane leaves her money in a bank account the amount grows by 4.5%. By what percentage does it grow in 3 years? Give your answer to the nearest 0.1%.

E6 (a) During 2003 the average wage earned by some factory workers in Barnsley rose from £350 to £372. What was the percentage increase?

(b) During 2003 the number of people out of work in Barnsley fell by 8%. At the end of the year there were 2576 people out of work in Barnsley. How many people were out of work at the beginning of the year?

AQA

E7 Kolleeg's Corn Flakes are sold in standard packs of 500 g for £1.20. During a promotion, the quantity in a pack is increased by 20%, but the cost stays the same.

Calculate the percentage reduction in the cost per kilogram during the promotion.

E8 Lord Elaudi is thinking of increasing the entrance fee to his castle by 15%. His advisers tell him that this will reduce the number of visitors by 14%. Should he increase the fee? Explain your answer.

E9 Items in a computer shop are priced to make a 37% profit. In a sale, the prices are reduced by 12%. Calculate the percentage profit on items sold in the sale.

AQA

Test yourself

T1 (a) Kelly invested £450 for 3 years at a rate of 6% per year compound interest.
Calculate the total amount that the investment is worth at the end of the 3 years.

(b) Kelly decides to buy a television.
After a reduction of 15% in the sale, the one she bought cost her £319.60.
What was the original price of the television?

OCR

T2 The price of a new television is £423.
This price includes value added tax (VAT) at $17\frac{1}{2}$%.

(a) Work out the cost of the television **before** VAT was added.

By the end of each year, the value of a television has
fallen by 12% of its value at the start of that year.
The value of a television was £423 at the start of the first year.

(b) Work out the value of the television at the end of the **third** year.
Give your answer to the nearest penny.

Edexcel

T3 In a sale all the prices are reduced by 30%.
The sale price of a jacket is £28.
Work out the price of the jacket before the sale.

Edexcel

T4 Joe put £5000 in building society savings account.
Compound interest at 4.8% was added at the end of each year.

(a) Calculate the total amount of money in Joe's savings account at
the end of 3 years. Give your answer to the nearest penny.

Sarah also put a sum of money in a building society savings account.
Compound interest at 5% was added at the end of each year.

(b) Work out the number by which Sarah has to multiply her sum of money
to find the total amount she will have after 3 years.

Edexcel

T5 The number of visitors to a theme park dropped by 18% between 2004 and 2005.
Improvements were made to the park and the number of visitors rose by 15%
between 2005 and 2006.

Calculate the overall percentage change in the number of visitors between
2004 and 2006.

T6 Liz estimated the cost of material needed to make herself a dress.
When Liz goes to a shop to buy the material, the cost per metre is 40%
more than she had estimated.
Liz is informed by the shopkeeper that she had miscalculated the amount
of material and she really needs 20% more material than she had estimated.

How much more than her original estimate does the dress material cost?
Give your answer as a percentage of Liz's original estimate.

AQA

Review 1

1 (a) Calculate the area of each shape.

(i)

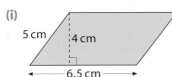
5 cm
4 cm
6.5 cm

(ii)

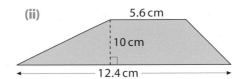
5.6 cm
10 cm
12.4 cm

(b) What is the perimeter of the parallelogram?

2 (a) Work out $1\frac{1}{4} \times \frac{4}{5}$.

(b) What does your result tell you about $1\frac{1}{4}$ and $\frac{4}{5}$?

3 Find the percentage increase in the price of a rail ticket that goes up from £89 to £92.

4 The table shows the results of a survey into the number of TV sets in people's homes.

(a) How many of these homes contain more than two TV sets?

(b) Calculate the mean number of sets in a home, correct to one decimal place.

(c) Find the median number of sets.

(d) What is the mode?

Number of sets	Number of homes
0	1
1	5
2	10
3	12
4	3

5 A charity appeal raised £157 000, correct to the nearest thousand pounds. What was the minimum possible amount raised?

6 These shapes are an equilateral triangle and a square.

What value of x gives both shapes the same perimeter?

x

$x - 5$

7 The population of a town is planned to increase by a total of 15% over the next three years. The present population is 24 600.
Find the planned population to an appropriate degree of accuracy.

8 Each exterior angle of a regular polygon is 15°.
How many sides does this polygon have?

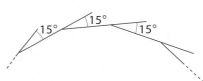
15° 15° 15°

9 In a village, the ratio of males to females is 3 : 5.
What fractions go in the gaps in the following statements?

(a) The number of males is … of the number of females.

(b) Females make up … of the population of the village.

10 Solve these equations.   (a) $4(n - 5) = n - 18$ (b) $3(x - 7) - 2(4 - x) = 26$

11 The triangle ABC is isosceles with AB = BC. Calculate, giving reasons, the size of angle x.

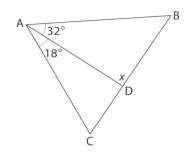

12 This stem-and-leaf table shows the typing speeds in words per minute of some people who took an audio-typing test.

2	9
3	2 2 4 7 8
4	0 1 1 3 4 5 5 9
5	1 3 4 4 6 7
6	2

Stem = 10 words per minute

   (a) How many people took the test?

   (b) What was the range of the typing speeds?

   (c) What was the median speed?

   (d) People with speeds of 38 words per minute or more had their work checked for accuracy. What percentage of the people was this?

13 Form and solve an equation to calculate the angles in this quadrilateral.

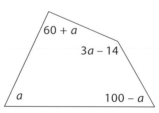

14 This metal tray has a square base x cm by x cm.

   (a) Write an expression for the area of the base in cm^2.

   The metal sides of the tray are 2 cm high.

   (b) Write an expression for the area of one side.

   (c) Show that the formula for the total area, y cm^2, of metal used for the tray is
   $$y = x^2 + 8x$$

   (d) On graph paper, draw a graph of this equation for values of x from 0 to 6.

   (e) Use your graph to find the length of the tray's base if the total area of metal is to be

   (i) 40 cm^2 (ii) 25 cm^2 (iii) 80 cm^2

15 How long will 24 tins of cat food last a cat if she eats $\frac{2}{3}$ of a tin each day?

16 Solve these equations.

   (a) $8 - \dfrac{n}{5} = 5$ (b) $\dfrac{2n}{3} - 5 = 1$ (c) $\dfrac{10 - 3n}{2} = n$

17 The diagram shows the end wall of a greenhouse.

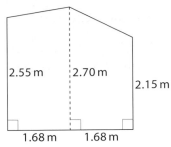

    (a) Calculate the area of the wall in m².

    (b) State the area of the wall in cm², correct to 2 s.f.

2.55 m   2.70 m   2.15 m

1.68 m   1.68 m

18 Rajeev invests £250 at a rate of 4% per annum compound interest.
How much will the investment be worth at the end of 5 years?

19 This table shows the distribution of the weights
of the pumpkins grown in a greenhouse.

Weight, w kg	Frequency
$0 < w \leq 1$	5
$1 < w \leq 2$	10
$2 < w \leq 3$	7
$3 < w \leq 4$	3

    (a) Draw a frequency polygon for this data.

    (b) Calculate an estimate of the mean weight
of the pumpkins.

    (c) What is the modal class of the weights?

20 In a sale, the cost of a dress is reduced by 15% to £25.50.
What was the cost of the dress before it was reduced?

21 A woman's weight is recorded as 70 kg, correct to the nearest kg.
What are the lower and upper bounds of this weight?

22 Work out these.

    (a) $5 \div \frac{1}{2}$ **(b)** $10 \div \frac{2}{5}$ **(c)** $\frac{1}{3} \div \frac{1}{6}$ **(d)** $3\frac{1}{2} \div \frac{1}{4}$ **(e)** $\frac{2}{3} \div \frac{5}{6}$

23 **(a)** Find the circumference of a circle with a diameter of 14 cm, correct to 1 d.p.

    (h) What is the **exact** area of a circle with a radius of 6 cm?

24 A video recorder cost £289.99 including VAT at $17\frac{1}{2}$%.
What was its cost before VAT was added?

25 Solve these equations.

    (a) $\dfrac{x+2}{2} = \dfrac{x-4}{4}$ **(b)** $\dfrac{x-5}{3} + \dfrac{x+1}{5} = 6$

    (c) $\dfrac{x+1}{4} + \dfrac{3x+2}{12} = \dfrac{11}{12}$ **(d)** $\dfrac{x+1}{2} - \dfrac{x+2}{3} = 1$

26 This is part of a 'ring' made by alternating
squares and regular pentagons.

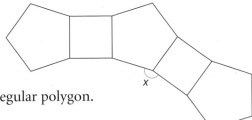

    (a) Calculate the angle x.

    (b) The inside of the completed ring forms a regular polygon.
How many sides does it have?

9 Transformations

You will revise how to transform points and shapes using reflection, translation, rotation and enlargement.

This work will help you

- use column notation for vectors
- describe fully how a shape has been transformed

A Reflection
level 6

A1 Give the shape that is the image after reflecting

(a) shape C in mirror line p (b) shape H in line m

(c) shape E in line q (d) shape A in line n

(e) shape F in line n (f) shape H in line p

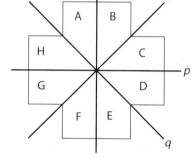

A2 Give the mirror line that is used to reflect

(a) F on to E   (b) A on to F

(c) H on to A   (d) G on to B

(e) A on to D   (f) F on to C

A3 (a) Is it possible to reflect shape H on to shape D?

(b) What transformation could be used to map shape F on to shape B?

(c) Is it possible to **translate** any of the shapes on to another shape?

Mirror lines are often described by their equations.

A4 Line a on this grid has the equation $y = x$.

(a) Give the equation of each of the other lines.

(b) Give the equation that can be used to describe the x-axis.

(c) Give the equation that can be used to describe the y-axis.

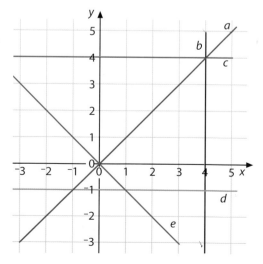

A5 On squared paper draw x- and y-axes, each marked from $^-5$ to 5. Draw a triangle with vertices (3, 3), (3, 4) and (1, 3). Label it A.

(a) Draw and label these lines.

$$y = x \qquad y = 2 \qquad x = {}^-1$$

Reflect triangle A in the line $y = x$. Label this image B.

Reflect triangle A in the line $y = 2$. Label this image C.

Reflect triangle A in the line $x = {}^-1$. Label this image D.

Reflect triangle A in the y-axis. Label this image E.

(b) What transformation will map D on to E?

A6 State the image produced by reflecting

(a) shape D in the line $y = 3$

(b) shape C in $y = x$

(c) shape I in $x = 0$

(d) shape E in $x = 4$

A7 Give the equation of the mirror line that reflects

(a) A on to D

(b) H on to G

(c) C on to H

(d) C on to B

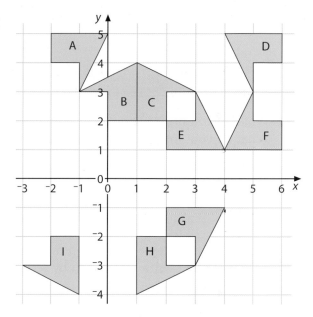

A8 (a) To what point will (7, 2) be mapped after a reflection in $y = x$?

(b) What happens to the coordinates of any point after reflection in $y = x$?

(c) What happens to the coordinates of any point after reflection in the x-axis?

(d) What happens to the coordinates of any point after reflection in the y-axis?

A9 Copy this diagram on to squared paper.

(a) Draw the image of the triangle T after a reflection in the line $x = 3$. Label this image U.

Now draw the image of U after a reflection in the line $x = 1$. Label this image V.

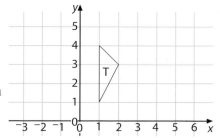

(b) Describe the **single** transformation that maps T to V directly.

B Translation

A **column vector** is a convenient way to describe how a point or shape has been translated.

The column vector $\begin{bmatrix} 3 \\ -2 \end{bmatrix}$ means 'move 3 units right and 2 units down.'

The column vector $\begin{bmatrix} -1 \\ 2 \end{bmatrix}$ means 'move 1 unit left and 2 units up.'

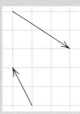

B1 Write a column vector for each of these translations.

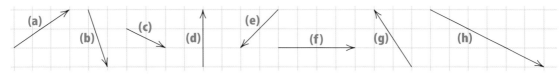

B2 What do you notice about translations (c) and (h) in B1?
What do you notice about their column vectors?

B3 What vector has been used to translate shape A to shape B?

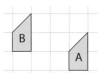

B4 Ben says that triangle T has been mapped on to triangle U by a translation by vector $\begin{bmatrix} 1 \\ -1 \end{bmatrix}$.

Comment on his claim.

B5 Give the trapezium that is the image of shape A after a translation by

(a) $\begin{bmatrix} 1 \\ 3 \end{bmatrix}$ (b) $\begin{bmatrix} -2 \\ -2 \end{bmatrix}$ (c) $\begin{bmatrix} 3 \\ -1 \end{bmatrix}$

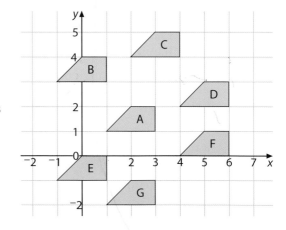

B6 Give the vector for the translation that maps

(a) B on to D (b) C on to D
(c) F on to G (d) G on to E

B7 Copy these axes and shape A only on to squared paper.

Draw the image of A after a translation by

(a) $\begin{bmatrix} 0 \\ 2 \end{bmatrix}$ (b) $\begin{bmatrix} -3 \\ -2 \end{bmatrix}$ (c) $\begin{bmatrix} 1 \\ -3 \end{bmatrix}$

C Rotation

C1 Shapes in this diagram are rotated about the centre *c*.

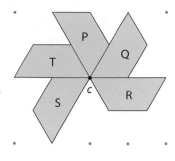

   (a) Give the shape that is the image after rotating

      (i) shape P by 60° clockwise

      (ii) shape S by 120° anticlockwise

      (iii) shape T by 120° clockwise

   (b) Tim says, 'To get from T to S rotate by 60° about centre *c*.' What's missing from his instruction?

   (c) Describe **fully** the rotation that maps

      (i) P on to T   **(ii)** P on to R

      (iii) Q on to T   **(iv)** Q on to S

      (v) Q on to R   **(vi)** R on to T

   (d) For which rotations do you not need to say 'clockwise' or 'anticlockwise'?

C2 (a) Which shape is the image of shape F after a 90° rotation clockwise, centre *n*?

   (b) Mary says:
'To get from I to J rotate about *q*.'
What's missing from her instruction?

   (c) Rafiq says:
'To get from G to C, rotate by 180°.'
What's missing from his instruction?

   (d) Find two letters that fill the blanks.

      Shape __ maps on to shape __ by a rotation through 180°, centre *p*.

   (e) What is needed in the blanks here?

      Shape __ maps on to shape J by a rotation 90° anticlockwise about __ .

   (f) How many shapes in the diagram can D be rotated on to, using the centres marked? Try to find them all.
For each shape you find, give the **centre**, **angle** and, where necessary, the **direction** of rotation.

   (g) Describe **fully** how to transform

      (i) I on to G   **(ii)** E on to G   **(iii)** J on to B

      (iv) I on to H   **(v)** A on to I   **(vi)** F on to C

   (h) Dave says, 'You can get to it by rotating shape E.'
Myra says, 'You can get to it by rotating shape A.'
They are talking about the same shape.
What shape is it and how should each of them describe their rotation fully?

The L method

When rotating a shape on a grid it helps to rotate each vertex using an 'L'.
Here is how you rotate a shape through 90° anticlockwise about point P.

Draw an 'L', using the grid, from the centre P to a vertex of the shape.

Rotate the L 90° anticlockwise. The end of the L marks the new position of the vertex. Repeat for every vertex until you can draw the shape.

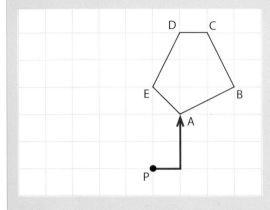

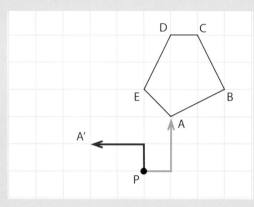

C3 (a) Copy the shape ABCDE above and point P on squared paper.
Complete the 90° anticlockwise rotation of ABCDE about point P.

(b) On the same diagram draw the 180° rotation of ABCDE about point P.

C4 Copy this diagram on to squared paper.
Using the L method, draw and label the images produced by the following mappings.

(a) A 90° clockwise rotation of triangle T about the centre $(0, 0)$

(b) A 90° clockwise rotation of T about the centre $(3, 2)$

(c) A 90° anticlockwise rotation of T about $(^-1, 0)$

(d) A 180° rotation of T with centre $(0, ^-1)$

(e) A 90° anticlockwise rotation of T with centre $(4, 2)$

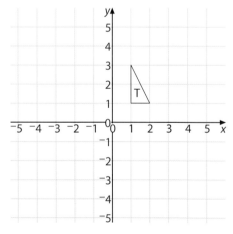

C5 P'Q'R' is the image of PQR after a 180° rotation about centre C.

(a) What do you notice about the position of centre C in relation to point P and its image P'?

(b) What about the position of centre C in relation to Q and Q'?

(c) What can you say in general about the position of the centre of a 180° rotation?

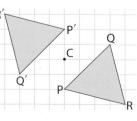

C6 Give the coordinates of the centre of the rotation that maps P on to Q.

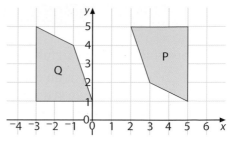

C7 A rotation through 180° maps the point (⁻4, ⁻2) on to the point (2, 0).
What is the centre of this rotation?

Finding the centre of a 90° rotation on a grid

In the diagrams below, shape B is the image of shape A after a 90° clockwise rotation.

To find the centre of rotation, first decide roughly where it lies.
Then try each point in this region as the centre, to see whether the
L method maps a vertex of A on to the corresponding vertex of B.

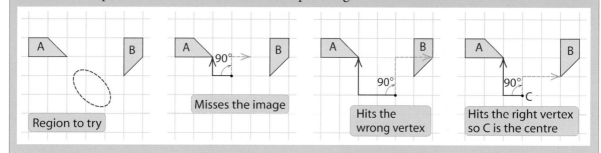

C8 Copy this diagram carefully on to squared paper.

Giving the coordinates of the centre of rotation in each case, describe fully the rotation that maps

(a) A on to B   (b) B on to C

(c) A on to C   (d) D on to B

(e) C on to D   (f) A on to E

(g) B on to E   (h) D on to E

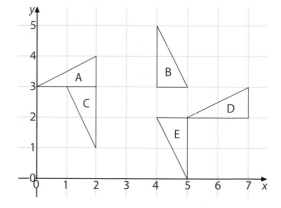

Congruent shapes

Two shapes are congruent if every length and angle on one equals a corresponding length or angle on the other.

The image of a shape after reflection, translation or rotation is congruent to the original shape. It doesn't matter that a reflection 'flips' the shape over.

D Enlargement

D1 Copy this diagram carefully on to squared paper.

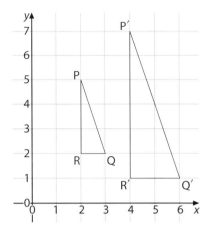

(a) Triangle P′Q′R′ is an enlargement of triangle PQR. What is the scale factor of the enlargement?

(b) Draw the line PP′.
Extend this line to the left and downwards.

Draw the lines QQ′ and RR′, extending each line to the left.

Your three lines should intersect at (0, 3). We call this point the **centre of enlargement**. Label it C.

(c) Write as a column vector the translation that takes C to P. (We call this vector $\overrightarrow{CP}$ for short.)

(d) Write $\overrightarrow{CP'}$ as a column vector. Compare it with $\overrightarrow{CP}$. What do you notice?

(e) Compare the column vectors $\overrightarrow{CQ}$ and $\overrightarrow{CQ'}$.
Compare $\overrightarrow{CR}$ and $\overrightarrow{CR'}$. What do you notice?

Drawing an enlargement of an object from a given centre, with a given scale factor

In this example, C is the centre of enlargement and the scale factor to be used is 3.

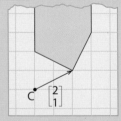
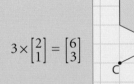

$$3 \times \begin{bmatrix} 2 \\ 1 \end{bmatrix} = \begin{bmatrix} 6 \\ 3 \end{bmatrix}$$

Draw the column vector from the centre of enlargement to a vertex of the object.

'Multiply' the vector by the scale factor and use the result to go from the **centre** to the corresponding point on the image.

Repeat this process for each vertex to obtain the complete image.

D2 Copy this diagram.

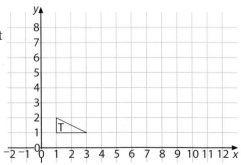

(a) Use the method above to draw an enlargement of T, with centre (0, 0) and scale factor 4 (so multiply each vector by 4).

(b) Draw an enlargement of T, with scale factor 3 and centre (2, 0).

(c) Draw an enlargement of T, with scale factor 2 and centre (⁻1, 2).

D3 Copy this diagram carefully.

(a) What transformation maps shape P on to shape Q? Describe it fully.

(b) Draw an enlargement of Q, with scale factor $1\frac{1}{2}$. and centre $(^-1, 2)$. Label the image R.

(c) What **single** transformation maps P directly on to R? Describe it fully.

(d) Draw an 'enlargement' of Q, with centre $(1, 0)$ and scale factor $\frac{1}{2}$ (so 'divide' each vector by 2). Label it S.

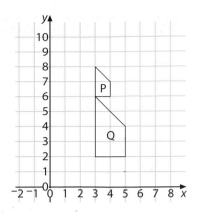

E Mixed questions

E1 Give the shape that is the image after

(a) shape C is reflected in the line $y = 0$

(b) shape E is rotated 90° clockwise about centre $(2, 1)$

(c) shape J is translated by $\begin{bmatrix} 1 \\ 3 \end{bmatrix}$

(d) shape C is reflected in the line $y = x$

E2 Describe fully the transformations that map

(a) D on to F   (b) G on to H

(c) E on to F   (d) I on to J

(e) I on to G   (f) A on to B

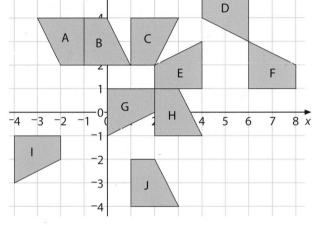

E3 Copy this diagram on to squared paper.

(a) Describe the transformation that maps the yellow triangle on to shape A.

(b) Give the scale factor and centre of the enlargement that maps the yellow triangle on to triangle B.

(c) Draw the image of the yellow triangle after a reflection in $y = 0$. Label this triangle C.

(d) Draw the image of the yellow triangle after an enlargement scale factor 2 with centre $(1, 1)$. Label this triangle D.

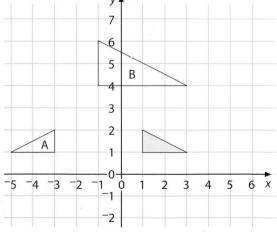

(e) Describe fully the single transformation that maps A on to C.

(f) Describe fully the single transformation that maps B on to D.

(g) Which shapes on your diagram are congruent?

Test yourself

T1 The grid shows several transformations of the shaded triangle.

(a) Write down the letter of the triangle

   (i) after the shaded triangle is reflected in the line $x = 3$,

   (ii) after the shaded triangle is translated by 3 squares to the right and 5 squares down,

   (iii) after the shaded triangle is rotated 90° clockwise about O.

(b) Describe fully the single transformation which takes triangle F on to triangle G.

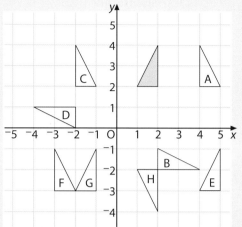

AQA

T2 (a) For these triangles, describe fully the single transformation that maps

   (i) A on to B

   (ii) A on to C

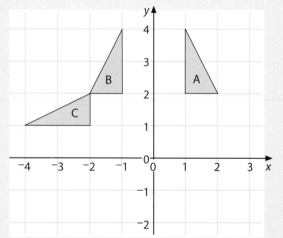

(b) For these quadrilaterals, describe fully the transformation that maps Q on to R.

(c) Q is reflected in $x = 4$, and then in $y = 1$. Describe fully the single transformation that is equivalent to these two transformations.

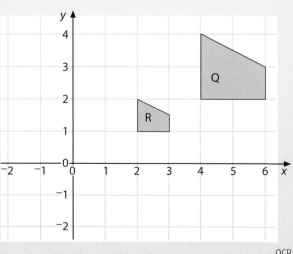

OCR

10 Powers and indices

You should know how to work out the value of powers such as 4^3 (4 to the power 3).

This work will help you

- work with negative indices (and evaluate, say, 7^0)
- use the rules for multiplying and dividing powers of the same number
- use the rules for indices to simplify algebraic expressions

You will need sheet H1–1.

A Calculating with powers

- What do you think is the next line of each pattern?

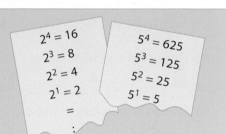

$$2^4 = 16$$
$$2^3 = 8$$
$$2^2 = 4$$
$$2^1 = 2$$
$$= \qquad$$

$$5^4 = 625$$
$$5^3 = 125$$
$$5^2 = 25$$
$$5^1 = 5$$

- What do you think is the value of 9^0?
  Check that your calculator gives the same result.

A1 Evaluate these.

    (a) $2^4 + 5$ (b) 3×2^3 (c) $3^2 \times 3^0$ (d) $5^2 + 2^5$

    (e) 10×3^4 (f) $10^2 \div 5$ (g) $3^3 \div 9$ (h) $5^1 \times 4^2$

A2 Find the missing number in the statement $4^{\blacksquare} = 1$.

A3 Work out the value of $2^n + 1$ when

    (a) $n = 3$ (b) $n = 5$ (c) $n = 0$ (d) $n = 1$

A4 For each of the following write down the value of n.

    (a) $3^n = 81$ (b) $6^n = 6$ (c) $n^3 = 64$ (d) $n^7 = 1$

    (e) $10^n = 100$ (f) $3^n = 243$ (g) $10^n = 1$ (h) $n^3 = 125$

A5 Work out the value of k in these statements.

    (a) $2^k + 9 = 17$ (b) $6 \times 10^k = 600\,000$ (c) $5^k + 4 = 5$

    (d) $2^k \times 3 = 48$ (e) $k^3 \div 4 = 16$ (f) $k \times 5^2 = 150$

    (g) $3^3 + 2^k = 29$ (h) $3^k \times 2 = 162$ (i) $5^3 - 4^k = 121$

A6 Work out the value of these expressions when $n = 3$.

    (a) $n^2 \times n^2$ (b) $2n^2$ (c) $n^2 + n^2$ (d) $n^2 \times n$

    (e) $n^2 + n^2 + n^2 + n^2$ (f) n^4 (g) $n^2 + n^1$ (h) n^3 (i) $4n^2$

B Multiplying powers

To **multiply** powers of the same number, **add** the indices.

Examples

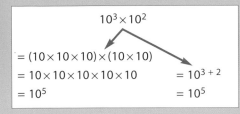

$$10^3 \times 10^2$$
$$= (10 \times 10 \times 10) \times (10 \times 10)$$
$$= 10 \times 10 \times 10 \times 10 \times 10 \qquad = 10^{3+2}$$
$$= 10^5 \qquad\qquad = 10^5$$

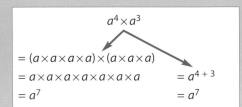

$$a^4 \times a^3$$
$$= (a \times a \times a \times a) \times (a \times a \times a)$$
$$= a \times a \times a \times a \times a \times a \times a \qquad = a^{4+3}$$
$$= a^7 \qquad\qquad = a^7$$

B1 Find three pairs of equivalent expressions.

A $3^5 \times 3^2$ **B** 3×3^7 **C** $3^3 \times 3^7$ **D** 3^{10} **E** 3^7 **F** 3^8

B2 Copy and complete these.

(a) $4^3 \times 4^2 = 4^{\blacksquare}$ (b) $3^4 \times 3^{\blacksquare} = 3^{11}$ (c) $7^{\blacksquare} \times 7^3 = 7^4$

B3 Write the answers to these using indices.

(a) $6^2 \times 6^7$ (b) $2^4 \times 2^9$ (c) $10^5 \times 10^7$ (d) $5^6 \times 5$

(e) $3^4 \times 3^2 \times 3^5$ (f) $8 \times 8^6 \times 8^2$ (g) $9^3 \times 9 \times 9^3$ (h) $2^4 \times 2^5 \times 2^3$

B4 This table shows some powers of 7.

7^2	7^3	7^4	7^5	7^6	7^7	7^8
49	343	2401	16 807	117 649	823 543	5 764 801

Use the results in the table to evaluate

(a) 49×343 (b) $343 \times 16\,807$ (c) 2401×343 (d) $823\,543 \times 7$

B5 In this wall, each expression is written as a power and is found by **multiplying** the two powers on the bricks below.

What should be on the top brick?

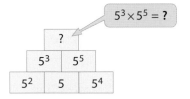

$5^3 \times 5^5 = ?$

?

| 5^3 | 5^5 |

| 5^2 | 5 | 5^4 |

B6 Copy and complete these multiplication walls.

(a)

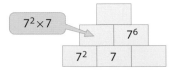

$7^2 \times 7$

| | 7^6 | |
| 7^2 | 7 | |

(b)

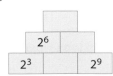

| 2^6 | |
| 2^3 | 2^9 |

(c)

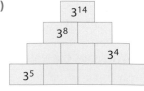

	3^{14}	
	3^8	
		3^4
3^5		

B7 Simplify each of these.

(a) $b \times b \times b \times b$ (b) $h^3 \times h^2$ (c) $a^4 \times a^5$ (d) $k \times k^5$

(e) $d^7 \times d$ (f) $m^2 \times m^4 \times m^6$ (g) $p \times p^9 \times p^3$ (h) $n \times n^7 \times n$

B8 Copy and complete these.

(a) $y^5 \times y^3 = y^\blacksquare$ (b) $n^2 \times n^\blacksquare = n^6$ (c) $h^\blacksquare \times h^2 \times h^5 = h^{11}$

(d) $k \times k^\blacksquare = k^6$ (e) $b^\blacksquare \times b^3 = b^3$ (f) $p^4 \times p^\blacksquare \times p^3 = p^{24}$

B9 Copy and complete these multiplication walls.

(a)  (b) 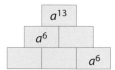 (c)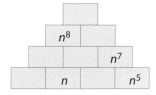

B10 Decide whether each statement is true or false.

(a) $(2^3)^2 = 2^3 \times 2^3$ (b) $(2^3)^2 = 2^3 + 2^3$ (c) $(4^2)^3 = 4^2 + 4^2 + 4^2$

(d) $(4^2)^3 = 4^2 \times 4^2 \times 4^2$ (e) $(5^4)^2 = 5^4 \times 5^4$ (f) $(5^4)^2 = 5^4 + 5^4$

B11 Copy and complete these statements.

(a) $(7^3)^2 = 7^3 \times 7^3 = 7^\blacksquare$ (b) $(2^4)^3 = 2^4 \times 2^4 \times 2^4 = 2^\blacksquare$

B12 Simplify these.

(a) $(3^3)^2$ (b) $(2^3)^3$ (c) $(4^5)^2$ (d) $(3^4)^3$

B13 Copy and complete $(x^5)^3 = x^5 \times x^5 \times x^5 = x^\blacksquare$.

B14 Simplify these.

(a) $(p^4)^2$ (b) $(x^2)^2$ (c) $(k^0)^4$ (d) $(n^3)^3$

B15 Copy and complete these statements.

(a) $(5^2)^\blacksquare = 5^8$ (b) $(10^\blacksquare)^3 = 10^{12}$ (c) $(n^5)^\blacksquare = n^{10}$ (d) $(x^\blacksquare)^7 = x^{14}$

B16 Copy and complete the rule $(a^m)^n = a^\blacksquare$.
Explain how you know your rule is correct.

*B17 Write each of these numbers as powers of 3.

(a) 9 (b) 9^5 (c) 27^4 (d) 81^2 (e) 27^n

*B18 Arrange the following numbers in order of size, smallest first.

$2^{31}, \; 4^{15}, \; 8^{11}, \; 16^7, \; 32^5$

*B19 Which of the numbers $2^4, 4^2, 2^7, 2^2$ is the same as half of 4^4?

C Multiplying expressions with powers

Order does not matter when you are multiplying.
For example, $2\times5\times7 = 7\times2\times5$.

This helps us multiply expressions in algebra.

Examples

$$5a\times3a = 5\times a\times3\times a$$
$$= 5\times3\times a\times a$$
$$= 15a^2$$

$$2p^2\times3p^5 = 2\times p^2\times3\times p^5$$
$$= 2\times3\times p^2\times p^5$$
$$= 6p^7$$

$$(5q^3)^2 = 5q^3\times5q^3$$
$$= 5\times q^3\times5\times q^3$$
$$= 5\times5\times q^3\times q^3$$
$$= 25q^6$$

C1 (a) Find four pairs of matching expressions.

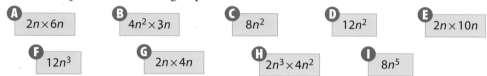

A $2n\times6n$ **B** $4n^2\times3n$ **C** $8n^2$ **D** $12n^2$ **E** $2n\times10n$

F $12n^3$ **G** $2n\times4n$ **H** $2n^3\times4n^2$ **I** $8n^5$

(b) Which is the odd one out?

C2 Simplify these.

(a) $3p\times5p$ (b) $n\times2n$ (c) $2m^2\times9m$ (d) $7d^3\times d^4$

(e) $2h^5\times3h^2$ (f) $4x^3\times5x^3$ (g) $3n^2\times n^4\times7n^3$ (h) $2n^3\times2n\times2n^5$

C3 Copy and complete these multiplication walls.

(a)

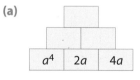

a^4 | $2a$ | $4a$

(b)

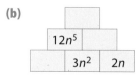

$12n^5$

$3n^2$ | $2n$

(c)

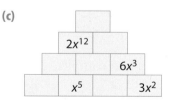

$2x^{12}$

$6x^3$

x^5 | $3x^2$

C4 Copy and complete these.

(a) $\blacksquare\times4p = 8p^2$ (b) $7m^2\times\blacksquare = 7m^3$ (c) $\blacksquare\times4d = 12d^3$

(d) $3h^5\times\blacksquare = 6h^{10}$ (e) $\blacksquare\times3h^6 = 18h^7$ (f) $5p^4\times\blacksquare = 15p^{12}$

C5 Solve the 'cover-up' puzzle on sheet H1–1.

C6 (a) Copy and complete $(2p)^3 = 2p\times2p\times2p = ?$

(b) Copy and complete $(3n^3)^2 = 3n^3\times3n^3 = ?$

C7 Simplify these.

(a) $(2y)^3$ (b) $(3n)^2$ (c) $(2p^5)^2$ (d) $(4m^3)^3$

D Dividing powers

$$5^6 \div 5^4 = \frac{5^6}{5^4}$$

$$= \frac{5 \times 5 \times 5 \times 5 \times 5 \times 5}{5 \times 5 \times 5 \times 5}$$

$$= \frac{\overset{1}{5} \times \overset{1}{5} \times \overset{1}{5} \times \overset{1}{5} \times 5 \times 5}{\underset{1}{5} \times \underset{1}{5} \times \underset{1}{5} \times \underset{1}{5}}$$

$$= 5 \times 5$$

$$= 5^2$$

$$3^7 \div 3^3 = \frac{3^7}{3^3}$$

$$= \frac{3 \times 3 \times 3 \times 3 \times 3 \times 3 \times 3}{3 \times 3 \times 3}$$

$$= \frac{3 \times 3 \times 3 \times 3 \times \cancel{3} \times \cancel{3} \times \cancel{3}}{\cancel{3} \times \cancel{3} \times \cancel{3}}$$

$$= 3 \times 3 \times 3 \times 3$$

$$= 3^4$$

> We usually leave out 1s as multiplying or dividing by 1 doesn't affect a number.

- What is the rule for dividing powers?

D1 (a) Find four pairs of equivalent expressions.

A $2^6 \div 2^2$

B $\frac{2^4}{2}$

C 2^3

D $\frac{2^5}{2^4}$

E 2^4

F $\frac{2^8}{2^6}$

G 2^2

H $2^{10} \div 2^5$

I 2

(b) Which is the odd one out?

D2 Write the answers to these using indices.

(a) $7^{10} \div 7^2$

(b) $2^9 \div 2^4$

(c) $10^7 \div 10^2$

(d) $5^6 \div 5$

(e) $\dfrac{3^9}{3^7}$

(f) $\dfrac{8^6}{8}$

(g) $\dfrac{10^{12}}{10^3}$

(h) $\dfrac{5^4}{5^4}$

D3 Find the value of n in each statement.

(a) $5^8 \div 5^2 = 5^n$

(b) $6^9 \div 6^n = 6^2$

(c) $9^n \div 9^8 = 9^3$

(d) $3^n \div 3^2 = 3^{12}$

(e) $\dfrac{9^{16}}{9^n} = 9^2$

(f) $\dfrac{2^n}{2} = 2^5$

(g) $\dfrac{7^7}{7^n} = 7^3$

(h) $\dfrac{3^n}{3^8} = 3^0$

D4 Write the answers to these using indices.

(a) $6^3 \times 6^5$

(b) $\dfrac{7^5}{7^3}$

(c) $\dfrac{2^5 \times 2^4}{2^3}$

(d) $\dfrac{3^5 \times 3^6}{3^9}$

(e) $\dfrac{(5^4)^2}{5^5}$

(f) $\dfrac{2^8}{2 \times 2^4}$

(g) $\dfrac{7 \times 7^6}{7^2 \times 7^3}$

(h) $\dfrac{8^3 \times 8^4}{8^2 \times 8^3}$

D5 This table shows some powers of 8.

8^2	8^3	8^4	8^5	8^6	8^7	8^8
64	512	4096	32 768	262 144	2 097 152	16 777 216

Use the results in the table to evaluate

(a) $\dfrac{32\,768}{512}$

(b) $\dfrac{262\,144}{512}$

(c) $\dfrac{16\,777\,216}{2\,097\,152}$

(d) $\dfrac{64 \times 262\,144}{16\,777\,216}$

D6 Work out $\dfrac{2^6 \times 2^2}{2^3 \times 2^5}$.

D7 Find the missing number in each statement.

(a) $\dfrac{p^5}{p^3} = p^{\blacksquare}$ (b) $\dfrac{x^7}{x^2} = x^{\blacksquare}$ (c) $\dfrac{n^{12}}{n^9} = n^{\blacksquare}$ (d) $\dfrac{a^{10}}{a} = a^{\blacksquare}$

D8 Write the answers to these using indices.

(a) $\dfrac{h^7}{h^3}$ (b) $\dfrac{n^9}{n^4}$ (c) $\dfrac{x^4}{x}$ (d) $\dfrac{d^{12}}{d^3}$ (e) $\dfrac{a^5}{a^4}$

D9 Find the missing number in each statement.

(a) $\dfrac{b^7}{b^{\blacksquare}} = b^5$ (b) $\dfrac{k^{10}}{k^{\blacksquare}} = k^2$ (c) $\dfrac{m^{\blacksquare}}{m} = m^3$ (d) $\dfrac{h^{\blacksquare}}{h^6} = h$

D10 Copy and complete each grid.
Each space should contain an expression using an index or one of the signs × or ÷.

Each row (from left to right) and each column (from top to bottom)
should show a true statement.

(a) 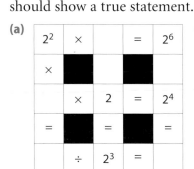   (b) 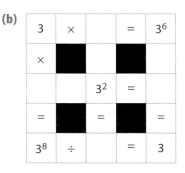   (c)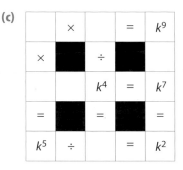

D11 Work out the value of each expression when $n = 3$.

(a) $\dfrac{n^4}{n^3}$ (b) $\dfrac{n^8}{n^6}$ (c) $\dfrac{n^{10}}{n^9}$ (d) $\dfrac{n^{14}}{n^{12}}$ (e) $\dfrac{n^6}{n^3}$

D12 Simplify each of these.

(a) $g^3 \times g^5$ (b) $\dfrac{w^6}{w^2}$ (c) $\dfrac{p^5 \times p}{p^2}$ (d) $\dfrac{h^5 \times h^6}{h^{10}}$

(e) $\dfrac{(y^3)^2}{y}$ (f) $\dfrac{h^8}{h \times h^3}$ (g) $\dfrac{q \times q^9}{q^3 \times q^4}$ (h) $\dfrac{z^5 \times z^3}{z^4 \times z^4}$

D13 Find the missing number in each statement.

(a) $\dfrac{n \times n^{\blacksquare}}{n^2} = n^3$ (b) $\dfrac{m^7}{m^{\blacksquare} \times m^2} = m^2$ (c) $\dfrac{(h^3)^{\blacksquare}}{h^5} = h$ (d) $\dfrac{7^5 \times 7^{\blacksquare}}{7 \times 7^7} = 7^3$

(e) $\dfrac{x^3 \times x^5}{x^{\blacksquare} \times x^4} = 1$ (f) $\dfrac{(3^{\blacksquare})^4}{3^7} = 3$ (g) $\dfrac{(5^3)^4}{(5^6)^{\blacksquare}} = 1$ (h) $\dfrac{2^4 \times 2^5}{2^2 \times 2^{\blacksquare}} = 8$

E Dividing expressions with powers

Here are two ways to think about simplifying the division $\dfrac{12p^7}{3p^2}$.

The result is the missing expression in

$$3p^2 \times \blacksquare = 12p^7$$

so the result is $4p^5$.

Write the multiplications out in full and 'cancel' common factors.

$$\dfrac{12p^7}{3p^2} = \dfrac{12 \times p \times p \times p \times p \times p \times p \times p}{3 \times p \times p}$$

$$= \dfrac{4p^5}{1}$$

$$= 4p^5$$

- Which method do you prefer?
  Can you think of a simpler one?

- Sort these into five pairs of equivalent expressions.

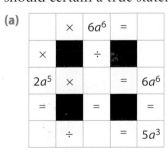

A $\dfrac{5p^5}{5p^2}$ **B** $\dfrac{6p^2}{2p}$ **C** $\dfrac{8p^5}{p^3}$ **D** $\dfrac{6p^5}{3p^3}$ **E** $\dfrac{12p^7}{4p^5}$ **F** $3p$ **G** $3p^2$ **H** p^3 **I** $8p^2$ **J** $2p^2$

E1 Simplify these.

(a) $\dfrac{5p^3}{p^2}$ (b) $\dfrac{8a^6}{4a^2}$ (c) $\dfrac{12y^4}{3y^3}$ (d) $\dfrac{8m^9}{8m^7}$ (e) $\dfrac{16n^7}{4n}$

E2 What are the missing numbers from each statement?

(a) $\dfrac{3p^1}{3p^\blacksquare} = p$ (b) $\dfrac{10x^9}{\blacksquare x^3} = 5x^6$ (c) $\dfrac{14n^\blacksquare}{7n^2} = 2n^3$ (d) $\dfrac{\blacksquare k^7}{3k^\blacksquare} - 9k$

E3 Copy and complete each grid so that each space contains an expression, × or ÷.

Each row (from left to right) and each column (from top to bottom)
should certain a true statement.

(a)
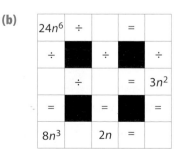

(b)

	×	$6a^6$	=	
×	■	÷	■	
$2a^5$	×		=	$6a^6$
=	■	=	■	=
	÷		=	$5a^3$

$24n^6$	÷		=	
÷	■	÷		÷
		÷		=	$3n^2$
=	■	=	■	=
$8n^3$		$2n$	=	

E4 Simplify these.

(a) $\dfrac{2n^3 \times 3n^2}{6n}$ (b) $\dfrac{3n^5 \times 4n^2}{2n^3}$ (c) $\dfrac{30n^8}{3n^2 \times 5n^3}$ (d) $\dfrac{20n^9}{(2n^4)^2}$

Sometimes cancelling common factors does not 'remove' the denominator.

Examples

$$\frac{3^2}{3^4} = \frac{3 \times 3}{3 \times 3 \times 3 \times 3}$$
$$= \frac{\cancel{3} \times \cancel{3}}{\cancel{3} \times \cancel{3} \times 3 \times 3}$$
$$= \frac{1}{3^2}$$

$$\frac{10p^2}{5p^5} = \frac{10 \times p \times p}{5 \times p \times p \times p \times p \times p}$$
$$= \frac{\cancel{10}^2 \times \cancel{p} \times \cancel{p}}{\cancel{5} \times \cancel{p} \times \cancel{p} \times p \times p \times p}$$
$$= \frac{2}{p^3}$$

$$\frac{6a^3}{10a^4} = \frac{6 \times a \times a \times a}{10 \times a \times a \times a \times a}$$
$$= \frac{\cancel{6}^3 \times \cancel{a} \times \cancel{a} \times \cancel{a}}{\cancel{10}^5 \times \cancel{a} \times \cancel{a} \times \cancel{a} \times a}$$
$$= \frac{3}{5a}$$

Cancelling is equivalent to dividing the 'top' and the 'bottom' by the same expression.

Examples

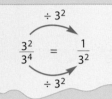

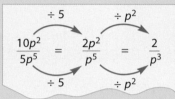

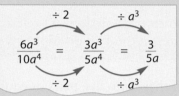

E5 Simplify these by cancelling.

(a) $\dfrac{5^2}{5^6}$ (b) $\dfrac{2^9}{2^{10}}$ (c) $\dfrac{p^2}{p^9}$ (d) $\dfrac{n^3}{n^{12}}$ (e) $\dfrac{y}{y^8}$

E6 Simplify these by cancelling.

(a) $\dfrac{3p^4}{p^7}$ (b) $\dfrac{10b^2}{5b^6}$ (c) $\dfrac{9x^3}{3x^8}$ (d) $\dfrac{m^8}{5m^5}$ (e) $\dfrac{a^{10}}{7a^9}$

(f) $\dfrac{12y^3}{24y^2}$ (g) $\dfrac{3n^7}{15n^5}$ (h) $\dfrac{30b^4}{3b^7}$ (i) $\dfrac{3x^7}{21x^{11}}$ (j) $\dfrac{6x^6}{18x^7}$

E7 Simplify these by cancelling.

(a) $\dfrac{8a^4}{6a^5}$ (b) $\dfrac{6n^7}{15n^5}$ (c) $\dfrac{12p^2}{28p^3}$ (d) $\dfrac{4x}{18x^3}$ (e) $\dfrac{15k^7}{25k^{10}}$

E8 Simplify these.

(a) $\dfrac{4x^3 \times 2x}{x^6}$ (b) $\dfrac{6k^8}{2k^3 \times 4k^7}$ (c) $\dfrac{4y^5 \times 3y^3}{12y^2 \times 2y^7}$ (d) $\dfrac{(2n^3)^5}{6n^{10} \times 2n^8}$

F Negative indices

- What do you think are the next three lines of each pattern?
- What do you think is the decimal value of 2^{-4}? What is 2^{-4} written as a fraction?

$2^4 = 16$
$2^3 = 8$
$2^2 = 4$
$2^1 = 2$
$2^0 = 1$
⋮

$5^4 = 625$
$5^3 = 125$
$5^2 = 25$
$5^1 = 5$
$5^0 = 1$
⋮

F1 (a) Find three matching pairs.

 3^{-4} 3^{-2} 2^{-3} 4^{-3} $\dfrac{1}{4^3}$ $\dfrac{1}{2^3}$ $\dfrac{1}{3^4}$

(b) Which is the odd one out?

F2 (a) Find four matching pairs.

 3^{-2} 2^{-3} 4^{-4} 6^{-1} 4^{-2} $\dfrac{1}{8}$ $\dfrac{1}{6}$ $\dfrac{1}{16}$ $\dfrac{1}{9}$

(b) Which is the odd one out?

F3 2^{-4} is equivalent to the fraction $\frac{1}{16}$.

Write these as fractions.

(a) 3^{-3} **(b)** 7^{-1} **(c)** 9^{-2} **(d)** 4^{-3} **(e)** 11^{-1}

We know that $n^0 = 1$ for any value of n. For example, $2^0 = 1$, $5^0 = 1$, $12^0 = 1$, …

F4 (a) Find four matching pairs.

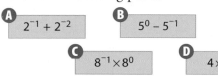

A $2^{-1} + 2^{-2}$ **B** $5^0 - 5^{-1}$ **E** $\dfrac{3}{4}$ **G** $\dfrac{-1}{5}$ **I** $\dfrac{4}{5}$

C $8^{-1} \times 8^0$ **D** 4×2^{-2} **F** $\dfrac{1}{8}$ **H** 1

(b) Which is the odd one out?

F5 $2^{-2} = \dfrac{1}{2^2} = \dfrac{1}{4} = 0.25$ as a decimal.

Work out the decimal value of these.

(a) 2^{-1} **(b)** 4^{-1} **(c)** 10^{-2} **(d)** 10^{-4} **(e)** 5^{-1}

F6 Write $5^{-1} + 5^0$ as a decimal.

F7 Write $10^{-1} + 10^{-3}$ as a decimal.

F8 a^{-2} is equivalent to $\dfrac{1}{a^2}$ in fractional form.

Write these in fractional form.

(a) x^{-3} **(b)** g^{-1} **(c)** n^{-2} **(d)** k^{-3} **(e)** p^{-1}

F9 Solve the following equations.

(a) $12^{-1} = \dfrac{1}{x}$ **(b)** $x^{-3} = 0.001$ **(c)** $4^x = \frac{1}{4}$ **(d)** $10^x = 1$

(e) $x^{-2} = \frac{1}{49}$ **(f)** $x^{-3} = \frac{1}{8}$ **(g)** $2^x = \frac{1}{32}$ **(h)** $4^x = 0.0625$

*F10 Do you think there is a solution to the equation $2^x = 0$?

G Extending the rules to negative indices

We know that $a^{-m} = \dfrac{1}{a^m}$. Examples are $2^{-4} = \dfrac{1}{2^4}$, $3^{-5} = \dfrac{1}{3^5}$, $5^{-1} = \dfrac{1}{5}$

The rules of indices that we have used to simplify expressions are

- To **multiply** powers of the same number, **add** the indices ($a^m \times a^n = a^{m+n}$).
  For example, $2^7 \times 2^3 = 2^{7+3} = 2^{10}$.

- To **divide** powers of the same number, **subtract** the indices ($a^m \div a^n = a^{m-n}$).
  For example, $2^7 \div 2^3 = 2^{7-3} = 2^4$.

- To **raise** a power **to a further power**, **multiply** the indices ($(a^m)^n = a^{mn}$).
  For example, $(2^4)^3 = 2^{4 \times 3} = 2^{12}$.

T Are these rules valid for negative indices?

$3^5 \times 3^{-2}$?	$\dfrac{5^2}{5^4}$?	$(7^{-3})^2$?
The definition of 3^{-2} gives	Cancelling gives	The definition of 7^{-3} gives
$3^5 \times 3^{-2} = 3^5 \times \dfrac{1}{3^2}$	$\dfrac{5^2}{5^4} = \dfrac{\cancel{5} \times \cancel{5}}{\cancel{5} \times \cancel{5} \times 5 \times 5}$	$(7^{-3})^2 = \left(\dfrac{1}{7^3}\right)^2$
$= \dfrac{3^5}{3^2}$	$= \dfrac{1}{5^2}$	$= \dfrac{1}{7^3} \times \dfrac{1}{7^3}$
$= 3^3$	$= 5^{-2}$	$= \dfrac{1}{7^6}$
Using a rule gives	**Using a rule** gives	$= 7^{-6}$
$3^5 \times 3^{-2} = 3^{5+{-2}}$	$\dfrac{5^2}{5^4} = 5^{2-4}$	**Using a rule** gives
$= 3^3$	$= 5^{-2}$	$(7^{-3})^2 = 7^{-3 \times 2}$
		$= 7^{-6}$

- Simplify each expression first without using a rule and then using a rule. Discuss your results.

A $2^{-5} \times 2^3 = ?$ **B** $2^{-3} \times 2^3 = ?$ **C** $2^{-1} \times 2^{-2} = ?$ **D** $\dfrac{2^3}{2^4} = ?$ **E** $\dfrac{7^2}{7^{-2}} = ?$ **F** $(2^5)^{-2} = ?$

G1 Write the answer to each of these as a single power.

(a) $3^4 \times 3^{-3}$ (b) $10^{-2} \times 10^5$ (c) $8^{-4} \times 8^4$ (d) $3^{-5} \times 3^3$

(e) $2^2 \times 2^{-7}$ (f) 9×9^{-2} (g) $2^{-4} \times 2^{-1}$ (h) $7^{-2} \times 7^9 \times 7^{-4}$

G2 Write the answer to each of these as a single power.

(a) $3^2 \div 3^4$ (b) $5^3 \div 5^6$ (c) $2^4 \div 2^5$ (d) $9 \div 9^6$

(e) $\dfrac{4^5}{4^7}$ (f) $\dfrac{7^3}{7^9}$ (g) $\dfrac{6^7}{6^8}$ (h) $\dfrac{10}{10^7}$

G3 Write the answer to each of these as a single power.

(a) $5^4 \times 5^{-2}$ (b) $2^3 \div 2^6$ (c) $7^{-9} \times 7^2 \times 7^6$ (d) $6 \div 6^8$

(e) $7^{-3} \times 7^{-2}$ (f) $\dfrac{4^3}{4^7}$ (g) $2^9 \times 2^{-9}$ (h) $\dfrac{5^2}{5^3}$

G4 Simplify each of these.

(a) $p^4 \times p^{-5}$ (b) $q^3 \times q^{-3}$ (c) $r^{-7} \times r^9$ (d) $s^{-3} \times s$

(e) $\dfrac{w^2}{w^7}$ (f) $\dfrac{x^3}{x^6}$ (g) $\dfrac{y^8}{y^8}$ (h) $\dfrac{z}{z^5}$

G5 Write each of these as a single power.

(a) $(2^{-4})^2$ (b) $(3^2)^{-3}$ (c) $(5^{-1})^2$ (d) $(a^2)^{-5}$ (e) $(x^{-3})^3$

G6 Copy and complete each of these statements.

(a) $2^{\blacksquare} \times 2^{-2} = 2^6$ (b) $\dfrac{3^2}{3^{\blacksquare}} = 3^{-5}$ (c) $a^2 \times a^{\blacksquare} \times a^{-4} = a^{-3}$

(d) $\dfrac{b^{\blacksquare}}{b^3} = b^{-2}$ (e) $(5^{\blacksquare})^3 = 5^{-12}$ (f) $(2^{-2})^{\blacksquare} = 2^{-10}$

G7 Simplify each of these.

(a) $4n^{-1} \times 2n^{-2}$ (b) $2r^{-7} \times 3r^9$ (c) $s^4 \times s^{-10} \times 5s$ (d) $\dfrac{10b^2}{b^7}$

(e) $\dfrac{4h}{h^9}$ (f) $\dfrac{4c^7}{12c^9}$ (g) $\dfrac{12a}{6a^3}$ (h) $\dfrac{6x}{15x^3}$

T These examples involve dividing by a fraction.

$3^5 \div 3^{-2}$?

The definition of 3^{-2} gives

$$3^5 \div 3^{-2} = 3^5 \div \frac{1}{3^2}$$

$$= 3^5 \times \frac{3^2}{1}$$

$$= 3^5 \times 3^2$$

$$= 3^7$$

Using a rule gives

$$3^5 \div 3^{-2} = 3^{5 - {-2}}$$

$$= 3^7$$

$(7^{-3})^{-2}$?

The definition of 7^{-3} gives

$$(7^{-3})^{-2} = \left(\frac{1}{7^3}\right)^{-2}$$

$$= \frac{1}{\left(\frac{1}{7^3}\right)^2}$$

$$= \frac{1}{\left(\frac{1}{7^6}\right)}$$

$$= 1 \div \frac{1}{7^6}$$

$$= 1 \times \frac{7^6}{1}$$

$$= 7^6$$

Using a rule gives

$$(7^{-3})^{-2} = 7^{-3 \times -2}$$

$$= 7^6$$

- Simplify each expression below, first without using a rule and then using a rule.
  Discuss your results.

A $10^{-2} \div 10^{-5} = ?$

B $3^{-2} \div 3^3 = ?$

C $5^{-4} \div 5^{-1} = ?$

D $(2^{-3})^{-1} = ?$

G8 Write each of these as a single power.

(a) $5^2 \div 5^{-3}$ (b) $2^{-3} \div 2^{-4}$ (c) $3^{-4} \div 3^{-3}$ (d) $(7^{-5})^{-3}$

G9 Simplify each of these. (a) $\dfrac{z}{z^{-5}}$ (b) $(a^{-2})^{-3}$ (c) $\dfrac{b^{-4}}{b^{-5}}$

G10 Copy and complete each grid.

Each space should contain an expression using an index or one of the signs $\times$ or $\div$.

Each row (from left to right) and each column (from top to bottom) should show a true statement.

(a)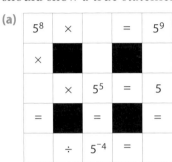
(b)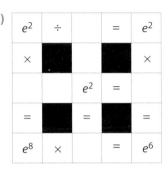
(c)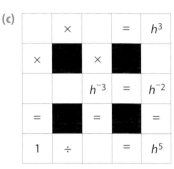

G11 Simplify each of these. (a) $\dfrac{5x^2}{10x^{-3}}$ (b) $\dfrac{20x^{-4}}{8x^{-3}}$ (c) $(2x^{-5})^{-1}$

H True, iffy, false

H1 In each statement below, m and n can be any integer.

Decide whether each statement is *always true*, *sometimes true* or *never true*.
Give reasons for each answer.

(a) $13^n \times 13^{-n} = 1$ (b) $(m + n)^2 = m^2 + n^2$ (c) $4n^2$ is a square number

(d) $(0.5)^n = 2^{-n}$ (e) $5^{2n} = 10^n$ (f) $2n^2$ is a square number

(g) $(2^m)^n = (2^n)^m$ (h) $2^n < n^3$ (i) $5^n \div 5^{-n} = 25^n$

(j) $2^{2n} = 4^n$ (k) $3^n = 9^m$ (l) $2^n < 0$

H2 In each statement below, a can be any integer, fraction or decimal except 0.

Decide whether each statement is *always true*, *sometimes true* or *never true*.
Give reasons for each answer.

(a) $a^4 + a^4 + a^4 = 3a^4$ (b) $2a^2 + 3a^3 = 5a^5$ (c) $5a^2 = 5a \times 5a$

(d) $3a^{-2} = \dfrac{1}{3a^2}$ (e) $6a^{-3} = \dfrac{6}{a^3}$ (f) $\dfrac{6a^{-1}}{2a} = \dfrac{3}{a^2}$

(g) $(4a)^2 = 4a^2$ (h) $5a^2 = 5 \times a \times a$ (i) $a^0 \times a^0 \times a^0 \times a^0 > 2$

(j) $(2a)^{-3} = \dfrac{8}{a^3}$ (k) $(3a)^{-2} = \dfrac{1}{9a^2}$ (l) $2a^2 = a$

H3 Decide whether each of the following statements is true or false.

(a) If $a^2 = 49$ then the only possible value for a is 7.

(b) If $x^2 = x$ then the only possible value for x is 1.

(c) If $0 < k < 1$ then $k^4 < k^3$ for all values of k in the range.

(d) If $^-1 < k < 1$ then $k^4 < k^3$ for all values of k in the range.

(e) $k^{-1} < 1$ for all possible values of k.

(f) $(2k)^{-1} < 2k^{-1}$ for all positive values of k.

Test yourself

T1 Solve the following equations.

(a) $2^n = 128$ (b) $n^3 = 64$ (c) $7^n = 7$ (d) $2^n \times 5 = 40$

T2 Evaluate these as whole numbers or fractions.

(a) 3^3 (b) 2^{-3} (c) 7^0

T3 Simplify

(a) $w^6 \times w^2$ (b) $x^3 \div x^5$ (c) $(y^3)^2$ AQA

T4 (a) Write as a power of 5

     (i) $5^4 \times 5^2$ (ii) $5^9 \div 5^6$

(b) $2^x \times 2^y = 2^{10}$ and $2^x \div 2^y = 2^4$

     Work out the value of x and the value of y.   Edexcel

T5 Write the answer to each of these as a single power.

(a) $\dfrac{2^3 \times 2^4}{2^5}$ (b) $7^9 \times 7^{-2}$ (c) $\dfrac{(6^2)^4}{6^9}$ (d) $\dfrac{3 \times 3^4}{3^{10}}$ (e) $3^5 \div 3^{-2}$

T6 Find the value of n in each of these statements.

(a) $2^n \times 2^3 = 2^{10}$ (b) $3^8 \times 3^n = 3^3$ (c) $4^2 \div 4^n = 4^{-3}$

(d) $5^n \div 5^{-2} = 5^5$ (e) $(9^2)^n = 9^{-8}$ (f) $(11^n)^{-2} = 11^6$

T7 Simplify these.

(a) $12m^6 \div 3m^2$ (b) $\dfrac{3b^2 \times 2b^6}{b^4}$ (c) $(2x^4)^3$ (d) $\dfrac{6x}{15x^2}$

T8 Solve the following equations.

(a) $10^n = 0.0001$ (b) $x^{-4} = \frac{1}{16}$ (c) $4^x = 0.25$ (d) $2^x = 1$

T9 Find the value of n in each of these statements.

(a) $6^n \times 6^2 = \dfrac{1}{6^3}$ (b) $3^n \div 3^{-4} = \frac{1}{3}$ (c) $(2^{2n})^{-4} = \dfrac{1}{2^8}$

11 Surveys and experiments

This work will help you plan and carry out a project in data handling.
You will need to be able to make frequency tables, draw bar charts or pie charts and use scatter diagrams.

You will learn how to

- write an effective questionnaire
- carry out experiments to get data

A The data handling cycle

Specifying the question	The starting point is a **question** or an area of interest, for example: • If the local library can be open for only ten hours a week, at what times would it be best to open? • Do people remember words better than numbers?

Collecting data	To answer the question, we have to decide what information or data we need. We have to plan how to **collect** it and how we will use it to help answer our question. If we have to collect the data ourselves, for example by asking people questions or by counting or measuring something, then the data is called **primary data**. If the data has already been collected by someone else, it is called **secondary data**.

Processing and representing the data	To help answer the question, the data has to be **processed** (for example, by working out percentages, finding frequencies, calculating means, and so on). It is often helpful to **represent** the data in pictorial form (for example, using a frequency chart, scatter diagram or pie chart).

Interpreting the data to answer the question	Processing and representing the data allows us to **interpret** it to help answer the question we started with. The result may suggest that some more data needs to be collected. It might also suggest other questions that need answering. So we may go back to an earlier stage of the cycle and repeat.

Primary data and secondary data

Primary data is data that you collect yourself.
For example, you are collecting primary data when you give people
a questionnaire to fill in. You are also collecting primary data when
you make measurements in an experiment.

Height	152 cm	172 cm
Weight	57 kg	78 kg
Pulse rate before exercise	89 b.p.m.	75 b.p.m.
Pulse rate after exercise	127 b.p.m.	133 b.p.m.

Secondary data is data that someone else has collected and organised.
For example, data about crime which is published by the government is
secondary data.

Vandalism, per 10 000 households			
Year	1981	1993	1995
Cases	1481	1638	1614

Sometimes data does not fit easily into either type.
For example, suppose you collect information about the prices of
secondhand cars from newspaper adverts. Is this primary or secondary data?
It feels more like primary data because although it's written by someone else,
it isn't organised in any way.

Toyota Yaris 1.4, 2003, 65 000 miles. Met blue vgc.
MOT. £2000 ovno.

Vauxhall Vectra 1.8, 02, 80k miles. Silver.
One owner. FSH. MOT, taxed to Aug. £1995 ono.

Lexus LS 4 litre, S reg. Fantastic cond. Leather.
Electric everything. FSH, tax, recent service.
150 000 miles. £4500.

School uniform   Report by Chris and Melanie

The school council discussed changing the school uniform. Some people didn't like the colour and some wanted sweatshirts instead of blazers. A lot of pupils thought that there shouldn't be a uniform at all.

We decided to find out what other students felt about the uniform. We thought that boys and girls might feel differently and so might different year groups. We wrote a questionnaire and we decided to give it to some students in every year group. (There are about 180 in each year.)

Here is our questionnaire.

1	What year group are you in? (Please tick.)	Y7	Y8	Y9	Y10	Y11	
2	Are you male or female?			Male		Female	
3	Do you think there should be a school uniform?			Yes		No	
4	If there has to be a uniform, would you prefer			blazer		sweatshirt	
5	What colours would you like the uniform to be?						

6   'Students should be allowed to wear jewellery.' What do you think?

     Strongly agree   Agree   Not sure   Disagree   Strongly disagree

Questions for discussion

- What do you think of the questions? Are they easy to answer?
  Are they clear – will they mean the same to everyone who answers them?
  Will the responses be easy to analyse?

- Who would you give the questionnaire to?
  How would you collect their responses?
  How many people would you give it to?

> I'll ask everyone in the school.

> I'll ask 5 people in each year.

> I'll ask all my friends.

> I'll ask everyone in the choir.

T The report continues like this.

Our teacher told us it was a good idea to pilot a questionnaire. This means giving it to a few people to see if there are any 'bugs' (problems).

We gave it to 10 people. Some of them thought there should be a question about ties. Two people said that 'jewellery' was too vague: ordinary rings could be allowed but not nose rings.

We also found that everybody had written different colours that they liked, sometimes three or four colours, e.g. dark blue, red, yellow. It would be difficult to analyse the answers to this question.

• Look back at the questionnaire.
  How could you improve it to avoid these problems?

In their report, Chris and Melanie made tables of the replies they got to the questions in their questionnaire.

This table shows the replies to the question 'Would you prefer a blazer or a sweatshirt?'

Year		7	8	9	10	11
Boys	Blazer	7	7	4	3	3
	Sweatshirt	8	11	12	11	13
Girls	Blazer	7	7	6	6	7
	Sweatshirt	5	8	9	10	9

B1 Draw a chart, or charts, to illustrate this data.
Explain why you chose your type of chart.

B2 What conclusions would you draw about the preferences?

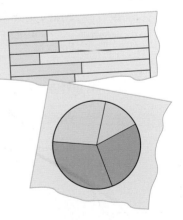

Question types

Here are some types of question that you could use in a questionnaire.
Questions which ask for boxes to be ticked (or letters to be ringed)
make it easier to collect all the data together afterwards.

Yes/no questions

A Have you passed the driving test?   YES ☐   NO ☐

The question must have a clear 'yes' or 'no' answer.
(If you think someone might not know the answer,
then you could include DON'T KNOW ☐).

Multiple-choice questions

B Which age group are you in?

0–19 ☐   20–39 ☐   40–59 ☐   60–79 ☐   80 or over ☐

C Which of these statements best describes how you plan what you will watch on TV?

A I plan days ahead.

B I decide on the day.

C I just flick around to see what's on.

Please ring   A   B   C

In examples B and C above, the person chooses one response.
In example D below, they can choose more than one.

D Which of these languages do you study for GCSE?

French ☐   German ☐   Spanish ☐   Gujerati ☐   Latin ☐

Questions that give a scale of responses

E Which statement best describes how you feel about maths?

A I like it a lot.

B I quite like it.

C It's all right.

D I don't like it very much.

E I hate it.

Please ring   A   B   C   D   E

Questions that ask for a number

| F | How many subjects are you taking at GCSE?   Number .... |

If you don't need to know the number exactly, then it is
better to give groups (as in example B).

Questions that ask for an order of preference

| G | What kind of music do you prefer?
Put in order of priority (1 for your favourite, 5 for your least).

Hard rock ☐   Pop ☐   Jazz ☐   Easy listening ☐   Classical ☐ |

Open questions

| H | What do you think about school lunches? |

This kind of question is good for finding out people's own ideas,
but it is hard to summarise the answers.

Things to avoid!

- Don't ask questions that could be embarrassing. ('How old are you?')

- Don't ask questions that try to lead people to answer in one way.
  ('Would you like to see the safety of our children improved by banning traffic
  from the road in front of the school?') These are called **leading questions**.

- Don't ask questions that are difficult to answer precisely.
  ('How many hours of TV do you usually watch each week?')

B3 Criticise these questions and try to improve them.

> How much do you earn?   £............
>
> How many are there in your family? ....
>
> Where do you shop? Please tick.
>
>   Asda ☐   Sainsbury's ☐   Safeway ☐   Tesco ☐
>
> How much do you spend a week on food?   £............
>
> How do you think supermarket fruit and vegetables compare with
> the real fruit and vegetables you buy direct from a farm?

Carrying out a survey

1 Be clear about the purpose of your survey.

2 Write a draft questionnaire.

3 Pilot your draft questionnaire with a small number of people.

4 Improve the questions if necessary.

5 Decide who to give the questionnaire to, and how many people to ask.

6 Decide whether you will see people and ask the questions, or give them the questionnaire to fill in.

7 Collect all the responses together, analyse them and write a **report**.

In your report
- State the purpose of your survey.
  Describe how you carried it out, any difficulties you had to overcome and any changes of plan.

- Include your final questionnaire.

- Say how many people responded.

- Summarise the responses to each question.
  Use tables and charts where appropriate.

  If you are comparing the responses of different groups (e.g. boys and girls), summarise them separately.
  You could use a table something like this.

Hours of TV	0–9	10–19	20–29	30+
Girls	17	12	15	9
Boys	12	10	19	10

- Write a conclusion.

Points for discussion

Music charts

January 1965

1 I FEEL FINE	Beatles
2 DOWNTOWN	Petula Clark
3 WALK TALL	Val Doonican
4 SOMEWHERE	P.J. Proby
5 I'M GONNA BE STRONG	Gene Pitney
6 YEH YEH	Georgie
7 I COULD EASILY FALL	
8 NO ARMS CAN EVER	
9 TERRY	
10 I UNDERSTAND	the Dreamers

January 1975

1 DOWN DOWN	Status Quo
2 NEVER CAN SAY GOODBYE	Gloria Gaynor
3 STREETS OF LONDON	Ralph McTell
4 THE BUMP	Kenny
5 MS GRACE	Tymes
6 I CAN HELP	Billy Swan

January 1985

1 DO THEY KNOW IT'S CHRISTMAS	Band Aid
2 EVERYTHING SHE WANTS	Wham!
3 NELLIE THE ELEPHANT	Toy Dolls
4 LIKE A VIRGIN	Madonna
5 WE ALL STAND TOGETHER	Paul McCartney & the Frog Chorus
6 . . . RANGE	Paul Young
. . . kie Goes To Hollywood	
. . .	Tears For Fears
. . .	Foreigner

The first British music chart was published in 1952.

In the early days the record charts were based on the number of records sold in only a few hundred shops. Nowadays there are over 5500 record stores involved, and downloaded singles are counted as well.

> **Why so many stores?**

US elections

Surveys got a bad name in 1936. In that year the US Presidential elections were held. There were two candidates, Landon (who represented the better off) and Roosevelt (for the less well off).

A magazine did a postal survey on who people would vote for. They obtained the names and addresses from telephone directories and car registrations.

Over 2 million of the 10 million sent questionnaires replied. These predicted a massive victory for Landon.

In fact Roosevelt won by a massive majority!

> **Why do you think the result was so different?**

Bluffing

About 60 years ago, an American survey contained the question

> What do you think of of the new metallic Metals Law?

The option boxes included 'I don't know' as an option, but fewer than 25% ticked it. Everyone else ticked an opinion.

In fact the 'new metallic Metals Law' was completely fictitious!

> **Why did over 75% of people express an opinion?**

Priya and Ben decided to investigate how good people are at remembering words, numbers and pictures.
They wrote a report on their findings.

Remembering words, pictures and numbers
by Priya and Ben

We wanted to see if there was any difference between how good young people are at remembering words, pictures and numbers.

We both thought it would be easiest to remember pictures.

We decided to test years 10 to 13, who are mostly between 14 and 18 years old.

How we got our results

We made up some experiments.

We chose:
- 10 words – we tried to make sure there were no links between them (like 'pencil' and 'paper')
- 10 pictures
- 10 numbers between 1 and 100

We showed our class the 10 words for 30 seconds and gave them 60 seconds to write down as many as they could remember. The order didn't matter.

We did the same with the pictures and the numbers.

Each correct word, picture or number scored 1 point.

Each student had three scores out of 10 and wrote them on a slip of paper. Our class is in year 10 and we wanted results from years 10 to 13. We couldn't use year 11 because they were on exam leave so we asked our teacher Mr Cassell to do the same experiment on his year 12 and 13 mathematics groups.

Our results

We collected all the slips of paper and chose 10 at random from each year so that we had the results for 30 students.

school
heather
lamp
sky
hate
spoon
necklace
birthday
hair
leaf

Here are some questions for discussion.
Explain each of your answers as fully as you can.

C1 Did you find Priya's and Ben's description of their memory experiments easy to follow?

C2 They made up a list of 10 words for one experiment.
Why do you think they tried to have no links between their words?

C3 Why do you think they used the same number of words, numbers and pictures in their experiments?

C4 Was it a good idea for Mr Cassell to collect the data from his year 12 and 13 mathematics groups?

C5 Why do you think they chose 10 students at random from each year?
Do you think this was a good idea?

Example

What is the average speed, in m.p.h., of a ship which travels 15 miles in 2.5 hours?

First method

15 miles in 2.5 hours
= 30 miles in 5 hours (doubling)
= 6 miles in 1 hour (dividing by 5)
So speed = **6 m.p.h.**

Second method

Speed in m.p.h. = $\dfrac{\text{Distance in miles}}{\text{Time in hours}}$

$= \dfrac{15}{2.5} = \dfrac{30}{5} = $ **6 m.p.h.**

A4 Calculate the average speed of each of these, stating the units.

(a) A ship that takes 5 hours to sail 75 km

(b) A plane that flies 210 km in $\frac{1}{2}$ hour

(c) A horse that runs 300 m in 20 seconds

A5 A ferry crosses an estuary, which is 18 miles wide, in $1\frac{1}{2}$ hours.
Calculate its average speed.

A6 A plane flying at a constant speed flies 200 miles in $1\frac{1}{4}$ hours.

(a) How far would it fly in $2\frac{1}{2}$ hours?

(b) How far in 5 hours at this speed?

(c) What is the speed of the plane, in m.p.h.?

A7 A coach takes $3\frac{1}{2}$ hours to travel from Hull to Birmingham, a distance of 140 miles.
Calculate the average speed of the coach.

A8 At the start of a journey, the mileometer on Sharmila's car reads 24752 miles.
At the end of the journey the mileometer reads 24941 miles.
The journey took $4\frac{1}{2}$ hours.
Calculate the average speed for the journey.

A9 A coach leaves Bristol at 10:45 and arrives in Birmingham at 13:00.
The distance from Bristol to Birmingham is 90 miles.
Calculate the average speed of the coach.

A10 This diagram shows a coach journey.

London   89 miles   Peterborough   51 miles   Lincoln

09:20   11:20   12:50

(a) Calculate the average speed of the coach between London and Peterborough.

(b) Calculate the average speed between Peterborough and Lincoln.

(c) Calculate the average speed between London and Lincoln.

B Distance–time graphs

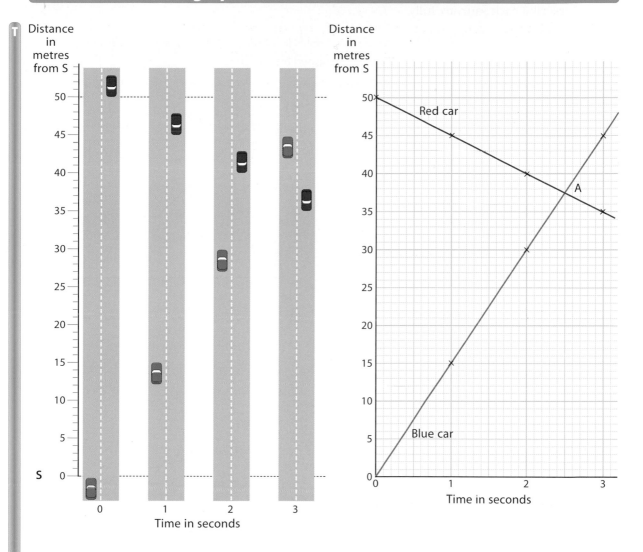

The red car and the blue car are travelling in different directions.

1 What is the speed of the blue car?

2 What is the speed of the red car?

3 Why is the line for the red car sloping downwards?

4 What does the point A on the graph show?

5 How far apart are the cars after 1.5 seconds?

6 How far apart are they after 3 seconds?

7 When will the red car reach the point where the blue car was to start with?

B1 Each graph below represents a journey.

Describe each journey fully.

For example, on graph (a),

> Stage 1: 20 miles in 1 hour = 20 m.p.h. away from home
> Stage 2: Stopped for 1 hour
> Stage 3:

(a)

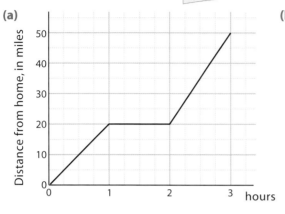

(b)

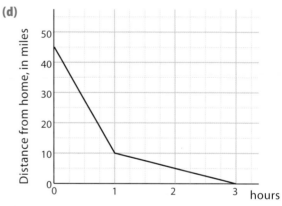

(c)

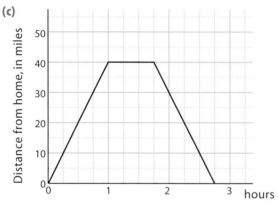

(d)

B2 This is a distance–time graph for three model cars, A, B and C.

(a) Which car is travelling fastest? How can you tell from the graph?

(b) What is the speed of car A?

(c) What is the speed of car B?

(d) What is the speed of car C? Comment on your answer.

(e) Which car does C pass first?

(f) At what time does car C pass car B?

(g) After 4 seconds how far apart are cars

(i) A and B   (ii) A and C   (iii) B and C

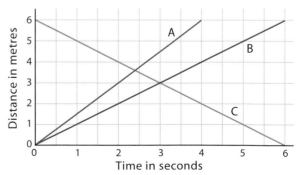

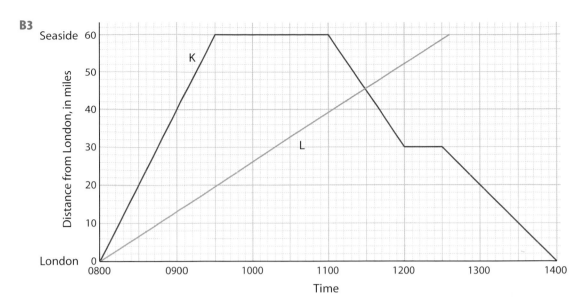

Kylie drives from London to the seaside and back. Graph K shows her journey.

(a) At what time did Kylie leave London?

(b) How long did it take her to reach the seaside?

(c) At what speed did she travel to the seaside?

(d) How long did she spend at the seaside?

(e) On the way home, Kylie stopped for a meal. For how long did she stop?

(f) At what speed was she travelling before she stopped for a meal?

(g) What was her speed for the last part of the journey home?

Kylie's brother Lee drives an old car.
Graph L shows his journey to the seaside.

(h) At what time did Kylie and Lee pass each other?

(i) How far were they from London when this happened?

(j) At what time did Lee get to the seaside?

B4 Make a copy of the axes above on graph paper.

(a) Rajesh leaves London at 0800 and cycles towards the seaside.
He travels at 10 m.p.h. for 2 hours and stops for an hour's rest.
He decides to return and arrives home at 1400.
Draw and label the graph of his journey.

(b) Nina leaves the seaside at 1100 and drives towards London at 40 m.p.h.
Draw and label the graph of her journey.

(c) At what time does Nina pass the place where Rajesh stopped for a rest?

(d) At what time does Nina overtake Rajesh?

13 Volume, surface area and density

You will revise how to find the volume of a cuboid.

This work will help you

- find the volume and surface area of a prism and cylinder
- use density
- convert between different units for volume and liquid measure

A Volume of a cuboid

Volumes are measured in cubic centimetres (cm³)
or for larger volumes cubic metres (m³).

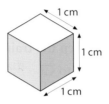

This cube has volume 1 cm³.

To find the volume of a cuboid use the formula

$$\text{volume} = \text{length} \times \text{width} \times \text{height}$$

This cuboid has volume $5 \times 3 \times 4 = 60$ cm³.

A1 Find the volume of each of these cuboids.

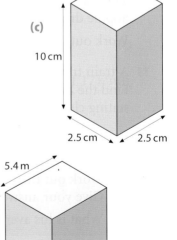

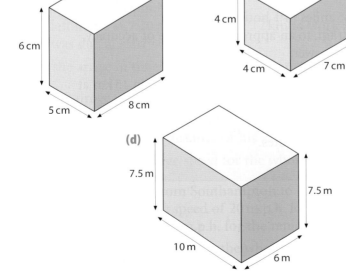

A2 These cuboids all have the same volume.
Find the missing measurements. (They are not drawn to scale.)

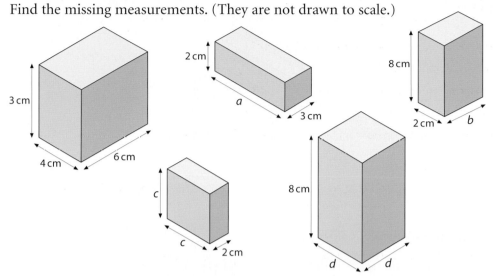

3 cm

4 cm   6 cm

2 cm

a

3 cm

8 cm

2 cm   b

c

c   2 cm

8 cm

d   d

B Volume of a prism

This solid is made up of 20 cuboids
of size 1 cm by 1 cm by 6 cm.

• What is its volume?

The prisms below are all made from similar
pieces, 6 cm long.

• Find their volumes.

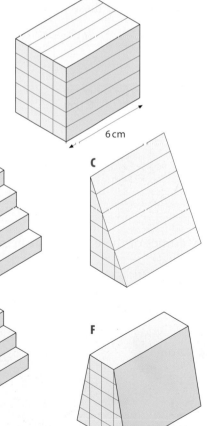

6 cm

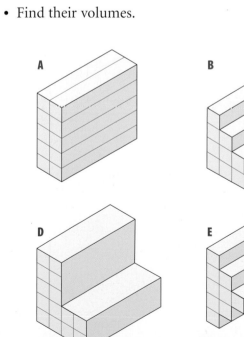

A

B

C

D

E

F

B1 Find the volume of each of these prisms.

(a)

(b)

(c)

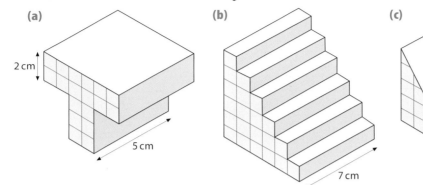

Finding the volume of a prism

A prism has the same cross-section throughout its length.

The volume of a prism is found by

    volume = area of cross-section × length

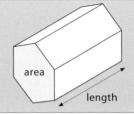

B2 Calculate the volume of these prisms. (Sketching the cross-section may help.)

(a)

(b)

(c)

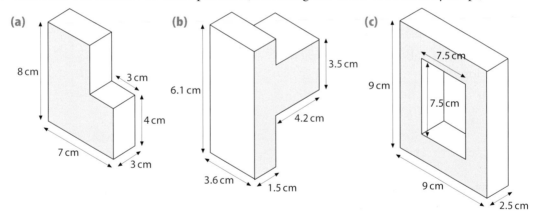

B3 Find the volumes of these triangular prisms.

(a)

(b)

(c)

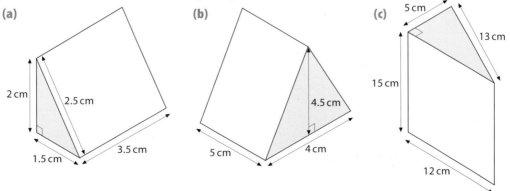

B4 Find the volumes of these prisms.

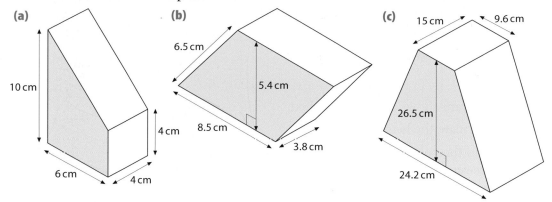

(a)
10 cm
4 cm
6 cm
4 cm

(b)
6.5 cm
5.4 cm
8.5 cm
3.8 cm

(c)
15 cm   9.6 cm
26.5 cm
24.2 cm

B5 For each of these prisms,
work in centimetres to get its volume in cm³,
then work in metres to get its volume in m³.

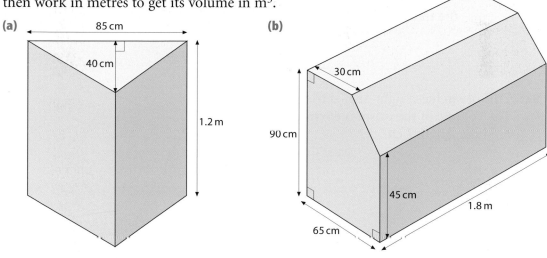

(a)
85 cm
40 cm
1.2 m

(b)
30 cm
90 cm
45 cm
65 cm
1.8 m

B6 A rubbish skip is made in the shape of a prism whose cross-section is a trapezium. Find the volume of this skip.

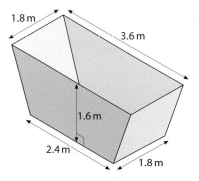

1.8 m
3.6 m
1.6 m
2.4 m
1.8 m

B7 A building site has area 150 m².
The topsoil on the site is 0.8 m deep throughout.
What is the volume of topsoil on the site?

B8 The cross-section of this prism is an isosceles triangle.

    (a) Use Pythagoras to work out the height h of the triangular cross-section.

    (b) Calculate the volume of the prism.

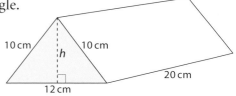

B9 The diagram shows a sketch of a shed.

    (a) Calculate the height marked h.

    (b) Find the volume of the shed. Give your answer to a reasonable degree of accuracy.

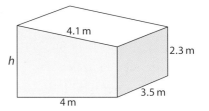

B10 For each of these cuboids, calculate

    (i) the length marked x cm

    (ii) the total surface area

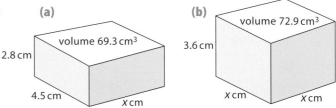

B11 This prism has a right-angled triangular cross-section.
The volume of the prism is 66 cm^3.
Find the length L cm.

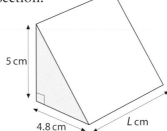

B12 A load of 15 m^3 of liquid concrete is poured over an area of 75 m^2, covering it to a constant depth everywhere.
Calculate the depth of the concrete   **(a)** in metres   **(b)** in centimetres

B13 A block of glass is a cube measuring 15 cm on each side.
The glass is melted into a sheet which is 0.5 cm thick.
What will be the area of the sheet of glass?

B14 The diagram shows a swimming pool which slopes from a maximum depth of 2 m to a minimum depth of 1.4 m.

    (a) Calculate the volume of the water in the pool when it is full.

    (b) By how much does the depth of water go down if 50 m^3 of water is pumped out of the pool?

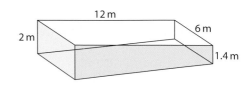

C Volume of a cylinder

You can think of a solid cylinder as a special kind of prism.

C1 A cylinder has a cross-section with radius 4.0 cm, and length 10.0 cm.

(a) Find the area of its cross-section to the nearest $0.1\,\text{cm}^2$.

(b) Find its volume to the nearest cm^3, treating it as a prism.

C2 A cylinder has radius r and length l.

(a) Write an expression for the area of its cross-section.

(b) Write an expression for its volume, treating it as a prism.

C3 Check the expression you wrote for C2(b) then use it as a formula to find the volume of each of these cylinders (to 3 s.f.).

(a) Radius 3.0 cm
Length 8.5 cm

(b) Radius 4.2 cm
Length 9.0 cm

(c) Radius 3.0 m
Length 4.7 m

For any cylinder, volume $= \pi r^2 h$

C4 Becca buys a large tin of coffee.
It is a cylinder with radius 7.5 cm.
It is filled to a depth of 14 cm.

Work out the volume of coffee in the tin.
State clearly the units of your answer.

OCR

C5 Ranjit has made a new circular fish pond in his garden.
The radius of the pond is 1.5 m.

(a) Calculate the circumference of the pond.

(b) The sides of the pond are vertical.
The water in the pond is 0.7 m deep.
Calculate the volume of the water in the pond.
Give your units in the answer.

OCR

C6 A cylinder has volume $210\,\text{cm}^3$ and length 6.0 cm. Find its radius.

C7 A cylinder has volume $150\,\text{cm}^3$ and radius 2.8 cm. Find its length.

C8 A cube of metal with edge length 3 cm has a hole of diameter 1 cm drilled through it as shown.
Find the volume of the remaining metal.

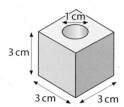

3 cm
3 cm   3 cm
1 cm

When you find the surface area of an object it is worth drawing
a net of the object to show clearly the areas that have to be calculated.

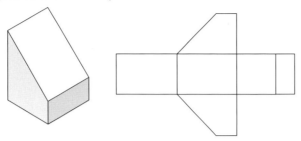

D1 For each of the objects below   **(i)** sketch the net adding any measurements you know
                                        (ii) find the surface area of the object

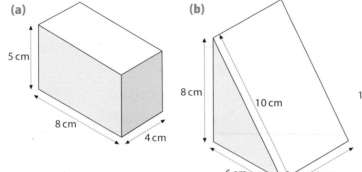

(a) 5 cm, 8 cm, 4 cm

(b) 8 cm, 10 cm, 6 cm, 4 cm

(c) 5 cm, 11 cm, 8 cm, 4 cm, 4 cm

D2 This is a label that just fits round a cylinder.
The length of the cylinder is 8.0 cm.
The radius of the cylinder is 2.0 cm.

(a) What is the other dimension of the label?

(b) What is the area of the label?

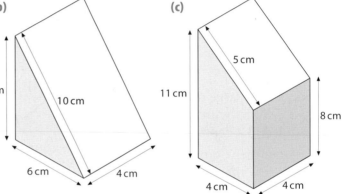

?   2.0 cm

8.0 cm

D3 This label just fits round a cylinder.
The length of the cylinder is l.
The radius of the cylinder is r.

(a) Write an expression (using π and r) for
the other dimension of the label.

(b) Write an expression for the area of the label.

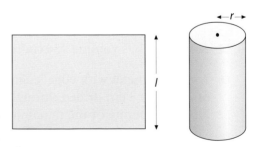

r

l

D4 Check the expression you wrote for D3(b) then use it as a formula to find the area of the curved surface of each of these cylinders.

    (a) Radius 3.0 cm   **(b)** Radius 7.6 cm   **(c)** Radius 18 m
           Length 5.0 cm   Length 12.3 cm   Length 5.2 m

D5 A cylinder has length 6.0 cm and curved surface area of 130 cm². Find its radius.

D6 A cylinder has radius 9.0 cm and curved surface area of 420 cm². Find its length.

D7 A cylinder has length 7.0 cm and radius 4.5 cm.
Find its total surface area (including the area of the circular ends).

D8 A cylinder has length l and radius r.
Write an expression for its total surface area (including the area of the ends).

D9 Check the expression you wrote for D8 then use it as
a formula to find the total surface area of each of these cylinders.

    (a) Radius 2.0 cm   **(b)** Radius 3.6 cm   **(c)** Radius 42 m
           Length 5.0 cm   Length 8.2 cm   Length 27 m

A food processing company wants a cylindrical can that holds exactly 1000 cm³.
It wants the surface area of the can to be as small as possible.
Use a spreadsheet to find the dimensions of a suitable can.

(See page 137 for a hint if you find it difficult to get started.)

D10 A can manufacturer designs a special can like this.
Its top and bottom surfaces consist of a rectangle with
a semicircle at each end. Its sides are vertical.
Calculate the total surface area of the can.

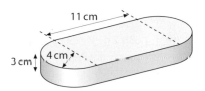

*D11 A cuboid has width 7 cm, height 8 cm and surface area 547 cm².
Calculate the length and the volume of the cuboid.

*D12 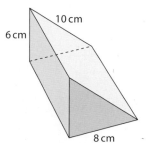 The surface area of this prism is 438 cm².
Calculate the volume of the prism.

E Density

The **density** of a substance tells you how heavy a standard volume of it is.

For example, the density of insulating foam is 0.1 g/cm³ (grams per cubic centimetre), while the density of lead is 11.4 g/cm³.

$$\text{density} = \frac{\text{mass}}{\text{volume}}$$

E1 **(a)** A glass ornament has mass 690 g and volume 240 cm³. Find its density in g/cm³.

(b) A statue has volume 1.5 m³ and mass 2.4 tonnes (1 tonne = 1000 kg). Find its density in kg/m³.

E2 Use the table on the right to work out the mass of these objects.

(a) A stone with volume 92 cm³

(b) A wooden cuboid 22 cm by 18 cm by 11 cm

(c) The water in a 25 m by 15 m swimming pool, which is 1.5 m deep everywhere

Material	Density
Wood	0.7 g/cm³
Stone	3.0 g/cm³
Water	1.0 g/cm³

E3 Density can help identify metals (or at least rule out fake metals).

One of these ingots is platinum, one is gold, one is silver and one is fake gold.

Work out the density of each ingot and use the table to say what each ingot is made of.

Material	Density
Platinum	21.5 g/cm³
Gold	19.3 g/cm³
Silver	10.5 g/cm³
Fake gold	9.8 g/cm³

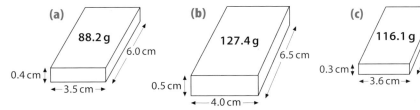

(a) 88.2 g, 6.0 cm, 0.4 cm, 3.5 cm

(b) 127.4 g, 6.5 cm, 0.5 cm, 4.0 cm

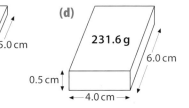

(c) 116.1 g, 5.0 cm, 0.3 cm, 3.6 cm

(d) 231.6 g, 6.0 cm, 0.5 cm, 4.0 cm

E4 An aluminium vase weighs 413 g. The density of aluminium is 2.6 g/cm³. What is the volume of the aluminium used to make the vase?

E5 This diagram shows a prism.
The cross-section of the prism is a trapezium.
The lengths of the parallel sides of the trapezium are 8 cm and 6 cm.
The distance between the parallel sides of the trapezium is 5 cm.
The length of the prism is 20 cm.

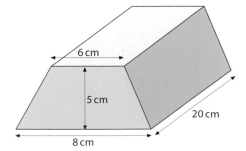

6 cm, 5 cm, 20 cm, 8 cm

(a) Work out the volume of the prism.

The prism is made out of gold. Gold has a density of 19.3 grams per cm³.

(b) Work out the mass of the prism. Give your answer in kilograms.

Edexcel

E6 A piece of copper wire has a **diameter** of 2 mm and is 1 m long.

　(a) Treating it as a cylinder, calculate its volume.

　(b) Given that copper has a density of 8.94 grams per cm^3, find its mass.

E7 A measuring cylinder has an internal base area of 6.5 cm^2.
It is partly filled with water. When a pebble is put into it the water rises by 18 mm.
The pebble has mass 32.8 g. What is its density?

Use information from the opposite page for the next two questions.

E8 As preparation for making a gold goblet, a goldsmith makes an actual size
wooden model on a lathe. The wooden model of the goblet weighs 27.25 g.
Calculate what the actual gold goblet will weigh.

E9 A silver ring and a platinum ring weigh the same.
The volume of the silver ring is 1.12 cm^3.
What is the volume of the platinum ring?

F Units of volume and liquid measure

F1 (a) Calculate the volume of this cuboid in m^3 and in cm^3.

　(b) How many cm^3 are there in 1 m^3?
(To check your answer makes sense, imagine filling a
metre cube with centimetre cubes.)

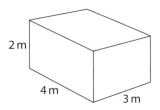

F2 Change these volumes in m^3 into cm^3.

　(a) 25 m^3　　　(b) 0.6 m^3　　　(c) 200 m^3　　　(d) 0.0008 m^3

F3 Change these volumes in cm^3 to m^3

　(a) 7 000 000 cm^3　(b) 3 200 000 cm^3　(c) 342 000 cm^3　(d) 8000 cm^3

The measurement system for the volume of solids is related
to the system for liquids and the capacity of containers.

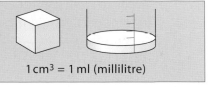

$1 cm^3 = 1 ml$ (millilitre)

F4 How many millilitres of liquid will this cylindrical beaker
hold when full to the brim?

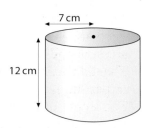

1 litre = 1000 millilitres ('milli' means a thousandth)

F5 How many litres will the full beaker hold?

F6 From the fact that there are 1 000 000 cm^3 in a m^3,
how many litres are there in a m^3?

Volume, liquid measure and capacity

In this summary, the arrows show how the relationships can be deduced.

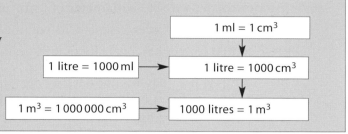

| 1 ml = 1 cm³ |

1 litre = 1000 ml → 1 litre = 1000 cm³

1 m³ = 1 000 000 cm³ → 1000 litres = 1 m³

F7 **(a)** How many litres of water does this fish tank hold when it is completely full?

(b) How deep will the water be (to the nearest cm) when the tank contains 50 litres?

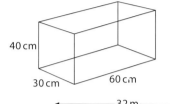

40 cm · 30 cm · 60 cm

F8 A tank to hold petroleum has these dimensions.

(a) How many litres can it hold, to the nearest 1000 litres?

(b) Petroleum is being pumped out of it at a rate of 10 000 litres per hour. How far, to the nearest centimetre, does the petroleum level fall in 3 hours?

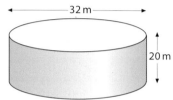

32 m · 20 m

F9 A litre of orange juice is spilt and spreads out to a depth of 1 mm. What area of floor, in m², is covered in orange juice?

F10 A 5 litre tin of paint is enough to cover an area of 24 m². How thick, in mm, should the layer of paint be when it is applied?

F11 The area of an ornamental pond is 4500 m². How many litres of water need to be added to the pond to increase the depth by 5 cm?

F12 A measuring cylinder for a science lab is being made. The radius on the inside is 1.50 cm. It needs to have a graduation mark for each ml of liquid poured in. How far apart should these graduation marks be?

Test yourself

T1 Find the volume and surface area of these objects.

(a) A cuboid   **(b)** A triangular prism   **(c)** A cylinder

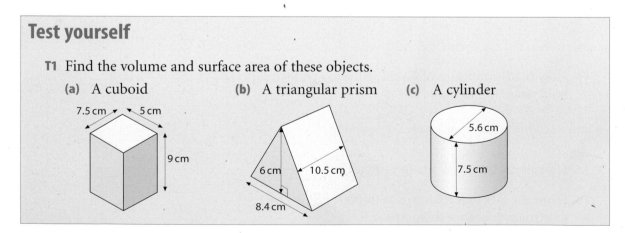

(a) 7.5 cm · 5 cm · 9 cm

(b) 6 cm · 10.5 cm · 8.4 cm

(c) 5.6 cm · 7.5 cm

T2 Chocomint is made in blocks as shown in the diagram.

The block is a prism and its cross-section is a trapezium.

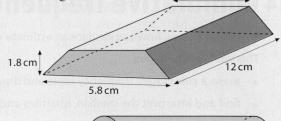

(a) Calculate the volume of a block of Chocomint.

Chocorock is made in cylindrical sticks as shown in the diagram.

The radius of the circular end is 1.2 cm.
The volume of the cylinder is 50 cm^3.

(b) Find the length of a stick of Chocorock.
Give your answer to a sensible degree of accuracy.

OCR

T3 The diagram represents a solid metal bar with a uniform cross-section in the form of the trapezium ABCD, in which AB = 9.3 cm and DC = 5.8 cm.

The height of the bar is 3.5 cm and the length of the bar, BE, is 14.7 cm.

The density of the metal is 5.6 g/cm^3.

Calculate the weight, in kilograms, of the bar.

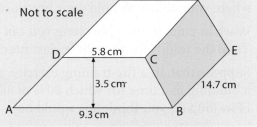

Not to scale

WJEC

T4 (a) Find an expression for the volume of each cuboid.

(b) What value of a gives them the same volume?

(c) What value of a gives them the same surface area?

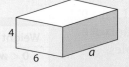
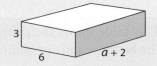

T5 Half a litre of water is poured into a tin.
The depth of the water is 8 cm.
What is the area of the base of the tin?

Hint for spreadsheet activity on page 133

Set up a formula that gives you the height of a 1000 cm^3 can for any value that you enter into a 'radius' cell.
Set up another formula that gives you the surface area of a can with the radius and height that are showing.

9 The bullet train in Japan covers the 120 miles between Hiroshima and Kokura at an average speed of 164 mph. How long does it take, to the nearest minute?

10 Draw a set of axes, each numbered from ⁻6 to 6.
Plot and join the points (1, 2), (1, 4), (3, 3) and (2, 2). Label the shape P.

   (a) **(i)** Draw the image of P after reflection in the x-axis. Label it Q.

      (ii) Draw the image of Q after a rotation of 90° anticlockwise about the point (0, 0). Label it R.

   (b) What single transformation maps shape R back onto shape P?

   (c) Draw the image of Q after the translation $\begin{bmatrix} 2 \\ -2 \end{bmatrix}$. Label the image S.

   (d) Describe fully the single transformation that maps shape R to shape S.

   (e) Draw the image of P after an enlargement with scale factor 3 and centre (4, 4). Label the image T.

11 Find the value of n in each of these equations.

   (a) $2^5 \times 2^n = 2^{15}$ **(b)** $3^n \times 3^6 = 3^2$ **(c)** $\dfrac{4^3}{4^n} = 4^{-5}$ **(d)** $\dfrac{5^n}{5^2} = 5^{-5}$

12 The diagram shows a triangular prism.

   (a) How many planes of symmetry does this prism have?

   (b) Calculate the perpendicular height (h) of the prism.

   (c) Find the volume of the prism.

   (d) Draw these full size.

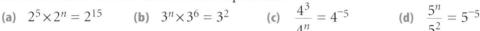

      (i) A plan view   **(ii)** A side view   **(iii)** A front view

   (e) Draw a full size net and calculate the surface area of the prism.

13 At the start of a journey a car's mileometer showed 042 786. At the end it showed 042 938. The journey took $3\frac{3}{4}$ hours.

   (a) Calculate the average speed in m.p.h, correct to one decimal place.

   (b) Given that 1 mile is approximately 1.6 kilometres, convert the speed to kilometres per hour, correct to one decimal place.

14 Simplify each of these.

   (a) $4x^3 \times 2x^2$ **(b)** $\dfrac{6x^6}{3x^2}$ **(c)** $5x^{-2} \times 2x^3$ **(d)** $\dfrac{6x}{3x^2 \times 3x^6}$ **(e)** $(2x^3)^{-2}$

15 If 1 litre of water is poured into this plastic container, how deep will the water be (to the nearest 0.1 cm)?

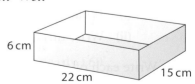

16 **(a)** Write 25^3 as a power of 5.   **(b)** Solve the equation $3^n = 27^4$.

15 Working with expressions

You should know how to

- multiply out expressions such as $4(2x - 3)$
- simplify expressions such as $4n^3 \times 2n$ and $4n^3 \div 2n$

This work will help you

- collect like terms in expressions involving powers
- simplify expressions such as $4ab^3 \times 2ab$ and $\dfrac{4ab^3}{2ab}$
- multiply out expressions such as $4x(xy + 3x)$ and simplify divisions such as $\dfrac{ab^2 + 3b}{b}$
- factorise expressions such as $6x^2y - 9xy^2$
- form and simplify formulas

You will need sheets H1–2 and H1–3.

A Collecting like terms
level 6

Sometimes a calculation can be simplified by collecting together like terms.
For example, $12 \times 23 - 2 \times 23 = 10 \times 23 = 230$

Sometimes algebraic expressions can be simplified in the same way.
For example, $3x^2 + 1 + 4x - 2x^2 + 6x - 7 = 3x^2 - 2x^2 + 4x + 6x + 1 - 7$
$$= x^2 + 10x - 6$$

This cannot be simplified any further.

A1 Simplify the following by collecting like terms.

    (a) $8 + 3n - 7 + 2n$ (b) $7p + 6 - 5p - 9$ (c) $5k - 7 - 9k + 12$

A2 Find four pairs of equivalent expressions.

A $x^2 + x^2$ **B** $3x^4 - 2x^4$ **C** $3x^3 + x$ **D** $2x^2 - x$

E $x^2 + 2x + x^2 - 3x$ **F** $2x^3 + 2x + x^3 - x$ **G** x^4 **H** $2x^2$

A3 Simplify the following by collecting like terms.

    (a) $n^2 + 3n + n^2 + 2n$ (b) $3a^2 + 5a - a^2$ (c) $k^2 - k + 2k^2 + 6k$

    (d) $7m + 4m^2 - 5m + 2$ (e) $g^2 + g^3 + 4g^2 + g^3$ (f) $5h^2 + 2h - 3h^2 - 5h$

    (g) $2x + 5x^2 - 3x + 2x^2$ (h) $y^2 + y + y^2 - 7y + 3$

A4 Find the value of each expression when $n = 5$.

    (a) $n^2 + n^2 + n^2 + n^2 - 2$ (b) $n^3 + 8n - n^3$

    (c) $8n^2 - 7n^2 + n + 1$ (d) $2n^2 + 3n - n^2 - 4n$

A5

    (a) Find pairs of the above expressions that add to give

        (i) $2a^2 + 4a - 1$ **(ii)** $a^2 + 3$ **(iii)** $2a^2 + 6$

        (iv) $4a^2 + a + 5$ **(v)** $3a - 1$ **(vi)** $a^2 + 2$

    (b) Find three of the above expressions that add to give $a + 2$.

B Multiplying and dividing expressions

Examples

$$p(2p + 3) = p \times 2p + p \times 3$$
$$= 2p^2 + 3p$$

$$3b(2b - 5) = 3b \times 2b - 3b \times 5$$
$$= 6b^2 - 15b$$

$$\frac{6n^2 - 8n^3}{2n} = \frac{6n^2}{2n} - \frac{8n^3}{2n}$$
$$= 3n - 4n^2$$

B1 Multiply out the brackets in these.

    (a) $n(n + 7)$ **(b)** $m(3 + m)$ **(c)** $3(2a - 5)$ **(d)** $h(h - 9)$

    (e) $k(10 - k)$ **(f)** $2w(w + 7)$ **(g)** $3x(x - 6)$ **(h)** $6n(2 - n)$

B2 Find the expressions missing from these statements.

    (a) $d(\blacksquare\blacksquare\blacksquare) = d^2 + 5d$ **(b)** $2n(\blacksquare\blacksquare\blacksquare) = 2n^2 - 8n$

    (c) $3p(\blacksquare\blacksquare\blacksquare) = 15p - 3p^2$ **(d)** $5k(\blacksquare\blacksquare\blacksquare) = 20k + 5k^2$

B3 Find five pairs of matching expressions.

B4 Multiply out the brackets in these.

    (a) $2h(7h - 5)$ **(b)** $3a(a^2 - 4)$ **(c)** $n^2(n^3 - 5)$ **(d)** $3k(4k + 5)$

    (e) $5d(3 - 2d^2)$ **(f)** $7p(3 - 4p)$ **(g)** $2b^2(3b + 1)$ **(h)** $3w^2(1 + 2w^2)$

B5 Multiply out the brackets in each of these and simplify where possible.

    (a) $x(x + 2) + 5(x - 3)$ **(b)** $2a(a^2 + 1) - a^2(a - 5)$ **(c)** $3h^2(2h - 3) - 4h(h^2 + 1)$

B6 Simplify each of these.

    (a) $\dfrac{10d^2 - 5}{5}$ **(b)** $\dfrac{8a^2 + 12a}{a}$ **(c)** $\dfrac{8a^2 + 12a}{4a}$ **(d)** $\dfrac{8a^2 + 12a^4}{2a^2}$

B7 Find the missing expressions.

    (a) $\dfrac{\blacksquare\blacksquare\blacksquare}{5} = d^2 + 2$ **(b)** $\dfrac{\blacksquare\blacksquare\blacksquare}{d^2} = d^2 + d$ **(c)** $\dfrac{\blacksquare\blacksquare\blacksquare}{2d^2} = 8d^3 + 4d$

B8 Find the missing expression for each diagram.

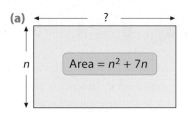

(a) Area = $n^2 + 7n$, height n, width ?

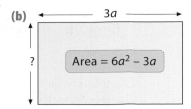

(b) Area = $6a^2 - 3a$, width $3a$, height ?

B9

| 3 | x | $2x$ | $5x$ | x^2 | $2x + 5$ | $x + 1$ |

Find pairs of the above expressions that multiply to give

(a) $6x + 15$ (b) $x^2 + x$ (c) $2x^2 + 5x$ (d) $2x^2 + 2x$

(e) $10x^2$ (f) $2x^3 + 5x^2$ (g) $10x^2 + 25x$ (h) $5x^2 + 5x$

C Factorising expressions

A number such as 15 can be written as 5×3, a product of two factors.

An algebraic expression can sometime be factorised into the product of two factors.

Examples

$3a - 12 = 3(a - 4)$

$6x - 15x^2 = 3x(2 - 5x)$

An expression is not completely factorised if any expression in brackets can be factorised further.

Example

$8k + 2k^2 = 2(4k + k^2)$
$ = 2k(4 + k)$

This is not completely factorised because $4k + k^2 = k(4 + k)$.

C1 Factorise these.

(a) $3m + 12$ (b) $4n - 6$ (c) $15 - 10p$ (d) $8q - 4$

(e) $9a^2 - 6$ (f) $b^2 + 3b$ (g) $5c + c^2$ (h) $d^2 - 7d$

(i) $11x - x^2$ (j) $y^2 + y$ (k) $w^3 - 2w$ (l) $7h^3 + h$

C2 Find the expressions missing from these statements.

(a) $2k(\blacksquare\blacksquare\blacksquare) = 2k^2 + 6k$ (b) $3p(\blacksquare\blacksquare\blacksquare) = 3p^2 - 6p$

(c) $5n(\blacksquare\blacksquare\blacksquare) = 20n^2 + 5n$ (d) $2x(\blacksquare\blacksquare\blacksquare) = 6x^2 + 4x$

(e) $h^2(\blacksquare\blacksquare\blacksquare) = h^3 + 2h^2$ (f) $y^2(\blacksquare\blacksquare\blacksquare) = 2y^3 + 3y^2$

C3 Factorise these completely.

(a) $3b^2 + 6b$ (b) $10a + 2a^2$ (c) $5d^2 - 15d$ (d) $21c + 7c^2$

(e) $6k^2 + 8k$ (f) $9h + 6h^2$ (g) $9x^2 - 3x$ (h) $2y + 10y^2$

E	L	R	G	U	A	S	B	W	D	H	O
5	7	n	$2n$	$3n$	$n+1$	$n-1$	$2n+3$	$2n-3$	$3n+2$	n^2+2	n^2-2

Completely factorise each expression below as the product of two factors.
Use the code above to find a letter for each factor.
Rearrange the letters in each part to spell an animal.

(a) $7n + 7$ $2n^2 - 3n$ $3n^2 - 3n$

(b) $14n - 21$ $5n - 5$ $5n + 5$

(c) $10n + 15$ $2n^2 + 2n$ $3n^2 + 2n$

(d) $5n^2 + 10$ $15n + 10$ $2n^3 + 4n$ $2n^3 - 4n$

C5 Factorise these completely.

(a) $n^3 + 4n^2$ (b) $6n^5 - n^3$ (c) $5n^3 + 7n^2$ (d) $2n^3 + 2n^2$

*C6 (a) Factorise $3n + 6$.

(b) Explain how the factorisation tells you that $3n + 6$ will be a multiple of 3 for any integer n.

*C7 (a) Factorise $n^2 + n$.

(b) Use the factorisation to show that $n^2 + n$ will always be even for any integer n.

D Dealing with more than one letter

Examples of substitution	Find the value of $3a^2b + b$ when $a = 4$ and $b = 5$.	Find the value of $5xy^2 - 2x$ when $x = 3$ and $y = 2$.
	$\begin{aligned} 3a^2b + b &= 3 \times a^2 \times b + b \\ &= 3 \times 4^2 \times 5 + 5 \\ &= 3 \times 16 \times 5 + 5 \\ &= 240 + 5 \\ &= 245 \end{aligned}$	$\begin{aligned} 5xy^2 - 2x &= 5 \times x \times y^2 - 2 \times x \\ &= 5 \times 3 \times 2^2 - 2 \times 3 \\ &= 5 \times 3 \times 4 - 2 \times 3 \\ &= 60 - 6 \\ &= 54 \end{aligned}$

D1 Find the value of each expression when $a = 2$ and $b = 5$.

(a) $2ab + a$ (b) $5a^2 - b$ (c) $a^2 + b^2 - 1$

(d) $3a + 2b^2 - 5b$ (e) $3ab + b^2 - a^2$ (f) $(ab)^2$

(g) a^2b (h) ab^2 (i) $a^3 + b$

D2 Find the value of each expression when $x = 3$, $y = 4$ and $z = {}^-6$.

(a) $x + y + z$ (b) $xy + yz$ (c) $3xy - z^2$

(d) $x^2 + 2x - y$ (e) $xy^2 - 3y + z$ (f) $\dfrac{xy}{z}$

D3 Solve the puzzles on sheet H1–2.

Examples of collecting like terms

$$3x + 2y + 7x - 5y = 3x + 7x + 2y - 5y$$
$$= 10x - 3y$$

$$ab + 4a^2 + 4ab - b - 7a^2 = ab + 4ab + 4a^2 - 7a^2 - b$$
$$= 5ab - 3a^2 - b$$

Neither of these can be simplified any further.

D4 Simplify the following expressions by collecting like terms.

(a) $2a + b + 3a - 5b$

(b) $ab + b^2 + 5ab + 3b^2 + 2$

(c) $a^2 + 5a + 2 - 8a$

(d) $8b - a^2 + 2b + 3a^2 - 7$

D5

A $x^2 - x$　　**B** $3x - y$　　**C** $5x + y$　　**D** $y^2 + x^2$　　**E** $5y - y^2$

Find pairs of the above expressions that add to give

(a) $y^2 + 2x^2 - x$

(b) $5y + x^2$

(c) $x^2 + 2x - y$

(d) $x^2 + 4x + y$

(e) $8x$

(f) $5x + 6y - y^2$

Examples of multiplying

$$3a \times 4b = 3 \times a \times 4 \times b$$
$$= 3 \times 4 \times a \times b$$
$$= 12ab$$

$$5zy \times 3z^2 = 5 \times z \times y \times 3 \times z \times z$$
$$= 5 \times 3 \times z \times z \times z \times y$$
$$= 15z^3y$$

D6 Find the result of each multiplication in its simplest form.

(a) $b \times 2a$

(b) $2x \times 3y$

(c) $4p \times 3q$

(d) $5c \times d$

(e) $5m \times 4n$

(f) $3v \times 5w$

D7 Find the result of each multiplication in its simplest form.

(a) $2a^2 \times 3b$

(b) $3xy \times 4x$

(c) $2pq \times 3pq$

(d) $4cd \times 5c^2$

(e) $2m^2n^2 \times 7mn^2$

(f) $4vw^4 \times 6v^3w^2$

D8 Find the expression missing from each statement.

(a) $5p \times \blacksquare = 10pq$

(b) $\blacksquare \times 7n = 21mn$

(c) $3a^2 \times \blacksquare = 9a^2b$

(d) $\blacksquare \times 2y^2 = 10x^2y^2$

(e) $3cd^2 \times \blacksquare = 15c^3d^2$

(f) $\blacksquare \times 7vw^3 = 28v^3w^4$

D9

$2a$　　$3b$　　$5ab$　　$3a^2$　　$2b^2$　　$5a^2b$　　ab^3

Find pairs of the above expressions that multiply to give

(a) $6ab$　　(b) $10ab^3$　　(c) $15a^4b$　　(d) $9a^2b$　　(e) $2ab^5$　　(f) $25a^3b^2$

D10 Solve the 'cover-up' puzzle on sheet H1–3.

D11 Multiply out the brackets in each of these and simplify where possible.

(a) $2(3x - y) + 3(x + y)$ (b) $5p(q + 2p^2) + 2p^2(p - 3q)$

(c) $2m(mn + 5) - n(n - m^2)$ (d) $3ab(4a + 3a^3b) - 2(6a^2b + 3)$

Examples of simplifying powers

$(2pq)^3 = 2pq \times 2pq \times 2pq$

$= 2 \times p \times q \times 2 \times p \times q \times 2 \times p \times q$

$= 2 \times 2 \times 2 \times p \times p \times p \times q \times q \times q$

$= 8p^3q^3$

$$\left(\frac{3p^3}{q}\right)^2 = \frac{3p^3}{q} \times \frac{3p^3}{q}$$

$$= \frac{3p^3 \times 3p^3}{q \times q}$$

$$= \frac{3 \times 3 \times p^3 \times p^3}{q \times q}$$

$$= \frac{9p^6}{q^2}$$

D12 Expand and simplify each of these.

(a) $(3pq)^2$ (b) $(2vw)^3$ (c) $(5x^2y)^2$ (d) $(2a^2b^3)^4$

(e) $\left(\dfrac{2p}{q}\right)^2$ (f) $\left(\dfrac{3vw}{5}\right)^2$ (g) $\left(\dfrac{x^2y}{z^3}\right)^4$ (h) $\left(\dfrac{2ab^2}{3c}\right)^3$

Examples of division

You can write out expressions in full and cancel.

$$\frac{8ab}{2b} = \frac{8 \times a \times b}{2 \times b}$$

$$= \frac{\overset{4}{8} \times a \times \cancel{b}}{\cancel{2} \times \cancel{b}}$$

$$= 4a$$

$$\frac{12a^2b}{4ab} = \frac{12 \times a \times a \times b}{4 \times a \times b}$$

$$= \frac{\overset{3}{12} \times a \times \cancel{a} \times \cancel{b}}{\cancel{4} \times \cancel{a} \times \cancel{b}}$$

$$= 3a$$

$$\frac{10a^4b^3}{15a^2b^4c} = \frac{10 \times a \times a \times a \times a \times b \times b \times b}{15 \times a \times a \times b \times b \times b \times b \times c}$$

$$= \frac{\overset{2}{10} \times a \times a \times \cancel{a} \times \cancel{a} \times \cancel{b} \times \cancel{b} \times \cancel{b}}{\underset{3}{15} \times \cancel{a} \times \cancel{a} \times \cancel{b} \times \cancel{b} \times \cancel{b} \times b \times c}$$

$$= \frac{2a^2}{3bc}$$

This is equivalent to dividing top and bottom by the same expressions.

$$\frac{8ab}{2b} \overset{\div 2}{=} \frac{4ab}{b} \overset{\div b}{=} \frac{4a}{1} = 4a$$

$$\frac{12a^2b}{4ab} \overset{\div 4}{=} \frac{3a^2b}{ab} \overset{\div b}{=} \frac{3a^2}{a} \overset{\div a}{=} \frac{3a}{1} = 3a$$

$$\frac{10a^4b^3}{15a^2b^4c} \overset{\div 5}{=} \frac{2a^4b^3}{3a^2b^4c} \overset{\div a^2}{=} \frac{2a^2b^3}{3b^4c} \overset{\div b^3}{=} \frac{2a^2}{3bc}$$

D13 Simplify each of these.

(a) $\dfrac{10pq}{2p}$ (b) $\dfrac{12xy}{6y}$ (c) $\dfrac{18mn}{6m}$ (d) $\dfrac{8ab^2}{2a}$

(e) $\dfrac{6p^2q}{2p}$ (f) $\dfrac{8x^2y}{4xy}$ (g) $\dfrac{12m^2n}{3mn}$ (h) $\dfrac{16a^3b^2}{4a^2b^2}$

D14

A	E	G	L	M	N	O	P	R
$2b$	$4bc$	bc^2	$4d$	cd	$2b^2$	$3bd$	$3c$	$2b^2d$

Simplify each expression below as far as you can.
Use the code above to find a letter for each expression.

Rearrange each set of letters to spell a fruit.

(a) $\dfrac{8cd}{2c}$ $\quad$ $\dfrac{12bc}{3}$ $\quad$ $\dfrac{15cd}{5d}$ $\quad$ $\dfrac{4bc}{2c}$ $\quad$ $\dfrac{9c^2b}{3cb}$

(b) $\dfrac{18b^2d}{6b}$ $\quad$ $\dfrac{10ab^2}{5a}$ $\quad$ $\dfrac{20b^2c^2}{5bc}$ $\quad$ $\dfrac{12cd^5}{3cd^4}$ $\quad$ $\dfrac{5c^2d}{5c}$

(c) $\dfrac{21bc^2}{7bc}$ $\quad$ $\dfrac{32b^2c^4}{8bc^3}$ $\quad$ $\dfrac{14bcd}{7cd}$ $\quad$ $\dfrac{6b^5d}{3b^3}$ $\quad$ $\dfrac{7b^5c^3}{7b^4c}$

(d) $\dfrac{5b^6c^7}{5b^5c^5}$ $\quad$ $\dfrac{16b^5d^2}{8b^3d}$ $\quad$ $\dfrac{8b^6c^3}{4b^5c^3}$ $\quad$ $\dfrac{2b^5d}{b^3d}$ $\quad$ $\dfrac{6b^2d^7}{2bd^6}$ $\quad$ $\dfrac{20b^2c^2d}{5bcd}$

D15 Simplify each of these.

(a) $\dfrac{ab}{bc}$ $\qquad$ (b) $\dfrac{bc}{6b}$ $\qquad$ (c) $\dfrac{6xy}{y^2}$ $\qquad$ (d) $\dfrac{16mn^2}{8mn^3}$

(e) $\dfrac{p^6q^4}{p^3q^6}$ $\qquad$ (f) $\dfrac{10ab^2c}{15abc}$ $\qquad$ (g) $\dfrac{3a}{9a^2b}$ $\qquad$ (h) $\dfrac{4gh^2}{8g^2h^2}$

D16 Simplify each of these.

(a) $\dfrac{2hk \times 6hk^2}{3h}$ $\qquad$ (b) $\dfrac{4m^2n \times 5mn^2}{10m^3}$ $\qquad$ (c) $\dfrac{4x^3y \times 3xz^3}{6x^2y}$

D17 Copy and complete: $\dfrac{ab^3 + 2a^2b^2}{ab^2} = \dfrac{ab^3}{ab^2} + \dfrac{2a^2b^2}{ab^2} = $ ⬤ + ⬤ .

D18 Simplify each of these.

(a) $\dfrac{cd^2 + c^2d}{cd}$ $\qquad$ (b) $\dfrac{8c^2d - 6c}{2c}$ $\qquad$ (c) $\dfrac{c^2d^3 + 7c^3d^2}{c^2d}$ $\qquad$ (d) $\dfrac{6c^2d^2 - 9cd^3}{3cd^2}$

D19 Find the missing expressions.

(a)
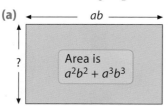
← ab →
? Area is $a^2b^2 + a^3b^3$

(b)
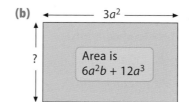
← $3a^2$ →
? Area is $6a^2b + 12a^3$

(c)
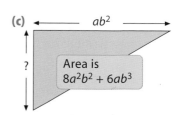
← ab^2 →
? Area is $8a^2b^2 + 6ab^3$

D20 Simplify each of these.

(a) $\dfrac{c^2d + 2d}{cd}$ $\qquad$ (b) $\dfrac{cd^2 + c^2d}{c^2d^2}$ $\qquad$ (c) $\dfrac{4cd^2 + 8c^2d}{12c^2d^2}$ $\qquad$ (d) $\dfrac{cd^2 + c^2d}{c^4d^4}$

E Expanding and factorising expressions

Examples

Expand $3a(b + a)$.

$$3a(b + a) = 3a \times b + 3a \times a$$
$$= 3ab + 3a^2$$

Factorise $6a^2 - 9ab$ completely.

$$6a^2 - 9ab = a(6a - 9b)$$
$$= 3a(2a - 3b)$$

This is not complete because $6a - 9b = 3(2a - 3b)$.

E1 Expand these.

(a) $4(a + b)$ (b) $3(x - y)$ (c) $5(m + 2n)$ (d) $4(3a - 5b)$

(e) $h(k + 1)$ (f) $p(p - q)$ (g) $b(3a + 5)$ (h) $c(2d + 3c)$

E2 Factorise these.

(a) $3p + 3q$ (b) $5k - 5h$ (c) $2a + 6b$ (d) $6n - 9m$

(e) $ab + a$ (f) $x^2 - xy$ (g) $7pq + 9p$ (h) $4ab + 5a^2$

E3 Expand these.

(a) $2a(b - a)$ (b) $3x(2y + 5)$ (c) $5m(n + 2m)$ (d) $xy(y - 1)$

(e) $ab(5a + 3b)$ (f) $p^2(3p - 1)$ (g) $3xy(2x + 9)$ (h) $2y^2(5x - 1)$

E4 Factorise these completely.

(a) $3m^2 - 3mn$ (b) $2x^2 + 4xy$ (c) $3p^2 - 6pq$ (d) $10mn + 15m^2$

(e) $ab^2 + 3ab$ (f) $x^2y - xy$ (g) $6y^2z + 10y^2$ (h) $10k^2h - 5k^2$

(i) $2x^2y + 2xy^2$ (j) $3a^2b - 15ab$ (k) $8hk + 4hk^2$ (l) $10p^2q + 5pq^2$

E5

E	H	P	S	O	A	I	L	G	R	T	U	N
5	$2a$	$3a$	$2b$	$7b$	a^2	ab	$3b^2$	$a + b$	$a - 5b$	$2a - b$	$ab + 1$	$2a + 3b$

Fully factorise each expression below as the product of two factors.
Use the code above to find a letter for each factor.

Rearrange each set of letters to spell a bird.

(a) $3a^2 - 15ab$ $2a^3 - a^2b$ $7ab - 35b^2$

(b) $4a^2 - 2ab$ $2a^2b + 2a$ $2ab - 10b^2$

(c) $7ab + 7b^2$ $5a - 25b$ $2ab^2 + 2b$

(d) $4ab - 2b^2$ $3b^2a + 3b^3$ $a^3 - 5a^2b$ $2a^2b + 3ab^2$

E6 Factorise these completely.

(a) $a^3b + 2a^2b^2$ (b) $7m^2n^2 + mn^2$ (c) $6x^2y^2 - 2xy^3$ (d) $3p^4q + 12p^2q^2$

F Finding and simplifying formulas

- Find and simplify formulas for the perimeter and area of each of these shapes.

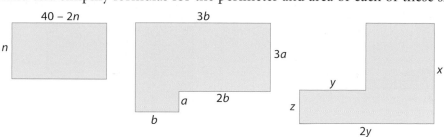

> It often helps to sketch the shape and mark any missing lengths.

- Find and simplify formulas for the volume and surface area of each of these cuboids.

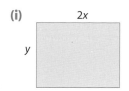

In the questions that follow, simplify each formula by expanding brackets and collecting like terms where appropriate.

F1 (a) Find a formula for the perimeter of each shape below.
Use P to stand for the perimeter each time. (Each formula begins $P = \ldots$)

(b) Find a formula for the area of each shape.
Use A to stand for the area each time.

(i)

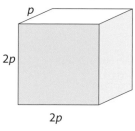

(ii)

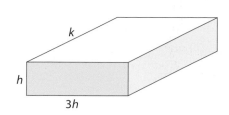

(iii)

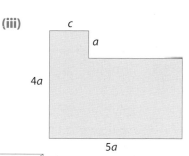

F2 Find formulas for the volume and surface area of this prism.
Use V to stand for the volume and S to stand for the surface area.

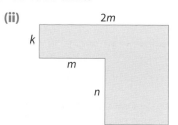

F3 Find a formula for the volume of this prism.

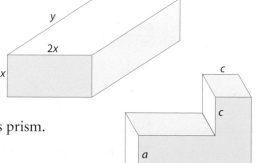

*F4 **(a)** Find a formula for the volume of each prism.

     (b) Find a formula for the surface area of each prism.

(i)

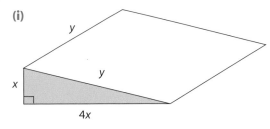

(ii)

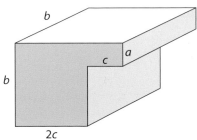

Test yourself

T1 Simplify each of these.

    (a) $4x + 2xy + 3x - 6xy$ **(b)** $a^2 - 4a - 1 + 3a - 2$ **(c)** $3h \times 5k$

    (d) $3a^2b \times 2ab$ **(e)** $\dfrac{10ab}{5b}$ **(f)** $\dfrac{4x^2 - 6x^3}{2x}$

T2 Multiply out these.

    (a) $2(p + q)$ **(b)** $x(x - 2)$ **(c)** $p^2(3p - p^4)$ **(d)** $5h(2h - k)$

T3 Expand and simplify

    (b) $3(x - 2) + 2(5x + 4)$ **(b)** $4(3x + 1) - 3(x - 1)$

T4 Factorise these completely.

    (a) $9y - 6$ **(b)** $4ab - 6a^2$ **(c)** $6x^3 - 15x^2$

T5 **(a)** Simplify $2a^3y^2 \times 5ay^4$.   **(b)** Factorise completely $14x^2y - 21xy^3$.

T6 Simplify $\dfrac{x^4y^2}{x^3y^5}$.

T7 Simplify these.

    (a) $\dfrac{3x^5y^3}{6xy^2}$ **(b)** $\dfrac{(2ab^2)^2}{10ab}$

T8 Find formulas for the volume and
surface area of this cuboid.

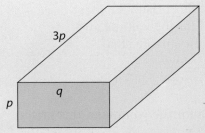

16 Coordinates in three dimensions

This work will help you identify points in three-dimensional space using coordinates.

You will need scissors, adhesive and sheets H1–4 and H1–5.

A Identifying points

To give the position of a point in 3-D space, a third axis is needed called the **z-axis**.
So each point has three coordinates, written in the form (x, y, z).

Making your own grid

- Cut out the 3-D grid from sheet H1–4 and stick it together.
  Place it on the desk with the x-axis and the y-axis on the desk
  and the z-axis pointing upwards.

- Here a rod 3 cm long has been placed on the grid.
  The bottom of the rod has coordinates $(2, 4, 0)$.
  What are the coordinates of the top of the rod?

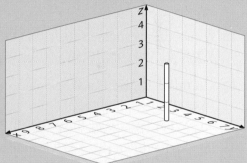

- Cut out the rectangle from sheet H1–5.
  Place it on the bottom of the 3-D grid with its x-axis and y-axis matching the grid.
  What are the 3-D coordinates of P, Q, R and S?

- Lift the rectangle up 3 units. What are the coordinates of P, Q, R and S now?

- Cut out the net for the cuboid from sheet H1–5 and glue it together.
  Place the cuboid on the 3-D grid like this
  (vertex B is at $(0, 0, 0)$ and face P is at the bottom).
  What are the coordinates of each corner
  that you can see?

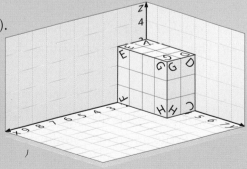

A1 Place the cuboid on the 3-D grid with corner A at $(0, 0, 0)$ and face M at the bottom.
Write down the coordinates of these vertices.

(a) F   (b) C   (c) E   (d) H

A2 Place the cuboid with corner C at $(0, 0, 0)$ and face N at the bottom.
Write down the coordinates of these vertices.

(a) B   (b) G   (c) E   (d) A

A3 Place the cuboid with face M at the bottom, corner A at $(5, 2, 0)$ and
corner D at $(1, 2, 0)$.
Write down the coordinates of these vertices.

(a) G   (b) B   (c) F   (d) H

A4 Place the cuboid so that face P is at the bottom, B is at $(1, 3, 0)$ and
C is at $(1, 7, 0)$.
Write down the coordinates of these points.

(a) H   (b) A   (c) D   (d) G

A5 If the cuboid is placed so that C is at $(3, 2, 1)$, E is at $(1, 6, 4)$ and
face P is facing downwards, what are the coordinates of these points?

(a) F   (b) B   (c) G   (d) A

A6 A cube has vertices at $(0, 0, 0)$, $(4, 0, 0)$ and $(0, 4, 0)$.
What are the coordinates of the other five vertices?

A7 On this 3-D grid is a shape made from
five centimetre cubes.

(a) What letter is at the point $(2, 2, 1)$?

(b) Write down the 3-D coordinates
of the other four labelled points.

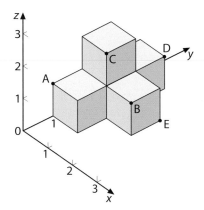

A8 This is a flight of steps with each step the same size.
The x, y and z-axes are shown.
Point A is at $(6, 0, 0)$. Point B is at $(6, 3, 2)$.

(a) How high is the flight of stairs?

(b) Write down the coordinates of these points.

(i) C   (ii) D

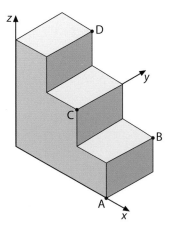

*A9 This shows a 3-D grid and a cube with sides 2 units long.
Point A is at (0, 1, 0).

The cube is reflected in the horizontal plane containing
the *x*-axis and *y*-axis.

What will be the images of these points after the reflection?

(a) A   **(b)** B   **(c)** C

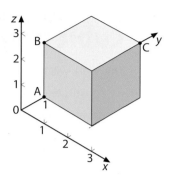

Test yourself

T1 The diagram shows eight
one-centimetre cubes fixed together.

Corner A has coordinates (1, 1, 0).

Write down the coordinates of
points B and C.

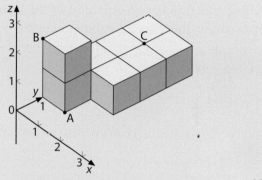

OCR

T2 This cuboid measures 3 units by 4 units by 2 units.
Vertex O is at (0, 0, 0) and vertex U is at (3, 4, 2).

(a) Give the coordinates of P, Q, R, S, T and V.

(b) Say whether each of these points lies on a
face of this cuboid, is inside the cuboid or is
outside the cuboid.

    (i) (2, 3, 2)   **(ii)** (1, 2, 1)

    (iii) (2, 3, 3)   **(iv)** (1, 4, 1)

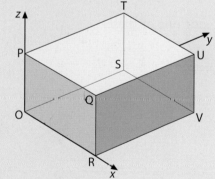

T3 This model is made of cubes of equal size.
The coordinates of A are (0, 6, 9).

Write the coordinates of B, C and D.

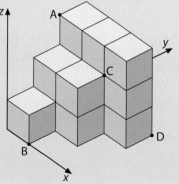

17 Cubic graphs and equations

This work will help you

- substitute positive and negative numbers into cubic expressions such as $x^3 - 2x^2 + x - 4$
- draw and use the graphs of cubic functions
- solve cubic equations using trial and improvement

A Cubic functions

A **cubic** function has an equation of the form $y = ax^3 + bx^2 + cx + d$ (where $a \neq 0$).
For example, these are all cubic functions: $y = x^3 + 2x^2 - 3$, $y = {}^-5x^3 + 2x$, $y = 8 + x - x^3$.

The graph of any cubic function will
look like one of these ...

... or one of these.

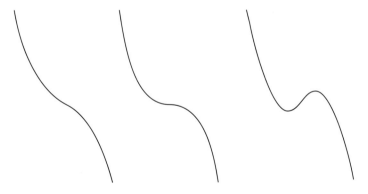

The graph of any cubic function has **rotation symmetry**.

Use a graph plotter to plot graphs of the form $y = ax^3 + bx^2 + cx + d$ for
various values of a, b, c and d.
Include examples where one or more of b, c and d take the value 0.
Include some negative values for a, b, c and d.
Comment on your findings.

To draw the graph of a cubic function, first draw up a table of values. Include a range of positive and negative values for x.

This is a table of values for $y = x^3 - 3x$.

x	$^-2$	$^-1.5$	$^-1$	$^-0.5$	0	0.5	1	1.5	2
$y = x^3 - 3x$	$^-2$	1.125	2	1.375	0	$^-1.375$	$^-2$	$^-1.125$	2

Plot the points shown by your table and join them with a smooth curve.

You may need to calculate a few more points to be sure of the shape of the graph.

Label your graph with its equation.

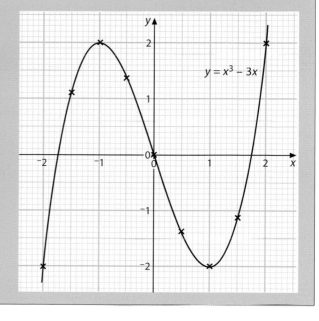

A1 Use the graph of $y = x^3 - 3x$ above to answer these.

   (a) Estimate the three solutions of the equation $x^3 - 3x = 0$, correct to 1 d.p.

   (b) Estimate the three solutions of the equation $x^3 - 3x = 1$, correct to 1 d.p.

   (c) What is the centre of rotation symmetry of the graph?

A2 (a) Copy and complete this table for $y = x^3 - 2x$.

x	$^-2$	$^-1.5$	$^-1$	$^-0.5$	0	0.5	1	1.5	2
$y = x^3 - 2x$	$^-4$								

   (b) On graph paper, draw axes as shown.

      Plot the points from your table. Join them up with a smooth curve to show the graph of $y = x^3 - 2x$.

   (c) Describe any symmetry that the graph has.

   (d) From the graph, estimate the three values of x for which $x^3 - 2x = 1$, correct to 1 d.p. where appropriate.

   (e) Use the graph to show that the equation $x^3 - 2x = 3$ has only one solution.

   (f) Use the graph to solve these equations, giving values to 1 d.p. where appropriate.

      (i) $x^3 - 2x = 2$ **(ii)** $x^3 - 2x = 0$

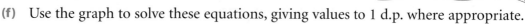

Go up from $^-4$ to 4.

Go across from $^-2$ to 2.

A3 **(a)** Copy and complete this table of values for $y = x^3 + \frac{1}{2}x + 1$.

x	-2	-1.5	-1	-0.5	0	0.5	1	1.5	2
$y = x^3 + \frac{1}{2}x + 1$	-8								

(b) On graph paper draw a pair of axes with x from -2 to 2, and y from -8 to 10. Draw the graph of $y = x^3 + \frac{1}{2}x + 1$.

(c) Use your graph to estimate the solution to $x^3 + \frac{1}{2}x + 1 = 0$, correct to 1 d.p.

B Trial and improvement

This sketch shows a small part of $y = x^3 + x - 1$. You can see that there is a solution to the equation $x^3 + x - 1 = 0$ between 0 and 1.

In order to find the value of this solution correct to one decimal place, say, we can use trial and improvement.

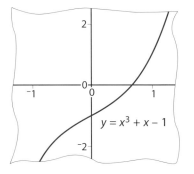
$y = x^3 + x - 1$

It is best to be systematic and use a table for this.

x	$x^3 + x - 1$	Comment
0.5	-0.375	Too low
0.6	-0.184	Too low
0.7	0.043	Too high
0.65	-0.075 375	Too low

0.5 is between 0 and 1 so is a suitable first trial.

The value of x must lie between 0.6 and 0.7

Try 0.65 which is the number halfway between 0.6 and 0.7.

0.65 is too low so the solution is closer to 0.7 than it is to 0.6. Hence the solution must be 0.7, correct to 1 d.p.

• Continue the table to find the solution correct to two decimal places.

B1 **(a)** Copy and complete this table.

x	-2	-1.5	-1	-0.5	0	0.5	1	1.5	2
$y = x^3 + 2x^2 - 2$	-2								

(b) Draw the graph of $y = x^3 + 2x^2 - 2$ for values of x from -2 to 2.

(c) Explain how your graph shows that there is a solution to $x^3 + 2x^2 - 2 = 0$ which lies between $x = 0$ and $x = 1$.

(d) Use trial and improvement to find the solution to $x^3 + 2x^2 - 2 = 0$, correct to 1 d.p. Show clearly your trials and their outcomes.

B2 Parveen is using trial and improvement to find a solution to the equation $x^3 + 7x = 30$. The table shows her first two trials.

x	$x^3 + 7x$	Comment
2	22	Too small
3	48	Too big

Copy and continue the table to find a solution to the equation.
Give your answer to one decimal place.

AQA

B3 The equation $x^3 + 2x = 50$ has one solution.

(a) Without drawing a graph, show that this solution lies between 3 and 4.

(b) Use trial and improvement to find the solution correct to 1 d.p.

B4 Use a trial and improvement method to find the value of x, correct to one decimal place, when $x^3 - 3x = 38$.
Show clearly your trials and their outcomes.

OCR

B5 The equation $x^3 + 8x - 40 = 0$ has a solution between 2 and 3.
Use trial and improvement to find this solution.
Give your answer correct to two decimal places.
Show clearly the outcome of all your trials.

OCR

B6 A cuboid has a square base of side x cm.
The height of the cuboid is 1 cm more than the length x cm.
The volume of the cuboid is $230\,\text{cm}^3$.

(a) Show that $x^3 + x^2 = 230$.

The equation $x^3 + x^2 = 230$ has a solution between $x = 5$ and $x = 6$.

(b) Use a trial and improvement method to find this solution.
Give your answer correct to one decimal place.
You must show **all** your working.

Edexcel

Test yourself

T1 The equation $x^3 + 4x = 100$ has one solution which is a positive number.
Use the method of trial and improvement to find this solution.
Give your answer correct to one decimal place.
You must show **all** working.

Edexcel

T2 (a) On graph paper, draw the graph of $y = x^3 - x^2$ for values of x from $^-1$ to 2.

(b) Use a trial and improvement method to find the value of x correct to one decimal place when $x^3 - x^2 = 3$.

T3 The equation $x^3 - x - 3 = 0$ has a solution between 1 and 2.
Use trial and improvement to find this solution correct to two decimal places.
You must show all your trials and their outcomes.

OCR

18 Gradients and rates

This work will help you

- calculate positive and negative gradients
- interpret gradients as rates
- calculate with rates

A Gradient of a sloping line

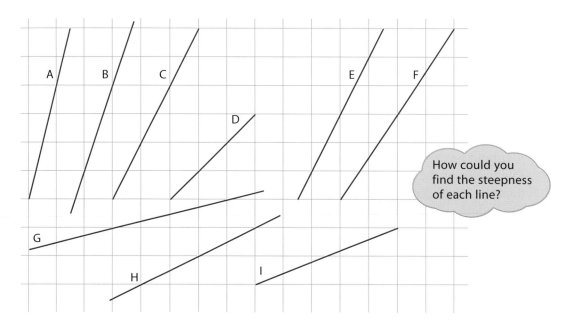

How could you find the steepness of each line?

A1 Find the gradient of each line in the diagram below.

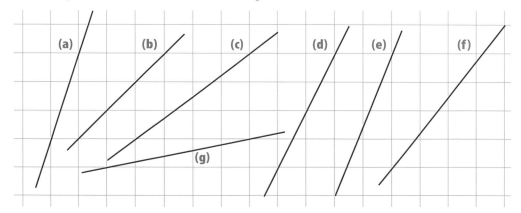

A2 Find the gradient of the line joining the points with coordinates $(1, 1)$ and $(6, 4)$.

A3 A county council uses the rule that the gradient of a wheelchair ramp must not be above 0.083.
Which of these ramps would be suitable for wheelchairs?

These sketches are not to scale.

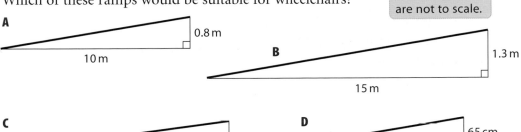

A4 Peter and Vicky are planning some walks.
They draw a sketch for each hill.
The gradient of each dotted line is the average gradient for the hill.

(a) Find the average gradient of each hill, correct to three decimal places.

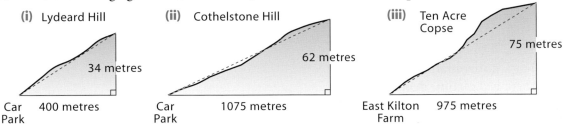

(i) Lydeard Hill — 34 metres — Car Park — 400 metres

(ii) Cothelstone Hill — 62 metres — Car Park — 1075 metres

(iii) Ten Acre Copse — 75 metres — East Kilton Farm — 975 metres

(b) Which hill has the highest average gradient?

A5 Stac Pollaidh is a mountain in Scotland.
The peak is 613 m above sea level.

Stephen and Carol are going to climb it starting at the car park at the foot of the mountain (90 m above sea level).

According to the map, the horizontal distance is 1050 m.

(a) What is the total height of their climb?

(b) What is the average gradient of the climb as a decimal?

A6 Scafell Pike is the highest mountain in England.
It is 977 m above sea level.

Becky and Ian are going to climb it starting at the car park at Wast Water (80 m above sea level).

According to the map, the horizontal distance is 3800 m.

What is the average gradient of the climb as a decimal?

OCR

B Positive and negative gradients

The gradient of a straight line is $\dfrac{\text{vertical change}}{\text{horizontal change}}$.

So lines that slope down from left to right have negative gradients.

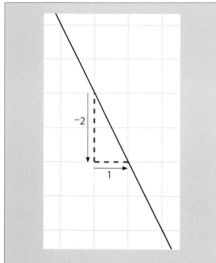

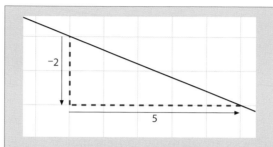

For a horizontal **increase** of 5
there is a vertical **decrease** of 2.

So the **gradient** is $\dfrac{^-2}{5} = ^-0.4$.

For a horizontal **increase** of 1
there is a vertical **decrease** of 2.

So the **gradient** is $\dfrac{^-2}{1} = ^-2$.

B1 Find the gradient of
each of these lines.

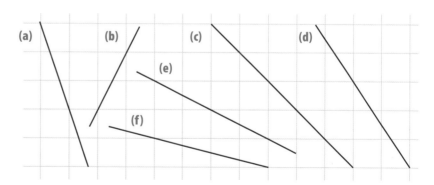

(a) (b) (c) (d) (e) (f)

B2 Find the gradients of the lines joining

(a) $(0, 1)$ and $(4, 5)$ (b) $(^-1, 0)$ and $(3, 8)$ (c) $(0, 8)$ and $(8, 0)$

(d) $(2, 1)$ and $(6, ^-1)$ (e) $(^-2, 5)$ and $(2, ^-1)$ (f) $(4, 5)$ and $(^-2, 5)$

B3 Draw a pair of intersecting lines where one has a gradient of 4 and
the other has a gradient of $^-4$. What do you notice about your lines?

B4 Draw a pair of intersecting lines where one has a gradient of 4 and
the other has a gradient of $^-\frac{1}{4}$. What do you notice about your lines?

C Interpreting a gradient as a rate

Water is added to a container over a period of 8 minutes.
Water flows in at a slow steady rate.

This graph shows the volume of water in the container during these 8 minutes.

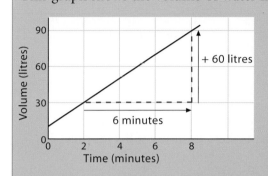

For a horizontal **increase** of 6 minutes there is a vertical **increase** of 60 litres.

The **gradient** is $\dfrac{60}{6} = 10$

> 60 **litres** and
> 6 **minutes** so
> 10 **litres per minute**.

So the rate of flow of the water is
10 litres per minute.

This graph shows the volume of water in a tank over a period of 4.5 seconds.

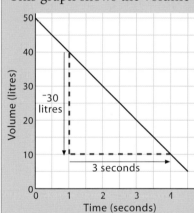

For a horizontal **increase** of 3 seconds there is a vertical **decrease** of 30 litres.

So **gradient** is $\dfrac{^-30}{3} = {}^-10$.

So the rate of flow is $^-10$ litres per second.
The volume of water is **decreasing**.

C1 What rates of flow are shown by the following graphs?

(a)

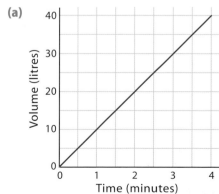

(b)

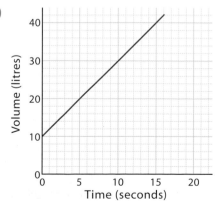

C2 What rates of flow are shown by the following graphs?

(a)

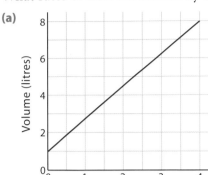

(b)

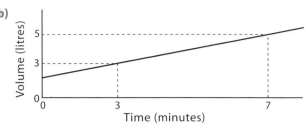

C3 This graph shows the distance Jamie cycled in the first 24 minutes of his journey.

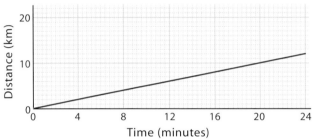

(a) Work out the gradient of this line.

(b) Which of these statements is true?

    A The gradient represents the speed in km per hour.

    B The gradient represents the speed in metres per minute.

    C The gradient represents the speed in km per minute.

C4 This graph shows the volume of oil in a tank.

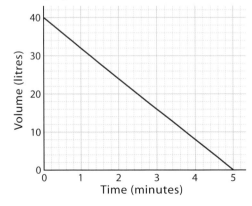

(a) Calculate the gradient of the line.

(b) What happens to the oil in the tank during these 5 minutes?

C5 (a) Work out the gradient of each line below.

(b) What does each gradient represent?

(i) Sue's swimming graph

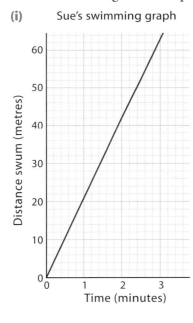

(ii) Mike's cycling graph

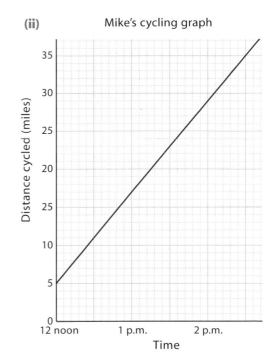

C6 (a) Work out the gradient of each line below, correct to 1 d.p.

(b) What does each gradient represent?

(i) Conversion graph for litres and pints

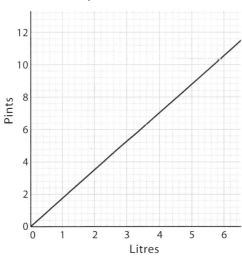

(ii) Conversion graph for Canadian dollars and pounds (£)

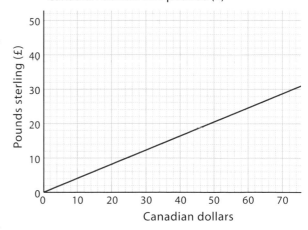

D7 An empty water tank has a leak.
Water flows into a tank at a rate of 2.4 litres per second.
After $2\frac{1}{2}$ minutes the quantity of water in the tank is 300 litres.
At what rate does the water leak from the tank?

D8 The fuel consumption of cars is measured in **litres per 100 km**.

   (a) On a test run of 40 km, a car used 3.8 litres of fuel.
   Calculate the fuel consumption of the car in litres/100 km.

   (b) The fuel consumption of a van is 13.6 litres/100 km.
   Calculate

   (i) the amount of fuel the van uses to travel 450 km

   (ii) the distance that the van can travel on 66 litres of fuel

Test yourself

T1 (a) Find the gradient of this ramp (to 2 d.p.).

   (b) A fork-lift truck can safely climb a ramp
   with a gradient of less than 0.17.
   Can the fork-lift truck safely use this ramp?

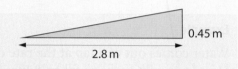

T2 Find the gradient of the line through the points A (1, 3) and B (3, 7).

T3 This graph shows the volume of water in
a container during 6 seconds.

   (a) Find the gradient of the line.

   (b) What does the gradient represent?

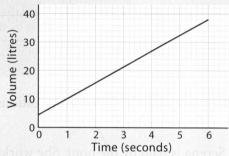

T4 This graph shows the volume of oil in
a tank during 6 minutes.

   (a) Find the gradient of the line,
   correct to 1 d.p.

   (b) What is happening to the oil in
   the tank during these 6 minutes?

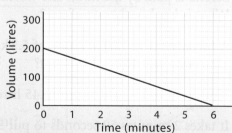

T5 A printer takes 35 minutes to print 80 copies of a leaflet.

   (a) What is the rate of printing

   (i) in copies per minute   **(ii)** in copies per hour

   (b) How long will the printer take to print 500 copies of the leaflet?
   Give your answer to a reasonable degree of accuracy.

19 Changing the subject

You should know how to solve equations like $\frac{6t}{5} = 12$, $\frac{a-2}{5} = 10$, $2k^2 = 18$ or $28 - 3a = 7$.

This work will help you rearrange formulas where the new subject appears once.

A Simple linear formulas

A formula connecting the number of white beads (w) and the number of black beads (b) in these patterns is $w = \frac{b+3}{2}$.

We can rearrange the formula to make b the subject like this.

$$w = \frac{b+3}{2}$$

$2w = b + 3$ [multiply both sides by 2]

$2w - 3 = b$ [take 3 from both sides]

We would usually write this with the subject on the left as $b = 2w - 3$.

A1 **(a)** Rearrange the formula $w = \frac{b+5}{3}$ to make b the subject.

    (b) **(i)** Find b when $w = 20$.   **(ii)** Find w when $b = 16$.   **(iii)** Find b when $w = 35$.

A2 Which of the following is a correct rearrangement of $P = \frac{Q-5}{2}$?

    | $Q = 5P + 2$ | $Q = 2P - 5$ | $Q = 2P + 5$ | $Q = 5P - 2$ |

A3 Rearrange each of these formulas to make the bold letter the subject.

    (a) $b = \frac{w+1}{3}$ **(b)** $w = \frac{\mathbf{b}-3}{2}$ **(c)** $w = \frac{7+\mathbf{b}}{5}$ **(d)** $b = \frac{\mathbf{w}-6}{7}$

A4 Match these up to give three pairs of equivalent formulas.

    A $x = \frac{y-3}{2}$ **B** $x = 2y - 3$ **C** $y = \frac{x-3}{2}$ **D** $y = 2x + 3$ **E** $y = \frac{x+3}{2}$ **F** $x = 2y + 3$

A5 Rearrange each of these formulas to make q the subject.

    (a) $p = 2q - 9$ **(b)** $p = \frac{q-5}{8}$ **(c)** $p = \frac{1+q}{11}$ **(d)** $p = 10 + 3q$

A6 Which of the following is a correct rearrangement of $a = \dfrac{3b - 5}{2}$?

$b = \dfrac{5a - 3}{2}$ $\quad$ $b = \dfrac{2a - 5}{3}$ $\quad$ $b = \dfrac{3a + 5}{2}$ $\quad$ $b = \dfrac{2a + 5}{3}$ $\quad$ $b = \dfrac{3a - 5}{2}$ $\quad$ $b = \dfrac{5a + 2}{3}$

A7 **(a)** Make x the subject of the formula $y = \dfrac{10 + 7x}{3}$.

(b) **(i)** Find x when $y = 8$. $\qquad$ **(ii)** Find y when $x = 3.5$. $\qquad$ **(iii)** Find x when $y = 15$.

When a formula uses brackets it is often useful to multiply them out first.

Example

Rearrange $t = 3(s + 5)$ to give s in terms of t.

$t = 3(s + 5)$

$t = 3s + 15$ $\qquad$ [multiply out brackets]

$t - 15 = 3s$ $\qquad$ [take 15 from both sides]

$\dfrac{t - 15}{3} = s$ $\qquad$ [divide both sides by 3]

$s = \dfrac{t - 15}{3}$ $\qquad$ [write the formula with the subject on the left]

A8 Rearrange each of these formulas so that the bold letter is the subject.

(a) $w = 5(\boldsymbol{u} + 1)$ $\qquad$ **(b)** $A = 3(\boldsymbol{B} - 5)$ $\qquad$ **(c)** $y = 2(7 + \boldsymbol{x})$

A9 Which of these formulas is equivalent to $h = 4(2k + 1)$?

$k = \dfrac{h - 1}{8}$ $\qquad$ $k = \dfrac{h - 4}{2}$ $\qquad$ $k = \dfrac{h - 4}{8}$ $\qquad$ $k = \dfrac{h - 4}{4}$

A10 Rearrange each of these formulas so that the bold letter is the subject.

(a) $p = 2(3\boldsymbol{q} + 5)$ $\qquad$ **(b)** $b = 3(2\boldsymbol{w} - 1)$ $\qquad$ **(c)** $F = 4(3 + 7\boldsymbol{G})$

Sometimes we need to use brackets in a rearranged formula.

Example

Rearrange $k = \dfrac{h}{2} - 7$ to give h in terms of k.

$k = \dfrac{h}{2} - 7$

$k + 7 = \dfrac{h}{2}$ $\qquad$ [add 7 to both sides]

$2(k + 7) = h$ $\qquad$ [multiply both sides by 2]

$h = 2(k + 7)$ $\qquad$ [write the formula with the subject on the left]

A11 Rearrange each of these formulas so that the bold letter is the subject.

(a) $a = \dfrac{b}{2} + 1$ (b) $D = \frac{1}{7}E - 4$ (c) $s = 9 + \dfrac{t}{5}$

A12 Which of these formulas is equivalent to $y = \dfrac{3x}{5} - 7$?

$x = \dfrac{5y - 7}{3}$ $x = \dfrac{5y + 7}{3}$ $x = \dfrac{5(y - 7)}{3}$ $x = \dfrac{5(y + 7)}{3}$

A13 Rearrange each of these formulas so that the bold letter is the subject.

(a) $H = \dfrac{4G}{3} + 1$ (b) $w = \dfrac{3b}{8} - 4$ (c) $m = 1 + \frac{5}{6}n$

A14 Rearrange each of these formulas so that the bold letter is the subject.

(a) $g = \dfrac{h + 5}{3}$ (b) $U = 3V - 4$ (c) $q = \dfrac{2p + 1}{7}$

(d) $m = \dfrac{n}{3} - 2$ (e) $y = 5(4x + 3)$ (f) $C = 6(f - 1)$

(g) $w = \frac{1}{4}Z + 2$ (h) $j = \dfrac{2h}{3} + 1$ (i) $y = 2(3x - 7)$

A15 A formula for converting a weight k in kilograms to a weight p in pounds is $p = \dfrac{11k}{5}$.

(a) How many pounds are equivalent to 4 kilograms?

(b) Make k the subject of the formula.

(c) Convert 20 pounds to kilograms, correct to two decimal places.

A16 The sum of the interior angles of a polygon is given by the formula

$S = 180(n - 2)$

where S is the sum in degrees and n is the number of sides.

(a) What is the sum of the interior angles of an octagon?

(b) Rearrange the formula to make n the subject.

(c) The sum of the interior angles of a polygon is 6120°.
How many sides does the polygon have?

(d) Show that it is impossible to draw a polygon where the sum of the interior angles is 500°.

A17 A formula for converting temperature in °F to temperature in °C is

$C = \dfrac{5F - 160}{9}$

(a) Make F the subject of the formula.

(b) Convert 30 °C to °F.

B Adding and subtracting algebraic expressions

Example

Make g the subject of $3g + 2h = 5$.

$3g + 2h = 5$ [take $2h$ from both sides]
$3g = 5 - 2h$ [divide both sides by 3]
$g = \dfrac{5 - 2h}{3}$

B1 You are given the formula $x + 2y = 10$.

   (a) Make x the subject of the formula.

   (b) Make y the subject of the formula.

   (c) What is the value of x when $y = 3$?

   (d) Find y when $x = {}^{-}2$.

B2 Rearrange each of these formulas to make the bold letter the subject.

   (a) $x + \boldsymbol{y} = 10$ **(b)** $2a + 3\boldsymbol{b} = 25$ **(c)** $\dfrac{\boldsymbol{p}}{2} + 5q = 8$

Examples

Make s the subject of $t = 12 - 2s$.

$t = 12 - 2s$ [add $2s$ to both sides]
$t + 2s = 12$ [take t from both sides]
$2s = 12 - t$ [divide both sides by 2]
$s = \dfrac{12 - t}{2}$

Make x the subject of $y = 5 - \dfrac{x}{2}$.

$y = 5 - \dfrac{x}{2}$ [add $\dfrac{x}{2}$ to both sides]
$y + \dfrac{x}{2} = 5$ [take y from both sides]
$\dfrac{x}{2} = 5 - y$ [multiply both sides by 2]
$x = 2(5 - y)$

B3 You are given the formula $y = 16 - 3x$.

   (a) Find the value of y when $x = 2$.

   (b) Make x the subject of the formula.

   (c) Check that your rearranged formula fits the values of x and y in part (a).

   (d) Find x when   **(i)** $y = 1$ **(ii)** $y = 5.5$ **(iii)** $y = {}^{-}36.5$

B4 **(a)** Make r the subject of the formula $s = 12 - 5r$.

   (b) Find r when $s = 9$.

B5 Rearrange each of these formulas to make the bold letter the subject.

   (a) $s = 8 - 7\boldsymbol{t}$ **(b)** $m = 3 - 8\boldsymbol{n}$ **(c)** $g = 66 - 5\boldsymbol{h}$ **(d)** $y = 12 - 3\boldsymbol{x}$

B6 You are given the formula $y = 15 - \frac{x}{3}$.

(a) Make x the subject of the formula.

(b) Find x when   (i) $y = 13$ (ii) $y = 1$ (iii) $y = 18$

B7 Rearrange each of these formulas to make x the subject.

(a) $y = 10 - \frac{x}{3}$ (b) $y = 3 - \frac{x}{5}$ (c) $y = 10 - \frac{x}{10}$ (d) $y = 100 - \frac{1}{2}x$

B8 Copy and complete this working to make a the subject of the formula $3b - 2a = 30$.

$$3b - 2a = 30$$
$$3b = 30 + \blacksquare$$
$$3b - \blacksquare = \blacklozenge$$
$$a = \frac{3b - \blacksquare}{\blacklozenge}$$

B9 Rearrange each of these formulas to make the bold letter the subject.

(a) $5s - \boldsymbol{t} = 40$ (b) $\boldsymbol{d} - 4j = 8$ (c) $6k - 8\boldsymbol{j} = 45$ (d) $3a - \frac{\boldsymbol{b}}{4} = 20$

B10 Rearrange each of these formulas to make the bold letter the subject.

(a) $5\boldsymbol{a} + 2b = 9$ (b) $p = 2 - 7\boldsymbol{q}$ (c) $2\boldsymbol{m} - 5n = 3$

(d) $h = 10 - \frac{\boldsymbol{k}}{5}$ (e) $4c - \frac{\boldsymbol{d}}{3} = 9$ (f) $h = 8 - \frac{3\boldsymbol{g}}{2}$

(g) $k = 5(4 - \boldsymbol{j})$ (h) $s = \frac{6 - \boldsymbol{t}}{3}$ (i) $y = \frac{1 - 3\boldsymbol{x}}{7}$

C Formulas connecting more than two letters

Some formulas have more than two letters in them, for example $y = 2x + wz$.

Since the letters in a formula stand for numbers, we can treat the letters just as we would numbers.

We would rearrange $y = 8 + 5z$ like this.

$$y = 8 + 5z$$
$$y - 8 = 5z \qquad \text{[take 8 from both sides]}$$
$$z = \frac{y - 8}{5} \qquad \text{[divide both sides by 5]}$$

We rearrange $y = 2x + wz$ like this.

$$y = 2x + wz$$
$$y - 2x = wz \qquad \text{[take } 2x \text{ from both sides]}$$
$$z = \frac{y - 2x}{w} \qquad \text{[divide both sides by } w\text{]}$$

C1 The formula $p = m + q$ connects p, m and q.

(a) Rearrange the formula to make m the subject.

(b) What is the value of m when $p = 15$ and $q = 12$?

(c) Check that this value of m and the values of p and q fit in the original formula.

C2 Copy and complete each of these to make m the subject.

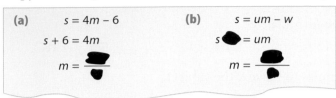

(a) $\quad s = 4m - 6$

$s + 6 = 4m$

$m = \dfrac{\blacksquare}{\blacktriangledown}$

(b) $\quad s = um - w$

$s \blacklozenge = um$

$m = \dfrac{\blacksquare}{\blacklozenge}$

C3 The formula $v = u + at$ is used when solving problems about moving objects. u stands for the initial speed of the object in m/s, v for the final speed in m/s, a for the acceleration in m/s^2 and t for the time in seconds. (m/s^2 means (m/s)/s so, for example, an acceleration of 5 m/s^2 means that every second the speed increases by 5 m/s.)

(a) Rearrange the formula $v = u + at$ to give a in terms of v, u and t.

(b) A dragster can accelerate from 20 m/s to 90 m/s in 5 seconds. Use your rearrangement to work out its acceleration.

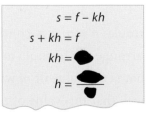

C4 Rearrange each of these formulas to make the bold letter the subject.

(a) $p = \boldsymbol{q} - r$ (b) $b = 5\boldsymbol{w} + k$ (c) $l = b\boldsymbol{v} - h$ (d) $y = m\boldsymbol{x} + c$

(e) $f = n\boldsymbol{d} + 8$ (f) $g = lk + 6\boldsymbol{j}$ (g) $a = c\boldsymbol{d} - 4f$ (h) $ak = b\boldsymbol{j} - nm$

C5 Copy and complete each of these to make q the subject.

(a) $\quad p = \dfrac{q}{2} + 3$

$p - 3 = \dfrac{q}{2}$

$q = \blacktriangledown(\blacksquare)$

(b) $\quad p = \dfrac{q}{s} + rt$

$p - \blacklozenge = \dfrac{q}{s}$

$q = \blacklozenge(\blacksquare)$

C6 Rearrange each of these formulas to make the bold letter the subject.

(a) $p = \dfrac{\boldsymbol{q}}{3} + r$ (b) $b = \dfrac{\boldsymbol{w}}{v} - k$ (c) $f = \dfrac{n + \boldsymbol{d}}{5}$ (d) $l = km + \dfrac{\boldsymbol{h}}{n}$

(e) $g = \dfrac{3\boldsymbol{k} - b}{v}$ (f) $a = \dfrac{5b + 8\boldsymbol{c}}{d}$ (g) $y = \dfrac{5\boldsymbol{x}}{m} + 2$ (h) $a = \dfrac{c\boldsymbol{d} + gf}{n}$

C7 (a) Copy and complete this working to make h the subject of the formula $s = f - kh$.

(b) Use your new formula to find h when $f = 30$, $s = 2$ and $k = 7$.

$s = f - kh$

$s + kh = f$

$kh = \blacklozenge$

$h = \dfrac{\blacklozenge}{\blacktriangledown}$

C8 (a) Copy and complete this working to make r the subject of the formula $p = 2q - \dfrac{r}{s}$.

(b) Use your new formula to find r when $q = 3.5$, $p = 1$ and $s = 8.5$.

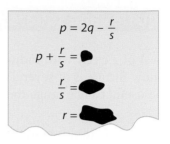

$$p = 2q - \frac{r}{s}$$
$$p + \frac{r}{s} = \bullet$$
$$\frac{r}{s} = \bullet$$
$$r = \bullet$$

C9 Rearrange each of these formulas to make the bold letter the subject.

(a) $y - 2\boldsymbol{x} = z$ (b) $a = b - \boldsymbol{c}$ (c) $j = p - q\boldsymbol{r}$ (d) $y = x - \dfrac{\boldsymbol{z}}{w}$

(e) $m = 3p - \dfrac{2\boldsymbol{q}}{r}$ (f) $v = \dfrac{u - \boldsymbol{b}}{5}$ (g) $v = \dfrac{5s - \boldsymbol{t}}{w}$ (h) $3k - m\boldsymbol{n} = p$

(i) $x - \dfrac{\boldsymbol{y}}{z} = m$ (j) $a = \dfrac{2\boldsymbol{d} - 7f}{n}$ (k) $a = \dfrac{b\boldsymbol{c} - de}{f}$ (l) $p = \dfrac{2(q - \boldsymbol{r})}{s}$

C10 The temperature in a cold store is given by the formula

$$T = T_0 - ah$$

T_0 stands for the starting temperature in °C;
T stands for the temperature in °C
in the store after h hours;
a is a constant and is the rate of cooling in degrees per hour.

> T_0 is a single symbol – a useful way of writing 'T at the start'.

(a) Rearrange the formula to make a the subject.

(b) What rate of cooling is needed to cool a store from 22 °C to ⁻18 °C in 5 hours?

C11 The mass of a brass bar in kilograms is given by

$$W = aV_1 + bV_2$$

W is the mass of the brass bar in kg;
a is the density of zinc in kilograms per cubic metre (kg/m³);
V_1 is the volume of zinc in m³;
b is the density of copper in kg/m³; V_2 is the volume of copper in m³.

(a) Rearrange the formula to give V_2 in terms of the other variables.

(b) What volume of copper needs to be added to 0.05 m³ of zinc to make a brass bar with mass 1000 kg? Give your answer to 2 s.f.
(Density of zinc = 7100 kg/m³; density of copper = 8900 kg/m³)

C12 Rearrange each of these formulas to make the bold letter the subject.

(a) $y = 5\boldsymbol{x} - z$ (b) $na + m\boldsymbol{b} = k$ (c) $f\boldsymbol{s} - t = j$ (d) $t = k + f\boldsymbol{g}$

(e) $f = 2a - m\boldsymbol{b}$ (f) $H = K - 8\boldsymbol{x}$ (g) $r = 5(\boldsymbol{s} - t_0)$ (h) $y = \dfrac{\boldsymbol{x}}{z} + c$

(i) $p = q - \dfrac{\boldsymbol{r}}{t}$ (j) $a = \dfrac{b\boldsymbol{c}}{3} - d$ (k) $a\boldsymbol{x} + by = r^2$ (l) $A_1 k - A_2 \boldsymbol{j} = 45$

(m) $\dfrac{cd - 4\boldsymbol{j}}{5} = e$ (n) $y = \dfrac{a(\boldsymbol{x} - 4)}{h}$ (o) $z = \dfrac{m(5 - \boldsymbol{y})}{x}$ (p) $z = a - \dfrac{b\boldsymbol{y}}{7}$

D Squares and square roots

The area A of a circle with radius r is given by the formula $A = \pi r^2$.
If you know the areas of several circles and want to know their radii
it may be useful to rearrange the formula to make r the subject.

$A = \pi r^2$ [divide both sides by π]

$\dfrac{A}{\pi} = r^2$ [take the positive square root of both sides]

$\sqrt{\dfrac{A}{\pi}} = r$

Here, r is positive as it is the value of the radius.

So use $\sqrt{\dfrac{A}{\pi}}$ as it represents the positive square root of $\dfrac{A}{\pi}$.

D1 Work out the radius of a circle with area

(a) $100\,\text{cm}^2$ (b) $5\,\text{m}^2$ (c) $1\,\text{mm}^2$ (d) $600\,\text{km}^2$

Give each answer to three significant figures.

D2 A cube has edges of length b.
Its total surface area A is $6b^2$.

(a) Copy and complete this working
to make b the subject of the formula.

(b) What is the length of the edge of a cube
with total surface area $10\,\text{cm}^2$?
(Give your answer to 3 s.f.)

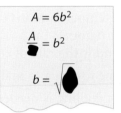

$A = 6b^2$

$\dfrac{A}{\blacksquare} = b^2$

$b = \sqrt{\blacksquare}$

D3 A stone is dropped from the top of a cliff.
Its distance (D metres) below the top of the cliff after t seconds is given by $D = 4.9t^2$.

(a) Rearrange this formula to give t in terms of D.

(b) How long will it take a stone to hit the ground from the top of a cliff $50\,\text{m}$ high?

D4 Pythagoras's theorem states that $c^2 = a^2 + b^2$ for this triangle.
Rearrange this formula to give a in terms of b and c.

D5 In each of these formulas x is a length and A is an area.
Make x the subject of each of these formulas.

(a) $A = 2x^2$ (b) $A = 5x^2$ (c) $A = \dfrac{x^2}{10}$ (d) $A = \dfrac{3x^2}{7}$

(e) $A = x^2 + 5$ (f) $A = 7x^2 - 3$ (g) $x^2 + A = 25$ (h) $A = \dfrac{x^2}{3} - 6$

D6 Find three pairs of equivalent formulas.

A $a = \sqrt{b} + 1$ **B** $b = (a - 1)^2$ **C** $a = \sqrt{b - 1}$ **D** $a = \sqrt{b} - 1$ **E** $b = a^2 + 1$ **F** $b = (a + 1)^2$

D7 Make x the subject of each of these formulas.

(a) $y = \sqrt{x} + 3$ (b) $y = \sqrt{x+3}$ (c) $y = \sqrt{x} - 7$ (d) $y = \sqrt{x-7}$

D8 Find four pairs of equivalent formulas.

A $p = \sqrt{2q}$ **B** $p = \sqrt{2q} + 1$ **C** $p = \sqrt{2q+1}$ **D** $p = \sqrt{\dfrac{q}{2}}$

E $q = \dfrac{(p-1)^2}{2}$ **F** $q = 2p^2$ **G** $q = \dfrac{p^2}{2}$ **H** $q = \dfrac{p^2-1}{2}$

D9 Make q the subject of each of these formulas.

(a) $h = \sqrt{5q}$ (b) $k = \sqrt{qn} + 1$ (c) $l = \sqrt{6q+1}$

(d) $t = \sqrt{\dfrac{q}{5}}$ (e) $r = \sqrt{\dfrac{aq}{s}}$

The equation of this graph is $y = x^2 - 3$. When rearranging, note that x can take any positive or negative value.

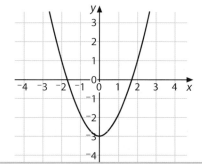

$y = x^2 - 3$

$y + 3 = x^2$

$x = \pm\sqrt{y+3}$

We use $\pm\sqrt{y+3}$ as it represents the positive **and** negative square roots of $y + 3$.

D10 Each of these is the equation of a graph where x can take any value.
Make x the subject of each one.

(a) $y = x^2 + 5$ (b) $y = 2x^2 - 1$ (c) $y = \dfrac{x^2}{5} + 2$ (d) $y = (x-5)^2$

D11 In each of these formulas, a, b and c can take positive and negative values.
Rearrange each one to make a the subject.

(a) $n = \dfrac{ba^2}{8}$ (b) $k = \dfrac{a^2 - b}{c}$ (c) $a^2 + b^2 = 1$ (d) $h = (2a - b)^2$

D12 Make t the subject of the formula $s = \frac{1}{2}at^2$.

D13 The equation of a graph is $y = 4x^2 - 1$.

(a) Make x the subject of the equation.

(b) What are the coordinates of the points where the graph intersects the x-axis?

D14 The equation of a graph is $y = (3x + 4)^2$.

(a) Make x the subject of the equation.

(b) Find the coordinates of the points where the graph intersects the line $y = 25$.

Test yourself

T1 Make t the subject of the formula $u = \dfrac{t}{3} + 5$.

AQA

T2 Make the bold letter the subject of each of these formulas.

    (a) $y = \dfrac{x - 4}{5}$ **(b)** $U = 3\mathbf{V} + 8$ **(c)** $h = \dfrac{4\mathbf{k} + 1}{9}$

    (d) $C = 2(\mathbf{f} - 3)$ **(e)** $m = \dfrac{\mathbf{n}}{5} + 3$ **(f)** $a = \dfrac{2\mathbf{b}}{3} - 5$

    (g) $t = 10 - 3\mathbf{q}$ **(h)** $w = \tfrac{3}{4}\mathbf{Z}$ **(i)** $y = 6 - \dfrac{\mathbf{x}}{5}$

T3 Make p the subject of the formula $\dfrac{4(p + 3)}{7} = r$.

AQA

T4 Make y the subject of the formula $x = 40 - 8y$.

AQA

T5 Rearrange each of these formulas so that the bold letter is the subject.

    (a) $h = s + a\mathbf{k}$ **(b)** $q = 2(e - \mathbf{f})$ **(c)** $t = 2r - w\mathbf{d}$ **(d)** $ax + b\mathbf{z} = cy$

    (e) $e = j(\mathbf{w} - t)$ **(f)** $R = p\mathbf{s} - fg$ **(g)** $q = \dfrac{u + a\mathbf{v}}{b}$ **(h)** $j = h - \dfrac{k}{\mathbf{l}}$

T6 Rearrange the equation $y + 7x = 3$ to make x the subject.

T7 You are given the formula $p = qr + t$.

    (a) Rearrange the formula to give q in terms of p, r and t.

    (b) Calculate q when $p = \tfrac{1}{2}$, $r = 2$ and $t = {}^{-}\tfrac{5}{6}$.

T8 You are given that $v = u + at$.

    (a) Make t the subject of this formula.

    (b) Find the value of t when $a = {}^{-}10$, $u = 12$ and $v = {}^{-}18$.

AQA

T9 Make x the subject of each of these formulas.

    (a) $y = x^2 + 9$ **(b)** $y = 5 - x^2$ **(c)** $y = 3(x^2 - 2)$

    (d) $y^2 + x^2 = 100$ **(e)** $y = \dfrac{x^2 - a}{b}$ **(f)** $y = \dfrac{a^2 - x^2}{100}$

T10 Make x the subject of the formula $y = \dfrac{x^2 + 4}{5}$.

Edexcel

T11 You are given the formula $w = \tfrac{3}{4}k^2$.

    Rearrange the formula to give k in terms of w.

T12 Make d the subject of the following formula.

    $h = \sqrt{t - d}$

WJEC

T13 Make x the subject of the formula $y = \dfrac{\sqrt{x} - 4}{5}$.

20 Probability

This work will help you

- estimate probabilities as relative frequencies
- calculate probabilities as fractions using equally likely outcomes
- find all equally likely outcomes by systematically listing or using a grid

A Relative frequency

Going potty

If you hold up a cottage cheese or similar shaped carton at nose height and drop it, it can land in one of three ways.

Which way do you think it is most likely to land?

How likely do you think it is to land the right way up?

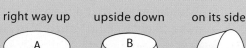
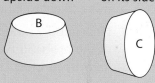

A simple way to find out which outcome is most likely is to do the experiment a large number of times.

For example, suppose the carton is dropped 120 times and lands as follows:

right way up	upside down	on its side
12	18	90

From this data it seems that 'on its side' is most likely.

The **relative frequency** of an event happening in a probability experiment is

$$\frac{\text{the number of times the event occurs}}{\text{the total number of trials}}$$

It gives an estimate of the probability of the event happening.

The relative frequency of the carton landing on its side $= \frac{90}{120} = 0.75$

This is an estimate of the probability that it lands on its side.
The probability that it does **not** land on its side is estimated as $1 - 0.75 = 0.25$.

For better estimates, the experiment must be done more often (say 200 times).

A1 From the data above, estimate the probability that the carton

   (a) lands the right way up   **(b)** lands upside down

   (c) does not land the right way up   **(d)** does not land upside down

A2 Martin carries out an experiment dropping pieces of toast to see whether they land 'jam-up' or 'jam-down'.

Here are the results of his experiment.

Total number of trials	10	20	30	40	50	60	70	80	90	100
Total number of 'jam-up's	3	8	12	18	23	27	32	36	40	45
Relative frequency	$\frac{3}{10} = 0.3$									

(a) Copy and complete the table above for Martin's experiment.

(b) Copy and complete this graph for the relative frequencies in Martin's experiment.

(c) From the results of Martin's experiment would you say that a piece of toast was more likely to land 'jam-up' or 'jam-down'?

(d) How good would you say Martin's estimate of the probability of a piece of toast landing 'jam-up' is after 100 trials?

(e) Calculate an estimate of the probability that a piece of Martin's toast lands 'jam-down'.

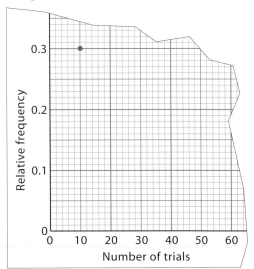

A3 Kay is recording which direction cars go when they reach a road junction near her school.

She writes right (R) or left (L) for each car and groups her results in tens.

Here are her results:

```
R R L R L R R L L L
R R R L L R L R L R
L R L L R R R R R L
L R L R L R R R L R
R L R R R L L R R R
```

(a) From Kay's results, what is the relative frequency of cars turning right after
  (i) 20 results   (ii) 40 results   (iii) 50 results

(b) If 800 cars a week drive over this junction, roughly how many would you expect to go right?

(c) How reliable do you think Kay's estimate of the probability of going right is?

A4 A cuboctahedron was rolled 400 times.
It landed with a square face on top 340 times.
As a decimal, estimate the probability that it will land with a square face on top.

A5 Steve has a spinner.
He spins it 140 times and it shows red 49 times.

(a) Calculate an estimate of the probability that it shows red.

(b) What is the probability that it will not show red?

(c) Estimate the number of times it will show red in 200 spins.

A6 Britalite is a company that makes light bulbs.
They tested 250 of their bulbs to see how long they lasted.

24 bulbs lasted less than 1000 hours.
208 lasted between 1000 and 2000 hours.
The rest lasted over 2000 hours.

(a) Estimate the probability that a Britalite bulb lasts

    (i) less than 1000 hours   (ii) over 2000 hours

(b) A company orders 2000 light bulbs.
Estimate how many of them will last 1000 hours or over.

B Equally likely outcomes

In working out probabilities it is often necessary to assume that different possibilities or **outcomes** are all equally likely.

The probability of an event happening is $\dfrac{\text{the number of 'successful' outcomes}}{\text{the total number of equally likely outcomes}}$.

For example, a bag holds 3 red and 5 black beads and each bead is equally likely to be chosen.

    Probability of choosing red $= \frac{3}{8}$

    Probability of **not** choosing red $= 1 - \frac{3}{8} = \frac{5}{8}$

Be careful about assuming that outcomes are equally likely.
In families we might assume that each child is equally likely to be a boy or girl.
In reality the probability of a child being born a boy is about $\frac{52}{100}$ or 0.52.

B1 In which of these are the possible outcomes equally likely?

A A card from a pack being of a particular suit (clubs, diamonds, hearts, spades)

B The next car to pass your window being of a particular colour (red, black, blue, …)

C A particular Lottery ball coming up first (1, 2, 3, 4, …, 49)

D Having a birthday in a particular month, (Jan, Feb, March, …)

B2 Sharmila takes a cube and writes these numbers on its six faces.

1   1   2   2   2   3

She rolls the cube.
What is the probability, as a fraction, that the number on top is

(a) 1   (b) 2   (c) 3   (d) 4

B3 This fair spinner is spun.

What is the probability that the spinner lands on

(a) yellow   (b) red   (c) blue

B4 An ordinary dice is rolled.
What is the probability that the number rolled is

(a) a six   (b) even   (c) odd   (d) a multiple of 3

B5 A set of 12 discs have the numbers 1 to 12 marked on them.
One disc is chosen at random.
What is the probability the number on the disc is

(a) a factor of 12   (b) a square number   (c) a prime number

B6 A pack of 24 cards have the numbers 1 to 24 marked on them.
The pack is shuffled and one card is chosen from the pack.
What is the probability the number on the card is

(a) even   (b) a square number   (c) a triangle number

(d) 5 or less   (e) a prime number   (f) not a prime number

B7 A box contains 3 red buttons, 4 blue buttons and 5 gold buttons.
A button is chosen at random.

(a) How many buttons are in the box?

(b) Find the probability that a button chosen is

(i) red   (ii) gold   (iii) not blue

B8 Ben has some coloured cubes in a bag.
The table shows the number of cubes of each colour.

Red	Blue	Yellow	Brown
7	4	8	6

Ben is going to take one cube at random from the bag.
Write down the probability that Ben

(a) will take a yellow cube   (b) will **not** take a brown cube   Edexcel

B9 A fair six-sided dice has its faces painted red, white or blue.
The dice is thrown 36 times.
Here are the results.

Colour	Frequency
Red	7
White	11
Blue	18

Based on the results, how many faces do you think are painted each colour?

B10 Ken has two spinners, each numbered 1 to 4.
Only one of them is a fair spinner.

These tables show the results of
spinning each spinner 80 times.

Which spinner do you think is fair,
spinner A or spinner B?
Explain your decision.

A

Score	Frequency
1	19
2	22
3	21
4	18

B

Score	Frequency
1	15
2	18
3	15
4	32

B11 These are some cakes.

(a) Copy and complete the table to show
the number of cakes in each category.

	Pink	White
Cherry		
No cherry		

(b) One of the cakes in the picture is chosen at random.
Write down the probability that the cake will have

  (i) white icing and a cherry   (ii) a cherry   (iii) pink icing

(c) If all the cakes with pink icing are put in a box and one is chosen at random,
what is the probability that it has a cherry?

B12 This table shows information about a group of children.

(a) How many children are in the group altogether?

(b) If a child is chosen from the group at random
what is the probability of that child

  (i) having blue eyes   (ii) being a boy?

	Boys	Girls
Blue eyes	3	6
Brown eyes	12	9

(c) If a boy is chosen from the group what is the probability that he has blue eyes?

In many situations, a **list** of equally likely possible outcomes is helpful.

Example

A coin is flipped and an ordinary dice rolled.
What is the probability of getting a head and a number greater than 4?

The outcomes can be listed:

H1	H2	H3	H4	(H5)	(H6)
T1	T2	T3	T4	T5	T6

There are 12 equally likely outcomes altogether.
Two of these outcomes give a head and a number greater than 4 (ringed).

So the probability of flipping a head and rolling a number greater than 4 $= \frac{2}{12} = \frac{1}{6}$.

C1 If a coin is flipped and an ordinary dice is rolled, what is the probability of getting

(a) a tail and a number less than 5

(b) a head and an even number

(c) a tail and a number other than 1

(d) a head and an even number or a tail and an odd number

C2 (a) Copy and complete this table to list all the outcomes when three different coins are flipped.

Coin 1	Coin 2	Coin 3
H	H	H

(b) How many outcomes are there altogether?

(c) What is the probability of all 3 coins showing a head?

(d) What is the probability of all 3 coins showing the same face?

(e) What is the probability of 2 or more coins showing a tail?

(f) What is the probability that there are more heads than tails showing?

C3 Tim writes the 3 letters of his name on pieces of card.
He turns the cards over and shuffles them.
He then turns them face up in a row.

(a) List all the possible outcomes.

(b) What is the probability the cards spell his name?

C4 Kate writes the letters E, A and P on pieces of card.
She turns the cards over and shuffles them.
She then turns them face up in a row.

What is the probability the cards spell a word?

C5 A and B are two fair spinners.

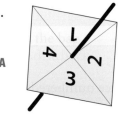 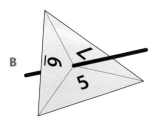

A   B

Jane spins the two spinners together at once.

(a) Copy the table below and show all the possible results and the total scores.

Spinner A	Spinner B	Total score

(b) Use your table to find the probability that Jane will get a total score of 7.

Tom spins the two spinners together 60 times.

(c) Work out the number of times you would expect Tom to get a total score of 7.

Edexcel

C6 Credit cards often have a PIN (Personal Identification Number) for security. This usually consists of a four-digit number.

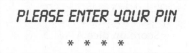

(a) Sarah knows that her PIN uses 1, 9, 6, 7 but cannot remember the correct order. Copy and complete this list of the possible PINs that she might have.

    1679   6179   7169

    1697   6197

    1769

(b) If Sarah tries to guess her number by using the numbers 1, 9, 6, 7 at random, what is the probability she guesses right first time?

(c) Elizabeth cannot remember her number either, but she knows it contains the digits 8, 3, 5, 5.

If Elizabeth tries to guess her number by putting in the digits 8, 3, 5, 5 in a random order, what is the probability she will be right?

D Using a calculator for large numbers in standard form

$p = 20\,000\,000$
$q = 1.2 \times 10^{14}$
$a = 5 \times 10^{17}$
$b = 2.96 \times 10^5$

Can you find the value of each expression?

p^2	q^2	pq	a^2	ab

$a + q$	$p + q$	$\dfrac{a}{b}$	$\dfrac{q}{b}$	$\frac{1}{2}b^2 p$

D1 Write the answer to each calculation in standard form.

(a) $2\,000\,000 \times 30\,000\,000$

(b) $4\,000\,000^2$

(c) $\dfrac{6\,200\,000}{0.0005}$

(d) $5\,000\,000^2 + 70\,000\,000^2$

D2 Give the answer to each calculation in standard form.

(a) $(2.31 \times 10^7) + (1.5 \times 10^6)$

(b) $(8.35 \times 10^6) \times (2.6 \times 10^8)$

(c) $\dfrac{4.2 \times 10^{19}}{8.4 \times 10^8}$

(d) $\dfrac{9.72 \times 10^9}{1.8 \times 10^3}$

D3 Write the answer to each calculation in standard form, correct to two significant figures.

(a) $(3.26 \times 10^9) \times 294$

(b) $\dfrac{1.47 \times 10^{13}}{5.39}$

(c) $(6.35 \times 10^6) \times (1.03 \times 10^7)$

(d) $(2.06 \times 10^9)^2$

D4 Find the value of each expression when $p = 2.3 \times 10^9$ and $q = 8.5 \times 10^8$.
Give each answer in standard form.

(a) $p + q$

(b) pq

(c) $2p + 5q$

D5 You are given the formula $P = \dfrac{xy}{x - y}$

Find the value of P when $x = 4.9 \times 10^{12}$ and $y = 2.8 \times 10^{11}$.
Give your answer in standard form, correct to three significant figures.

D6 In 1991 an estimated 1.6×10^7 kg of oil entered the sea each day.
Estimate how much oil entered the sea during 1991.
Give your answer in standard form, correct to two significant figures.

D7 Until it became illegal in 1990, an estimated 6×10^9 kg of rubbish was dumped from ships each year.
Estimate the weight of rubbish that was dumped each day.
Give your answer in ordinary form, correct to one significant figure.

Here is some information about the planets in the Solar System.

Planet	Equatorial radius (km)	Mass (kg)	Mean distance from Sun (km)
Earth	6378	5.98×10^{24}	1.496×10^8
Jupiter	71942	1.90×10^{27}	7.783×10^8
Mars	3397	6.39×10^{23}	2.279×10^8
Mercury	2439	3.29×10^{23}	5.791×10^7
Neptune	25269	1.03×10^{26}	4.497×10^9
Pluto	1162	1.31×10^{22}	5.914×10^9
Saturn	60268	5.69×10^{26}	1.427×10^9
Uranus	25559	8.72×10^{25}	2.871×10^9
Venus	6052	4.87×10^{24}	1.082×10^8

D8 Copy and complete the following statements.

(a) The mass of ...... is about 18 times the mass of Mercury.

(b) The mass of Venus is about ...... times the mass of Pluto.

(c) The mass of Jupiter is about ...... times the mass of Earth.

(d) The mass of Neptune is about 160 times the mass of ......

D9 Ken wants to put models in a park to show how far away from the Sun the planets are.

Mercury is to be 1 metre from the Sun.

This is Ken's calculation for the Earth.

$(1.496 \times 10^8) \div (5.791 \times 10^7) = 2.58$ (to 2 d.p.)

Earth: 2.58 metres from Sun

(a) Explain why Ken divides by 5.791×10^7.

(b) How far will each model be from the Sun?

D10 A formula for the approximate mean density (D) of each planet in kg/m^3 is

$$D = \frac{3m}{4\pi(1000r)^3}$$

where m is the mass in kg and r is the radius in km.

(a) Work out the mean density of each planet to two significant figures.

(b) An object floats in water when its density in kg/m^3 is less than 1000.
Which planets would float in water (if you could find a bowl big enough!)?

E Standard form for small numbers

Standard form can be used for very small numbers.

$\vdots$

$3 \times 10^2 = 3 \times 100$	$= 300$	$426 = 4.26 \times 100$	$= 4.26 \times 10^2$
$3 \times 10^1 = 3 \times 10$	$= 30$	$42.6 = 4.26 \times 10$	$= 4.26 \times 10^1$
$3 \times 10^0 = 3 \times 1$	$= 3$	$4.26 = 4.26 \times 1$	$= 4.26 \times 10^0$
$3 \times 10^{-1} = 3 \times \frac{1}{10} = \frac{3}{10}$	$= 0.3$	$0.426 = \frac{4.26}{10} = 4.26 \times \frac{1}{10}$	$= 4.26 \times 10^{-1}$
$3 \times 10^{-2} = 3 \times \frac{1}{10^2} = \frac{3}{100}$	$= 0.03$	$0.0426 = \frac{4.26}{100} = 4.26 \times \frac{1}{10^2}$	$= 4.26 \times 10^{-2}$
$3 \times 10^{-3} = 3 \times \frac{1}{10^3} = \frac{3}{1000}$	$= 0.003$	$0.00426 = \frac{4.26}{1000} = 4.26 \times \frac{1}{10^3}$	$= 4.26 \times 10^{-3}$

$\vdots$

E1 Write each number as   **(i)**   a fraction   **(ii)**   a decimal

     (a) 10^{-1} **(b)** 10^{-5} **(c)** 10^{-3} **(d)** 10^{-6}

E2 **(a)**   Which of these are ways to write the number 0.000 045 3?

A 0.453×10^{-5} **B** 4.53×10^{-5} **C** 4.53×10^{-4}

D 453×10^{-7} **E** $4.53 \div 10^5$ **F** $45.3 \div 1\,000\,000$

     (b)   What is 0.000 045 3 written in standard form?

E3 Write these numbers in ordinary form.

     (a) 9.1×10^{-3} **(b)** 6.21×10^{-5} **(c)** 3.4×10^{-10}

     (d) 5×10^{-7} **(e)** 3.01×10^{-8} **(f)** 1×10^{-21}

E4 Write these numbers in standard form.

     (a)   0.000 000 002 9   **(b)**   0.000 000 428   **(c)**   0.092 34

     (d)   0.000 000 006   **(e)**   0.000 000 000 001   **(f)**   0.000 000 000 000 000 000 08

E5 A jawa is a coin that was used in Nepal.
It is the smallest coin ever issued and weighed 0.014 grams.

Write the weight of this coin in **kilograms**

     (a)   in ordinary form   **(b)**   in standard form

E6 Write 6.7×10^{-9} kg in **grams** in ordinary form.

E7 The patu marplesi spider is the smallest in the world.
It is found in Samoa and is 0.43 mm long.

Write the length of this spider in **metres**

     (a)   in ordinary form   **(b)**   in standard form

E8 The masses of some living creatures are given below.

Blue whale: 130 000 kg   Pygmy shrew: 1.5×10^{-3} kg   Giraffe: 1200 kg

Kitti's hog-nosed bat: 1.7 grams   House mouse: 1.2×10^{-2} kg   House spider: 10^{-4} kg

Bee hummingbird: 0.0016 kg   Helena's hummingbird: 2×10^{-3} kg

(a) List the creatures in order of mass, starting with the heaviest.

(b) Copy and complete the following statements

(i) The mass of a giraffe is ...... times the mass of a house mouse.

(ii) ...... house spiders would weigh the same as a bee hummingbird.

(iii) A ...... weighs the same as 800 thousand pygmy shrews.

E9 A transmission electron microscope can examine features of width 2×10^{-9} metres or more. Which of these could be detected using a transmission electron microscope?

A A grain of pollen that is 0.0039 cm in diameter

B A particle of tobacco smoke that is 5×10^{-7} metres wide

C The nucleus of a carbon atom about 5×10^{-15} metres in diameter

D A virus that is 0.000 024 cm wide

E A distance of 0.000 000 019 7 centimetres between two calcium atoms

F Using a calculator for small numbers in standard form

Example

A molecule of water has a mass of about 3×10^{-23} grams.

About how many water molecules are in a drop of water with a mass of 0.25 grams?
(Give your answer in ordinary form correct to three significant figures.)

$0.25 \div (3 \times 10^{-23}) \approx 8.33 \times 10^{21}$
$= 8\,330\,000\,000\,000\,000\,000\,000$

Make sure you can work this out on **your** calculator.

F1 Write each answer to three significant figures

(i) in standard form   (ii) in ordinary form

(a) $(2.4 \times 10^{-5}) \times (6.9 \times 10^{-4})$

(b) $\dfrac{2.3 \times 10^{-10}}{6}$

(c) $\dfrac{4.2 \times 10^{-5}}{2.01 \times 10^{-20}}$

F2 Write the answer to each calculation in standard form, correct to two significant figures.

(a) $\sqrt{0.000005}$

(b) $(5.3 \times 10^{-9}) \times (4.82 \times 10^{-3})$

(b) $\dfrac{6.8 \times 10^{-8}}{2.3 \times 10^{-2}}$

(c) $\dfrac{(7.8 \times 10^{-5})^2}{300}$

D8 This is an isosceles triangle.
Find the missing length.

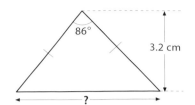

3.2 cm

86°

?

D9 The lengths of the diagonals of this rhombus are shown.
Calculate the angles at the vertices of the rhombus
(to the nearest 0.1°).

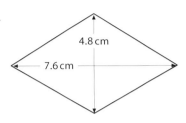

4.8 cm

7.6 cm

D10 This is an equilateral triangle.

   (a) How long is the dotted line (to 2 d.p.)?

   (b) What is the area of the equilateral triangle
(to 2 d.p.)?

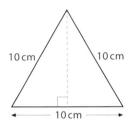

10 cm 10 cm

10 cm

*D11 This is a regular octagon.
O is the centre.

Calculate

   (a) angle AOC

   (b) length OB (to 2 d.p.)

   (c) the area of the whole octagon (to 1 d.p.)

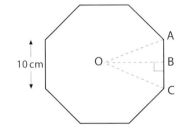

10 cm

O A B C

*D12 This is a regular hexagon with sides 2 cm long.

Explain why the area of the hexagon is $(6 \tan 60°) \, \text{cm}^2$.

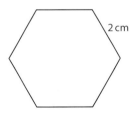

2 cm

*D13 Find the missing length here, to 1 d.p.

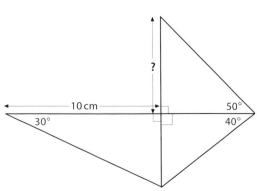

?

10 cm

30° 50° 40°

Test yourself

T1 Find the missing quantity in each of these. Give each answer to 1 d.p.

(a) ?

17.0 cm

32°

(b) 10.0 cm 21.0 cm ?

(c) 14.2 cm ? 53°

(d) 9.4 cm 13.8 cm ?

T2 A fisherman F, at sea in a small boat, looks at a vertical cliff.
The angle of elevation to the top of the cliff is 18°.
The fisherman knows the cliff is 23 m high.
How far is his boat from
the foot of the cliff?

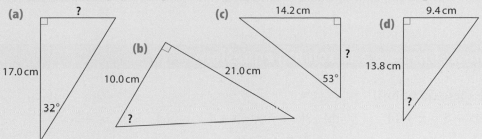

F 18°

23 m

T3 This is a symmetrical trapezium.
Calculate the angle marked *b*,
to the nearest 0.1°.

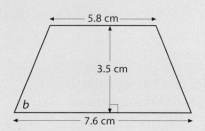

5.8 cm

3.5 cm

b

7.6 cm

T4 The diagonals of rectangle ABCD cross at O.
Find the angles *x* and *y*.

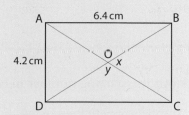

A 6.4 cm B

4.2 cm

O *x*

y

D C

T5 The shorter diagonal of this rhombus is 10 cm long.
How long is the longer diagonal?

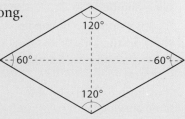

120°

60° 60°

120°

23 Linear equations 2

This work will help you form equations to solve problems, including problems expressed in words.

A Review: forming and solving equations

A1 Solve these equations.

(a) $4x + 5 = x + 14$

(b) $2(x + 3) = 7x - 4$

(c) $10 - 3x = 2(x - 2)$

(d) $\dfrac{x}{5} + 1 = 7$

(e) $\dfrac{3x + 5}{4} = 2x$

(f) $2(3x + 1) = 4(2x - 5)$

(g) $6 - 5x = 2x + 27$

(h) $2 - 3x = 7 - 5x$

(i) $5(1 - x) = 2(2x + 3)$

A2 Form and solve an equation to calculate the angles of this triangle.

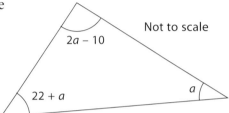

Not to scale

$2a - 10$

$22 + a$

a

OCR

A3 This parallelogram has a perimeter of 67. Find the length of the longest side.

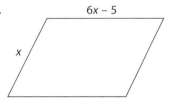

$6x - 5$

x

A4 Work out the starting number in each of these 'think of a number' puzzles.

(a)
> Fi and Clare both think of the same number.
>
> Fi adds 4 and then multiplies by 3.
>
> Helen multiplies by 5 and then subtracts 1.
>
> They both end up with the same answer.

(b)
> Walt and Wilf both think of the same number.
>
> Walt adds 6 to his number and then divides the result by 3.
>
> Wilf takes 10 off his number and then halves the result.
>
> They both end up with the same answer.

B Forming equations to solve word problems

Jan has some pencils.
Mary has 2 more pencils than Jan.
Altogether they have 50 pencils.
How many do they have each?

Let **n** stand for the number
of pencils that Jan has.

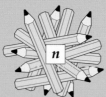

Then Mary has **n + 2** pencils.

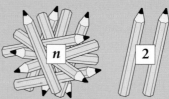

Altogether they have **2n + 2** pencils.

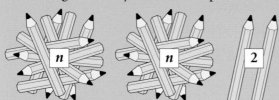

We are told they have **50** pencils.

So $2n + 2 = 50$
$2n = 48$
$n = 24$

Jan has 24 pencils and Mary has 26.

B1 Alan has some DVDs.
Beth has 8 fewer than Alan.

Let *n* stand for the number of DVDs that Alan has.

(a) Write an expression for the number of DVDs that Beth has.

(b) Write an expression, in terms of *n*, for the number of DVDs they have altogether.

(c) Altogether they have 100 DVDs.
Use your expression from (b) to form an equation in *n*.
Solve your equation and write down how many DVDs they have each.

B2 Chloe has two sisters, Becky and Emily.
Becky is 4 years younger than Chloe.
Emily is twice as old as Chloe.

Let *y* stand for Chloe's age, in years.

(a) How old is Becky, in terms of *y*?

(b) How old is Emily, in terms of *y*?

(c) Write an expression for the sum of the three ages.

(d) Their ages add up to 24.
Form an equation in *y* and solve it.
How old is each of the girls?

B3 Maria buys two chocolate bars costing x pence each
and one packet of sweets costing $(x + 2)$ pence.
She spends a total of 56 pence.

    (a) Write down an equation in x.

    (b) Solve your equation.   OCR

B4 An apple costs y pence.
An orange costs 5 pence more than an apple.

    (a) Write down an expression, in terms of y, for the cost of one orange.

    (b) Write down an expression, in terms of y, for the
total cost of three apples and one orange.

    (c) The total cost of three apples and one orange is 61 pence.
Form an equation in terms of y and solve it to find the cost of one apple.   OCR

B5 The apple in my fruit bowl weighs x grams.
The orange weighs $2x$ grams.
The banana weighs 13 grams more than the orange.

    (a) Write an expression, in terms of x, for the weight of the banana.

    The total weight of all three pieces of fruit is 163 grams.

    (b) (i) Form an equation and find the value of x.

        (ii) What is the weight of the orange?

B6 Twins Susan and Stephen both have some money.
Stephen has £80 more than Susan.

    Suppose that n is the amount of money (in pounds) that Susan has.

    (a) Write down an expression for the amount of money that Stephen has.

    Their aunt then gives them both £20 for their birthday.

    (b) (i) Write an expression for the amount of money Susan has after her birthday.

        (ii) Write an expression for the amount of money Stephen has after his birthday.

    After his aunt's birthday present, Stephen now has three times as much money as Susan.

    (c) (i) Write an equation and solve it to find the value of n.

        (ii) How much money does Stephen have now?

B7 Mary's mum is 24 years older than Mary is.
In 6 years time, Mary's mum will be exactly four times as old as Mary.

    (a) Suppose that Mary's age now is m years.
Write down an expression for Mary's mum's age now.

    (b) (i) Write down an expression for Mary's age in 6 years time.

        (ii) Write down an expression for Mary's mum's age in 6 years.

    (c) Use your answer to part (b) to write an equation in m.
Solve the equation and thus find how old Mary and her mum are now.

B8 Alex's dad is 30 years older than Alex.
In four years time, Alex's dad will be three times as old as Alex.
Work out how old Alex and his dad are now.

B9 Abbas is two years younger than Brad.
Two years ago, the sum of their ages was the same as Brad's age now.
How old are the boys now?

C Mixed questions

C1 Hattie has two sisters, Molly and Emily.
Molly is 5 years younger than Hattie.
Emily is three times as old as Hattie.

Let x stand for Hattie's age in years.

(a) In terms of x, write expressions for

    (i) Molly's age   (ii) Emily's age

(b) The sum of their ages in 25.

    (i) Form an equation in x and solve it.   (ii) How old is Emily?

C2 Find the size of each angle in this triangle.

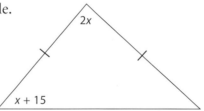

C3 The diagram shows a rectangle with
length $3x + 2$ and width $2x$.
All measurements are given in centimetres.

The perimeter of the rectangle is P centimetres.
The area of the rectangle is A square centimetres.

(a) Write down an expression in its simplest form,
in terms of x, for

    (i) P (ii) A

(b) $P = 44$. Work out the value of A.

Edexcel

C4 A stone is thrown up with velocity u metres per second.
After t seconds the stone's velocity, v metres per second, is given by the formula

$$v = u + gt$$

Calculate t when $u = 8.5$, $g = {}^-9.8$ and $v = 3.6$.

Test yourself

T1 Do a scale drawing to solve this puzzle and mark the position of the treasure with a cross.

> The treasure is in a rectangular field ABCD.
> Side AB is 11 m long and side BC is 8 m long.
>
> The treasure is equidistant from corners A and C.
> It is along one of the edges of the field.
> It is closer to corner B than to corner D.

T2 This is the plan of a square garden.
The tree is at the centre.

Grass is to be planted. It must be at least 3 m from the tree and at least 4 m from the wall of the house. It can go right up to the edge on the other sides.

Draw the plan to scale and shade the part where the grass goes.

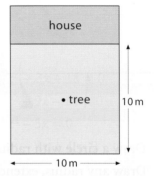

T3 A tree is to be planted in this rectangular garden.
The tree must be equidistant from sides AB and AD.
The tree must also be exactly 3.0 m from corner C.

Draw the plan to scale, showing clearly how you find the position for the tree.

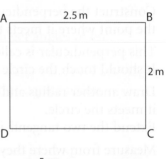

T4 Copy this diagram using the lengths shown.

Shade the region containing points that satisfy all three of these conditions.

- They must be more than 4 cm from Y.
- They must be closer to line YX than line YZ.
- They must be closer to Z than X.

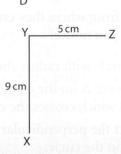

T5 Draw the rhombus ABCD such that the sides are each 4 cm and the angle between AB and AD is 60°.

Construct and shade the region consisting of all points inside the rhombus that are nearer to B than to any other vertex.

25 Equations of linear graphs

You should know how to

- plot points and draw the graph of a straight line, given its equation
- calculate the gradient of a straight line
- rearrange simple formulas

This work will help you find

- the equation of any straight line, including a line of best fit
- the gradient and y-intercept of a straight line from its equation
- the equations of lines parallel or perpendicular to a line with a given equation

A Gradient and intercept of a linear graph

A1 (a) On the same set of axes, plot the graphs of $y = x$, $y = 2x$, $y = 3x$ and $y = {}^-4x$ for values of x between $^-1$ and 3.

(b) What is the gradient of each line?

(c) What do you notice? Can you explain it?

A2 (a) On the same set of axes, plot the graphs of $y = x + 1$, $y = 4 + x$ and $y = x - 2$ for values of x between $^-1$ and 3.

(b) What is the gradient of each line?

(c) Where does each line cross the y-axis?

(d) What do you notice? Can you explain it?

A3

A
$y = x + 3$
$y = 3 + 2x$
$y = 3x + 3$

B
$y = 2x + 2$
$y = 2x - 1$
$y = 5 + 2x$

C
$y = {}^-x + 1$
$y = 5 - x$
$y = {}^-x - 3$

D
$y = 1 - 2x$
$y = {}^-2x + 2$
$y = {}^-2x - 1$

(a) For each set of equations above

(i) draw the graphs on the same set of axes

(ii) find the gradient of each line

(iii) write down where each line crosses the y-axis

(b) Briefly summarise your results.

A4 (a) Where do you think the line with equation $y = 2x + 1$ crosses the y-axis?

(b) What do you think is the gradient of the line with equation $y = 2x + 1$?

A5 What do you think is the equation of the line with gradient 5 that goes through $(0, 3)$?

Sometimes you need to **rearrange** the equation of a straight line to express it in the form $y = mx + c$.

Examples

A line has equation $2y + 4x = 3$.

$$2y + 4x = 3$$
$$2y = 3 - 4x \qquad \text{[− 4x]}$$
$$\qquad\qquad \text{[÷ 2]}$$
$$y = \tfrac{3}{2} - 2x \qquad \text{[rearrange]}$$
$$y = {}^-2x + \tfrac{3}{2}$$

So the gradient is **−2** and the y-intercept is $\tfrac{3}{2}$.

A line has equation $3y - 6 = 2x$.

$$3y - 6 = 2x$$
$$3y = 2x + 6 \qquad \text{[+ 6]}$$
$$\qquad\qquad \text{[÷ 3]}$$
$$y = \frac{2x}{3} + \frac{6}{3}$$
$$y = \tfrac{2}{3}x + 2$$

So the gradient is $\tfrac{2}{3}$ and the y-intercept is **2**.

E1 What is the gradient of the line with equation $y - 7x = 5$?

E2 (a) Match the equations below to give four pairs of parallel lines.

A $y - x = 2$ B $y + 3x = 1$ C $y = 5 + 3x$ D $y = 5 - 3x$ E $y - 4x = 5$

F $y = 6 - 4x$ G $y = 4x - 2$ H $3x - y = 8$ I $y + 6 = x$

(b) Which equation is the odd one out?

E3 Find the gradient and y-intercept of each of these lines.
(a) $y - x = 5$ (b) $y - 2x = 4$ (c) $3x + y = 6$ (d) $2x - y = 3$

E4 Show that the lines $y = 2(3 + x)$ and $y - 2x = 10$ are parallel.

E5 Find the gradient and y-intercept of each of these lines.
(a) $y = 2(x - 5)$ (b) $y = 3(3 - 4x)$ (c) $y = 4\left(1 - \tfrac{1}{2}x\right)$ (d) $2(y - 1) = 4x$

E6 Find the gradient and y-intercept of each of these lines.
(a) $3y = 6x + 1$ (b) $4y = 8x - 3$ (c) $4y = x + 8$ (d) $3y = 2x - 6$

E7 (a) Match the equations below to give four pairs of parallel lines.

A $y = \tfrac{1}{2}x - 3$ B $6y + 3x = 6$ C $2y = 3 - x$ D $6y = 3 + 2x$

E $3y = 2x - 1$ F $3y - x = 6$ G $3y = 9 - x$ H $2y + 8 = x$ I $y + \tfrac{1}{3}x = 1$

(b) Which equation is the odd one out?

E8 Show that the lines $2x + 6y = 1$ and $3y = 9 - x$ are parallel.

E9 Show that the lines $3y - 6x = 2$ and $6y + x = 4$ intersect on the y-axis.

E10 Find the gradient and y-intercept of lines with the following equations.

(a) $2y - 5x = 4$ (b) $x = 3y + 12$ (c) $2y + 3x = 2$

(d) $2y = x - 3$ (e) $3(y + 2x) = 1$ (f) $x = 2(y - 1)$

(g) $3y + x + 2 = 0$ (h) $7y = 2x + 21$ (i) $3x = 4(1 - y)$

E11 Show that $10x = 2y - 2$ and $6y - 30x = 6$ are equations for the same line.

E12 (a) Show that the two lines in the sketch are not parallel.

(b) Which is the steeper line?

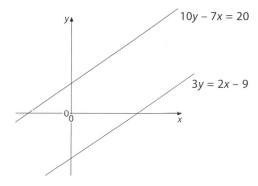

E13 (a) Give an equation for the line parallel to $y - 3x = 2$ through $(0, 3)$.

(b) Give an equation for the line parallel to $y - 3x = 2$ through $(1, 11)$.

E14 Give an equation for the line parallel to $2y + 3x = 1$ through $(3, {}^-1)$.

E15 Give an equation for the line parallel to $3y = 2(3 - x)$ through $(6, 1)$.
Give the equation in the form $ax + by = c$, where a, b and c are integers.

E16 Give an equation for the line through each pair of points in the form $ax + by = c$, where a, b and c are integers.

(a) $(6, 1)$ and $({}^-2, 5)$ (b) $(3, 1)$ and $(6, 0)$ (c) $({}^-1, {}^-1)$ and $(9, 3)$

F Perpendicular lines

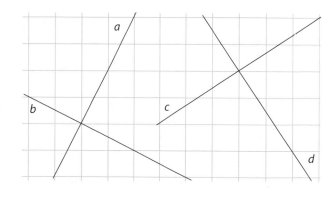

- What is the gradient of line a?

  Line b is perpendicular to line a. What is its gradient?

- What is the gradient of line c?

  Line d is perpendicular to line c. What is its gradient?

- On squared paper, draw a line with gradient 3.
  Draw a line perpendicular to this line and find its gradient.

- Investigate the relationship between the gradients of perpendicular lines.

Perpendicular lines and gradients

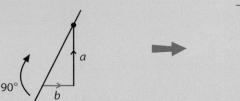 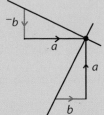

The gradient of the line is $\frac{a}{b}$.　　　The gradient of the perpendicular is $\frac{^-b}{a}$.

The product of the gradients of two perpendicular lines is $^-1$.

For example, lines with gradients $\frac{2}{3}$ and $\frac{^-3}{2}$ are perpendicular as $\frac{2}{3} \times \frac{^-3}{2} = ^-1$.

So, if the gradient of a line is g, then the gradient of a perpendicular is $\frac{^-1}{g}$.

F1 (a) Write down the gradient of the line whose equation is $y = 4x - 3$.

　　(b) What is the gradient of any line perpendicular to $y = 4x - 3$?

F2 (a) What is the gradient of any line perpendicular to $y = 2x + 1$?

　　(b) State the equation of the line perpendicular to $y = 2x + 1$ that passes through $(0, 9)$.

F3 Find the equation of the line　(a) perpendicular to $y = 5 - 3x$ through $(0, 1)$

　　　　　　　　　　　　　　　　(b) perpendicular to $y = \frac{1}{3}x + 6$ through $(0, ^-4)$

　　　　　　　　　　　　　　　　(c) perpendicular to $y = 10 - \frac{1}{5}x$ through $(0, 7)$

F4 Lines a and b intersect at right angles on the y-axis.
The equation of line a is $y = \frac{3}{4}x + 3$. What is the equation of line b?

F5 Which of these lines is perpendicular to $y + 2x = 9$?

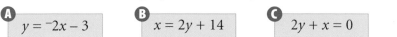

A $y = ^-2x - 3$　　　**B** $x = 2y + 14$　　　**C** $2y + x = 0$　　　**D** $y + 2x = \frac{^-1}{9}$

F6 Give an equation for the line perpendicular to $2y + 3x = 7$ through $(0, ^-5)$.

F7 Find the equation of the line　(a) perpendicular to $y = 2x + 5$ through $(6, 8)$

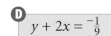

　　　　　　　　　　　　　　　　(b) perpendicular to $y = \frac{4}{5}x - 1$ through $(^-4, 2)$

F8 Give an equation for the line perpendicular to $3y - 5x = 4$ through $(10, ^-3)$.

F9 ABCD is a rectangle.

C is the point with coordinates $(0, ^-8)$.

The equation of the straight line through AB is $x + 2y = 4$.

Find the equations of the lines DC, AD and BC.

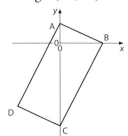

F10 A is the point (8, 9) and B is (12, 10).

    (a) Find the equation of the line AB.

    (b) Find the equation of the line through A perpendicular to AB.

G Line of best fit

A pan of water was heated and the temperature measured at various intervals.

Time from start (minutes)	1	2	4	6	8
Temperature (°C)	32	40	53	75	85

We can investigate the relationship between time (t) and temperature (T).

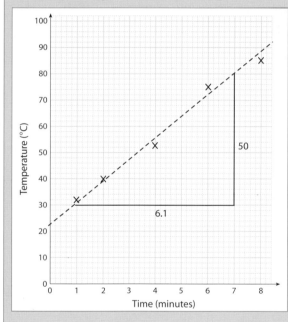

- Plot these pairs of values.
- They lie close to a straight line so draw the line of best fit.
- Choose two suitable points on the line and use them to estimate the gradient.

$$\frac{50}{6.1} \approx 8.2$$

- Estimate where it cuts the vertical axis.

  The line cuts this axis at about 22.

- So the equation of the line of best fit is approximately

$$T = 8.2t + 22$$

G1 Nigel lit a small candle and put a beaker upside down over it. He counted how many seconds it took for the flame to go out.

He repeated the experiment with larger containers. Here are his results.

Capacity (V ml)	200	250	500	750	1000
Time taken (t s)	12	17	32	48	60

    (a) Plot the points and draw a line of best fit. Estimate its gradient and y-intercept to one significant figure. Hence find an approximate equation for your line of best fit.

    (b) Use your equation to estimate how long it would take for the flame to go out in a beaker with capacity of 600 ml.

G2 For each of set of data

- plot the pairs of values and draw a line of best fit
- estimate the gradient and vertical intercept correct to two significant figures
- hence find an approximate equation for the line of best fit

(a) Here are the results of an experiment where different loads were added to a helical spring to see how much it stretched.

Load (L newtons)	1.7	3.2	5.0	6.7	8.3	10.0
Extension (E cm)	5.1	9.6	14.8	20.2	25.0	29.9

(i) Use your equation to estimate the stretch in cm for a load of 7.5 newtons.

(ii) Would you use this equation to estimate the stretch for a load of 1000 newtons? Explain your answer.

(b) Here are the some of the world records for women's indoor running events.

Distance run (s m)	200	400	800	1000
Time taken (t s)	21.87	49.59	116.36	150.94

(i) Use your equation to estimate what the world record would be for 600 m.

(ii) The world record for the 50 m race is 5.96 seconds.
Does this fit your equation? Comment on your answer.

G3 **(a)** For each set of values, plot the pairs of values and, where appropriate, draw a line of best of fit and find an approximate equation for it.

(i) This table shows the mean wing length of a group of ducks at various ages.

Age (d days)	2	4	6	8	10	13	16	19	22
Wing length (W mm)	26	29.2	33.9	37	41.6	57.4	73.7	81.5	105

(ii) This table shows fat as a percentage of body weight for a group of adult men.

Age (y years)	23	39	41	49	50	53	54	56	57	60	61
Percentage of fat (F)	23	26	21	20	26	30	37	24	28	29	36

(iii) This table shows the results of aerial surveys carried out on each of 11 days in a particular part of Alaska.
The average wind speed and the number of black bears sighted on each day are given.

Wind speed (w knots)	2.1	21.1	4.9	23.6	21.5	10.5	20.3	11.9	6.9	14	27.2
Number of bears (B)	99	30	82	43	49	79	54	69	87	72	23

(b) Decide, giving reasons, which of the following you can estimate with reasonable confidence.

   (i) The wing length of a 100-day-old duck

   (ii) The percentage of a 40-year-old man's body that is fat

   (iii) The number of bears sighted on a day when the average wind speed is 15 knots

   (iv) The wing length of a 12-day-old duck

   (v) The number of bears sighted on a day when the average wind speed is 40 knots

Test yourself

T1 (a) What are the gradient and y-intercept of the line with equation $y = 4x - 7$?

   (b) What is the equation of the line parallel to $y = {}^-2x + 5$ going through $(0, 9)$?

T2 The line with equation $x + 2y = 6$ has been drawn on the grid.

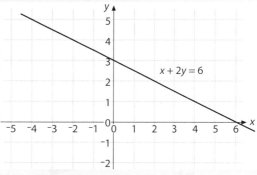

(a) Rearrange the equation $x + 2y = 6$ to make y the subject.

(b) Write down the gradient of the line with equation $x + 2y = 6$.

(c) Write down the equation of the line which is parallel to the line with equation $x + 2y = 6$ and passes through the point with coordinates $(0, 7)$.   Edexcel

T3 Find an equation of the straight line passing through the point $(0, 5)$ which is perpendicular to the line $y = \frac{2}{3}x + 3$.   AQA

T4 Here are the world records for men's outdoor running events.

Distance run (s m)	200	400	800	1000
Time taken (t s)	19.32	43.29	101.11	132.18

(a) Plot the pairs of values and find an approximate equation of the line of best fit.

(b) Use your equation to estimate what the world record would be for 600 m.

(c) Would you use this equation to estimate the world record for 100 metres? Explain your answer.

T5 A straight line L passes through the point with coordinates $(4, 7)$ and is perpendicular to the line with equation $y = 2x + 3$.
Find an equation of the straight line L.   Edexcel

26 Quadratic expressions and equations

This work will help you

- multiply out expressions such as $(x + 1)(x + 3)$ and $(x + 1)(x - 3)$
- write expressions such as $x^2 + 4x + 3$ as the product of two linear expressions
- solve quadratic equations such as $x^2 + 4x + 3 = 0$
- solve problems by forming and solving a quadratic equation
- use algebra to prove simple general statements

A Multiplying out expressions such as $(x + 1)(x + 3)$

We can sometimes break down a multiplication into simpler calculations.

For example,

52×58

×	50	8
50	2500	400
2	100	16

52×58
$= 2500 + 400 + 100 + 16$
$= 3016$

We can set it out like this:

$$52 \times 58 = (50 + 2) \times (50 + 8)$$
$$= (50 \times 50) + (50 \times 8) + (2 \times 50) + (2 \times 8)$$
$$= 2500 + 400 + 100 + 16$$
$$= 3016$$

We can sometimes break down an algebraic multiplication in the same way.

For example,

$(n + 2)(n + 8)$

×	n	8
n	n^2	$8n$
2	$2n$	16

$(n + 2)(n + 8)$
$= n^2 + 8n + 2n + 16$
$= n^2 + 10n + 16$

We can set it out like this:

$$(n + 2)(n + 8) = (n \times n) + (n \times 8) + (2 \times n) + (2 \times 8)$$
$$= n^2 + 8n + 2n + 16$$
$$= n^2 + 10n + 16$$

The statement $n^2 = 9$ (called an equation) is true for only two values, $n = 3$ and $n = {}^-3$.

However, a statement such as $(n + 2)(n + 8) = n^2 + 10n + 16$ is true for **all** values of n. A statement like this is called an **identity**.

A1 In each of these, multiply out the brackets and write the result in its simplest form.

(a) $(n + 2)(n + 6)$ (b) $(n + 12)(n + 1)$ (c) $(n + 4)(n + 1)$

(d) $(n + 4)(n + 2)$ (e) $(n + 6)(n + 3)$ (f) $(n + 2)(n + 9)$

A2 Copy and complete $(x + 3)^2 = (x + 3)(x + 3)$

$$= \dots\dots\dots\dots$$

Simplify your result.

A3 Multiply out each expression and write the result in its simplest form.

(a) $(x + 4)^2$ (b) $(x + 5)^2$ (c) $(x + 1)^2$

A4 Show that the area of this rectangle is $x^2 + 8x + 15$.

$x + 5$

$x + 3$

A5 Write an expression for the area of each rectangle below
- with brackets, for example $(x + 2)(x + 8)$
- without brackets, for example $x^2 + 10x + 16$

(a) $x + 4$

$x + 3$

(b) $x + 8$

$x + 1$

(c) $x + 2$

$x + 2$

A6 Find pairs of expressions from the loop that multiply to give these.

(a) $n^2 + 6n + 5$ (b) $n^2 + 7n + 12$

(c) $n^2 + 7n + 6$ (d) $n^2 + 5n + 6$

> $n + 2$ $n + 1$ $n + 3$
> $n + 4$ $n + 5$ $n + 6$

A7 Find pairs of expressions from the loop that multiply to give these.

(a) $n^2 + 9n + 8$ (b) $n^2 + 9n + 20$

(c) $n^2 + 14n + 40$ (d) $n^2 + 13n + 40$

> $n + 1$ $n + 2$ $n + 4$
> $n + 5$ $n + 8$ $n + 10$

A8 Solve these equations.

(a) $(x + 2)(x + 3) = x^2 + 11$ (b) $(x + 1)(x + 6) = x(x + 8)$

(c) $(x + 3)(x + 1) = 4x + 7$ (d) $(x + 2)^2 = x^2$

A9 Decide whether each statement is an identity or an equation that can be solved.
Solve each equation.
Show that each identity is true.

(a) $(n + 2)(n + 4) = n^2 + 8n + 6$ (b) $(n + 9)(n + 4) = n^2 + 13n + 36$

(c) $(n + 3)(n + 10) = n(n + 13) + 30$ (d) $(n + 5)(n + 9) = n(n + 11)$

B Opposite corners investigation

1	2	3	4	5	6	7	8	9	10
11	12	13	14	15	16	17	18	19	20
21	22	23	24	25	26	27	28	29	30
31	32	3	34	35	36	37	38	39	40
4		43	44	45	46	47	48		

This grid of numbers has ten columns.
A 3 by 3 square outlines some numbers.

14	15	16
24	25	26
34	35	36

- Multiply the numbers in opposite corners.

$14 \times 36 = 504$
$16 \times 34 = 544$

- Find the difference between the results.

$544 - 504 = 40$

- Let's call this the 'opposite-corners number'.

The opposite-corners number
for this square is **40**.

B1 Find the opposite-corners number for some 3 by 3 squares in
different positions on this grid.
What do you think is true about these opposite-corners numbers?

B2 (a) Copy this square for the grid above.
Fill in the corner squares.

(b) Find and simplify an expression for the
opposite-corners number for this square.

(c) What does this prove?

B3 (a) Investigate for 2 by 2 squares on this grid.

(b) What do you think is true about the opposite-corners number this time?

(c) Can you prove your result?

B4 Investigate for squares of different size on this grid.

*B5 Investigate for grids with different numbers of columns.

A table can be used when the multiplication involves subtraction.

Examples

$(n - 2)(n + 8)$ →

$\times$	n	8
n	n^2	$8n$
$^-2$	^-2n	$^-16$

→ $(n - 2)(n + 8)$
$= n^2 + 8n - 2n - 16$
$= n^2 + 6n - 16$

$(n - 2)(n - 8)$ →

$\times$	n	$^-8$
n	n^2	^-8n
$^-2$	^-2n	16

→ $(n - 2)(n - 8)$
$= n^2 - 8n - 2n + 16$
$= n^2 - 10n + 16$

Another way to approach $(n - 2)(n + 8)$ is:

$$(n - 2)(n + 8) = n(n + 8) - 2(n + 8)$$
$$= n^2 + 8n - (2n + 16)$$
$$= n^2 + 8n - 2n - 16$$
$$= n^2 + 6n - 16$$

C1 Multiply out each expression and write the result in its simplest form.

(a) $(n - 2)(n + 5)$ (b) $(n + 6)(n - 3)$ (c) $(n + 9)(n - 1)$

(d) $(n - 6)(n + 2)$ (e) $(n + 2)(n - 7)$ (f) $(n - 10)(n + 1)$

(g) $(n - 3)(n - 4)$ (h) $(n - 5)(n - 3)$ (i) $(n - 1)(n - 7)$

(j) $(n - 10)(n + 9)$ (k) $(n - 3)(n - 1)$ (l) $(n + 2)(n - 12)$

C2 Show that the area of this rectangle
is equivalent to $x^2 + 4x - 12$.

$x + 6$

$x - 2$

C3 Copy and complete $(x - 4)^2 = (x - 4)(x - 4)$
$= \ldots\ldots\ldots\ldots$

Simplify your result.

C4 Multiply out each expression and write the result in its simplest form.

(a) $(x - 3)^2$ (b) $(x - 1)^2$ (c) $(x - 6)^2$

C5 (a) Multiply out and simplify these expressions.

(i) $(n + 7)(n - 7)$ **(ii)** $(n + 5)(n - 5)$ **(iii)** $(n - 3)(n + 3)$

Comment on your results.

(b) Write down the expansion of $(n + 4)(n - 4)$.

C6 Find pairs of expressions from the loop that multiply to give these.

(a) $n^2 + 2n - 3$ **(b)** $n^2 - n - 2$

(c) $n^2 - 5n + 6$ **(d)** $n^2 - 4n + 3$

(e) $n^2 - 4$ **(f)** $n^2 - 1$

$$\boxed{\; n + 2 \qquad n + 1 \qquad n + 3 \atop n - 1 \quad n - 2 \qquad n - 3 \;}$$

C7 Copy and complete each identity.

(a) $(n + 3)(\,\ldots\ldots\,) = n^2 + 4n + 3$ **(b)** $(n - 2)(\,\ldots\ldots\,) = n^2 + 4n - 12$

(c) $(n + 7)(\,\ldots\ldots\,) = n^2 + 6n - 7$ **(d)** $(n - 3)(\,\ldots\ldots\,) = n^2 - 11n + 24$

C8 The area of the square is $5\,\text{cm}^2$ less than the area of the rectangle. Find x.

C9 The area of the square is $5\,\text{cm}^2$ more than the area of the rectangle. What is the area of each shape?

*C10 If n is a whole number, show that the tinted area is always a multiple of 10.

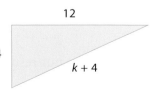

*C11 Find the length of each side for these right-angled triangles.

(a)

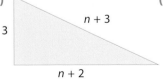

(b) $b - 1$, 12, $b + 5$

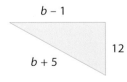

(c) 12, $k - 4$, $k + 4$

*C12 Copy and complete these identities.

    (a) $(\ldots\ldots)(n + 1) = n^2 - 9n \ldots\ldots$ **(b)** $(n - 5)(\ldots\ldots) = n^2 - 11n \ldots\ldots$

    (c) $(n + 6)(\ldots\ldots) = n^2 - 36$ **(d)** $(\ldots\ldots)^2 = n^2 + 8n \ldots\ldots$

D Factorising quadratic expressions

An expression that can be written in the form $ax^2 + bx + c$ is called a **quadratic expression**.

A quadratic expression written as the product of two simple linear expressions is said to be **factorised**.

For example, the expression $n^2 + 9n + 14$ can be factorised to give $(n + 2)(n + 7)$. However, the expression $n^2 + 9n + 13$ **cannot** be factorised like this.

- Can you factorise these quadratic expressions?

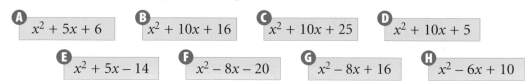

A $x^2 + 5x + 6$ **B** $x^2 + 10x + 16$ **C** $x^2 + 10x + 25$ **D** $x^2 + 10x + 5$

E $x^2 + 5x - 14$ **F** $x^2 - 8x - 20$ **G** $x^2 - 8x + 16$ **H** $x^2 - 6x + 10$

D1 Factorise these.

    (a) $x^2 + 3x + 2$ **(b)** $x^2 + 5x + 4$ **(c)** $x^2 + 4x + 4$

    (d) $x^2 + 16x + 28$ **(e)** $x^2 + 11x + 28$ **(f)** $x^2 + 11x + 30$

D2 Factorise these.

    (a) $n^2 - 4n + 3$ **(b)** $n^2 - 6n + 8$ **(c)** $n^2 - 9n + 14$

    (d) $n^2 - 12n + 32$ **(e)** $n^2 - 6n + 9$ **(f)** $n^2 - 10n + 25$

D3 Factorise these.

    (a) $x^2 + 4x - 5$ **(b)** $x^2 - 4x - 5$ **(c)** $x^2 + 3x - 10$

    (d) $x^2 - 3x - 10$ **(e)** $x^2 + 9x - 10$ **(f)** $x^2 + 9x - 22$

    (g) $x^2 - 3x - 18$ **(h)** $x^2 - 11x - 12$ **(i)** $x^2 + x - 12$

D4 Factorise these.

    (a) $n^2 + 6n + 5$ **(b)** $n^2 + 12n + 36$ **(c)** $n^2 - 9n + 20$

    (d) $n^2 + 2n - 3$ **(e)** $n^2 - 7n - 8$ **(f)** $n^2 - 2n + 1$

    (g) $n^2 + 3n - 18$ **(h)** $n^2 - 5n - 14$ **(i)** $n^2 - n - 20$

D5 Which two of these expressions cannot be factorised?

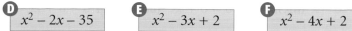

A $x^2 + 13x + 40$ **B** $x^2 + 10x + 12$ **C** $x^2 + 5x - 50$

D $x^2 - 2x - 35$ **E** $x^2 - 3x + 2$ **F** $x^2 - 4x + 2$

G2 A rectangular garden is made up of a square lawn of side x m and two paths 1.5 m wide, as shown in the diagram.

The total area of the garden is 88 m².

Write down an equation in x and solve it to find the dimensions of the lawn.

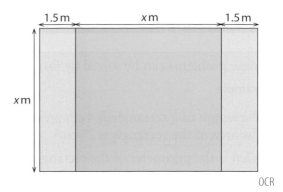

OCR

G3 The width of a rectangle is 3 cm less than its length.
The area of the rectangle is 54 cm².
What is the length of this rectangle?

G4 The area of this shape is 91 cm².
Find the value of x.

3 cm

G5 These two rectangles have the same area.

What is the area of each rectangle?

*G6 Find the area of this right-angled triangle.

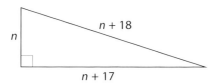

*G7 The expression for the nth term of a sequence is $n^2 + n - 11$.

    (a) What is the 10th term of the sequence?

    (b) Which term of the sequence is 261?

Test yourself

T1 Multiply out and simplify these.

(a) $(n + 4)(n + 5)$ (b) $(a + 5)(a - 3)$ (c) $(y - 6)(y + 1)$

(d) $(k - 4)(k - 2)$ (e) $(x + 6)(x - 6)$ (f) $(p - 5)^2$

T2 Factorise these expressions.

(a) $n^2 + 4n + 3$ (b) $n^2 + 7n + 6$ (c) $n^2 + 8n + 15$

T3 Factorise $x^2 - 11x + 30$.

T4 Factorise these.

(a) $x^2 - 16$ (b) $x^2 - 6x - 16$ OCR

T5 (a) Solve the equation $x^2 + 3x = 0$.

(b) Factorise $x^2 - 7x + 12$. OCR

T6 (a) Factorise $x^2 + 7x - 30$.

(b) Hence solve the equation $x^2 + 7x - 30 = 0$.

T7 (a) Factorise $x^2 - 6x + 8$.

(b) Solve the equation $x^2 - 6x + 8 = 0$. Edexcel

T8 Solve the equation $x^2 - 10x = 0$.

T9 Solve the equation $x^2 - 4x - 21 = 0$.

T10 Solve the equation $x^2 + 2x - 15 = 0$. OCR

T11 Solve the equation $x^2 - 8x + 15 = 0$. OCR

T12 The dimensions of a rectangle are shown.

$(x + 7)$ cm

$(x - 2)$ cm

The rectangle has an area of 36 cm^2.

(a) Form an equation, in terms of x, for the area of the rectangle and show that it can be written in the form $x^2 + 5x - 50 = 0$.

(b) Solve the equation in part (a) and hence write down the dimensions of the rectangle.

B Percentages from a two-way table

This two-way table shows gender and age
breakdowns for the population of a small town.

Many different percentages can be found
using this data. Examples are given below.

	Age 0–59	Age 60+	Total
Males	358	82	440
Females	309	112	421
Total	667	194	861

What percentage of the whole population are male?

The whole population is 861, of whom 440 are male.

$\frac{440}{861} = 0.511$ (to 3 d.p.), so the percentage who are males is 51.1% (to 1 d.p.).

What percentage of the females are aged 60+?

The number of females is 421, of whom 112 are aged 60+.

$\frac{112}{421} = 0.266$ (to 3 d.p.), so the percentage of the females who are aged 60+ is 26.6% (to 1 d.p.).

What percentage of the people aged 60+ are male?

The number of people aged 60+ is 194, of whom 82 are male.

$\frac{82}{194} = 0.423$ (to 3 d.p.), so the percentage of the 60+ group who are male is 42.3% (to 1 d.p.).

B1 What percentage of the whole population are females aged 60+?

B2 What percentage of the people aged 0–59 are female?

B3 What percentage of the males are aged 0–59?

B4 What percentage of the whole population are aged 60+?

B5 This table gives information about the people who
work for a company.

Use the data to compare the proportions of part-time
workers among the men and among the women.

	Full-time	Part-time
Men	42	28
Women	33	57

B6 A researcher examined data relating to car accidents.
She found that in only 25% of accidents the driver had been drinking
and in 75% the driver had not been drinking.

She drew the conclusion that driving was more dangerous if
the driver had not been drinking.
Was she correct? If not, why not?

Here is some data published by the Home Office.

Selected offences recorded by the police: England and Wales			
			thousands
	1971	**1982**	**1983**
Fraud and forgery	99.8	123.1	121.8
Criminal damage (vandalism)	27.0	417.8[a]	443.3
Other offences	5.6	3.8[b]	8.7[b]

Source: Criminal Statistics, Home Office

[a] Before 1982 vandalism causing less than £20 of damage was not recorded.

[b] The offence of 'abstracting electricity', of which there were 5688 in 1983, was included among 'other offences' in 1971 and 'theft' in 1982 and 1983.

This data was used for a newspaper article. Here is part of the article.

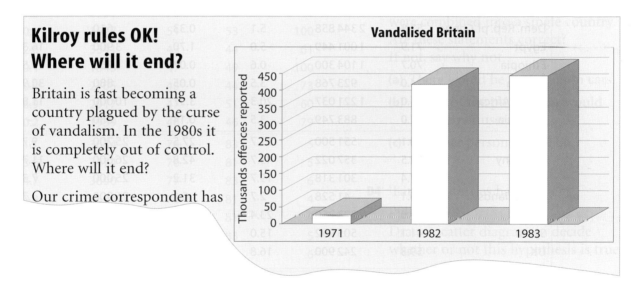

Kilroy rules OK!
Where will it end?

Britain is fast becoming a country plagued by the curse of vandalism. In the 1980s it is completely out of control. Where will it end?

Our crime correspondent has

Vandalised Britain

(Bar chart: Thousands offences reported vs year 1971, 1982, 1983)

C1 Does the article give an accurate account of the Home Office data?

C2 'When writing a report you should give the source of the data.'
Why do you think this is?

The data on these two pages is from a secondary school in England.

All the students in a year 11 group are shown.
The table gives their sex, their GCSE mathematics grade and whether they chose AS/A2 mathematics in the sixth form (Y = yes).

To be qualified to do AS/A2 mathematics, a student needs to have achieved at least a grade C at GCSE.

- What conclusions can you draw from this data?

Reference number	Sex	GCSE mathematics	A level mathematics
1	M	A	
2	M	E	
3	F	C	
4	F	E	
5	M	A	Y
6	M	B	
7	M	C	
8	F	B	
9	F	B	
10	F	B	
11	M	B	
12	F	A	Y
13	F	B	
14	F	A*	
15	M	A	Y
16	M	C	
17	M	C	
18	M	C	Y
19	M	G	
20	M	A	Y
21	M	D	
22	M	D	
23	M	A*	Y
24	M	E	
25	M	D	

Reference number	Sex	GCSE mathematics	A level mathematics
26	M	F	
27	F	B	
28	F	B	
29	F	B	
30	F	A*	Y
31	F	A	
32	F	E	
33	M	D	
34	M	B	
35	M	E	
36	F	A*	Y
37	F	B	Y
38	F	F	
39	M	B	Y
40	M	D	
41	M	B	
42	M	C	
43	F	A	
44	F	B	
45	M	C	
46	M		
47	M	C	
48	F	B	
49	M	E	
50	M	C	

Reference number	Sex	GCSE mathematics	A level mathematics
51	M	C	
52	M	C	
53	F	C	
54	F	C	
55	F	A	
56	F	C	
57	F	B	
58	M	D	
59	M	C	
60	M	A*	Y
61	M	F	
62	M	F	
63	M	D	
64	M	A	Y
65	M	B	
66	F	D	
67	M	D	
68	F	E	
69	F	B	
70	F	D	
71	M	F	
72	M	C	
73	M	E	
74	M	E	
75	F	B	

Reference number	Sex	GCSE mathematics	A level mathematics
76	F	A	
77	F	C	
78	F	B	
79	F	B	
80	F	C	
81	F	B	
82	F	B	
83	F	D	
84	F	C	
85	F	A	
86	F	C	
87	F	A	
88	F	A	
89	M	B	
90	F	A	Y
91	M	A*	Y
92	F	D	
93	F	D	
94	F	B	
95	F	E	
96	F	E	
97	F	B	
98	F	B	
99	F	B	
100	F	C	

101	F	C		147	F	A		193	M	B	Y	239	F	D	
102	F	C		148	F	E		194	M	A		240	M	C	
103	F	B		149	F	B		195	F	E		241	F	A	Y
104	F	A	Y	150	F	B		196	M	G		242	F	B	
105	F	E		151	F	B		197	F	C		243	F	E	
106	M	B		152	F	E		198	F	C		244	F	A	Y
107	M	A	Y	153	M	E		199	M	A		245	F	A	
108	M	C		154	F	E		200	M	B		246	M	B	
109	F	E		155	F	C		201	F	C		247	F	B	
110	M	E		156	F	D		202	F	A	Y	248	F	C	
111	M	B		157	F	C		203	M	C		249	F	D	
112	M	C		158	F	G		204	M	A		250	F	E	
113	M	E		159	F	A*	Y	205	M	B		251	F	C	
114	M	B	Y	160	F	D		206	M	E		252	M	D	
115	M	A*	Y	161	F	D		207	M	A		253	M	D	
116	M	E		162	F	A	Y	208	M	C		254	F	F	
117	M	E		163	F	D		209	M	A	Y	255	M	F	
118	M	D		164	M	D		210	M			256	F	B	Y
119	M	B	Y	165	F	B		211	F	B		257	M	D	
120	M	B	Y	166	F	D		212	F	B		258	F	D	
121	M	F		167	M	F		213	F	E		259	F	B	
122	M	C		168	M	E		214	M	B	Y	260	F	E	
123	M	F		169	M	A	Y	215	F	A		261	M		
124	F	D		170	F	G		216	F	B		262	M	U	
125	F	C		171	F	A	Y	217	F	A		263	M	D	
126	F	A*		172	F	C		218	F	C		264	M	D	
127	F	E		173	F	B		219	F	B	Y	265	M		
128	M	D		174	F	F		220	F	D		266	M	D	
129	F	B		175	F	B		221	F	B		267	M	G	
130	F	B		176	F	C		222	F	D		268	M	D	
131	F	D		177	F	C		223	F	C		269	F	B	
132	F	B		178	F	A	Y	224	F	C		270	M	D	
133	F	A*		179	F	F		225	F	C		271	M	A	Y
134	F	E		180	M	C		226	M	C		272	M	B	Y
135	F	A		181	M	C		227	M	B	Y	273	F	E	
136	M	D		182	M	B		228	M	A	Y	274	M	B	
137	M	A	Y	183	M	D		229	M	D		275	M	D	
138	M	A	Y	184	M	C		230	M	C		276	M	E	
139	M	A*		185	M	D		231	F	E		277	M	F	
140	M	A		186	M	A*	Y	232	M	E		278	F	A	
141	F	C		187	M	B		233	F	A	Y	279	F	A	
142	M	D		188	F	D		234	F	F		280	F	A	Y
143	F	E		189	M	D		235	M	C		281	F	D	
144	M	A	Y	190	M	D		236	M	E		282	M	A	Y
145	M	D		191	M	B		237	F	A	Y	283	F	A	Y
146	M	B	Y	192	M	B		238	M	E					

If your own school has a sixth form, you could do a similar survey.

28 Solving inequalities

You will revise the notation for inequalities, and how to represent them on a number line.

This work will help you to solve inequalities.

A Review: writing and interpreting inequalities

- $x < 3$ means 'x is less than 3'.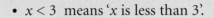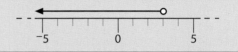

- $x \geq {}^-2$ means 'x is greater than or equal to $^-2$'.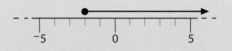

- ${}^-2 \leq x < 3$ means 'x is greater than or equal to $^-2$ and less than 3'.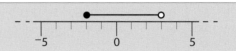

A1 For each of these inequalities, say whether it is true or false.

(a) $3 > {}^-5$ 　　　(b) ${}^-1 < {}^-3$ 　　　(c) $2 \leq 2$ 　　　(d) ${}^-1.9 \leq {}^-2$

A2 Write an inequality, using x, for each of these diagrams.

(a) 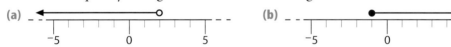　　　(b)

(c) 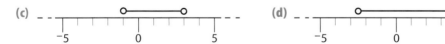　　　(d)

A3 Draw number lines to show these inequalities.

(a) $n \geq 3$ 　　　(b) $n < {}^-1$ 　　　(c) $0 < n < 5$ 　　　(d) ${}^-4 < n \leq 1.5$

A4 (a) List four different numbers, x, such that $1 \leq x < 3$.

(b) List four different numbers, n, such that ${}^-1 < n \leq 1$.

The **integers** are the positive and negative whole numbers, including 0.

A5 List all the integers, x, such that

(a) $3 \leq x \leq 6$ 　　　(b) $5 < x \leq 10$ 　　　(c) ${}^-4 \leq x < 1.5$ 　　　(d) ${}^-6 < x < 2$

A6 There are seven integers, n, such that $n^2 \leq 9$. What are they?

A7 List all the prime numbers, p, such that $0 < p^2 < 100$.

A8 If w stands for the weight of my suitcase in kg, then $w \leq 20$ means that my suitcase weighs 20 kg or less.

Write inequalities for each of these.
Choose your own letters, but say what they stand for.

   (a) Maximum number of passengers 65   **(b)** Children must be at least 12 years old

   (c) Baggage must weigh less than 40 kg   **(d)** Free travel for the over 60s

B Manipulating inequalities

This diagram shows the set
of numbers where $n \leq 4$.

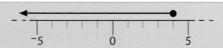

- Which of these inequalities gives the above set of numbers?

$2n \leq 8$ $n + 1 \leq 4$ $3n \leq 10$ $n + 1 \leq 5$ $n - 3 \leq 1$ $n - 1 \leq 5$ $\dfrac{n}{2} \leq 3$ $\dfrac{n}{4} \leq 1$

- Match up these inequalities.

A $2x < 10$ **C** $\dfrac{x}{2} > 3$ **E** $x + 1 < 5$ **G** $x + 3 < 7$

B $x > 4$ **D** $x + 3 > 7$ **F** $x < 5$ **H** $x > 6$

B1 Which one of the following is equivalent to $n \leq 8$?

$n + 2 \leq 16$ $n + 5 \leq 3$ $n + 6 \leq 14$ $n + 4 \leq 2$ $n + 1 \leq 10$

B2 Which two of the following are equivalent to $m > 6$?

$2m > 8$ $\dfrac{m}{2} > 12$ $3m > 2$ $2m > 12$ $\dfrac{m}{3} > 2$ $\dfrac{m}{2} > 4$

B3 Which of the following are equivalent to $n \leq 3$?

A $n + 1 \leq 4$ **B** $3n \leq 6$ **C** $3 \leq n$ **D** $\dfrac{n}{2} \leq 1\frac{1}{2}$ **E** $2n \leq 6$

B4 Which of the following are equivalent to $p < 10$?

A $p - 10 < 0$ **B** $2p < 12$ **C** $2p < 20$ **D** $\dfrac{p}{2} < 20$ **E** $p + 10 < 20$

B5 Which of the following inequalities are equivalent to $a \geq 10$?

A $a - 5 \geq 5$ **B** $2a \geq 20$ **C** $a + 5 \geq 5$ **D** $\frac{1}{2}a \geq 5$ **E** $a + \frac{1}{2} \geq 10\frac{1}{2}$

B6 Find the four equivalent pairs in these eight inequalities.

$p \leq 8$ $4p \leq 24$ $2p \leq 18$ $p - 2 \leq 6$ $p \leq 9$ $p + 4 \leq 14$ $3p \leq 18$ $2p \leq 20$

C Solving simple inequalities

- If we are given an inequality, we can add or subtract any number on both sides.
  For example,

$$x \leq 12$$ [add 1]
$$so \quad x + 1 \leq 13$$

$$n + 4 > 9$$ [subtract 4]
$$so \quad n > 5$$

- We can multiply or divide both sides of an inequality by the same **positive** number.
  For example,

$$\frac{x}{2} \leq 12$$ [multiply by 2]
$$so \quad x \leq 24$$

$$2n > 8$$ [divide by 2]
$$so \quad n > 4$$

- You can **solve** inequalities using the rules above.

  To solve is to find, in its simplest form, the set of all numbers that satisfy the inequality.
  This is sometimes called the **solution set**.
  For example,

$$2x + 17 \geq 25$$ [subtract 17]
$$2x \geq 8$$ [divide by 2]
$$x \geq 4$$

> Checking a few values in the solution set can help you spot mistakes.
> For example, when $x = 5$,
> $$2x + 17 = 2 \times 5 + 17$$
> $$= 27$$
> which **is** greater than or equal to 25.

We can show the solution set on a number line.

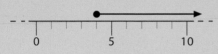

C1 (a) Solve the inequality $x + 4 > 6$.

(b) Show the solution set on a number line.

C2 Solve each of these inequalities.

(a) $n + 5 \leq 11$	**(b)** $n + 3 < 10$	**(c)** $n - 5 \geq 11$	**(d)** $n - 1 > 6$
(e) $2x \leq 12$	**(f)** $3x > 24$	**(g)** $\frac{x}{2} \geq 5$	**(h)** $\frac{x}{3} < 9$
(i) $2p \geq 7$	**(j)** $3p > {}^-6$	**(k)** $t + 3 < 2$	**(l)** $t - 4 \leq 0$

C3 (a) Solve the inequality $2x + 3 \leq 11$.

(b) Show the solution set on a number line.

(c) Write down three integers that satisfy the inequality.

C4 Solve each of these inequalities.

(a) $4r + 1 \geq 17$	**(b)** $2t - 1 \leq 13$	**(c)** $1 + 2f > 11$	**(d)** $3d - 2 \leq 10$
(e) $2n + 1 > 10$	**(f)** $4k - 3 \leq 7$	**(g)** $x + 9 < 5$	**(h)** $t - 1 \leq {}^-6$
(i) $6f + 1 > {}^-11$	**(j)** $5n + 11 \geq 1$	**(k)** $7y + 14 < 0$	**(l)** $2h - 6 \geq {}^-5$

C5 Multiply out the brackets in $2(x-3)$.
Use this to help you solve the inequality $2(x-3) \leq 14$.

C6 Solve these by first multiplying out any brackets.

    (a) $3(n+1) > 15$ **(b)** $2(x-5) \geq 1$ **(c)** $4(n+1) < 2$

C7 Find the largest possible integer value of x if   **(a)** $2(4x-1) < 11$ **(b)** $3(2x+1) < 20$

C8 **(a)** Solve the inequality $\frac{a}{2} + 2 \geq 8$.

    (b) Show the solution set on a number line.

C9 Solve each of these inequalities.

    (a) $\frac{a}{5} - 1 > 1$ **(b)** $\frac{s}{3} + 2 \leq 5$ **(c)** $\frac{m+1}{2} \geq 3$ **(d)** $\frac{p-5}{4} < 2$

D Unknown on both sides

When solving inequalities, sometimes the unknown is on both sides.

Examples

$7 + 3a < 25 + a$	[subtract a]
$7 + 2a < 25$	[subtract 7]
$2a < 18$	[divide by 2]
$a < 9$	

$10 + n < 4n - 5$	[add 5]
$15 + n < 4n$	[subtract n]
$15 < 3n$	[divide by 3]
$5 < n$	

or $n > 5$ We usually write the inequality with the letter on the left.

D1 Solve each of these.

    (a) $2x < x + 7$ **(b)** $7y \geq 5y + 2$ **(c)** $9w < 6w + 21$ **(d)** $4r - 12 \geq 3r$

D2 **(a)** Solve $5x + 7 > 3x + 19$ by first subtracting $3x$ from both sides.

    (b) Write down two integers in the solution set.

D3 Solve each of these inequalities.

    (a) $4s + 2 < 3s + 12$ **(b)** $7n + 1 \geq 3n + 29$ **(c)** $4x + 1 < 4 + x$

    (d) $5a - 3 \leq 4a + 1$ **(e)** $6b - 9 < 6 + b$ **(f)** $5z - 4 \leq 3z + 7$

    (g) $3y - 6 > 2y - 4$ **(h)** $5y + 7 \leq 2y + 1$ **(i)** $7t + 1 > 5t - 7$

D4 Solve $2x + 8 \geq 4x + 2$ by first subtracting $2x$ from each side.

D5 Solve each of these inequalities.

    (a) $6t + 11 > 10t + 3$ **(b)** $6n < 8n - 18$ **(c)** $b + 2 \geq 17 + 4b$

D6 Solve these by first multiplying out any brackets.

    (a) $4n > 3(n+3)$ **(b)** $3(n-1) < n + 6$ **(c)** $4(n-3) \geq 6n$

D7 By first multiplying both sides by 3, solve the inequality $\dfrac{n+2}{3} > n$.

D8 Copy and complete this working to solve $\dfrac{x-3}{5} \le x+1$.

$$\dfrac{x-3}{5} \le x+1$$
$$x - 3 \le 5(x + 1)$$

D9 Solve these.   (a) $\dfrac{x+6}{4} \le x$ (b) $\dfrac{x+5}{4} \le x-1$

D10 Solve the inequality $\dfrac{r+1}{3} \le r-2$.   Edexcel

D11 By first multiplying both sides by 15, solve $\dfrac{x+2}{3} > \dfrac{x+3}{5}$.

D12 Solve these.   (a) $\dfrac{n-2}{2} > \dfrac{n-1}{3}$ (b) $\dfrac{2n-3}{3} \ge \dfrac{2n-5}{4}$

E Multiplying or dividing by a negative number

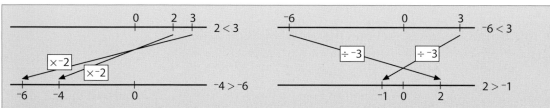

When we divide or multiply both sides of an inequality by a **negative** number, the inequality sign 'turns round'.

For example, **5** is the **largest** number that satisfies the inequality $^{-}2x \ge ^{-}10$.
Anything larger does not satisfy the inequality so the solution is $x \le 5$.

$$^{-}2x \ge ^{-}10$$
$$x \le 5$$
[divide both sides by $^{-}2$ and 'turn around' the sign]

E1 Solve each of these by multiplying or dividing by a negative number.

(a) $^{-}2x \le ^{-}8$ (b) $^{-}6t \ge 12$ (c) $^{-}4r < ^{-}12$ (d) $\dfrac{^{-}n}{2} > ^{-}7$

One strategy is to always aim to get a positive number in front of the unknown.
This avoids having to divide or multiply by a negative number.

Example

$$11 - 2b < b - 7 \quad \text{[add } 2b\text{]}$$
$$11 < 3b - 7 \quad \text{[add 7]}$$
$$18 < 3b \quad \text{[divide by 3]}$$
$$6 < b$$
$$\text{or} \quad b > 6$$

E2 Solve $6 < 10 - x$ by first adding x to both sides.

E3 Solve $2n + 3 \geq 13 - 3n$ by first adding $3n$ to both sides.

E4 Solve each of these.

(a) $3 > 7 - p$

(b) $7 \leq 13 - 2d$

(c) $2 + f < 20 - 2f$

(d) $6n - 2 \leq 18 - 2n$

(e) $22 - 5w \geq 2w + 1$

(f) $5 - z > 7 - 2z$

E5 Solve each of these.

(a) $2(n + 3) > 9 - n$

(b) $12 - 2m \leq 3(m + 1)$

(c) $5(k + 1) < 3(9 - 2k)$

E6 Solve each of these.

(a) $7 - 5t > 7t + 1$

(b) $4 - 5f \geq 4(1 - 2f)$

(c) $1 - 5p \leq 3(3 - p)$

E7 Solve these.

(a) $\dfrac{7 - n}{2} > 1$

(b) $\dfrac{10 - 3n}{4} \leq 1$

(c) $\dfrac{9 - n}{2} \geq n$

(d) $\dfrac{6 - 5n}{2} < 8$

(e) $\dfrac{5 - n}{3} \leq 1 - n$

(f) $\dfrac{2 - n}{4} < \dfrac{1 - n}{8}$

F Combined inequalities

To solve a combined inequality we can do the same thing to each part.

Example

$5 \leq 2x - 1 < 11$ [add 1 to each part]

$6 \leq 2x < 12$ [divide all parts by 2]

$3 \leq x < 6$

We can show the solution on a number line.

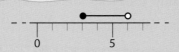

F1 (a) Solve $4 \leq x + 1 < 9$.

(b) Show your solution on a number line.

F2 (a) Solve $6 < 2x \leq 10$ and show your solution on a number line.

(b) Write down all the integers that satisfy this inequality.

F3 Solve these inequalities.

(a) $7 \leq x + 4 < 20$

(b) $0 < n - 2 < 7$

(c) $^-1 \leq x + 2 < 11$

(d) $12 \leq 3z < 24$

(e) $3 \leq \dfrac{n}{2} \leq 5$

(f) $^-8 \leq 4z < 10$

F4 Solve $10 \leq 3n + 1 \leq 25$ and show your solution on a number line.

F5 Solve these inequalities.

(a) $2 \leq 3x - 4 < 8$

(b) $4 < 3x + 1 \leq 16$

(c) $^-8 \leq 2x + 4 < 7$

F6 (a) Solve $9 \leq 2x + 1 < 21$.

  (b) List the values of x, where x is an **integer**, such that $9 \leq 2x + 1 < 21$.

F7 (a) Find the integer values of n which satisfy the inequality $7 < 5n < 34$.

  (b) Solve the inequality $5x - 2 < 18$.   OCR

F8 List the values of a, where a is an integer, such that $1 \leq 3a - 5 < 7$.

F9 (a) Solve these.   (i) $2x - 3 < 10$ (ii) $3 - 4x < 10$

  (b) Write down all the integers that satisfy both inequalities in part (a).

F10 Solve these inequalities.

  (a) $80 < 4(2x + 1) \leq 100$ (b) $^-2 < 2(x + 3) < 7$ (c) $0 \leq \dfrac{5x - 1}{2} \leq 7$

F11 Find the integer values of n which satisfy each of these inequalities.

  (a) $^-8 \leq 2(3n - 1) < 9$ (b) $^-1 < \frac{1}{2}(4 + n) < 1$

Test yourself

T1 List all the integers, n, such that   (a) $^-2 < n \leq 5$ (b) $n^2 \leq 4$

T2 Solve each of these inequalities.

  (a) $3x + 8 \geq 29$ (b) $4x - 3 < 9$ (c) $2x - 7 > 2$ (d) $\dfrac{x}{2} + 5 \leq 8$

T3 Solve $3x + 19 > 4$.   OCR

T4 Solve these inequalities and show each solution set on a number line.

  (a) $12n - 13 \leq 7n + 2$ (b) $2(6 + n) > 11n - 6$ (c) $7n + 2 < 12n - 1$

T5 Solve these inequalities.   (a) $5 - 2h \leq 3h$ (b) $3(x + 3) > 2(2 - x)$

T6 (a) (i) Solve the inequality $5x - 7 < 2x - 1$.

      (ii) On a copy of this number line, represent the solution set to part (i).

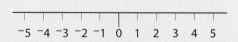

  n is an integer such that $^-4 \leq 2n < 3$.

  (b) Write down the possible values of n.   Edexcel

T7 (a) Solve the inequality $2x + 3 \geq 1$.

  (b) Write down the inequality shown by the following diagram.

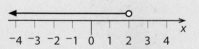

  (c) Write down all the integers that satisfy both inequalities shown in parts (a) and (b).   AQA

T8 Solve these inequalities.   (a) $9 < 2x - 1 < 15$ (b) $^-4 \leq 3x + 2 < 5$

29 Simultaneous equations

You should know how to

- draw the graph of a straight line given its equation
- rearrange a simple formula

This work will help you

- solve simultaneous equations using the algebraic methods of elimination and substitution
- solve problems by forming and solving simultaneous equations
- interpret the solution of simultaneous equations as the point of intersection of two graphs

A Puzzles involving two statements

A1 All weights in these balance pictures are in grams.

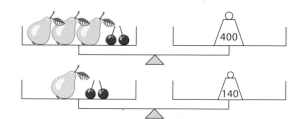

- **(a)** Find the weight of a pear.
- **(b)** What is the weight of a cherry?

A2 In a café, three coffees and a biscuit cost £4.10.
Three coffees and four biscuits cost £5.60.
How much is a biscuit and how much is a coffee?

A3 In this puzzle, each different symbol stands for a number.
What does each symbol stand for?

$$\bigstar + \text{✎} + \bigstar + \text{✎} + \text{✎} = 22$$
$$\text{✎} + \bigstar + \heartsuit + \heartsuit + \heartsuit = 39$$
$$\text{✎} + \bigstar + \bigstar = 14$$

A4 All weights in these balance pictures are in grams.

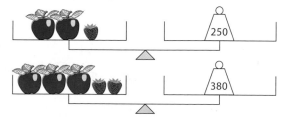

- **(a)** Explain how you can find the weight of 4 apples and 2 strawberries.
- **(b)** Find the weight of an apple.
- **(c)** What is the weight of a strawberry?

A5 The cost of 4 cups of coffee and a bun is £6.90.
The cost of 6 cups of coffee and 3 buns is £11.70.

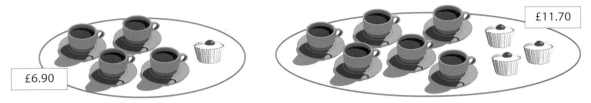

£11.70

£6.90

How much is a coffee and how much is a bun?

A6 Jupiter chocolate bars are made in two sizes, regular and king-size.
2 regular bars and 5 king-size bars weigh 760 g altogether.
1 regular bar and 7 king-size bars weigh 920 g altogether.

(a) How much does a king-size bar weigh?

(b) How much does a regular bar weigh?

A7 The cost of 3 sodas and 2 burgers is £4.21.
The cost of 2 sodas and 5 burgers is £6.40.

£6.40

£4.21

(a) Find the missing number in the following:
'The cost of 6 sodas and … burgers is £8.42.'

(b) Find the cost of 6 sodas and 15 burgers.

(c) How much is a burger and how much is a soda?

A8 In this puzzle, each different symbol stands for a number.

$$\bigstar + \bigstar + \clubsuit + \clubsuit + \clubsuit = 31$$
$$\bigstar + \bigstar + \bigstar + \bigstar + \bigstar + \clubsuit + \clubsuit + \clubsuit + \clubsuit = 46$$

What does each symbol stand for?

A9 Jamie has a pile of gold and silver coins.
The weight of 3 gold coins and 8 silver coins is 100 grams.
The weight of 5 gold coins and 3 silver coins is 84 grams.

Find the weight of a gold coin.

B Solving equations 1

The equation $\boxed{4a + 2b = 460}$ is true for many pairs of values of a and b.

The equation $\boxed{a + 2b = 220}$ is also true for many pairs of values of a and b.

However, only one pair of values can fit both of these equations.
Finding these values is called solving a pair of **simultaneous equations**.

If we subtract the equations, the terms involving b on
the left-hand side will 'disappear'.

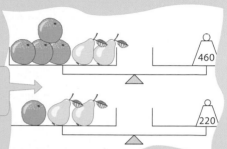

$$4a + 2b = 460$$
$$\underline{a + 2b = 220}$$
$$3a = 240$$
Subtract

> You can think of these equations as shorthand for a balance problem.

so $a = 80$

To find the value of b, substitute a in one equation.
Choosing the second equation gives

$$80 + 2b = 220$$
$$2b = 140$$
$$b = 70$$

So the solution is $a = 80$, $b = 70$.

The solution fits both pairs of equations so substitute in the other equation to check:
$4a + 2b = 4 \times 80 + 2 \times 70 = 460$ ✓

B1 Solve the following pairs of simultaneous equations to find the values of a and b.

(a) $5a + b = 21$
     $3a + b = 13$

(b) $6a + 3b = 21$
     $4a + 3b = 19$

(c) $3a + 2b = 10$
     $4a + 2b = 12$

(d) $a + 7b = 24$
     $a + 3b = 12$

(e) $2a + b = 27$
     $2a + 6b = 62$

(f) $3a + 8b = 79$
     $3a + 2b = 31$

B2 Solve the following pairs of simultaneous equations.

(a) $2c + 3d = 10$
     $2c + 2d = 7$

(b) $3h + 4k = 12$
     $3h + 2k = 9$

(c) $4p + 2q = 9$
     $p + 2q = 6$

B3 Solve the following pairs of simultaneous equations.

(a) $4a + b = 7$
     $2a + b = 3$

(b) $5p + 2q = 18$
     $p + 2q = 2$

(c) $4x + 2y = 12$
     $4x + y = 2$

(d) $5a + b = 2$
     $3a + b = 4$

(e) $5x + 3y = 2$
     $2x + 3y = 8$

(f) $3k + h = 9$
     $3k + 4h = 0$

You often need to multiply both sides of one or both equations before you can eliminate one of the terms in each equation.

Examples

Solve this pair of simultaneous equations.

(A) $2x + y = 17$
(B) $3x + 4y = 28$

If we multiply both sides of equation (A) by 4, the coefficients of y will be the same size.

$$(A) \times 4 \quad 8x + 4y = 68$$
$$(B) \qquad\quad 3x + 4y = 28$$
$$\text{Subtract}$$
$$5x = 40$$
$$\text{so} \quad x = 8$$

Substitute in equation (A) to give

$$16 + y = 17$$
$$y = 1$$

So the solution is $x = 8$, $y = 1$.

Substitute in equation (B) to check:
$3x + 4y = 3 \times 8 + 4 \times 1 = 28$ ✓

Solve this pair of simultaneous equations.

(A) $5x + 11y = 3$
(B) $2x + 3y = 4$

If we multiply both sides of equation (A) by 2 and both sides of equation (B) by 5, the coefficients of x will be the same size.

$$(A) \times 2 \quad 10x + 22y = 6$$
$$(B) \times 5 \quad 10x + 15y = 20$$
$$\text{Subtract}$$
$$7y = {}^-14$$
$$\text{so} \quad y = {}^-2$$

Substitute in equation (B) to give

$$2x - 6 = 4$$
$$2x = 10$$
$$\text{so} \quad x = 5$$

So the solution is $x = 5$, $y = {}^-2$.

Substitute in equation (A) to check:
$5x + 11y = 5 \times 5 + 11 \times {}^-2 = 3$ ✓

B4 Here is a pair of equations.

$$11x + 4y = 42$$
$$3x + 2y = 16$$

(a) Multiply both sides of the second equation by 2.

(b) Find the values of x and y.

B5 Solve the following pairs of simultaneous equations.

(a) $p + 3q = 12$
$3p + 2q = 22$

(b) $3m + 2n = 10$
$7m + 6n = 24$

(c) $2c + 9d = 1$
$5c + 3d = 22$

B6 Here is a pair of equations.

$$2m + 5n = 9$$
$$3m + 2n = 8$$

(a) Multiply both sides of the first equation by 3.

(b) Multiply both sides of the second equation by 2.

(c) Find the values of m and n.

B7 Solve each pair of simultaneous equations.

(a) $3p + 7q = 19$
$4p + 2q = 18$

(b) $2v + 3w = 8$
$3v + 4w = 12$

(c) $2m + 9n = 11$
$5m + 2n = 7$

(d) $7k + 3h = 37$
$2k + 5h = 23$

(e) $5y + 3x = 31$
$5x + 3y = 25$

(f) $7a + 2b = 23$
$11b + 2a = 17$

B8 Solve each pair of simultaneous equations.

(a) $2v + w = 1$
$3v + 5w = 19$

(b) $3p + 5q = 1$
$7p + 2q = 12$

(c) $5m + 2n = 6$
$3n + 10m = 4$

c Forming and solving equations

C1 Three chocolate bars and four chocolate eggs weigh 465 grams.
Three chocolate bars and two chocolate eggs weigh 315 grams.

(a) Which of these pairs of equations is correct for the chocolate bars and eggs?

A
$3b + 2e = 465$
$3b + 4e = 315$

B
$b + 4e = 465$
$b + 2e = 315$

C
$3b + 4e = 465$
$3b + 2e = 315$

(b) Solve the correct pair of simultaneous equations to find the values of b and e.

C2 The weight of a blue brick is b grams.
The weight of a red brick is r grams.

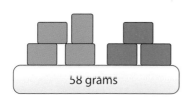
58 grams

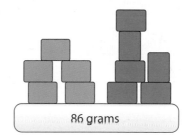
86 grams

4 blue bricks and 3 red bricks weigh 58 grams.
5 blue bricks and 6 red bricks weigh 86 grams.

(a) (i) Write an equation for the first diagram.

(ii) Write an equation for the second diagram.

(b) Find the weight of a blue brick and the weight of a red brick.

(c) What is the total weight of 2 blue bricks and 5 red bricks?

C3 Julie and Rosa buy some candy bars and ice creams.

Julie spends 90p on two ice creams and a candy bar.
Rosa spends 95p on one ice cream and three candy bars.

With the cost of an ice cream p pence and the cost of a candy bar q pence,
form two equations and solve them to find the cost of a candy bar.

C4 A discount shop is selling tapes and CDs.
The tapes are all at one price.
The CDs are all at another price.

Jane buys three CDs and a tape and pays £8.92.
Paul buys two CDs and five tapes and pays £12.23.

How much does one CD cost?
Show your equations and working clearly.

OCR

C5 Three geese and five golden eggs weigh 14 kg.
Two geese and seven golden eggs weigh 13 kg.
Find the weight of a golden egg and the weight of a goose.

C6 Two people were in front of me in the queue for ice cream.
The man bought 5 cones and 7 tubs for £6.70.
The woman bought 3 cones and 5 tubs for £4.50.
How much will it cost me for my cone?

C7 Some hens and a herd of cows are in a field.
Between them they have 50 heads and 180 legs.
How many cows and how many hens are in the field?

C8 In a pet shop there are some mice and some budgies.
Altogether they have 27 heads and 70 legs.
How many mice and how many budgies are there?

C9 A bag contains a mixture of 5p coins and 1p coins.
There are 17 coins in the bag and their total value is 61p.
How many of each type of coin are there?

C10 A drinks machine takes 20p and 50p coins.
In the machine, there are 31 coins altogether.
They are worth £12.20.
How many of each type of coin are there?

D Solving equations 2

If one of a pair of simultaneous equations involves subtraction, it is often simpler to **add** the equations.

Example

Solve this pair of simultaneous equations.   (A) $4x + 3y = 27$
(B) $x - 3y = 3$

If we add the equations, the y-terms will be eliminated.

$$\begin{array}{ll}
\text{(A)} & 4x + 3y = 27 \\
\text{(B)} & \underline{x - 3y = 3} \quad \text{Add} \\
& 5x = 30
\end{array}$$

so $x = 6$

Substitute in equation (A) to give $24 + 3y = 27$
$$3y = 3$$
$$y = 1$$

So the solution is $x = 6$, $y = 1$

Substitute in equation (B) to check: $x - 3y = 6 - 3 \times 1 = 3$ ✓

D1 Solve each pair of simultaneous equations.

(a) $3p + q = 13$
     $2p - q = 2$

(b) $2c + d = 4$
     $2c - d = 2$

(c) $h - 4k = 1$
     $h + 4k = 21$

D2 Ahmet and Baljeet each think of a number.

Adding twice Baljeet's number to Ahmet's gives 11.
Subtracting twice Baljeet's number from Ahmet's gives 3.

Let Ahmet's number be a.
Let Baljeet's number be b.

Form two equations and solve them to find the values of a and b.

D3 Solve each pair of simultaneous equations.

(a) $3p + 2q = 10$
     $4p - 2q = 18$

(b) $2a + 3b = 2$
     $4a - 3b = 22$

(c) $3c - 4d = 17$
     $4d + c = 3$

D4 The sum of two numbers is 36 and the difference between them is 9.
If x is the smaller number and y is the larger, find x and y.

D5 Carol is heavier than her daughter.
The sum of their weights is 78 kg.
The difference between their weights is 50 kg.
How much does Carol weigh?

As before, you often need to multiply both sides of one or both equations before you can eliminate one of the terms in each equation by adding.

Example

Solve this pair of simultaneous equations.   (A) $2x - 3y = 5$
                                               (B) $5x + 2y = 22$

Multiply both sides of equation (A) by 2 and both sides of equation (B) by 3 so that the coefficients of y will be the same size.

$$(A) \times 2 \qquad 4x - 6y = 10$$
$$(B) \times 3 \qquad \underline{15x + 6y = 66} \qquad \text{Add}$$
$$19x = 76$$
$$\text{so} \qquad x = 4$$

Substitute in equation (B) to give $20 + 2y = 22$
$$2y = 2$$
$$\text{so} \qquad y = 1$$

So the solution is $x = 4$, $y = 1$

Substitute in equation (A) to check: $2x - 3y = 2 \times 4 - 3 \times 1 = 5$ ✓

D6 Here is a pair of equations.
$$7a - 6b = 9$$
$$3a + 2b = 13$$

(a) Multiply both sides of the second equation by 3.

(b) Find the values of a and b.

D7 Solve each pair of simultaneous equations.

(a) $3v + w = 18$ (b) $p + 3q = 29$ (c) $m + 2n = 4$
     $2v - 3w = 1$ $2p - q = 23$ $3m - 4n = 7$

(d) $3k - 2h = 8$ (e) $2x + y = 9$ (f) $a + 8b = {}^-5$
     $k + 4h = 5$ $x - 2y = 7$ $3a - 4b = 13$

D8 Here is a pair of equations.
$$x - 2y = 2$$
$$2x + 5y = 22$$

(a) Multiply both sides of the first equation by 5 and multiply both sides of the second equation by 2.

(b) Find the values of x and y.

D9 Solve each pair of simultaneous equations.

(a) $p + 2q = 3$
$5p - 3q = 2$

(b) $5a - 2b = 11$
$3a + 5b = 19$

(c) $5c - 4d = 19$
$2c + 3d = 3$

(d) $3y + 2x = 5$
$3x - 2y = 14$

(e) $4h - 5k = {}^-6$
$h + 2k = 5$

(f) $5n + 3m = 24$
$m - 3n = 1$

If both equations involve subtraction, you need to be careful with signs.

Example

Solve this pair of simultaneous equations.
(A) $4x - 2y = 18$
(B) $5x - 3y = 23$

Multiply both sides of equation (A) by 5 and both sides of equation (B) by 4 so that the coefficients of x will be the same size.

(A)$\times 5$ $20x - 10y = 90$
(B)$\times 4$ $20x - 12y = 92$
         $2y = {}^-2$ Subtract

Be careful.
${}^-10y - ({}^-12y)$
$= {}^-10y + 12y$
$= 2y$

so $y = {}^-1$

Substitute in equation (A) to give $4x + 2 = 18$
           $4x = 16$
so $x = 4$

So the solution is $x = 4$, $y = {}^-1$

Substitute in equation (B) to check: $5x - 3y = 5 \times 4 - 3 \times {}^-1 = 20 - ({}^-3) = 23$ ✓

D10 Solve each pair of simultaneous equations.

(a) $5p - 2q = 21$
$2p - 3q = 4$

(b) $5a - 2b = 8$
$3a - 5b = 1$

(c) $4x - y = 19$
$3x - 2y = 18$

D11 Here is a pair of equations.

$5x - 3y = 24$
$3x - 4y = 10$

(a) (i) Multiply both sides of the first equation by 3 and both sides of the second by 5.

(ii) Subtract to find the value of y and then substitute to find the value of x.

(b) (i) Multiply both sides of the first equation by 4 and both sides of the second by 3.

(ii) Subtract to find the value of x and then substitute to find the value of y.

(c) Which method did you find easier?

D12 Solve each pair of simultaneous equations.

(a) $3c - 4d = 5$
$2c - 3d = 3$

(b) $y - 2x = 8$
$3y - 5x = 22$

(c) $3a - 4b = 21$
$4a - 3b = 14$

D13 (a) Rearrange the equation $3x = 4 - 2y$ into the form $ax + by = c$.

(b) Use your rearrangement to solve the simultaneous equations
$$3x = 4 - 2y$$
$$5x - 2y = 12$$

D14 Solve each pair of simultaneous equations.

(a) $x + y = 14$
$x = 6 + y$

(b) $9y = 49 - 5x$
$5x - 2y = 38$

(c) $2x - 3y = 29$
$5x = 2y + 56$

E Substitution

Sometimes the most efficient way to solve a pair of simultaneous equations is to **substitute** an expression for one unknown in terms of the other.

Example

Solve this pair of simultaneous equations.

(A) $3y + 2x = 0$
(B) $y = \frac{1}{3}x - 2$

Substitute the expression for y given by the second equation into the first equation.
$$3y + 2x = 0$$
$$3\left(\frac{1}{3}x - 2\right) + 2x = 0$$
$$x - 6 + 2x = 0$$
$$3x - 6 = 0$$
$$x = 2$$

Leave this value as a fraction as it is the exact solution.

Substitute in equation (B) to give $y = \frac{1}{3} \times 2 - 2 = \frac{-4}{3}$

So the solution is $x = 2$, $y = \frac{-4}{3}$

Substitute in equation (A) to check: $3y + 2x = 3 \times \frac{-4}{3} + 2 \times 2 = -4 + 4 = 0$ ✓

E1 Solve each pair of simultaneous equations using substitution.

(a) $y = 2x$
$y + 8x = 20$

(b) $p = 5q$
$2p - 9q = 2$

(c) $6w - 5v = 18$
$w = \frac{1}{3}v$

(d) $n = m + 5$
$3n + 11m = 57$

(e) $4j - k = 0$
$j = \frac{1}{2}k - 3$

(f) $x + 6y = 3$
$y = \frac{1}{3}x - 2$

(g) $h = 2g + 1$
$5g - 3h = 2$

(h) $y = 5x - 4$
$y + x = 1$

(i) $y = 1 - 2x$
$x - 3y = 1$

E2 Here is a pair of equations.
$$p + q = 220$$
$$\frac{p}{q} = 19$$

(a) Rearrange the second equation to make p the subject.

(b) Now solve the simultaneous equations using substitution.

There is more than one way to solve any pair of simultaneous equations.
Sometimes it is clear which way is the most straightforward but not always.

Example

Solve this pair of simultaneous equations.

(A) $4x + 7y = 6$
(B) $y - 3x = 8$

Method 1

Rearrange equation (B) to make y the subject and then substitute into equation (A).

Rearrange (B)
$$y - 3x = 8$$
so $$y = 3x + 8$$

Substitute in (A):
$$4x + 7(3x + 8) = 6$$
$$4x + 21x + 56 = 6$$
$$25x + 56 = 6$$
$$25x = {}^-50$$
$$x = {}^-2$$

You then can complete each solution by substituting to find the value of y or x.

Method 2

Multiply both sides of equation (B) by 7 and then subtract.

(A) $\qquad$ $4x + 7y = 6$
(B)$\times 7$ $\qquad$ $\underline{7y - 21x = 56}$ $\quad$ Subtract
$\qquad\qquad\qquad$ $25x = {}^-50$
$\qquad\qquad\qquad\qquad$ $x = {}^-2$

Method 3

Multiply both sides of equation (A) by 3, both sides of (B) by 4 and then add.

(A)$\times 3$ $\quad$ $12x + 21y = 18$
(B)$\times 4$ $\quad$ $\underline{4y - 12x = 32}$ $\quad$ Add
$\qquad\qquad\quad$ $25y = 50$
$\qquad\qquad\qquad$ $y = 2$

*E3 Solve each pair of simultaneous equations choosing your own method.
Where appropriate, give values as fractions.

(a) $h = 3g + 1$
$5g - 2h = 3$

(b) $5b - 3a = 8$
$20 - 9b = 3a$

(c) $y - 2x = 0$
$3y = 10x - 14$

(d) $d = 4c - 1$
$d + 5c = 11$

(e) $2f - 10e = {}^-1$
$2f + 5e = 5$

(f) $\frac{1}{4}h + 5g = 15$
$3h + 2g = 35$

(g) $\frac{p}{q} = 10$
$5q + p = 3$

(h) $\frac{3a + b}{4} = 5$
$b = 35 - 6a$

(i) $\frac{3p - 2q}{5} = 3$
$2p = 3(q + 5)$

F Graphs and simultaneous equations

Ⓐ $x + 2y = 9$ $\qquad$ Ⓑ $2x + 2y = 10$ $\qquad$ Ⓒ $x + y = 5$ $\qquad$ Ⓓ $x + y = 2$

- Use the equations above to form pairs of simultaneous equations.
  What happens when you try to solve them?

- On the same pair of axes, draw the graphs for the equations above.
  Do the graphs explain what happened when you tried to solve the equations?

The solution to any pair of simultaneous equations fits both equations.

It follows that the solution gives the coordinates of the point of intersection of their graphs. Conversely, the coordinates of the point of intersection of their graphs gives the solution.

For example, the graphs shown are for this pair of equations.

$$10y + 7x = 64$$
$$y = 2x + 1$$

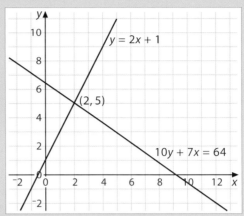

The point of intersection is $(2, 5)$ and the solution is $x = 2$, $y = 5$.

A pair of simultaneous linear equations can have ...

one solution, ...

$$x + y = 6$$
$$2x + y = 10$$

no solution, ...

$$2x + y = 6$$
$$4x + 2y = 15$$

or **infinitely many** solutions.

$$2x + y = 6$$
$$4x + 2y = 12$$

F1 (a) Where do the lines with equations $3x + 4y = 22$ and $x + 2y = 2$ intersect?

(b) Where do the lines with equations $x + 2y = 6$ and $y - x = 2$ intersect?

F2 The lines with equations $y = 2x + 5$ and $y = 3x - 2$ intersect.

(a) Explain why the x-coordinate of the point of intersection can be found by solving the equation $2x + 5 = 3x - 2$.

(b) Find the coordinates of the point of intersection.

F3 Where do the lines with equations $y = 3x - 2$ and $y = 1 - 4x$ intersect?

F4 Show that there is no solution to each of these pairs of simultaneous equations.

(a) $y = 2x + 4$
     $y = 2x - 1$

(b) $2y + 4x = 9$
     $y + 2x = 1$

(c) $y = \frac{1}{3}x - 1$
     $3y - x = 4$

F5 Here is a pair of simultaneous equations.

$y = 3 + 2x$
$2y - 4x = 6$

(a) Show that there are infinitely many solutions to this pair of simultaneous equations.

(b) Find three of these solutions.

F6 For each graph below,

(i) estimate the coordinates of the point of intersection

(ii) use algebra to find the exact coordinates

(a)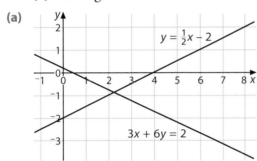

(b)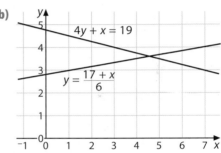

G Mixed questions

G1 Solve each pair of simultaneous equations.

(a) $3a - b = 12$
     $4a + 2b = 6$

(b) $3e + 2f = {}^-8$
     $4e + 5f = 1$

(c) $4n + 5m = 12$
     $9m - 3n = 42$

(d) $2(p - q) = 6$
     $3p + 7q = 4$

(e) $2r - 3s = 0$
     $s = 2 - r$

(f) $u = 5t + 6$
     $u = 3t - 10$

Solve each of the following problems by forming and solving a pair of simultaneous equations.

G2 Two people were in front of me in the queue at the theatre.
The man bought 2 tubs of ice cream and 3 programmes for £8.40.
The woman bought 5 tubs of ice cream and 2 programmes for £11.10.
How much will it cost me for my tub of ice cream?

G3 If you take Poppy's age away from Daniel's age you get 7.
If you take Poppy's age away from three times Daniel's you get 40.
How old is Daniel?

G4 Lorna has 5p stamps and 6p stamps.
She sticks 11 stamps on a parcel, with a total value of 63p.
How many of each type of stamp does she use?

G5 Find the weight of an apple and the weight of a strawberry.
(The weights are in grams.)

G6 The difference between two numbers is 40.
The result of dividing the larger number by the smaller is 6.
What are the numbers?

G7 A line has gradient 2 and cuts the y-axis at $(0, 1)$.
Another line has equation $9y = 17x - 9$.

  (a) Without drawing them, show that the two lines are not parallel.

  (b) What is the point of intersection of these two lines?

G8 A fraction is equivalent to $\frac{1}{3}$.
The sum of the numerator and the denominator is 36.
Find the fraction.

G9 At what point do the lines with equations $3y + 2x = 7$ and $y = \dfrac{13 + 2x}{2}$ intersect?

G10 Rory has some 2-litre bottles of lemonade.
Sarah has some 3-litre bottles of lemonade.
Altogether they have 27 litres.
Rory has 6 bottles more than Sarah.
How many bottles does each person have?

G11 A box contains £110 in £2 coins and £5 notes.
There are three times as many coins as there are notes.
How many coins are there?

*G12 In 5 years time a dog will be as old as his owner was 3 years ago.
Now, the sum of their ages is 17 years. How old is the dog now?

*G13 A fraction is equivalent to $\frac{2}{7}$.
Increasing both the numerator and denominator by 1 gives a fraction equivalent to $\frac{3}{10}$.
Find both fractions.

*G14 A motorist drives at one speed for $2\frac{1}{2}$ hours and at a different speed for $1\frac{1}{2}$ hours.
She drives 190 kilometres in total.
If she had driven at the first speed for 3 hours and the second speed for 1 hour
she would have travelled 180 kilometres.
What was the faster of the two speeds?

*G15 In seven years time a father will be three times as old as his son.
Three years ago he was five times as old as his son.
How old is each person now?

*G16
> A ship is twice as old as its boilers were when the ship was as old as its boilers are.

The ship is now 40 years old.
How old are its boilers?

Test yourself

T1 Solve the simultaneous equations.
$$4p + q = 22$$
$$3p + 5q = 25$$

T2 Solve $x + 2y = 4$
$$3x - 4y = 7$$

T3 Solve the simultaneous equations.
$$4x + 3y = 14$$
$$2x + y = 5$$

You must show your working.
Do not use trial and improvement.

AQA

T4 Solve $2x - 3y = 11$
$$5x + 2y = 18$$

Edexcel

T5 Solve the simultaneous equations.
$$2x + 3y = {}^-3$$
$$3x - 2y = 28$$

Edexcel

T6 Solve the simultaneous equations
$$5x + 3y = 13$$
$$3x + 5y = 3$$

You must show your working.
Do not use trial and improvement.

AQA

T7 Solve the simultaneous equations.
$$6x - 2y = 33$$
$$4x + 3y = 9$$

Edexcel

T8 A goose lays gold and silver eggs.
A gold egg weighs three times as much as a silver egg.

One day she lays 9 gold and 5 silver eggs.
Their total weight is 1200 grams.

How heavy is a gold egg?

29 Simultaneous equations   295

A4 (a) Find sin 28° on your calculator.

Use this result to find the lengths of the opposite sides here (to 1 d.p.).

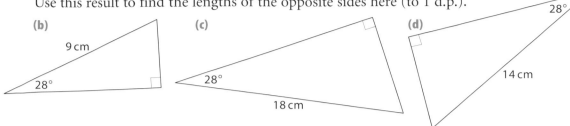

(b)

9 cm

28°

(c)

28°

18 cm

(d)

28°

14 cm

A5 For each of these, state the letter for the opposite side, then use sine on your calculator to find its length. Give your answers to 1 d.p.

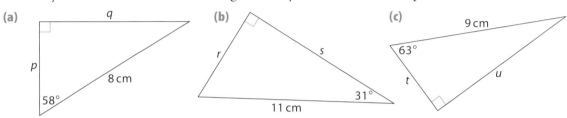

(a)

q

p

8 cm

58°

(b)

r

s

11 cm

(c)

9 cm

63°

t

u

31°

A6 Go back to your drawing experiment.

Check that the base (adjacent side) for the 10° angle is about 9.8 cm.

Measure the adjacent side for each other triangle and record your results in a table like the one below.

10°

9.8 cm

Angle	Hypotenuse	×?	Adjacent side
10°	10 cm		9.8 cm
20°	10 cm		
30°	10 cm		
40°	10 cm		

Work out the numbers that go in here and write them in your table.

Each multiplier in your table is called the **cosine** of its angle ('cos', for short).

So cos 10° = 0.98 to a degree of accuracy possible from a drawing.

For any acute angle *a*, hypotenuse ─│×cos *a*│→ adjacent side

hyp

a

adj

A7 Use the cos function on your calculator to check the multipliers in your table in A6.

A8 (a) Find $\cos 35°$ on your calculator.

Use this result to find the missing lengths here (to 1 d.p.).

(b)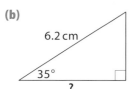

(c)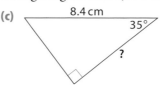

(d)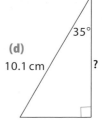

A9 (a) Find $\cos 67°$ on your calculator.

Use this result to find the lengths of the adjacent sides here (to 1 d.p.).

(b)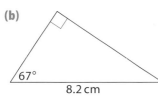

(c)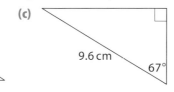

(d)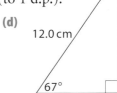

A10 For each of these, state the letter for the adjacent side, then use cosine on your calculator to find its length. Give your answers to 1 d.p.

(a)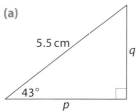

(b)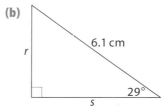

(c)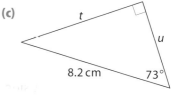

Summary

Like the tangent, the sine and cosine are **trigonometric** functions of an angle.

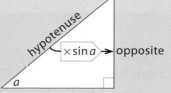

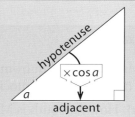

A11 For each of these problems,

   (i) decide whether the opposite side or the adjacent side is required

   (ii) choose the correct calculation from one of the boxes

   (iii) do the calculation as a key sequence on your calculator
      (calculators vary: make sure you know what yours requires)

$25 \times \sin 32°$
$25 \times \cos 32°$
$32 \times \sin 25°$
$32 \times \cos 25°$

(a)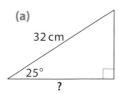

(b)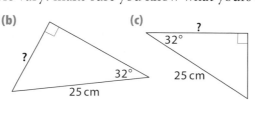

(c)

(d)

B Finding the hypotenuse from another side and an angle

You know how to use the sine as a multiplier.

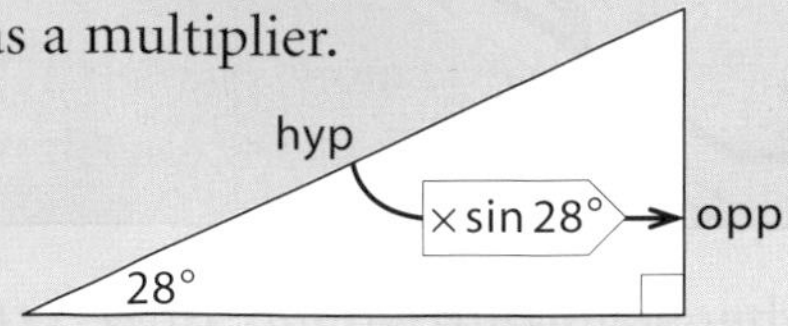

hyp
×sin 28° → opp
28°

So how do you find the length of the hypotenuse here?

?
?
7 cm
28°

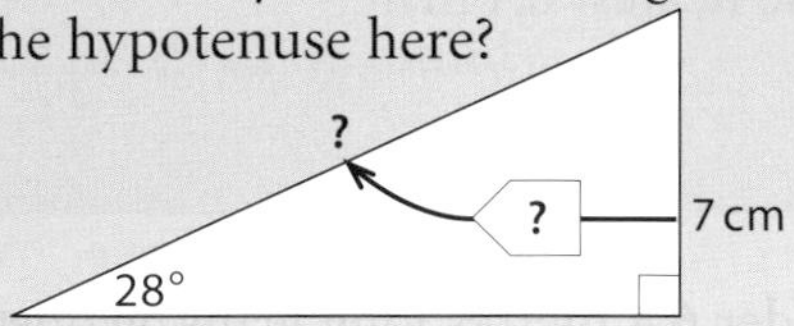

B1 Find the length of the hypotenuse in each of these triangles, to 1 d.p. (Check that you are using the right key sequence for your calculator.) Remember that the hypotenuse is the **longest** side of a right-angled triangle.

(a)
?
5.0 cm
64°

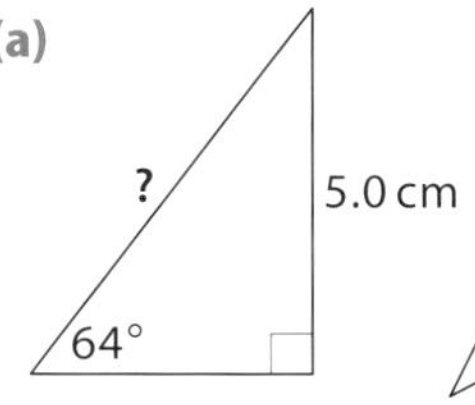

(b)
6.0 cm
40°
?

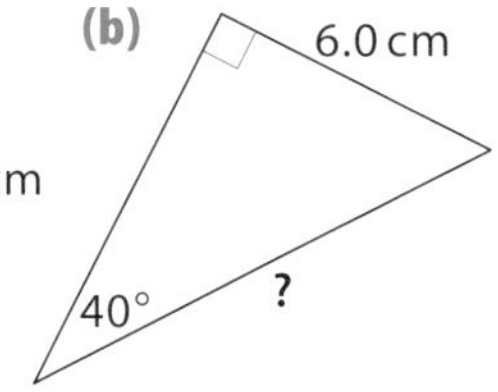

B2 Find the length of each hypotenuse, to 1 d.p.

(a)
7.1 cm
?
50°

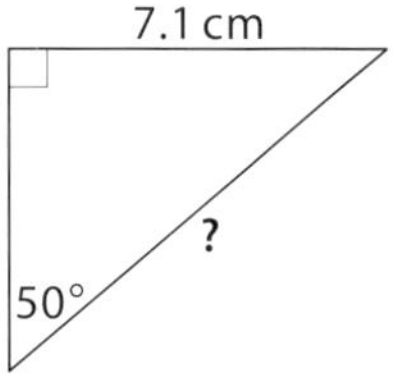

(b)
18°
2.6 cm
?

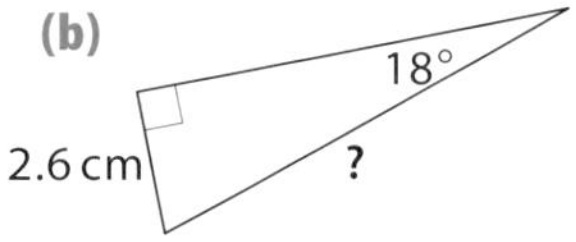

(c)
14.6 cm
66°
?

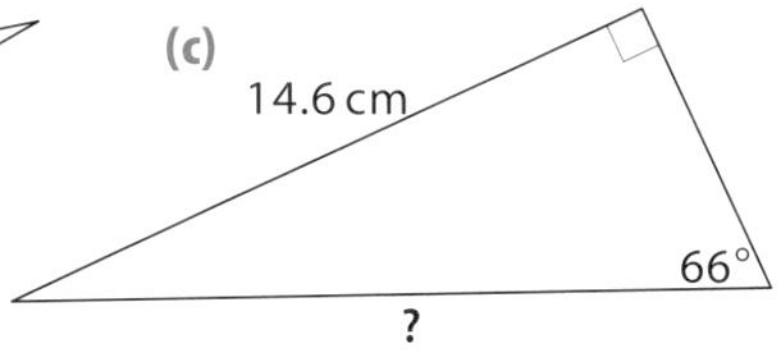

You also know how to use the cosine as a multiplier.

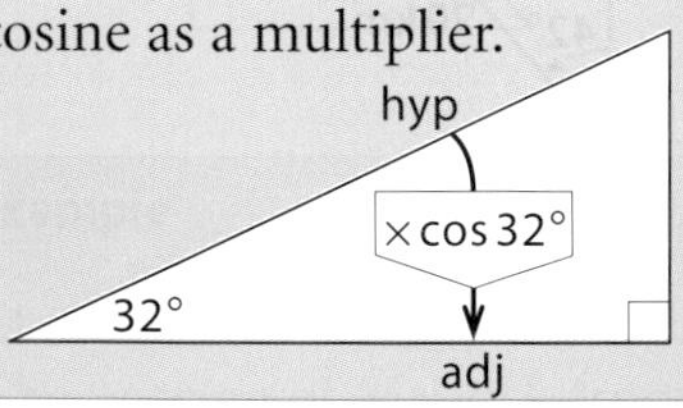

hyp
×cos 32°
32°
adj

So how do you find the length of the hypotenuse here?

?
?
32°
11 cm

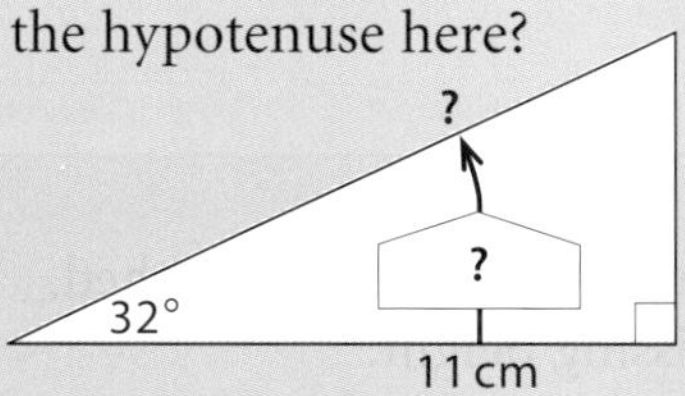

B3 Find the length of the hypotenuse in each of these triangles. Give your answers to 1 d.p.

(a)
?
59°
7.0 cm

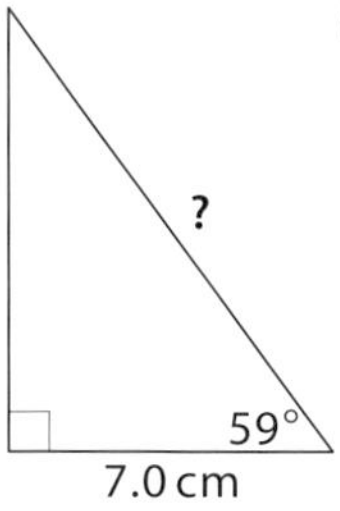

(b)
10.2 cm
24°
?

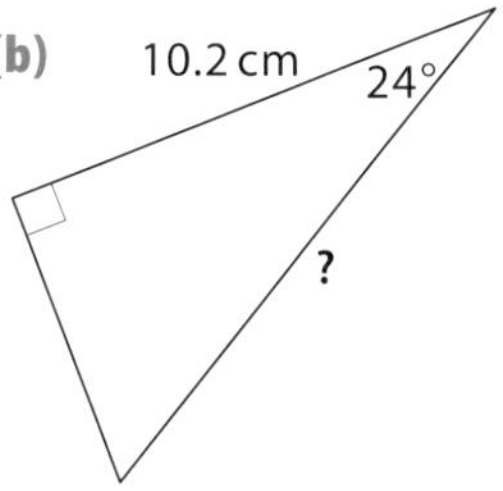

B4 Find the length of each hypotenuse, to 1 d.p.

(a)
35°
7.0 cm

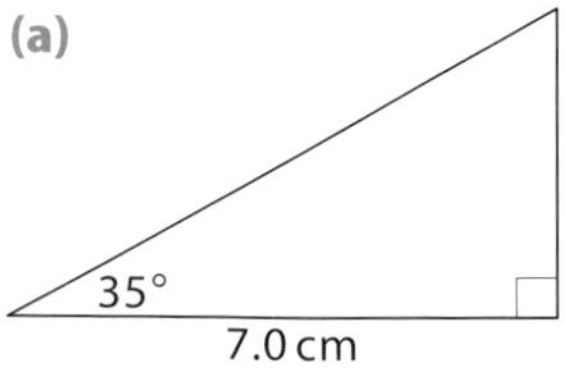

(b)
4.0 cm
64°

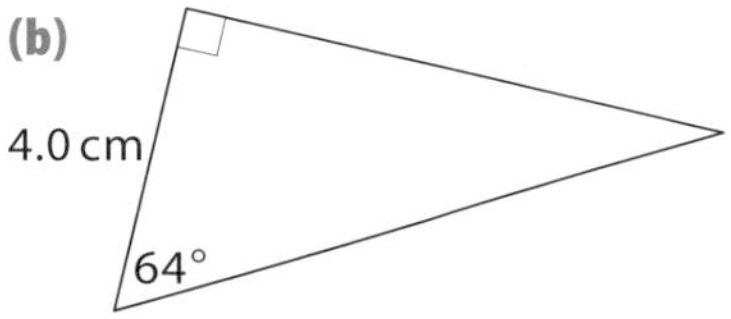

(c)
7.5 cm
32°

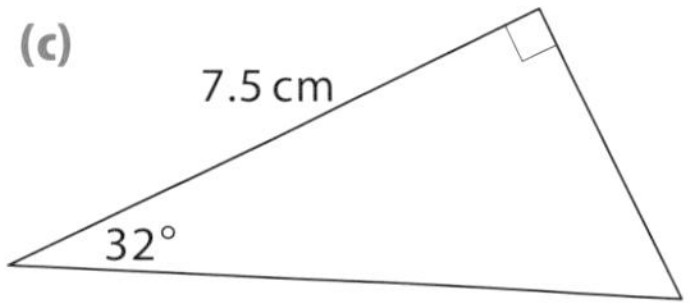

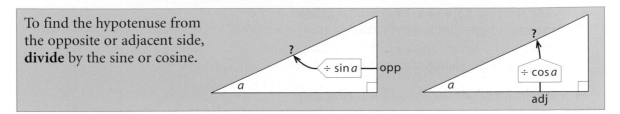

To find the hypotenuse from the opposite or adjacent side, **divide** by the sine or cosine.

÷ sin a — opp

÷ cos a

adj

B5 Find the length of the hypotenuse in each of these triangles.
Decide carefully whether to use sine or cosine.
Give your answers to 1 d.p.

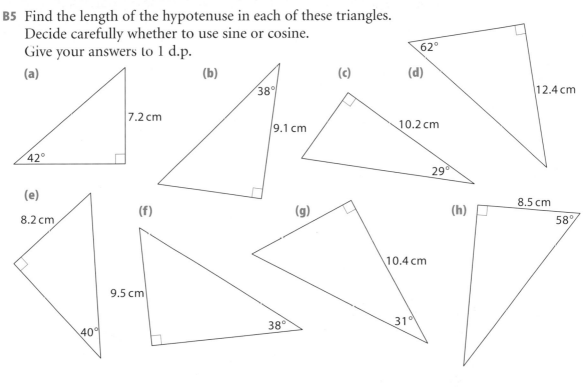

(a) 7.2 cm 42°

(b) 38° 9.1 cm

(c) 10.2 cm

(d) 62° 12.4 cm 29°

(e) 8.2 cm 40°

(f) 9.5 cm 38°

(g) 10.4 cm 31°

(h) 8.5 cm 58°

Example

Find the length up the ramp.

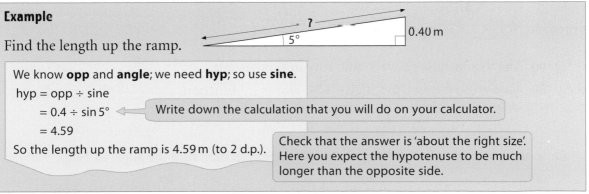

? 5° 0.40 m

We know **opp** and **angle**; we need **hyp**; so use **sine**.

hyp = opp ÷ sine

= 0.4 ÷ sin 5° ← Write down the calculation that you will do on your calculator.

= 4.59

So the length up the ramp is 4.59 m (to 2 d.p.).

Check that the answer is 'about the right size'. Here you expect the hypotenuse to be much longer than the opposite side.

For each of the next four questions make a labelled sketch.

B6 A ladder leans against a vertical wall.
The foot of the ladder is 2.2 m from the wall and makes an angle of 72° with the horizontal ground.
How long is the ladder, to the nearest 0.1 m?

B7 A kite is flying 32 m above horizontal ground.
Its string is tight and is fixed to the ground.
The string makes an angle of 25° with the ground.
How long is the string, to the nearest metre?

B8 Find the length of the sides of this rhombus.

64°   7.2 cm

B9 How long are the sides of this kite?

72°   110°   8.8 cm

C Finding an angle

Consider this rule that you have been using:

hypotenuse × sin a = opposite

Dividing both sides by 'hypotenuse' gives the formula

$$\sin a = \frac{\text{opposite}}{\text{hypotenuse}}$$

C1 (a) Use the formula above to find sin a in this triangle.

(b) Find angle a using 'the angle whose sine is …' function on your calculator. This is usually $\sin^{-1}$ and it will work on your calculator the way $\tan^{-1}$ did.

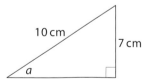
10 cm   7 cm a

C2 In these triangles find the sine of the marked angle, then find the angle to 1 d.p.

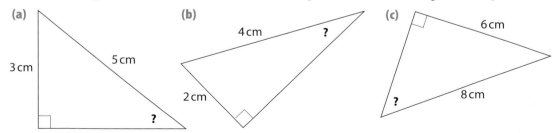

(a) 3 cm   5 cm   ?

(b) 4 cm   ?   2 cm

(c) 6 cm   8 cm   ?

You have also been using this rule:

hypotenuse $\times \cos a$ = adjacent

Dividing both sides by 'hypotenuse' gives the formula

$$\cos a = \frac{\text{adjacent}}{\text{hypotenuse}}$$

C3 **(a)** Use the formula above to find $\cos a$ in this triangle.

(b) Find angle a using 'the angle whose cosine is …' function on your calculator.

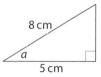

C4 In these, find the cosine of the marked angle, then find the angle to 1 d.p.

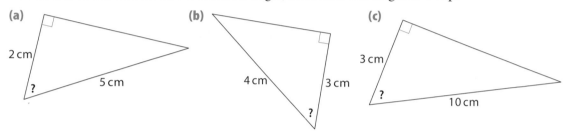

C5 A triangle with sides these lengths is right-angled (as a check using Pythagoras will confirm).

(a) Calculate $\sin x$ from lengths given.

(b) Find $\sin^{-1}$ of this value to get the angle x.

(c) Calculate $\cos x$ from lengths given.

(d) Find $\cos^{-1}$ of this value to get the angle x. Is this the same result as in part (b)?

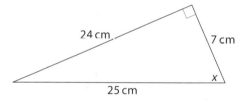

C6 To find each of these angles,

(i) choose the correct calculation from one of the boxes

(ii) do the calculation as a key sequence that works on your calculator

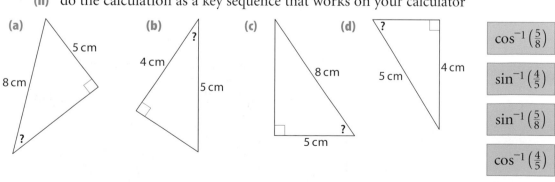

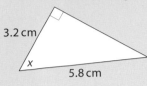

Example

Find the marked angle.

You know **hyp** and **adj**; you need the **angle**. So use **cosine**.

$\cos x = \dfrac{3.2}{5.8}$

so $x = \cos^{-1}\left(\dfrac{3.2}{5.8}\right)$

$= 56.5°$ (to 1 d.p.)

Write down the calculation that you will do on your calculator, to help with checking later.

C7 Find the marked angles, giving your answers to 1 d.p.

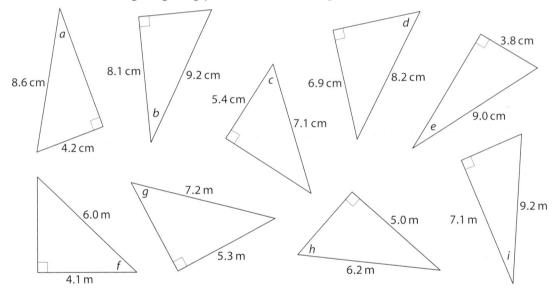

C8 What angle, to the nearest degree, does this bridge make with the horizontal when point P is 3.8 metres above road level?

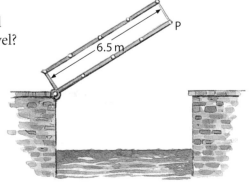

C9 A board 2 m long is used as a ramp to rise a vertical distance of 0.4 m.
What is the angle between the board and the horizontal?

C10 A ladder 6.5 m long leans against a wall with its foot on horizontal ground.
The foot of the ladder is 2.2 m from the wall.
What is the angle between the ladder and the ground?

C11 Calculate the lettered angles in these isosceles triangles.

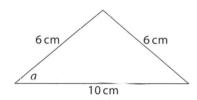

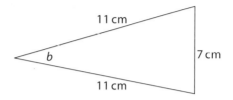

C12 A parallelogram has lengths of sides and
perpendicular height as shown.
Calculate the angles at its vertices.

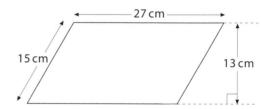

*C13 A kite has sides of length 5 cm and 3 cm.
The vertices with the same size angle are joined by a diagonal 4 cm long.
Find the angles at all the vertices and the length of the other diagonal.

Some people prefer to use the formulas $\sin a = \dfrac{\text{opp}}{\text{hyp}}$ and $\cos a = \dfrac{\text{adj}}{\text{hyp}}$

for problems like those in sections A and B instead of using sine and cosine as
multipliers that you apply to the hypotenuse to get the opposite and adjacent sides.

Example

Find the length AB.

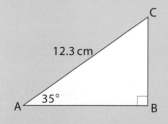

We know **hyp** and **angle**, we need **adj**, so use **cosine**.

$$\cos a = \frac{\text{adj}}{\text{hyp}}$$

so $\cos 35° = \dfrac{AB}{12.3}$

$$AB = 12.3 \times \cos 35°$$
$$= 10.1 \text{ cm (to 1.d.p.)}$$

However, thinking of sine and cosine as multipliers can help with later work in maths.

It may seem that in trigonometry there are a lot of rules to remember.
This summary may help.

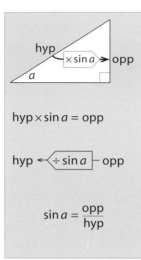

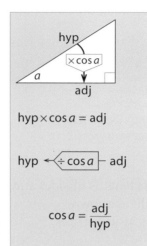

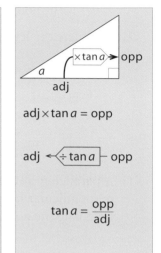

Remember each of the 'main' rules.

$$\text{hyp} \times \sin a = \text{opp}$$

$$\text{hyp} \times \cos a = \text{adj}$$

$$\text{adj} \times \tan a = \text{opp}$$

Reverse the main rule when you need to.

$$\text{hyp} \leftarrow \div \sin a \vdash \text{opp}$$

$$\text{hyp} \leftarrow \div \cos a \vdash \text{adj}$$

$$\text{adj} \leftarrow \div \tan a \vdash \text{opp}$$

Rearrange the main rule so the trigonometric ratio is the subject (good for finding angles).

$$\sin a = \frac{\text{opp}}{\text{hyp}}$$

$$\cos a = \frac{\text{adj}}{\text{hyp}}$$

$$\tan a = \frac{\text{opp}}{\text{adj}}$$

D1 For each of the quantities shown by a question mark,

    (i) choose the correct calculation from the boxes on the right

    (ii) do the calculation as a key sequence on your calculator

(a)

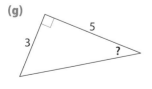

(b)

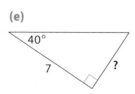

(c)

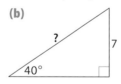

$$7 \times \sin 40°$$

$$7 \div \sin 40°$$

$$\sin^{-1}\left(\tfrac{3}{5}\right)$$

(d)

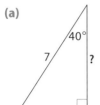

(e)

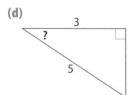

(f)

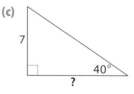

$$7 \times \cos 40°$$

$$7 \div \cos 40°$$

$$\cos^{-1}\left(\tfrac{3}{5}\right)$$

(g)

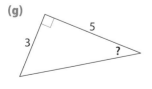

(h)

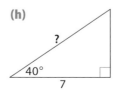

(i)

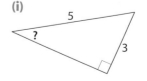

$$7 \times \tan 40°$$

$$7 \div \tan 40°$$

$$\tan^{-1}\left(\tfrac{3}{5}\right)$$

D2 Find the missing lengths and angles here. Give your answers to 1 d.p.

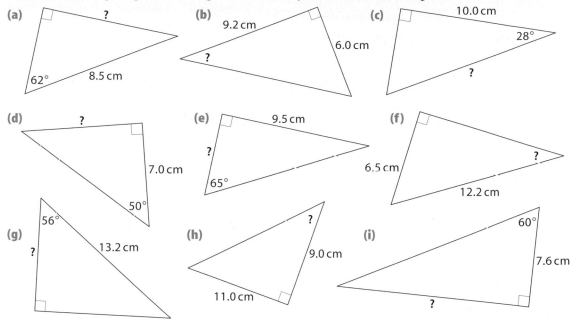

(a) ? 62° 8.5 cm

(b) 9.2 cm 6.0 cm ?

(c) 10.0 cm 28° ?

(d) ? 7.0 cm 50° 56° 13.2 cm

(e) 9.5 cm ? 65°

(f) ? 6.5 cm 12.2 cm

(g) ?

(h) ? 9.0 cm 11.0 cm

(i) 60° 7.6 cm ?

D3 **(a)** What special kind of triangle is this?

(b) Work out the length of the side AC.
(Make a sketch and add information to it if you need to.)

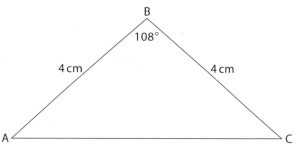

B 108° 4 cm 4 cm A C

D4 Calculate these.

(a) The length QK to 2 d.p.

(b) The length PK to 2 d.p.

(c) The length KR to 2 d.p.

(d) The area of triangle PQR to 1 d.p.

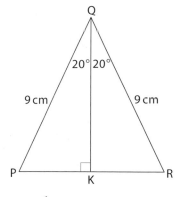

Q 20° 20° 9 cm 9 cm P K R

D5 Calculate angle *x*.

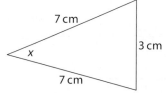

7 cm 3 cm *x* 7 cm

Sometimes Pythagoras's theorem is useful in work where you are using trigonometry:

$$hyp^2 = adj^2 + opp^2$$

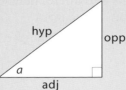

D6 **(a)** Sketch this right-angled triangle (including its labels). What is special about it?

(b) How big is angle x? Mark the value on your sketch.

(c) Use Pythagoras to work out length DE and mark it on your sketch.

(d) Work out $\sin x$ from two of the lengths given on your sketch. Do you get the same by keying the sine of this angle on your calculator?

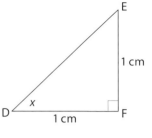

D7 **(a)** What special kind of triangle is triangle ABC?

(b) What are the values of angles w, x, y and z?

(c) Use Pythagoras to work out the length AN.

(d) Use your answer to (c) and the lengths in the diagram to work out these.

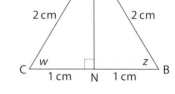

(i) $\sin 30°$	**(ii)** $\cos 30°$	**(iii)** $\tan 30°$
(iv) $\sin 60°$	**(v)** $\cos 60°$	**(vi)** $\tan 60°$

(e) Check your answers using the sin, cos and tan functions on your calculator.

D8 **(a)** Calculate the area of an equilateral triangle with sides 10 cm long.

(b) What is the area of a regular hexagon with sides 10 cm long?

D9 A rocket is fired from ground level at an angle of 68° to the horizontal.
It travels in a straight line.
After 8 seconds it is 106 metres above ground level.
How far has it travelled?

D10 Calculate the area of this triangle.

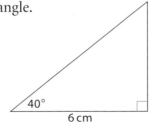

D11 A boat travels for 24 km on a bearing of 080°.
It then travels for 18 km on a bearing of 043°.

   (a) How much further north is it from when it started?

   (b) How much further east?

D12 A speedboat travels 475 metres in a straight line starting from a jetty.
It is now 345 metres west from the jetty.
What bearing could it have been travelling on?

D13 The diagonals of a rhombus are 14 cm and 8 cm long.
Calculate the angles at the vertices of the rhombus.

*D14 This is a regular pentagon.

   (a) Use tangent to calculate the length h to 2 d.p.

   (b) Calculate the area of one of the isosceles triangles
   to 1 d.p.

   (c) Calculate the area of the whole pentagon to 1 d.p.

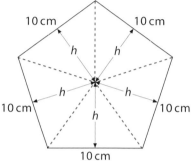

*D15 A regular nonagon is drawn by spacing nine points equally
around a circle of radius 10 cm.
Calculate the length of one side of the nonagon.

*D16 Nick wants to draw a regular decagon by spacing ten points
equally around a circle. He wants each side to be 6 cm long.
What radius circle should he use?

Test yourself

T1 Find the values of these to 1 d.p.

   (a) The angle whose tangent is 0.04   **(b)** The angle whose sine is 0.56

   (c) The angle whose cosine is 0.82   **(d)** The angle whose tangent is 156

T2 Find the missing lengths.

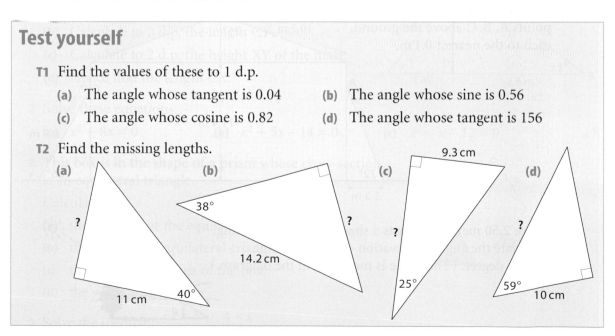

1 Triangles and polygons

A Special triangles and quadrilaterals (p 11)

A1 (a) 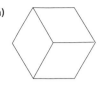 (b)

(c) etc.

(d)   (e)

(f)   (g)

A2 (a)  (b)

(c) etc.   (d)

(e)   (f) etc.

(g) etc.

A3 (a) A square

(b) Some of the following properties:
It has four lines of reflection symmetry.
All four sides are the same length.
All four angles are the same, 90°.
The diagonals bisect one another.
The diagonals cross at right angles.

B Angles of a triangle (p 12)

B1 $a = 35°$, $b = 25°$, $c = 60°$, $d = 45°$

B2 $a = 71°$, $b = 71°$, $c = 54°$, $d = 67°$, $e = 46°$, $f = 47°$, $g = 86°$

B3 $a = 40°$ ($\angle ACE = 80°$, angles on straight line,
so $a = 180° - 60° - 80°$)
$b = 70°$ ($\angle FGE = 40°$. The angle at E is also equal to b.
So $2b = 180° - 40° = 140°$)
$c = 30°$ (Angle IKJ = 70°, isosceles triangle.
So $\angle LKI = 110°$, so $c = 180° - 40° - 110°$)
$d = 55°$ (isosceles triangle)
$e = 70°$ (interior angles of a triangle)
$f = 110°$ (angles on a straight line)
$g = 50°$ (interior angles of a triangle)

B4 $x = 31$; an equation leading to $y = 26$

C Angles of a polygon (p 13)

C1 (a) 180° (b) 180° (c) 360°

C2 (a) $p = 25°$ (sum of interior angles of quadrilateral is 360°)

(b) $q = 80°$ (angle EFH = 25°, angles on a straight line. $q = 360 - (90 + 25 + 165)$, interior angles of a quadrilateral add up to 360°)

(c) $s = 70°$ (angle MJK = 60°, exterior = sum of other two interior. $s = 360 - (150 + 60 + 80)$, interior angles of a quadrilateral add up to 360°)

C3 Steps leading to the formula $180(n-2)°$ for the total of the interior angles

C4 1620°

C5 (a) (i) 5 (ii) 540° (iii) 110°

(b) (i) 6 (ii) 720° (iii) 150°

(c) (i) 7 (ii) 900° (iii) 115°

C6 $a = 75°$, $b = 124°$, $c = 142°$, $d = 142°$, $e = 105°$, $f = 105°$

C7 14

C8 (a) 120° (b) 140°

C9 (a) 360° (b) 360°

C10 (a) (i) $w = 110°$ (ii) A 112°, B 98°, C 70°, D 80°
(iii) Total of interior angles = 360°
This is the same as $180(4-2)°$.

(b) (i) $x = 63°$
(ii) E 117°, F 84°, G 130°, H 103°, I 106°
(iii) Total of interior angles = 540°
This is the same as $180(5-2)°$.

(c) (i) $y = 43°$
(ii) J 137°, K 137°, L 137°, M 78°, N 137°, O 137°, P 137
(iii) Total of interior angles = 900°
This is the same as $180(7-2)°$.

(d) (i) $z = 31°$

  (ii) Q 115°, R 118°, S 149°, T 105°, U 146°, V 87°

  (iii) Total of interior angles $= 720°$
    This is the same as $180(6 - 2)°$.

C11 $e = 30°$

C12 (a) 72° **(b)** 15° **(c)** 12° **(d)** 8°

C13 150°

C14 (a) 108° **(b)** 165° **(c)** 168° **(d)** 172°

C15 144°

C16 9

C17 (a) 40 **(b)** 15 **(c)** 36 **(d)** 20

C18 (a) 8 **(b)** 18 **(c)** 72 **(d)** 60

C19 (a) $\dfrac{360}{n}$ **(b)** $180 - \dfrac{360}{n}$ or an equivalent expression

D Mixed questions (p 16)

D1 (a) Exterior angle of pentagon $= \dfrac{360}{5} = 72°$
    $a = 180 - 72 = 108°$

  (b) One possible explanation is:
    $\triangle$TPS is isosceles, so $\angle$TSP $= \angle$TPS.
    So $\angle$TSP $= \frac{1}{2}(180° - a)$ (angles of $\triangle$TPS)
      $= 36°$
    $b = \angle$TSR $- \angle$TSP $= 108 - 36 = 72°$

D2 With explanatory diagrams:
  100° and 90°, or two 95° angles, or 70° and 120°

D3 30°

D4 The six-sided polygon can be divided
  into four triangles whose vertices
  are all vertices of the polygon.
  So the formula $180(n - 2)$ for
  an n-sided polygon does apply.

  However, when the dividing lines do not all go through
  one vertex of the polygon it is no longer obvious that
  the number of triangles must be $n - 2$.

Test yourself (p 17)

T1 $a = 140°$, $b = 126°$, $c = 36°$, $d = 36°$, $e = 111°$, $f = 69°$,
  $g = 44°$, $h = 67°$

T2 20

T3 From the fact that the nonagon is regular, $\triangle$ADG is
  equilateral, so $x = 60°$.
  Exterior angle of nonagon $= \dfrac{360}{9} = 40°$
  $y =$ interior angle $= 180 - 40 = 140°$
  $z = 40°$ (explained either in terms of $\angle$IAB or the sum
  of the angles of symmetrical quadrilateral IAGH)

2 Drawing and using quadratic graphs

A Parabolas and quadratic functions (p 18)

A1 (a) (i) 1.4 **(ii)** 3.6

  (b) $x = 1.6$ and $^-1.6$

  (c) 1.4

  (d) $x = 0$

A2 (a)

x	-2	-1	0	1	2
x^2	4	1	0	1	4
$x^2 - 2$	2	-1	-2	-1	2

  (b)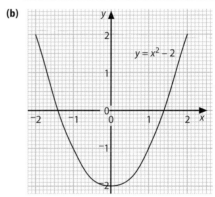

  (c) $x = {}^-1.4$ and 1.4

  (d) $x = 0$

A3 (a)

x	-2	-1	0	1	2
x^2	4	1	0	1	4
$2x^2$	8	2	0	2	8
y	9	3	1	3	9

  (b)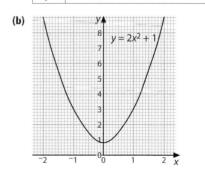

  (c) $y = 1$; the graph is symmetrical about $x = 0$.

  (d) $x = {}^-1.2$ and 1.2

  (e) The whole of the graph lies above the line $y = 0$.

A4 (a)

x	-2	-1	0	1	2
x^2	4	1	0	1	4
$x^2 + x$	2	0	0	2	6

(b)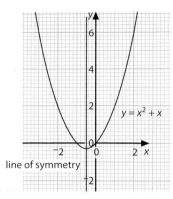

(c) $x = 0.6$ and $^-1.6$

(d) $x = ^-0.5$

(e) (i) $x = ^-0.5$ (ii) $^-0.25$

(iii) Comment on accuracy

A5 (a)

x	$^-4$	$^-3$	$^-2$	$^-1$	0	1	2	3
x^2	**16**	**9**	**4**	1	0	1	**4**	**9**
$2x$	$^-$**8**	$^-$**6**	$^-$**4**	$^-2$	0	**2**	**4**	**6**
$^-4$	$^-$**4**	$^-$**4**	$^-$**4**	$^-$**4**	$^-$**4**	$^-$**4**	$^-$**4**	$^-$**4**
$x^2 + 2x - 4$	**4**	$^-$**1**	$^-$**4**	$^-$**5**	$^-$**4**	$^-$**1**	**4**	**11**

(b)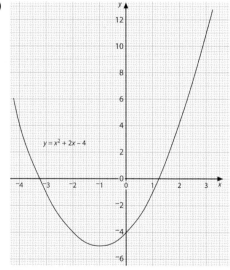

(c) $^-5$

(d) $x = 1.2$ and $^-3.2$

(e) $x = 1.4$ and $^-3.4$

A6 (a)

x	$^-3$	$^-2$	$^-1$	0	1	2	3
x^2	**9**	**4**	**1**	**0**	1	**4**	**9**
$6 - x^2$	$^-$**3**	**2**	**5**	**6**	**5**	**2**	$^-$**3**

(b)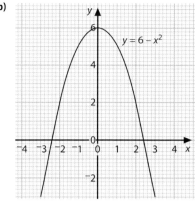

(c) $x = 1.7$ and $^-1.7$

(d) $x = 0$

A7 (a)

x	$^-1$	0	1	2	3	4	5	6
$6x$	$^-$**6**	**0**	**6**	**12**	**18**	24	**30**	**36**
x^2	**1**	**0**	**1**	**4**	**9**	16	**25**	**36**
$6x - x^2$	$^-$**7**	**0**	**5**	**8**	**9**	8	**5**	**0**

(b)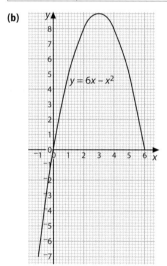

(c) 9

(d) $x = 1.3$ and 4.7

(e) No, the maximum value of $6x - x^2$ is 9.

A8 (a)

x	$^-1$	0	1	2	3	4
$2x^2$	2	**0**	2	8	18	**32**
$6x$	$^-$6	**0**	6	12	18	**24**
$2x^2 - 6x$	8	**0**	$^-$**4**	$^-$**4**	**0**	**8**

(b)

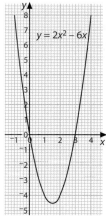

$y = 2x^2 - 6x$

(c) $x = 0.2$ and 2.8

(d) (i) $^-4.5$ (when $x = 1.5$)

   (ii) Comment on accuracy

A9 (a)

x	$^-2$	$^-1$	0	1	2	3	4	5
y	**16**	**9**	**4**	**1**	**0**	**1**	**4**	**9**

(b)

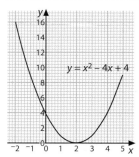

$y = x^2 - 4x + 4$

(c) 0

(d) $x = ^-0.2$ and 4.2

A10 (a)

x	$^-4$	$^-3$	$^-2$	$^-1$	0	1	2	3	4
y	$^-4$	$^-0.5$	**2**	**3.5**	**4**	**3.5**	**2**	$^-0.5$	$^-4$

(b)

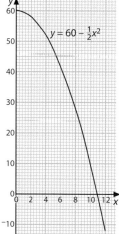

$y = 4 - \frac{1}{2}x^2$

(c) 4

(d) $x = ^-2.8$ and 2.8

A11 (a)

x	$^-2$	$^-1$	0	1	2	3
y	15	**5**	$^-1$	**$^-3$**	$^-1$	5

(b)

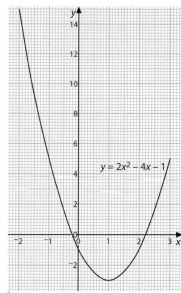

$y = 2x^2 - 4x - 1$

(c) (i) Read off the x-values at the points where the graph intersects the x-axis. $x = 2.2$ is one of these values.

   (ii) $x = ^-0.2$

B Using graphs to solve problems (p 23)

B1 (a)

x	0	2	4	6	8	10	12
$\frac{1}{2}x^2$	0	2	8	18	**32**	**50**	**72**
$60 - \frac{1}{2}x^2$	60	58	52	42	**28**	**10**	**$^-12$**

(b)

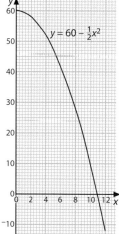

$y = 60 - \frac{1}{2}x^2$

(c) 60 m

(d) 11 m

(e) $y = ^-68$. The stone won't follow the same path in the sea.

B2 (a) (i) 4   **(ii)** 1.5 m

    (b) (i) 0   **(ii)** 24 m

B3 (a)

t	0	1	2	3	4	5
s	125	120	105	80	45	0

    (b)

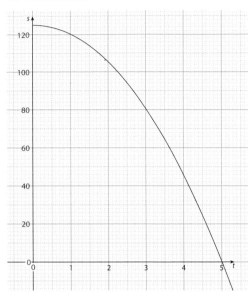

    (c) About 94 m; by calculation 93.75 m

    (d) (i) About 3.2 seconds.

         (ii) The stone is 75 m high after 3.2 seconds.

B4 (a)

t	0	0.25	0.5	0.75	1	1.25	1.5
h	0	1.19	1.75	1.69	1	⁻0.31	⁻2.25

    (b)

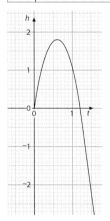

    (c) 1.8 metres

    (d) 0.6 second

    (e) About 1.3 or 1.4 seconds

B5 (a) $A = x(20 - x)$ or $20x - x^2$

    (b) (table may not be needed)

x	0	5	10	15	20
A	0	75	100	75	0

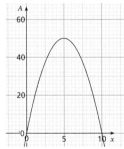

    (c) About 2.3 and 17.7

    (d) Between about 6.8 and 13.2

    (e) 100 m² , with both sides 10 metres

B6 If the short side is x m, then $A = x(20 - 2x)$ or $20x - 2x^2$. The graph of this is drawn below.

The maximum enclosed area is 50 m², achieved when $x = 5$.

The enclosure will measure 5 m by 10 m.

Test yourself (p 25)

T1 (a)

x	⁻1	0	1	2	3	4
x^2	1	0	**1**	4	9	**16**
$-3x$	3	0	⁻**3**	⁻6	⁻9	⁻**12**
$x^2 - 3x$	4	0	⁻**2**	⁻2	**0**	**4**

(b)

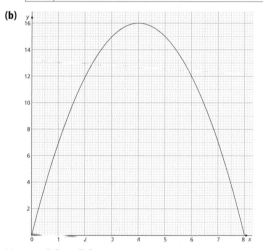

$y = x^2 - 3x$

(c) **(i)** $x = 0$ and 3 **(ii)** $x = 3.3$ and $^-0.3$

(d) $x = 1.5$

T2 (a)

x	0	1	2	3	4	5	6	7	8
y	**0**	7	12	**15**	**16**	15	12	7	0

(b)

(c) $x = 0.8$ or 7.2

T3 (a) $3.75 \, \text{m}$

(b) **(i)** 3.75 **(ii)** 0 **(iii)** 5

(c) $10 \, \text{m}$

3 Distributions and averages

A Review: mean, median, range and mode (p 26)

A1 (a) 34   **(b)** 21

(c) Median 32.5, range 17

(d) The coaches to Sheffield had more passengers on the whole. The number in a coach was more spread out for the Sheffield coaches.

(e) To Sheffield: 36
To Liverpool: 33.1 (to 1 d.p.)

(f) Yes

A2 (a) 35   **(b)** 43   **(c)** 20–29

A3 (a)

2	4 8 8
3	0 1 5 9 9
4	1 4 4 7 7 7 9
5	1 5 5 6 6 8
6	3 3 6 8 9
7	0 0 1 2

(b) Median 50, range 48

A4 (a)

0.	8
1.	5 7 7 7 8 9
3.	2 5 6 6 7 7 8 8 8 9
3.	0 1 2 3 3 5 5 6 6 7 8
4.	0 2

(b) Median 2.8 kg, range 3.4 kg

A5 Boys: median = 56, range = 33
Girls: median = 65, range = 37
The girls did better on the whole. The girls' marks were more spread out than the boys'.

A6 (a) 78 kg   **(b)** 76.8 kg

A7 (a) 32   **(b)** 88   **(c)** 2.75   **(d)** 2

A8 (a) 58   **(b)** 212   **(c)** 3.7 (to 1 d.p.)

A9 1.56

A10 (a) 2   **(b)** 2.9 (to 1 d.p.)   **(c)** 3

B Grouped frequencies (p 29)

B1 (a)

Distance (d units)	Tally	Frequency
$0 \leq d < 10$	II	2
$10 \leq d < 20$	JHI III	8
$20 \leq d < 30$	JHI II	7
$30 \leq d < 40$	JHI III	8
$40 \leq d < 50$	JHI JHI I	11
$50 \leq d < 60$	JHI JHI IIII	14
Total		50

(b) $50 \leq d < 60$ **(c)** $40 \leq d < 50$

B2 (a) $40 < w \leq 50$ **(b)** $30 < w \leq 40$

(c)

Weight (w kg)	Frequency
$30 < w \leq 40$	4
$40 < w \leq 50$	11
$50 < w \leq 60$	8
$60 < w \leq 70$	6
$70 < w \leq 80$	1
Total	30

(d) $40 < w \leq 50$

(e)

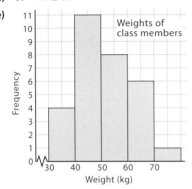

Weights of class members

B3 (a)

Height (h cm)	Tally	Frequency
$5 \leq h < 10$	JHT I	6
$10 \leq h < 15$	JHT JHT	10
$15 \leq h < 20$	JHT II	7
$20 \leq h < 25$	JHT IIII	9
$25 \leq h < 30$	JHT III	8

(b)

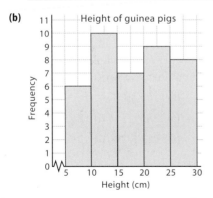

Height of guinea pigs

(c) 16 **(d)** $10 \leq h < 15$

B4 (a)

Max. temp. (°C)	Frequency
$12.0 \leq t < 13.0$	9
$13.0 \leq t < 14.0$	8
$14.0 \leq t < 15.0$	12
$15.0 \leq t < 16.0$	1
$16.0 \leq t < 17.0$	1
Total	31

(b) $14.0 \leq t < 15.0$ **(c)** 17

C Choosing class intervals (p 32)

C1 (a)

Foot length (f cm)	Frequency
$15 \leq f < 20$	2
$20 \leq f < 25$	3
$25 \leq f < 30$	3
$30 \leq f < 35$	6
$35 \leq f < 40$	7
$40 \leq f < 45$	10
$45 \leq f < 50$	8
$50 \leq f < 55$	4
$55 \leq f < 60$	1
Total	44

The modal group is $40 \leq f < 45$

(b)

Foot length (f cm)	Frequency
$10 \leq f < 20$	2
$20 \leq f < 30$	6
$30 \leq f < 40$	13
$40 \leq f < 50$	18
$50 \leq f < 60$	5
Total	44

The modal group is $40 \leq f < 50$

(c) The first grouping gives more detail but the second gives a clearer shape of the distribution.

C2 Answers will vary but these are possible groups:

(a) $10 \leq t < 13$, $13 \leq t < 16$, $16 \leq t < 19$ etc.

(b) $62 < w \leq 64$, $64 < w \leq 66$ etc.

D Estimating a mean using mid-interval values (p 34)

D1 (a) 12

(b)

Speed (s m.p.h.)	Freq.	Mid-interval	Group total
$20 < s \leq 30$	7	25	$7 \times 25 = 175$
$30 < s \leq 40$	21	35	$21 \times 35 = 735$
$40 < s \leq 50$	8	45	$8 \times 45 = 360$
$50 < s \leq 60$	3	55	$3 \times 55 = 165$
$60 < s \leq 70$	1	65	$1 \times 65 = 65$
Total	40		1500

(c) $1500 \div 40 = 37.5$ m.p.h.

D2 (a) 54

(b)

Temp. (t °C)	Frequency
$36.0 < t \leq 36.2$	1
$36.2 < t \leq 36.4$	2
$36.4 < t \leq 36.6$	3
$36.6 < t \leq 36.8$	8
$36.8 < t \leq 37.0$	17
$37.0 < t \leq 37.2$	13
$37.2 < t \leq 37.4$	8
$37.4 < t \leq 37.6$	2
Total	54

(c) Estimated mean (using 36.1, 36.3 …)
    = 1994.8 ÷ 54 = 36.9 °C

D3 Estimated mean = 270 ÷ 16 = 16.875 minutes,
    17 minutes (to the nearest minute)

D4 **(a)** 3, since the numbers 1, 2, 3, 4 and 5 will go in that
        group
    (b) Estimated mean = 434 ÷ 33 = 13.2 (to 1 d.p.)

E Frequency polygons (p 36)

E1 **(a)** The missing frequencies are: 3, 4, 6, 2, 1
    (b) $60 < t \leq 70$

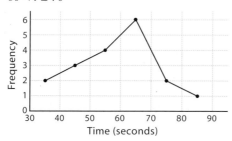

E2 **(a)** Girls 1.63 m, boys 1.71 m
    (b) Girls 0.24 m, boys 0.29 m
    (c)

Height (h m)	Frequency (girls)	Frequency (boys)
$1.5 < h \leq 1.6$	8	3
$1.6 < h \leq 1.7$	9	7
$1.7 < h \leq 1.8$	3	5
$1.8 < h \leq 1.9$	0	5

(d)

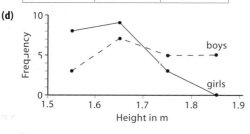

(e) For both groups the modal interval is $1.6 < h \leq 1.7$.
    There are more girls than boys with heights up to
    1.7 m and more boys than girls with heights over
    1.7 m.

E3 **(a)**

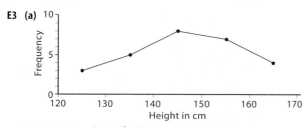

(b) 146.5 cm (to 1 d.p.)

E4 51.6 kg (to 1 d.p.)

E5 114 cm (to the nearest cm)

Test yourself (p 38)

T1 **(a)**

```
6 | 5 8 9
7 | 0 0 5 6 6
8 | 0 3 6 8 8
9 | 0 2            Stem = 10 b.p.m.
```

(b) Median = 76 b.p.m. Range = 27 b.p.m.
(c) Median = 68 b.p.m. Range = 54 b.p.m.
(d) The median of the smokers was higher.
    The range of the non-smokers was twice as big but
    that was largely due to just one student with a very
    high pulse rate.

T2 **(a)**

Time (t seconds)	Tally	Frequency
$0 \leq t < 5$	III	3
$5 \leq t < 10$	ЖΙ II	7
$10 \leq t < 15$	ЖΙ IIII	9
$15 \leq t < 20$	IIII	4
$20 \leq t < 25$	II	2

(b) $10 \leq t < 15$

T3 **(a)** 52
(b)

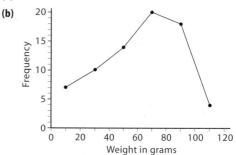

(c) 62.1 g

4 Fractions

A Review: adding, subtracting and multiplying (p 39)

A1 (a) $\frac{5}{6}$ (b) $\frac{13}{15}$ (c) $\frac{13}{30}$ (d) $1\frac{1}{24}$ (e) $1\frac{17}{40}$

     (f) $2\frac{5}{12}$ (g) $3\frac{19}{20}$ (h) $2\frac{7}{15}$ (i) $4\frac{5}{12}$ (j) $3\frac{23}{30}$

A2 (a) $\frac{1}{6}$ (b) $\frac{11}{20}$ (c) $\frac{5}{24}$ (d) $\frac{1}{30}$ (e) $\frac{9}{40}$

     (f) $\frac{2}{3}$ (g) $1\frac{5}{8}$ (h) $\frac{19}{24}$ (i) $2\frac{1}{24}$ (j) $2\frac{5}{12}$

A3 (a) $\frac{23}{24}$ (b) $\frac{17}{24}$ (c) $\frac{17}{20}$ (d) $1\frac{13}{20}$ (e) $3\frac{1}{6}$

     (f) $1\frac{2}{5}$ (g) $1\frac{19}{24}$ (h) $1\frac{1}{24}$ (i) $3\frac{17}{35}$ (j) $\frac{32}{35}$

A4 (a) $\frac{1}{2}$ (b) $\frac{3}{10}$ (c) $\frac{5}{8}$ (d) $\frac{4}{15}$ (e) $\frac{6}{25}$

A5 (a) $1\frac{1}{8}$ (b) $\frac{8}{9}$ (c) 2 (d) $1\frac{7}{8}$ (e) $3\frac{3}{4}$

A6 (a) 1 (b) 1 (c) 1 (d) 1 (e) 1

B Reciprocals (p 40)

B1 (a) $\frac{1}{3}$ (b) 3 (c) $\frac{1}{5}$ (d) $\frac{5}{2}$ (e) $\frac{6}{5}$

     (f) 8 (g) $\frac{7}{5}$ (h) $\frac{4}{5}$ (i) $\frac{1}{8}$ (j) 1

B2 (a) $\frac{3}{2}$ (b) $\frac{2}{3}$

B3 (a) $\frac{2}{7}$ (b) $\frac{3}{4}$ (c) $\frac{4}{9}$ (d) $\frac{5}{7}$ (e) $\frac{3}{8}$

B4 (a) 1.6
     (b) (i) 10 (ii) 2.5 (iii) 8 (iv) 0.8 (v) 0.4

B5 (a) A (b) 0

C Dividing by a fraction (p 40)

C1 (a) 8 (b) 15 (c) 16 (d) 20 (e) 18

C2 (a) 24 (b) 8 (c) 18 (d) 9 (e) 10

C3 (a) $\frac{15}{2}$ (b) $\frac{8}{3}$ (c) $\frac{20}{3}$ (d) $\frac{4}{3}$ (e) $\frac{40}{3}$

C4 (a) 24 (b) 12

C5 8 hours

C6 $25\,\text{kg}$

C7 (a) $\frac{10}{9}$ (b) $\frac{10}{3}$ (c) $\frac{8}{9}$ (d) $\frac{3}{4}$ (e) $\frac{6}{5}$

C8 (a) $\frac{5}{6}$ (b) $\frac{2}{9}$ (c) $\frac{8}{15}$ (d) $\frac{10}{9}$ (e) $\frac{9}{8}$

C9 (a) 6 (b) $\frac{15}{4}$ or $3\frac{3}{4}$ (c) $\frac{1}{2}$ (d) $\frac{3}{2}$ or $1\frac{1}{2}$

D Mixed questions (p 42)

D1 (a) 2 (b) 3 (c) $2\frac{1}{2}$ (d) 0 (e) $4\frac{1}{2}$
     (f) $\frac{1}{6}$ (g) 12 (h) 12 (i) $\frac{3}{2}$ (j) $\frac{2}{3}$

D2 (a) 4 (b) 6 (c) 1 (d) $2\frac{1}{2}$ (e) $\frac{2}{3}$
     (f) $\frac{1}{2}$ (g) $\frac{3}{2}$ (h) $\frac{4}{3}$ (i) $\frac{8}{9}$ (j) $\frac{9}{8}$

D3 (a) $\frac{13}{10}$ or $1\frac{3}{10}$ (b) $\frac{3}{10}$ (c) $\frac{2}{5}$
     (d) $\frac{8}{5}$ (e) $\frac{5}{8}$

D4 $x = \frac{8}{15}$

D5 (a) $x = \frac{3}{10}$ (b) $x = \frac{10}{9}$ (c) $x = \frac{4}{3}$ (d) $x = \frac{25}{12}$

D6 30

D7 $\frac{1}{32}$

D8 $\frac{32}{243}$

Test yourself (p 42)

T1 (a) $\frac{1}{4}$ (b) 5 (c) $\frac{7}{4}$ (d) $\frac{2}{9}$ (e) 50

T2 (a) 18 (b) $\frac{18}{5}$ (c) 4 (d) $\frac{4}{5}$ (e) $\frac{15}{16}$

T3 (a) $x = \frac{15}{4}$ (b) $x = \frac{2}{9}$ (c) $x = \frac{9}{16}$ (d) $x = \frac{24}{25}$

5 Accuracy

A Lower and upper bounds (p 43)

A1 (a) $12.5\,°\text{C}$ (b) $13.5\,°\text{C}$

A2 $346.5\,\text{ml}, 347.5\,\text{ml}$

A3 $77.5\,\text{kg}, 78.5\,\text{kg}$

A4 $169.5\,\text{ml}, 170.5\,\text{ml}$

A5 $265\,\text{g}, 275\,\text{g}$

A6 $415\,\text{km/h}, 425\,\text{km/h}$

A7 $3750\,\text{km}, 3850\,\text{km}$

Test yourself (p 44)

T1 $25.5\,\text{kg}, 24.5\,\text{kg}$

T2 $201.5\,\text{cm}, 202.5\,\text{cm}$

6 Linear equations 1

A Solving equations (p 45)

A1 (a) $x = 4.5$ (b) $x = {}^-2$ (c) $x = 4.2$
    (d) $x = 1$ (e) $x = {}^-1$ (f) $x = {}^-4$

A2 (a) $n = 3$ (b) $n = {}^-1$ (c) $n = 2$
    (d) $n = {}^-2$ (e) $n = 2.25$ (f) $n = 4$
    (g) $n = 3$ (h) $n = 1.25$ (i) $n = {}^-1.5$

A3 (a) $x = {}^-1$ (b) $x = 6$ (c) $x = 1$
    (d) $x = {}^-2$ (e) $x = 0$ (f) $x = {}^-3$
    (g) $x = {}^-7.5$ (h) $x = 2.5$ (i) $x = {}^-11$

A4 (a) $k = \frac{1}{5}$ (b) $k = \frac{1}{3}$ (c) $k = \frac{1}{4}$
    (d) $k = \frac{1}{2}$ (e) $k = \frac{2}{3}$ (f) $k = \frac{-1}{2}$

A5 $3(x - 4) + 2(3x \diagup 2) = 19$
       $3x - 12 + 6x + 4 = 19$
            $9x - 8 = 19$
               $9x = 27$
                $x = 3$

A6 (a) $n = 2$ (b) $m = 5$ (c) $k = {}^-3$
    (d) $h = \frac{14}{3}$ or $4\frac{2}{3}$

A7 $2(3x + 2) - 2(2x - 1) = 8$
      $(6x + 4) - (4x - 2) = 8$
        $6x + 4 - 4x + 2 = 8$
              $2x + 6 = 8$
                $2x = 2$
                 $x = 1$

A8 (a) $x = {}^-3$ (b) $x = \frac{5}{2}$ or $2\frac{1}{2}$

B Forming equations (p 46)

B1 (a) $20°, 80°, 80°$ (b) $35°, 55°, 90°$
    (c) $60°, 60°, 60°$ (d) $95°, 70°, 80°, 115°$

B2 (a) 22, 19, 25, 34   (b) Length: 30, width: 20

B3 $^-1.5$

B4 (a) $120 - 4x$ (b) $x = 13$

B5 (a) $^-2$ (b) 2   (c) 0.25 or $\frac{1}{4}$ (d) $^-1$

B6 2θ

B7 (a) Blue rectangle: length 13, width 4
        Orange rectangle: length 13, width 3
    (b) When $x = 14$, $42 - 3x = 0$ and 0 is not possible for
        a length.
    (c) 8   (d) 6   (e) 12   (f) 10   (g) 10.5
    (h) $60 - 2x = 100$ has a negative solution.

B8 $24°$

B9 (a) 2   (b) 33   (c) $^-1$

B10 $135°$

C Equations that involve a fraction (p 49)

C1 (a) $y = 15$ (b) $k = 8$ (c) $m = 10$
    (d) $x = 20$ (e) $p = {}^-4$ (f) $q = 8$
    (g) $v = 6$ (h) $w = {}^-10$ (i) $n = \frac{4}{3}$ or $1\frac{1}{3}$

C2 (a) $x = 11$ (b) $x = 13$ (c) $x = 2$
    (d) $x = {}^-5$ (e) $x = \frac{11}{3}$ or $3\frac{2}{3}$ (f) $x = \frac{1}{5}$ or 0.2

C3 (a) $n = 9$ (b) $n = {}^-6$ (c) $n = 61$
    (d) $n = \frac{14}{3}$ or $4\frac{2}{3}$ (e) $n = {}^-3$ (f) $n = 5$

C4 (a) $\frac{n + 5}{3} = 6$ (b) 13

C5 (a) 15   (b) 21   (c) $^-10$

C6 (a) $h = 8$ (b) $k = 5$ (c) $j = \frac{3}{11}$
    (d) $f = {}^-3$ (e) $g = 4$ (h) $d = 3$

C7 (a) $a = 5$ (b) $b = {}^-5$ (c) $c = 7.5$
    (d) $d = 2$ (e) $e = \frac{2}{3}$ (f) $f = 2$

C8 5

C9 (a) 2   (b) $^-7$ (c) 5   (d) $^-2$

D More than one fraction (p 51)

D1 (a) $x = 5$ (b) $x = 0.25$ or $\frac{1}{4}$ (c) $x = {}^-5$
    (d) $x = 4$ (e) $x = {}^-3$ (f) $x = 6$

D2 (a) 7   (b) $^-5$

D3 (a) $x = 5$ (b) $x = 2$ (c) $x = 4$

D4 $x = 3.5$ or $\frac{7}{2}$ or $3\frac{1}{2}$

D5 $x = {}^-3$

D6 (a) $x = 11$ (b) $x = 2$ (c) $x = 7$

D7 (a) $x = 5$ (b) $x = {}^-7$ (c) $x = {}^-2$
    (d) $x = \frac{4}{3}$ or $1\frac{1}{3}$ (e) $x = {}^-1$ (f) $x = {}^-1$

E Mixed questions (p 52)

E1 $x = {}^-4$

E2 (a) $x = 15$ (b) $y = 6$ (c) $z = 4$
    (d) $f = 0.4$ (e) $g = {}^-3$ (f) $h = 3$
    (g) $p = 13$ (h) $q = {}^-4$ (i) $r = 2$

E3 $38°, 71°, 71°$

E4 (a) $a = 4$ (b) $x = 0.5$ or $\frac{1}{2}$

E5 (a) $x = 17$ (b) $x = 1.2$ or $\frac{6}{5}$ or $1\frac{1}{5}$

E6 (a) $x = 7$ (b) $x = {}^-3$

E7 (a) $^-5$ (b) 17   (c) 7

E8 (a) $x = 2$ (b) $x = {}^-17$ (c) $x = 0.125$ or $\frac{1}{8}$
    (d) $x = 7$ (e) $x = 5$ (f) $x = {}^-1$

E9 (a) $c = 60$ (b) $e = 80$

Test yourself (p 53)

T1 $x = 5.5$ or $5\frac{1}{2}$ or $\frac{11}{2}$

T2 (a) $a = 1.5$ or $\frac{3}{2}$ or $1\frac{1}{2}$ (b) $b = {}^-3$

   (c) $c = 1.2$ or $\frac{6}{5}$ or $1\frac{1}{5}$

T3 48.8

T4 (a) $x = 5.6$ or $\frac{28}{5}$ or $5\frac{3}{5}$ (b) $y = 0.2$ or $\frac{1}{5}$

T5 $x = \frac{^-15}{11}$

T6 (a) $y = {}^-3$ (b) $x = 0.5$ or $\frac{1}{2}$

T7 (a) $x = {}^-0.25$ or $\frac{^-1}{4}$ (b) $x = 3$

7 Area and perimeter

A Parallelogram (p 54)

A1 (a) $24\,\text{cm}^2$ (b) $63\,\text{mm}^2$ (c) $17.5\,\text{cm}^2$ (d) $49.5\,\text{m}^2$
   (e) $19.2\,\text{cm}^2$ (f) $43.9\,\text{m}^2$ (g) $30.2\,\text{cm}^2$

A2 (a) $22\,\text{cm}$ (b) $34\,\text{mm}$ (c) $18\,\text{cm}$ (d) $30\,\text{m}$
   (e) $20.8\,\text{cm}$ (f) $39\,\text{m}$ (g) $24\,\text{cm}$

A3 (a) pq or qp (b) $2f^2$ (c) $m(n + 1)$

A4 (a) $6.5\,\text{cm}$ (b) $3\,\text{cm}$ (c) $5\,\text{cm}$

A5 No, you can work out that its perpendicular height is
4 cm but that does not give the other side length. All you
know is that the other side length must be at least
4 cm, so the perimeter must be at least 14 cm.

A6 (a) $1.5\,\text{cm}$ (b) $1.6\,\text{cm}$ (c) $4.0\,\text{cm}$ (d) $12\,\text{cm}$

A7 (a) $9600\,\text{cm}^2, 0.96\,\text{m}^2$ (b) $12\,000\,\text{cm}^2, 1.2\,\text{m}^2$
   (c) $17\,000\,\text{cm}^2, 1.7\,\text{m}^2$

A8 (a) $28\,\text{cm}^2$ (b) $22.9\,\text{cm}$ (or $23.0\,\text{cm}$)

B Triangle (p 56)

B1 (a) $104.5\,\text{cm}^2$ (b) $120\,\text{mm}^2$ (c) $105\,\text{cm}^2$ (d) $76.5\,\text{m}^2$
   (e) $31.9\,\text{cm}^2$ (f) $32.4\,\text{m}^2$ (g) $30.4\,\text{cm}^2$ (h) $39.8\,\text{cm}^2$

B2 $22.8\,\text{cm}^2$ from
base = 6.0 cm and height = 7.6 cm or
base = 8.0 cm and height = 5.7 cm or
base = 11.4 cm and height = 4.0 cm
However slight differences in the measured values can
produce an appreciable difference in the calculated area.
For example, if the base is measured as 11.5 cm and the
height as 4.1 cm then the area is calculated as $23.575\,\text{cm}^2$.
Compared with $22.8\,\text{cm}^2$ (given above) there is already a
difference in the second significant figure. So there is no
point in giving an answer for this kind of area
calculation to many significant figures.

B3 (a) $2m$ (b) $\frac{pq}{2}$ or $\frac{qp}{2}$ (c) $6de$ or $6ed$

B4 (a) $4600\,\text{cm}^2, 0.46\,\text{m}^2$ (b) $2700\,\text{cm}^2, 0.27\,\text{m}^2$
   (c) $3900\,\text{cm}^2, 0.39\,\text{m}^2$

B5 (a) $66 = 6h$ (b) $11\,\text{cm}$

B6 (a) $9\,\text{cm}$ (b) $3.5\,\text{cm}$ (c) $7\,\text{cm}$

B7 (a) $4\,\text{cm}$ (b) $15\,\text{cm}$

B8 (a) A parallelogram
   (b) bh
   (c) A triangle has half the area of the parallelogram so
the triangle's area is $\frac{1}{2}bh$.

C Composite shapes and algebra (p 58)

C1 (a) $15\,\text{cm}^2$ (b) $26\,\text{cm}^2$ (c) $8.4\,\text{m}^2$ (d) $2.0\,\text{m}^2$
   (e) $16\,\text{cm}^2$ (f) $22\,\text{m}^2$ (g) $19\,\text{cm}^2$

C2 (a) $6s$ (b) $4w$ (c) $15g$ (d) $12.5p$
   (e) $13b$ (f) $7d$

C3 (a) $6 + 3a, 7a$ (b) 1.5

C4 (a) $10x + 5, 12x$ (b) 2.5

C5 $\frac{1}{2}ah + \frac{1}{2}bh$ or an equivalent expression

D Trapezium (p 60)

D1 (a) $28\,\text{cm}^2$ (b) $35\,\text{cm}^2$ (c) $22.5\,\text{cm}^2$
   (d) $68\,\text{cm}^2$ (e) $50.6\,\text{cm}^2$ (f) $108.3\,\text{cm}^2$

D2 (a) $71.1\,\text{m}^2$ (b) £1280 to the nearest £

D3 785 square units

D4 (a) $4000\,\text{mm}^2, 40\,\text{cm}^2$ (b) $14\,700\,\text{mm}^2, 147\,\text{cm}^2$

D5 6

D6 (a) $14a - 6, 10a + 2$ (b) 2

D7 (a) $16 = 4h$ (b) $4\,\text{cm}$

D8 (a) $5\,\text{cm}$ (b) $4.4\,\text{cm}$ (c) $8.3\,\text{m}$

E Circle (p 62)

E1 (a) (i) $18.8\,\text{cm}$ (ii) $28.3\,\text{cm}^2$
   (b) (i) $20.1\,\text{m}$ (ii) $32.2\,\text{m}^2$
   (c) (i) $50.3\,\text{mm}$ (ii) $201.1\,\text{mm}^2$
   (d) (i) $47.1\,\text{cm}$ (ii) $176.7\,\text{cm}^2$
   (e) (i) $125.7\,\text{m}$ (ii) $1256.6\,\text{m}^2$

E2 (a) (i) $25.1\,\text{m}$ (ii) $50.3\,\text{m}^2$
   (b) (i) $15.1\,\text{cm}$ (ii) $18.1\,\text{cm}^2$
   (c) (i) $15.7\,\text{cm}$ (ii) $19.6\,\text{cm}^2$
   (d) (i) $22.0\,\text{mm}$ (ii) $38.5\,\text{mm}^2$
   (e) (i) $314.2\,\text{m}$ (ii) $7854.0\,\text{m}$

E3 A with R, B with Q, C with S, D with P, E with T

E4 (a) 30π (b) 36π (c) 10π (d) $\frac{49}{4}\pi$ (e) $\frac{9}{2}\pi$

E5 31.8 cm

E6 (a) 5.7 cm (b) 11.5 cm (or 11.4 cm)

E7 (a) 4.0 cm (b) 5.6 cm (c) 2.8 m

E8 64 km

E9 (a) 8.0 m (b) 50.1 m

E10 (a) 28.2 m
  (b) The square needs 200 m. The circle needs 177.2 m.
  So the square needs more fencing.

E11 Circle B

E12 (a) 1 unit (b) 6 units

F Population density (p 64)

F1 (a) 244 people per km^2 (b) India

F2 6 760 000

F3 27 or 28

F4 (a) 53 chickens (b) 15 of each type of bird

G Converting units of area (p 65)

G1 (a) 20 000 cm^2 (b) 2 m^2 (c) 10 000

G2 (a) 650 m^2 (b) 48 m^2 (c) 5 m^2 (d) 0.05 m^2

G3 100

G4 1 000 000 (1000×1000)

G5 (a) 30 000 cm^2 (b) 72 000 cm^2 (c) 0.005 m^2
  (d) 0.104 m^2 (e) 7000 cm^2 (f) 0.0302 m^2
  (g) 11 000 000 m^2 (h) 0.008 km^2 (i) 90 000 m^2
  (j) 0.000 72 km^2 (k) 6 km^2

G6 (a) 100 m (b) 100

G7 3840

H Mixed questions (p 65)

H1 (a) 3600 m^2 (b) 3200 m^2 (c) 4584 m^2 (d) 2400 m^2

H2 (a) 74.6 cm^2 (to 1 d.p.)
  (b) 216 cm^2 to the nearest whole number

H3 (a) 2.645 cm^2 (b) 10.58 cm^2
  (c) 1.5 cm^2 (to 1 d.p.)

H4 (a) 168 cm^2 (b) 25 cm (c) 13.44 cm

H5 (a) 63 m (b) 3571 m^2

H6 (a) $2\pi + 4$ square units (b) $\frac{9}{4}\pi + 3$ square units
  (c) $16 - 2\pi$ square units

Test yourself (p 67)

T1 (a) 21 cm^2 (b) 37.9 cm^2

T2 (a) 19.6 cm^2 (b) 23.9 cm^2
  (c) 37.7 cm^2 (d) 24.6 cm^2

T3 (a) 1960 mm^2 (b) 2390 mm^2
  (c) 3770 mm^2 (d) 2460 mm^2

T4 22.3 m^2

T5 64 cm

T6 (a) 5.2 kg/m^2 (b) 11 180 kg (or about 11 000 kg)

8 Percentages

A Review: percentage change (p 68)

A1 (a) 0.72 (b) 0.06 (c) 0.145 (d) 0.035

A2 42%

A3 (a) 30.6% (b) 75.4% (c) 7.8% (d) 61.4%

A4 (a) 1.04 (b) 0.93 (c) 12 (d) 12.5

A5 (a) £48.59 (b) £79.18 (c) £31.92

A6 (a) 1.15 (b) 15%

A7 (a) 28% (b) 5% (c) 27.5%

A8 (a) 0.94 (b) 6%

A9 (a) 15% (b) 28% (c) 17.5%

A10 (a) £703.83 (b) £85.25

A11 (a) 12.5% (b) £56

A12 (a) 25% (b) 14.8% (c) 6.5% increase

A13 (a) 33.3% (b) 43.2% (c) 7.4% increase

A14 125%

B Successive percentage changes (p 69)

B1 (a) 50% increase (b) 32.2% increase

B2 (a) 40% decrease (b) 43.6% decrease

B3 (a) 4% increase (b) 4% increase
  (c) 1.44% decrease (d) 3.03% increase

B4 £8428

B5 28 430

B6 3.5% increase

B7 (a) 33.1% (b) 21%

B8 12%

C Compound interest (p 71)

C1

Number of years	Amount
0	£500.00
1	£525.00
2	**£551.25**
3	**£578.81**
4	**£607.75**

C2 (a) £980.03   (b) £790.82   (c) £1324.58   (d) £893.42

C3 (a) £506.71   (b) £1499.25   (c) £2329.45   (d) £436.40

C4 6 years

C5 (a) 2 years   (b) 4 years   (c) 12 years

C6 The amount on 1 January 2010 is £3293.09.

C7 (a) 31 May   (b) £106.14

C8 (a) 1 minute 39 seconds   (b) Day 6
(c) 5 minutes 17 seconds

C9 298

C10 44.9%

C11 26.8%

C12 19.6%

C13 156%

C14 (a) A 78%, B 93.2%, C 103.9%, D 112.9%, E 116.9%
(b) 118.0% (hourly 118.1%)

D Percentage change in reverse (p 73)

D1 £12.50

D2 £84

D3 (a) £329   (b) £360

D4

Price excluding VAT	Price including VAT
£1430	**£1680.25**
£480	£564
£740	**£869.50**
£2550	£2996.25

D5 £16.80

D6 £32.50

D7 (a) £25   (b) £45   (c) £96   (d) £80.80

E Mixed questions (p 74)

E1 (a) 82 300   (b) 74393

E2 £152.81

E3 (a) 50%   (b) $33\frac{1}{3}$%   (c) 25%   (d) 20%
(e) $66\frac{2}{3}$%   (f) 100%   (g) 150%

E4 (a) £32.86   (b) £25.01   (c) £14.50   (d) £18.50
(e) up 35%   (f) down 8%

E5 14.1%

E6 (a) 6.3%   (b) 2800

E7 16.7%

E8 He should not increase the fee.
$1.15 \times 0.86 = 0.989$, so the total money taken will go down.

E9 20.6%

Test yourself (p 76)

T1 (a) £535.96   (b) £376

T2 (a) £360   (b) £288.26

T3 £40

T4 (a) £5755.11   (b) 1.157 625

T5 5.7% reduction

T6 68%

Review 1 (p 77)

1 (a) (i) 26 cm^2 (ii) 90 cm^2
(b) 23 cm

2 (a) 1   (b) $1\frac{1}{4}$ and $\frac{4}{5}$ are the reciprocals of each other.

3 3.4% or 3%

4 (a) 15   (b) 2.4   (c) 2   (d) 3 sets

5 £156 500

6 20

7 28 300 or 28 000

8 24

9 (a) $\frac{3}{5}$ (b) $\frac{5}{8}$

10 (a) $n = \frac{2}{3}$ (b) $x = 11$

11 $\angle BAC = 32 + 18 = 50°$
$\angle ABC = 180 - (2 \times 50) = 80°$ ($\triangle ABC$ is isosceles)
So $x = 180 - (32 + 80) = 68°$ (The sum of the angles of a triangle is 180°.)

12 **(a)** 21   **(b)** 33 words per minute
(c) 44 words per minute   **(d)** 76.2% or 76%

13 $4a + 146 = 360$, so $a = 53.5$
The angles are 53.5°, 113.5°, 146.5°, 46.5°.

14 **(a)** x^2 **(b)** $2x$
(c) In cm², the area of the four sides is $2x \times 4 = 8x$ and the area of the base is x^2 so the total area of metal is given by $y = x^2 + 8x$.

(d)

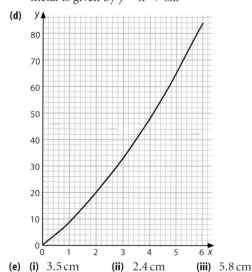

(e) **(i)** 3.5 cm   **(ii)** 2.4 cm   **(iii)** 5.8 cm

15 36 days

16 **(a)** $n = 15$ **(b)** $n = 9$ **(c)** $n - 2$

17 **(a)** 8.484 m²   **(b)** 85 000 cm²

18 £304.16

19 **(a)**

(b) 1.8 kg   **(c)** $1 < w \le 2$

20 £30

21 69.5 kg, 70.5 kg

22 **(a)** 10   **(b)** 25   **(c)** 2   **(d)** 14   **(e)** $\frac{4}{5}$

23 **(a)** 44.0 cm   **(b)** 36π cm²

24 £246.80

25 **(a)** $x = ^-8$ **(b)** $x = 14$ **(c)** $x = 1$ **(d)** $x = 7$

26 **(a)** 162°   **(b)** 20

9 Transformations

A Reflection (p 80)

A1 **(a)** D   **(b)** C   **(c)** D   **(d)** D   **(e)** G   **(f)** G

A2 **(a)** m **(b)** p **(c)** q **(d)** q **(e)** n **(f)** q

A3 **(a)** No
(b) Rotation through 180° about the point where the mirror lines intersect
(c) No

A4 **(a)** a is $y = x$; b is $x = 4$; c is $y = 4$; d is $y = ^-1$; e is $y = ^-x$.
(b) $y = 0$
(c) $x = 0$

A5 **(a)**

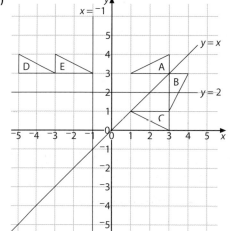

(b) A translation 2 units to the right

A6 **(a)** F   **(b)** E   **(c)** H   **(d)** F

A7 **(a)** $x = 2$ **(b)** $y = x$ **(c)** $y = 0$ **(d)** $x = 1$

A8 **(a)** $(2, 7)$
(b) The x- and y-coordinates are interchanged.
(c) The x-coordinate stays the same; the y-coordinate changes it sign.
(d) The x-coordinate changes its sign; the y-coordinate stays the same.

A9 **(a)**

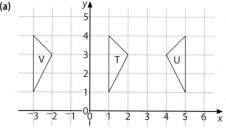

(b) A translation 4 units to the left

B Translation (p 82)

B1 (a) $\begin{bmatrix} 3 \\ 2 \end{bmatrix}$ (b) $\begin{bmatrix} 1 \\ -3 \end{bmatrix}$ (c) $\begin{bmatrix} 2 \\ -1 \end{bmatrix}$ (d) $\begin{bmatrix} 0 \\ 3 \end{bmatrix}$

   (e) $\begin{bmatrix} -2 \\ -2 \end{bmatrix}$ (f) $\begin{bmatrix} 4 \\ 0 \end{bmatrix}$ (g) $\begin{bmatrix} -2 \\ 3 \end{bmatrix}$ (h) $\begin{bmatrix} 6 \\ -3 \end{bmatrix}$

B2 They both go in the same direction but (h) goes three times as far as (c) does. The numbers in the column vector for (h) are three times those in the vector for (c).

B3 $\begin{bmatrix} -3 \\ 1 \end{bmatrix}$

B4 He is wrong. The vector is $\begin{bmatrix} 1 \\ -2 \end{bmatrix}$.

The vertices connected by the vector in his diagram do not correspond.

B5 (a) C   (b) E   (c) F

B6 (a) $\begin{bmatrix} 5 \\ -1 \end{bmatrix}$ (b) $\begin{bmatrix} 2 \\ -2 \end{bmatrix}$ (c) $\begin{bmatrix} -3 \\ -2 \end{bmatrix}$ (d) $\begin{bmatrix} -2 \\ 1 \end{bmatrix}$

B7

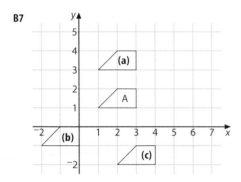

C Rotation (p 83)

C1 (a) (i) Q   (ii) R   (iii) Q

   (b) 'anticlockwise'

   (c) (i) 60° anticlockwise about centre c

      (ii) 120° clockwise about centre c

      (iii) 120° anticlockwise about centre c

      (iv) 180° about centre c

      (v) 60° clockwise about centre c

      (vi) 180° about centre c

   (d) Those where the angle is 180°

C2 (a) G

   (b) '90° clockwise' (or '270° anticlockwise'; in the answers that follow, 90° will be given rather than 270° in the opposite direction, though the latter is also correct.)

   (c) 'about point n'

   (d) F, H (in either order)

   (e) G, q

(f) A (90° clockwise about m)

     B (180° about m)

     C (90° anticlockwise about m)

     H (180° about n)

(g) (i) 180° rotation about q

     (ii) 90° rotation anticlockwise about n

     (iii) 180° rotation about n

     (iv) 90° rotation anticlockwise about q

     (v) 180° rotation about n

     (vi) 90° rotation anticlockwise about n

(h) C; Dave should add '90° clockwise about n'; Myra should add '180° about m'. D is also a possible answer, though the centre of rotation for Dave (where D and E touch) does not have a letter in the diagram.

C3

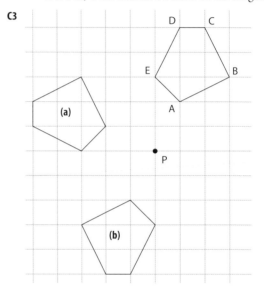

C4

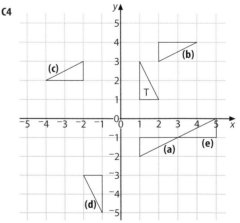

C5 (a) It is the mid-point of PP′.

   (b) It is the mid-point of QQ′.

   (c) It is the mid-point of a line joining any point to its image point.

C6 $(1, 3)$

C7 $(^-1, ^-1)$

C8 **(a)** 90° clockwise about $(3, 2)$

  (b) 180° about $(3, 3)$

  (c) 90° anticlockwise about $(2, 3)$

  (d) 90° clockwise about $(6, 4)$

  (e) 90° clockwise about $(4, 0)$

  (f) 90° anticlockwise about $(4, 4)$

  (g) 180° about $(4\frac{1}{2}, 2\frac{1}{2})$

  (h) 90° anticlockwise about $(6, 1)$

D Enlargement (p 86)

D1 **(a)** 2

  (b) A diagram showing 'rays' coming from centre C at $(0, 3)$ and going through the vertices of the triangles

  (c) $\begin{bmatrix} 2 \\ 2 \end{bmatrix}$

  (d) $\overrightarrow{CP'} = \begin{bmatrix} 4 \\ 4 \end{bmatrix}$

  The top and bottom numbers are twice those for $\overrightarrow{CP}$.

  (e) In each case the vector is 'doubled' (its top and bottom numbers are doubled).

D2

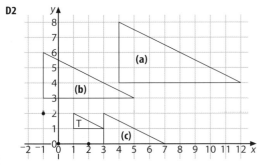

D3 **(a)** An enlargement scale factor 2, centre $(3, 10)$

  (b), (d)

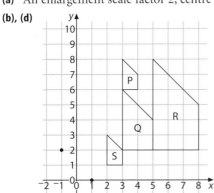

  (c) An enlargement scale factor 3, centre $(2, 8)$

  (d) 9...

  (e) Transla...

  (f) 180° rotation a...

E3 **(a)** Reflection in the line...

  (b) Scale factor 2, centre $(3, ^-2)$

  (c), (d)

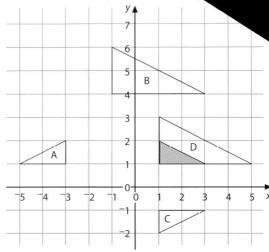

  (e) 180° rotation about $(^-1, 0)$

  (f) Translation with vector $\begin{bmatrix} 2 \\ -3 \end{bmatrix}$

  (g) The yellow triangle, A and C are congruent. B and D are congruent.

Test yourself (p 88)

T1 **(a)** **(i)** A   **(ii)** E   **(iii)** B

  (b) Reflection in the line $x = ^-2$

T2 **(a)** **(i)** Reflection in $x = 0$

    (ii) 90° anticlockwise rotation centre $(0, 0)$

  (b) Enlargement scale factor $\frac{1}{2}$, centre $(0, 0)$

  (c) 180° rotation centre $(4, 1)$

(b) False   (c) False

(e) True   (f) False

$= 7^3 \times 7^3 = 7^6$ (b) $(2^4)^3 = 2^4 \times 2^4 \times 2^4 = 2^{12}$

(b) 2^9 (c) 4^{10} (d) 3^{12}

$= x^5 \times x^5 \times x^5 = x^{15}$

p^8 (b) x^4 (c) k^0 or 1   (d) n^9

a) $(5^2)^4 = 8$ (b) $(10^4)^3 = 10^{12}$

(c) $(n^5)^2 = n^{10}$ (d) $(x^2)^7 = x^{14}$

.6 $(a^m)^n = a^{mn}$ with explanation

B17 (a) 3^2 (b) 3^{10} (c) 3^{12} (d) 3^8 (e) 3^{3n}

B18 $32^5, 16^7, 4^{15}, 2^{31}, 8^{11}$

B19 2^7

C Multiplying expressions with powers (p 92)

C1 (a) A and D, B and F, C and G, H and I

(b) E

C2 (a) $15p^2$ (b) $2n^2$ (c) $18m^3$ (d) $7d^7$

(e) $6h^7$ (f) $20x^6$ (g) $21n^9$ (h) $8n^9$

C3 (a)

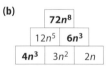

(b)

(c)

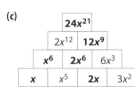

C4 (a) $2p \times 4p = 8p^2$ (b) $7m^2 \times m = 7m^3$

(c) $3d^2 \times 4d = 12d^3$ (d) $3h^5 \times 2h^5 = 6h^{10}$

(e) $6h \times 3h^6 = 18h^7$ (f) $5p^4 \times 3p^8 = 15p^{12}$

C5

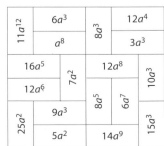

E Mixed questions

E1 (a) J

E2 (a) 180° rotation about (-1, 3)

(b) 90° anticlockwise rotation about (2, 1)

(c) H

(b) H

(b) 90° anticlockwise rotation about (0, 0)

(c) Reflection in the line $x = 5$

(d) E

...tion with vector $\begin{bmatrix} 4 \\ 2 \end{bmatrix}$

$x = -1$

(p 87)

C and

B2 (a) $4^3 \times 4^2 =$

(c) $7^1 \times 7^3 = 7^4$ or

B3 (a) 6^9 (b) 2^{13} (c) 10

(f) 8^9 (g) 9^7 (h) 2^{12}

B4 (a) 16 807   (b) 5 764 801   (c) ... 3

(d) 5 764 801

B5 5^8

B6 (a)

(b)

(c)

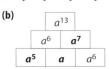

B7 (a) b^4 (b) h^5 (c) a^9 (d) k^6 (e) d^8

(f) m^{12} (g) p^{13} (h) n^9

B8 (a) $y^5 \times y^3 = y^8$ (b) $n^2 \times n^4 = n^6$

(c) $h^4 \times h^2 \times h^5 = h^{11}$ (d) $k \times k^5 = k^6$

(e) $b^0 \times b^3 = b^3$ (f) $p^4 \times p^{17} \times p^3 = p^{24}$

B9 (a)

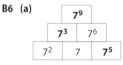

(b)

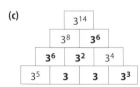

332 Answers: Chapter 10

C6 (a) $(2p)^3 = 2p \times 2p \times 2p = \mathbf{8p^3}$

(b) $(3n^3)^2 = 3n^3 \times 3n^3 = \mathbf{9n^6}$

C7 (a) $8y^3$ (b) $9n^2$ (c) $4p^{10}$ (d) $64m^9$

D Dividing powers (p 93)

D1 (a) A and E $(2^6 \div 2^2 = 2^4)$, B and C $\left(\dfrac{2^4}{2} = 2^3\right)$,

D and I $\left(\dfrac{2^5}{2^4} = 2\right)$, F and G $\left(\dfrac{2^8}{2^6} = 2^2\right)$

(b) H

D2 (a) 7^8 (b) 2^5 (c) 10^5 (d) 5^5 (e) 3^2

(f) 8^5 (g) 10^9 (h) 5^0

D3 (a) 6   (b) 7   (c) 11   (d) 14   (e) 14

(f) 6   (g) 4   (h) 8

D4 (a) 6^8 (b) 7^2 (c) 2^6 (d) 3^2 (e) 5^3

(f) 2^3 (g) 7^2 (h) 8^2

D5 (a) 64   (b) 512   (c) 8   (d) 1

D6 2^0 or 1

D7 (a) 2   (b) 5   (c) 3   (d) 9

D8 (a) h^4 (b) n^5 (c) x^3 (d) d^9 (e) a^1 or a

D9 (a) 2   (b) 8   (c) 4   (d) 7

D10 (a)   (b)

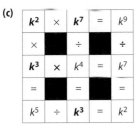

(c)

D11 (a) 3   (b) 9   (c) 3   (d) 9   (e) 27

D12 (a) g^8 (b) w^4 (c) p^4 (d) h^1 or h

(e) y^5 (f) h^4 (g) q^3 (h) z^0 or 1

D13 (a) 4   (b) 3   (c) 2   (d) 6

(e) 4   (f) 2   (g) 2   (h) 4

E Dividing expressions with powers (p 95)

E1 (a) $5p$ (b) $2a^4$ (c) $4y$ (d) m^2 (e) $4n^6$

E2 (a) 3   (b) 2   (c) 5   (d) 27, 6

E3 (a)

$5a^3$	$\times$	$6a^6$	$=$	$30a^9$
$\times$	■	$\div$	■	$\div$
$2a^5$	$\times$	$3a$	$=$	$6a^6$
$=$	■	$=$	■	$=$
$10a^8$	$\div$	$2a^5$	$=$	$5a^3$

(b)

$24n^6$	$\div$	$2n^2$	$=$	$12n^4$
$\div$	■	$\div$	■	$\div$
$3n^3$	$\div$	n	$=$	$3n^2$
$=$	■	$=$	■	$=$
$8n^3$	$\div$	$2n$	$=$	$4n^2$

E4 (a) n^4 (b) $6n^4$ (c) $2n^3$ (d) $5n$

E5 (a) $\dfrac{1}{5^4}$ (b) $\dfrac{1}{2}$ (c) $\dfrac{1}{p^7}$ (d) $\dfrac{1}{n^9}$ (e) $\dfrac{1}{y^7}$

E6 (a) $\dfrac{3}{p^3}$ (b) $\dfrac{2}{b^4}$ (c) $\dfrac{3}{x^5}$ (d) $\dfrac{m^3}{5}$ (e) $\dfrac{a}{7}$

(f) $\dfrac{y}{2}$ (g) $\dfrac{n^2}{5}$ (h) $\dfrac{10}{b^3}$ (i) $\dfrac{1}{7x^4}$ (j) $\dfrac{1}{3x}$

E7 (a) $\dfrac{4}{3a}$ (b) $\dfrac{2n^2}{5}$ (c) $\dfrac{3}{7p}$ (d) $\dfrac{2}{9x^2}$ (e) $\dfrac{3}{5k^3}$

E8 (a) $\dfrac{8}{x^2}$ (b) $\dfrac{3}{4k^2}$ (c) $\dfrac{1}{2y}$ (d) $\dfrac{8}{3n^3}$

F Negative indices (p 96)

F1 (a) A and G $\left(3^{-4} = \dfrac{1}{3^4}\right)$, C and F $\left(2^{-3} = \dfrac{1}{2^3}\right)$,

D and E $\left(4^{-3} = \dfrac{1}{4^3}\right)$

(b) B

F2 (a) A and I $\left(3^{-2} = \tfrac{1}{9}\right)$, B and F $\left(2^{-3} = \tfrac{1}{8}\right)$,

D and G $\left(6^{-1} = \tfrac{1}{6}\right)$, E and H $\left(4^{-2} = \tfrac{1}{16}\right)$

(b) C

F3 (a) $\tfrac{1}{27}$ (b) $\tfrac{1}{7}$ (c) $\tfrac{1}{81}$ (d) $\tfrac{1}{64}$ (e) $\tfrac{1}{11}$

F4 (a) A and E $\left(2^{-1} + 2^{-2} = \tfrac{3}{4}\right)$, B and I $\left(5^0 - 5^{-1} = \tfrac{4}{5}\right)$,

C and F $\left(8^{-1} \times 8^0 = \tfrac{1}{8}\right)$, D and H $(4 \times 2^{-2} = 1)$

(b) G

F5 (a) 0.5   (b) 0.25   (c) 0.01   (d) 0.001   (e) 0.2

F6 1.2

F7 0.101

F8 (a) $\dfrac{1}{x^3}$ (b) $\dfrac{1}{g}$ (c) $\dfrac{1}{n^2}$ (d) $\dfrac{1}{k^3}$ (e) $\dfrac{1}{p}$

F9 (a) $x = 12$ (b) $x = 10$ (c) $x = {-}1$ (d) $x = 0$

(e) $x = 7$ (f) $x = 2$ (g) $x = {-}5$ (h) $x = {-}2$

F10 No, $2^x > 0$ for all x

G Extending the rules to negative indices (p 98)

G1 (a) 3^1 (or 3)   (b) 10^3 (c) 8^0 (or 1)   (d) 3^{-2}

(e) 2^{-5} (f) 9^{-1} (g) 2^{-5} (h) 7^3

G2 (a) 3^{-2} (b) 5^{-3} (c) 2^{-1} (d) 9^{-5}

(e) 4^{-2} (f) 7^{-6} (g) 6^{-1} (h) 10^{-6}

G3 (a) 5^2 (b) 2^{-3} (c) 7^{-1} (d) 6^{-7}

(e) 7^{-5} (f) 4^{-4} (g) 2^0 (or 1)   (h) 5^{-1}

G4 (a) p^{-1} or $\dfrac{1}{p}$ **(b)** q^0 or 1 **(c)** r^2

(d) s^{-2} or $\dfrac{1}{s^2}$ **(e)** w^{-5} or $\dfrac{1}{w^5}$ **(f)** x^{-3} or $\dfrac{1}{x^3}$

(g) y^0 or 1 **(h)** z^{-4} or $\dfrac{1}{z^4}$

G5 (a) 2^{-8} **(b)** 3^{-6} **(c)** 5^{-2} **(d)** a^{-10} **(e)** x^{-9}

G6 (a) $2^8 \times 2^{-2} = 2^6$ **(b)** $\dfrac{3^2}{3^7} = 3^{-5}$

(c) $a^2 \times a^{-1} \times a^{-4} = a^{-3}$ **(d)** $\dfrac{b^1}{b^3} = b^{-2}$

(e) $(5^{-4})^3 = 5^{-12}$ **(f)** $(2^{-2})^5 = 2^{-10}$

G7 (a) $8n^{-3}$ or $\dfrac{8}{n^3}$ **(b)** $6r^2$ **(c)** $5s^{-5}$ or $\dfrac{5}{s^5}$

(d) $10b^{-5}$ or $\dfrac{10}{b^5}$ **(e)** $4h^{-8}$ or $\dfrac{4}{h^8}$ **(f)** $\frac{1}{3}c^{-2}$ or $\dfrac{1}{3c^2}$

(g) $2a^{-2}$ or $\dfrac{2}{a^2}$ **(h)** $\frac{2}{5}x^{-2}$ or $\dfrac{2}{5x^2}$

G8 (a) 5^5 **(b)** 2^1 **(c)** 3^{-1} **(d)** 7^{15}

G9 (a) z^6 **(b)** a^6 **(c)** b^1 or b

G10 (a)

5^8	$\times$	5	$=$	5^9
$\times$	■	$\div$	■	$\div$
5^{-4}	$\times$	5^5	$=$	5
$=$	■	$=$	■	$=$
5^4	$\div$	5^{-4}	$=$	5^8

(b)

e^2	$\div$	e^0	$=$	e^2
$\times$	■	$\div$	■	$\times$
e^6	$\div$	e^2	$=$	e^4
$=$	■	$=$	■	$=$
e^8	$\times$	e^{-2}	$=$	e^6

(c)

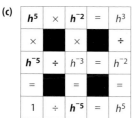

h^5	$\times$	h^{-2}	$=$	h^3
$\times$	■	$\times$	■	$\div$
h^{-5}	$\div$	h^{-3}	$=$	h^{-2}
$=$	■	$=$	■	$=$
1	$\div$	h^{-5}	$=$	h^5

G11 (a) $\frac{1}{2}x^5$ **(b)** $\dfrac{5}{2x}$ **(c)** $\frac{1}{2}x^5$

H True, iffy, false (p 100)

H1 (a) Always true

(b) Sometimes true
(but only when m or $n = 0$, otherwise it is false)

(c) Always true   **(d)** Always true

(e) Sometimes true
(but only when $n = 0$, otherwise it is false)

(f) Never true (unless you count 0 as a square number)

(g) Always true

(h) Sometimes true (for $2 \le n \le 9$ only)

(i) Always true   **(j)** Always true

(k) Sometimes true (whenever $n = 2m$)

(l) Never true

H2 (a) Always true

(b) Sometimes true (but only when $a = 1$)

(c) Never true   **(d)** Never true

(e) Always true   **(f)** Always true

(g) Never true   **(h)** Always true

(i) Never true   **(j)** Never true

(k) Always true

(l) Sometimes true (but only when $a = \frac{1}{2}$ (or 0))

H3 (a) False, a could be $^-7$ **(b)** False, x could be 0

(c) True   **(d)** False, for example $k = \frac{-1}{2}$

(e) False, for example $k = \frac{1}{2}$

(f) True

Test yourself (p 101)

T1 (a) $n = 7$ **(b)** $n = 4$ **(c)** $n = 1$ **(d)** $n = 3$

T2 (a) 27   **(b)** $\frac{1}{8}$ **(c)** 1

T3 (a) w^8 **(b)** x^{-2} or $\dfrac{1}{x^2}$ **(c)** y^6

T4 (a) (i) 5^6 **(ii)** 5^3 **(b)** $x = 7, y = 3$

T5 (a) 2^2 **(b)** 7^7 **(c)** 6^{-1} **(d)** 3^{-5} **(e)** 3^7

T6 (a) 7   **(b)** $^-5$ **(c)** 5   **(d)** 3   **(e)** $^-4$

(f) $^-3$

T7 (a) $4m^4$ **(b)** $6b^4$ **(c)** $8x^{12}$

(d) $\frac{2}{5}x^{-1}$ or $\dfrac{2}{5x}$

T8 (a) $n = ^-4$ **(b)** $x = 2$ **(c)** $x = ^-1$ **(d)** $x = 0$

T9 (a) $^-5$ **(b)** $^-5$ **(c)** 1

11 Surveys and experiments

Most questions are for discussion with the whole class or in small groups and do not have a single 'right' answer. So answers to only some questions are given.

B Surveys (p 104)

B1 The choice of chart depends on the features of the data that are to be brought out.

To compare year groups and boys and girls, two divided bar charts could be drawn:

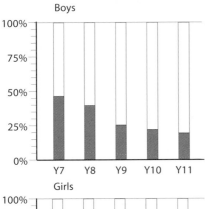

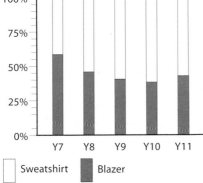

These could be combined into a single divided bar chart if year groups as a whole are to be compared. Two pie charts could be used to compare all boys and all girls.

B3 'How much do you earn?' may be thought rude. It is also unclear: per week, per year?

'How many are there in your family?' is unclear and could also be embarrassing in some circumstances.

'Where do you shop?' gives only four choices, none of which may apply.

'How much do you spend a week on food?' will result in people approximating in different ways. It would be better to give groups. Also, what is covered by 'food'?

'How do you think supermarket fruit …?' is a leading question.

C Experiments (p 110)

All the data used in the report is authentic. The words used were: car, pencil, cake, hoover, love, elephant, fire, data, cloud, history. The pictures used were: lamp, eye, heart, mug, bottle, dice, flower, cake, boat, pencil. The numbers used were: 92, 47, 81, 24, 5, 48, 30, 12, 55, 76

C2 Items are more easily remembered if they can be linked. One way to help remember unrelated items is to make up a story that links them, for example: 'I was sitting in a **car** with a **cake** in the shape of a **pencil**. When the cake disintegrated and had to be **hoover**ed up …'

C4 There is a possibility of bias in the sample: sixth-form maths groups might be better at remembering numbers.

C6 5 words, 7 numbers

C7 5

C8 2

C9 14

C14 When the same data-pair has to be plotted twice on a scatter diagram, two crosses can be plotted very close to each other.

The technique of 'quartering' can be used: lines are drawn at the medians and the crosses in each pair of diagonally opposite corners are counted (ignoring those on a line).

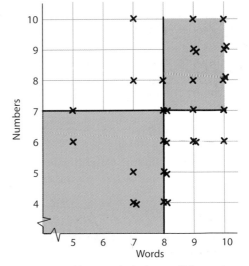

13 crosses in the 'upward' diagonal

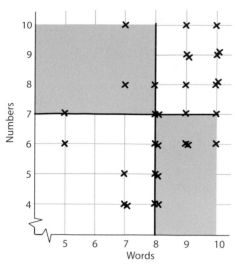

5 crosses in the 'downward' diagonal

There are more crosses in the upward diagonal than in the downward. This indicates a positive correlation.

C15

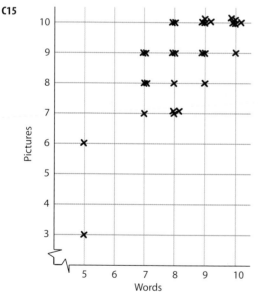

There is a stronger positive correlation between memory for words and pictures for this sample.

12 Speed, distance and time

A Calculating speed (p 115)

A1 8 m/s

A2 A: 25 km/h, B: 30 km/h, C: 29 km/h, D: 48 km/h

A3 (a) 70 km/h   (b) 10 m/s   (c) 280 m.p.h.
     (d) 40 m.p.h.   (e) 35 m.p.h.

A4 (a) 15 km/h   (b) 420 km/h   (c) 15 m/s

A5 12 m.p.h.

A6 (a) 400 miles   (b) 800 miles   (c) 160 m.p.h.

A7 40 m.p.h.

A8 42 m.p.h.

A9 40 m.p.h.

A10 (a) 44.5 m.p.h.   (b) 34 m.p.h.   (c) 40 m.p.h.

B Distance–time graphs (p 117)

B1 (a) Stage 1   20 miles in 1 hour
              = 20 m.p.h. away from home
      Stage 2   Stopped for 1 hour
      Stage 3   30 m.p.h. for 1 hour away from home

     (b) Stage 1   30 miles in $1\frac{1}{2}$ hours
              = 20 m.p.h. towards home
      Stage 2   Stopped for $\frac{1}{2}$ hour
      Stage 3   40 m.p.h., arriving at home at $2\frac{1}{2}$ hours

     (c) Stage 1   40 m.p.h. away from home
      Stage 2   Stopped for $\frac{3}{4}$ hour
      Stage 3   40 m.p.h. towards home

     (d) Stage 1   35 m.p.h. towards home
      Stage 2   5 m.p.h. towards home

B2 (a) A, because the line is steeper.
     (b) 1.5 m/s
     (c) 1 m/s
     (d) 1 m/s. The speed of car C is the same as the speed of car B, but car C is travelling in the opposite direction.
     (e) A
     (f) 3 seconds
     (g) (i) 2 m   (ii) 4 m   (iii) 2 m

B3 (a) 0800   (b) $1\frac{1}{2}$ hours   (c) 40 m.p.h.
     (d) $1\frac{1}{2}$ hours   (e) $\frac{1}{2}$ hour   (f) 30 m.p.h.
     (g) 20 m.p.h.   (h) 1130   (i) 45 miles
     (j) About 1235

B4 (a), (b)

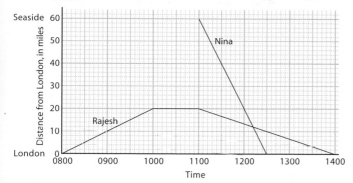

(c) 1200   (d) About 1212

B5 (a) 20 km   (b) $\frac{2}{3}$ km/min

    (c) 40 km/h   (d) 30 km/h

B6 (a) A: 14 km/h, B: 17.5 km/h, C: 28 km/h, D: 35 km/h

    (b) A is overtaken by C

    (c) B, C, D, A

    (d) Approximately 12 km and 16 km

    (e) B, A, D

C Calculating distance and time (p 121)

C1 90 m

C2 720 miles

C3 (a) 12.5 cm   (b) 30 cm   (c) 75 cm

C4 165 miles

C5 18 miles

C6 3 hours

C7 4 hours

C8 6 hours

C9 $2\frac{1}{2}$ hours

C10 $2\frac{1}{2}$ hours

D Mixing units (p 122)

D1 32 m.p.h.

D2 (a) 600 m   (b) 3000 m   (c) 9000 m

D3 (a) 150 miles   (b) 10 miles   (c) 5 miles

D4 16 minutes

D5 (a) 10 km   (b) 2.5 km   (c) 20 km   (d) 22.5 km

D6 (a) 84 km/h   (b) 48 km/h   (c) 82.5 km/h

D7 (a) 720 m   (b) 12.5 km   (c) 13.5 miles

D8 (a) 22.5 minutes   (b) 4 minutes   (c) 2.5 minutes

D9 1 hour 20 minutes

D10 33 miles

E Time on a calculator (p 123)

E1 8.3 km/h

E2 16.4 m.p.h.

E3 6.6 miles

E4 9.3 km

E5 31.25 miles

E6 7.6 m/s

E7 34 minutes

E8 2 hours 20 minutes

E9 (a) 2 hours 20 minutes   (b) 50 minutes

E10 (a) 40.4 m.p.h.   (b) 23.4 m.p.h.   (c) 29.6 m.p.h.

E11 No, she was 2 minutes late.

E12 (a) 32.5 miles   (b) 35.5 m.p.h.

E13 46.7 m.p.h.

Test yourself (p 125)

T1 (a) 10:16

    (b) 28 km

    (c) Between B and C because the line is steepest.

    (d) 50 km/h

T2 45 m.p.h.

T3 103 m.p.h. (to the nearest 1 m.p.h.)

T4 (a) 1 hour 9 minutes   (b) 21.7 km/h

13 Volume, surface area and density

A Volume of a cuboid (p 126)

A1 (a) $240 \, \text{cm}^3$ (b) $112 \, \text{cm}^3$ (c) $62.5 \, \text{cm}^3$
(d) $450 \, \text{m}^3$ (e) $105.3 \, \text{m}^3$

A2 $a = 12 \, \text{cm}, b = 4.5 \, \text{cm}, c = 6 \, \text{cm}, d = 3 \, \text{cm}$

B Volume of a prism (p 127)

B1 (a) $90 \, \text{cm}^3$ (b) $147 \, \text{cm}^3$ (c) $50 \, \text{cm}^3$

B2 (a) $132 \, \text{cm}^3$ (b) $85.86 \, \text{cm}^3$ (c) $61.875 \, \text{cm}^3$

B3 (a) $5.25 \, \text{cm}^3$ (b) $45 \, \text{cm}^3$ (c) $450 \, \text{cm}^3$

B4 (a) $168 \, \text{cm}^3$ (b) $174.42 \, \text{cm}^3$ (c) $6717.75 \, \text{cm}^3$

B5 (a) $204\,000 \, \text{cm}^3, 0.204 \, \text{m}^3$ (b) $911\,250 \, \text{cm}^3, 0.911\,25 \, \text{m}^3$

B6 $8.64 \, \text{m}^3$

B7 $120 \, \text{m}^3$

B8 (a) $8 \, \text{cm}$ (b) $960 \, \text{cm}^3$

B9 (a) $3.2 \, \text{m}$ (b) 38 or $39 \, \text{m}^3$

B10 (a) (i) $5.5 \, \text{cm}$ (ii) $105.5 \, \text{cm}^2$
(b) (i) $4.5 \, \text{cm}$ (ii) $105.3 \, \text{cm}^2$

B11 $5.5 \, \text{cm}$

B12 (a) $0.2 \, \text{m}$ (b) $20 \, \text{cm}$

B13 $6750 \, \text{cm}^2$

B14 (a) $122.4 \, \text{m}^3$ (b) $0.69 \, \text{m}$

C Volume of a cylinder (p 131)

C1 (a) $50.3 \, \text{cm}^2$ (b) $503 \, \text{cm}^3$

C2 (a) πr^2 (b) $\pi r^2 l$

C3 (a) $240 \, \text{cm}^3$ (b) $499 \, \text{cm}^3$ (c) $133 \, \text{cm}^3$

C4 $2474 \, \text{cm}^3$

C5 (a) $9.4 \, \text{m}$ (b) $4.95 = 5 \, \text{m}^3$

C6 $3.3 \, \text{cm}$

C7 $6.1 \, \text{cm}$

C8 $24.6 \, \text{cm}^3$

D Surface area (p 132)

D1 (a) (i) Sketch of net   (ii) $184 \, \text{cm}^2$
(b) (i) Sketch of net   (ii) $144 \, \text{cm}^2$
(c) (i) Sketch of net   (ii) $188 \, \text{cm}^2$

D2 (a) $12.6 \, \text{cm}$ (b) $101 \, \text{cm}^2$

D3 (a) $2\pi r$ (b) $2\pi r l$

D4 (a) $94 \, \text{cm}^2$ (b) $587 \, \text{cm}^2$ (c) $588 \, \text{m}^2$

D5 $3.4 \, \text{cm}$

D6 $7.4 \, \text{cm}$

D7 $325 \, \text{cm}^2$

D8 $2\pi r l + 2\pi r^2$ or $2\pi r(l + r)$

D9 (a) $88 \, \text{cm}^2$ (b) $267 \, \text{cm}^2$ (c) $18\,209 \, \text{m}^2$

D10 $418 \, \text{cm}^2$

D11 Length $14.5 \, \text{cm}$, volume $812 \, \text{cm}^3$

D12 $390 \, \text{cm}^2$

E Density (p 134)

E1 (a) $2.875 \, \text{g/cm}^3$ (b) $1600 \, \text{kg/m}^3$

E2 (a) $276 \, \text{g}$ (b) $3049 \, \text{g}$ (to the nearest gram)
(c) $562\,500 \, \text{kg}$ (or 562.5 tonnes)

E3 (a) Silver   (b) Fake gold
(c) Platinum   (d) Gold

E4 $159 \, \text{cm}^3$ (to the nearest cm^3)

E5 (a) $700 \, \text{cm}^3$ (b) $13.51 \, \text{kg}$

E6 (a) $3.14 \, \text{cm}^3$ (b) 28 grams

E7 $2.8 \, \text{g/cm}^3$

E8 $751 \, \text{g}$

E9 $0.59 \, \text{cm}^3$

F Units of volume and liquid measure (p 135)

F1 (a) $24 \, \text{m}^3 = 24\,000\,000 \, \text{cm}^3$ (b) $1\,000\,000$

F2 (a) $25\,000\,000 \, \text{cm}^3$ (b) $600\,000 \, \text{cm}^3$
(c) $200\,000\,000 \, \text{cm}^3$ (d) $800 \, \text{cm}^3$

F3 (a) $7 \, \text{m}^3$ (b) $3.2 \, \text{m}^3$ (c) $0.342 \, \text{m}^3$ (d) $0.008 \, \text{m}^3$

F4 $1847 \, \text{ml}$

F5 1.847 litre

F6 1000

F7 (a) 72 litres   (b) $28 \, \text{cm}$

F8 (a) $16\,085\,000$ litres   (b) $4 \, \text{cm}$

F9 $1 \, \text{m}^2$

F10 $0.2 \, \text{mm}$

F11 $225\,000$ litres

F12 $0.141 \, \text{cm}$

Test yourself (p 136)

T1 (a) $337.5 \, \text{cm}^3, 300 \, \text{cm}^2$ (b) $264.6 \, \text{cm}^3, 292.4 \, \text{cm}^2$
(c) $184.73 \, \text{cm}^3, 181.2 \, \text{cm}^2$

T2 (a) $99.36 \, \text{cm}^3$ (b) $11.1 \, \text{cm}$

T3 $2.18 \, \text{kg}$

T4 (a) $24a, 18a + 36$ (b) $a = 6$ (c) $a = 12$

T5 $62.5 \, \text{cm}^2$

14 Cumulative frequency

A How long can you hold your breath? (p 138)

The results can first be recorded on a dot plot:

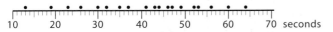

Then suitable class intervals (e.g. 10–20, 20–30, …) can be chosen and the number of students who held their breath for up to (and including), say, 60 seconds, 70 seconds, etc. can be recorded:

Time (t seconds)	Cumulative frequency
$t \le 20$	2
$t \le 30$	5

This leads to questions such as 'How many (or what percentage) held their breath for more than 60 seconds, 50 seconds, etc., until the time for which 90% of the class can hold their breath is reached?'

B Cumulative frequency tables (p 138)

B1 (a) 51, 60   (b) The total number of babies

B2 (a) 31   (b) 45   (c) 50   (d) 52

B3

Height (h cm)	Cumulative frequency
$h \le 65$	2
$h \le 70$	11
$h \le 75$	23
$h \le 80$	29
$h \le 85$	33

B4 (a)

Age (a years)	Cumulative frequency
$a \le 20$	4
$a \le 30$	9
$a \le 40$	19
$a \le 50$	26
$a \le 60$	28

(b)

Height (h cm)	Cumulative frequency
$h \le 150$	3
$h \le 160$	10
$h \le 170$	24
$h \le 180$	44
$h \le 190$	56

B5 (a) 55   (b) 11   (c) 9   (d) 37

B6 36.6 cm

C Cumulative frequency graphs (p 140)

Estimates from graphs may differ slightly from values given here.

C1 (a) 8   (b) 18   (c) 32   (d) 39

C2 About 24

C3 About 22

C4 About 20%

C5 90% of the people can hold their breath for more than **40** seconds.

In the cumulative frequency graphs that follow it is also permissible to join the points with straight line segments. This is equivalent to assuming that the distribution in each interval is uniform.

C6 (a)

Waist (w cm)	Cumulative frequency
$w \le 65$	12
$w \le 70$	32
$w \le 75$	60
$w \le 80$	72
$w \le 85$	80

(b)

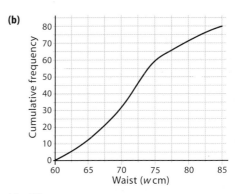

(c) 65

C7 (a) 250

(b)

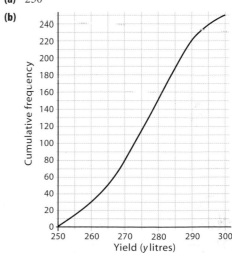

(c) (i) 188   (ii) 199

(d) About 190

C8 (a)

Number of marks, m	Cumulative frequency
$m \leq 10$	4
$m \leq 20$	11
$m \leq 30$	23
$m \leq 40$	46
$m \leq 50$	84
$m \leq 60$	130
$m \leq 70$	150
$m \leq 80$	166
$m \leq 90$	177
$m \leq 100$	180

(b)

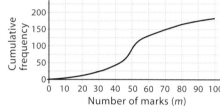

(c) 25   **(d)** About 65

D Median, quartiles and interquartile range (p 141)

D1 (a) 169 cm   **(b)** 163 cm   **(c)** 177.5 cm   **(d)** 14.5 cm

D2 (a) 25% of the boys have an armspan below **163 cm**.

    (b) 50% of the boys have an armspan below **169 cm**.

    (c) 75% of the boys have an armspan below **177.5 cm**.

    (d) 25% of the boys have an armspan above **177.5 cm**.

D3 (a)

Lifetime (x hours)	Cumulative frequency
$x \leq 500$	20
$x \leq 1000$	100
$x \leq 1500$	240
$x \leq 2000$	420
$x \leq 2500$	470
$x \leq 3000$	500

(b)

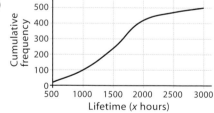

(c) (i) 1530 hours **(ii)** 1100 hours **(iii)** 1810 hours

    (iv) 710   **(v)** 11%

D4

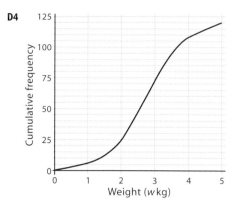

Median = 2.75 kg
Lower quartile = 2.2 kg
Upper quartile = 3.4 kg
Interquartile range = 1.2 kg

D5 (a)

Weight (w g)	Cumulative percentage
$w \leq 60$	8%
$w \leq 70$	21%
$w \leq 80$	45%
$w \leq 90$	72%
$w \leq 100$	88%
$w \leq 110$	97%
$w \leq 120$	100%

(b)

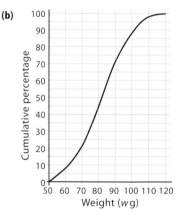

(c) Median = 82 g
Lower quartile = 72 g
Upper quartile = 92 g
Interquartile range = 20 g

E Box-and-whisker plots (p 144)

E1

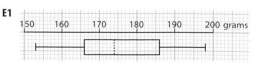

E2 (a) 44 years   **(b)** 32 years   **(c)** 50%

    (d) Town B: they have a higher median age (and a higher maximum age).

(e) Town A: you can tell because it has the wider box. This tells you that the ages in Town A are more spread out on the whole.

E3 The girls' handspans are more varied, and the boys' handspans are generally larger.

E4 (a)

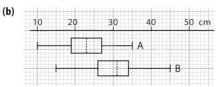

(b) 15 kg

E5 (a) E, because it has the greatest median.

(b) E, because it has the greatest interquartile range, or A, which has the greatest range.

E6 (a)

(length in cm)	A	B
Median	23	31
Upper quartile	27	34
Lower quartile	19	26

(b)

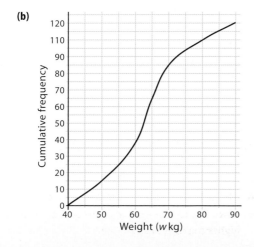

(c) 8 cm for both groups

(d) Although both groups have the same interquartile range, the worms in group B are on the whole larger and have a greater range of lengths.

Test yourself (p 146)

T1 (a)

Weight (w kg)	Cumulative frequency
$w \le 50$	15
$w \le 60$	37
$w \le 70$	85
$w \le 80$	110
$w \le 90$	120

(b)

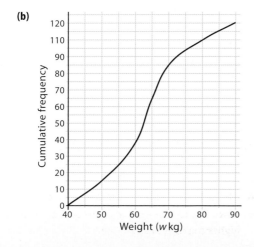

(c) 64 kg

(d) Lower quartile = 57 kg
Upper quartile = 72 kg
Interquartile range = 15 kg

(e)

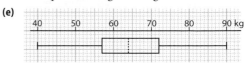

T2 (a) 25%　　　　　**(b)** 25%

(c) Variety B is generally heavier than variety A (from comparing the medians). The weight of variety A apples is generally more variable than for variety B (from the interquartile range and the range).

T3 (a) About £60

(b)

Money received (£)	≤ 0	≤ 50	≤ 100	≤ 150	≤ 200	≤ 250	≤ 300	≤ 350
Cumulative frequency	0	32	44	48	50	51	51	52

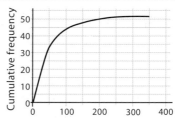

(c) Median = £40
Upper quartile = £70
Lower quartile = £20

(d) An appropriate comment

Review 2 (p 147)

1 (a) 2^6 **(b)** 4^6 **(c)** 3^3 **(d)** 7^6 **(e)** 5^{-6}

2 (a) 23 m.p.h. **(b)** 70 m.p.h.

3 (a) 135 000 cm^3 **(b)** 0.135 m^3

4 (a) $156 = 2^2 \times 3 \times 13$, $288 = 2^5 \times 3^2$

 (b) 3744 **(c)** 12

5 (a)

Number of hours (h)	Cumulative frequency
$h \le 5$	2
$h \le 10$	7
$h \le 15$	21
$h \le 20$	39
$h \le 25$	71
$h \le 30$	86
$h \le 35$	89
$h \le 40$	90

(b)

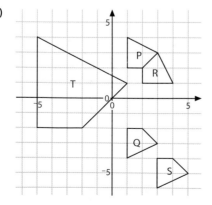

(c) About 21 hours

(d) Upper quartile 24 hours, lower quartile 15 hours

6 (a) $n = 2$ **(b)** $n = 1$ **(c)** $n = 0$ **(d)** $n = 10$

7 (a) 810.7 cm^3 (to the nearest 0.1 cm^3)

 (b) (i) 2700 cm^2 **(ii)** 0.27 m^2

8 (a) a^5 **(b)** a^{-6} **(c)** a^{-4} **(d)** a^5 **(e)** a^6

9 44 minutes

10 (a), (c), (e)

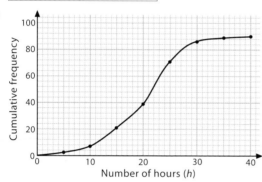

(b) Reflection in the line $y = x$

(d) Rotation of 90° clockwise about the point $(0, {-2})$

11 (a) $n = 10$ **(b)** $n = {-4}$ **(c)** $n = 8$ **(d)** $n = {-3}$

12 (a) 2 **(b)** 3 cm **(c)** 72 cm^3

 (d) (i)

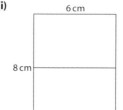

(ii)

(iii)

(e)

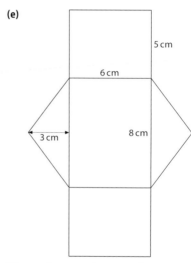

The surface area is 132 cm^2

13 (a) 40.5 mph

 (b) 64.9 km/h (or 64.8 km/h if the rounded value used)

14 (a) $8x^5$ **(b)** $2x^4$

 (c) $10x$ **(d)** $\dfrac{2}{3x^7}$ or $\dfrac{2x^{-7}}{3}$ or $\frac{2}{3}x^{-7}$

 (e) $\dfrac{1}{4x^6}$ or $\dfrac{x^{-6}}{4}$ or $\frac{1}{4}x^{-6}$

15 3.0 cm

16 (a) 5^6 **(b)** $n = 12$

15 Working with expressions

A Collecting like terms (p 149)

A1 (a) $5n + 1$ (b) $2p - 3$ (c) $5 - 4k$

A2 A and H, B and G, C and F, D and E

A3 (a) $2n^2 + 5n$ (b) $2a^2 + 5a$ (c) $3k^2 + 5k$
  (d) $4m^2 + 2m + 2$ (e) $5g^2 + 2g^3$ (f) $2h^2 - 3h$
  (g) $7x^2 - x$ (h) $2y^2 - 6y + 3$

A4 (a) 98 (b) 40 (c) 31 (d) 20

A5 (a) (i) B and D (ii) B and E (iii) A and C
  (iv) C and D (v) A and D (vi) D and E
  (b) A, D and E

B Multiplying and dividing expressions (p 150)

B1 (a) $n^2 + 7n$ (b) $3m + m^2$ (c) $6a - 15$
  (d) $h^2 - 9h$ (e) $10k - k^2$ (f) $2w^2 + 14w$
  (g) $3x^2 - 18x$ (h) $12n - 6n^2$

B2 (a) $d + 5$ (b) $n - 4$ (c) $5 - p$ (d) $4 + k$

B3 A and J, B and H, C and F, D and I, E and G

B4 (a) $14h^2 - 10h$ (b) $3a^3 - 12a$ (c) $n^5 - 5n^2$
  (d) $12k^2 + 15k$ (e) $15d - 10d^3$ (f) $21p - 28p^2$
  (g) $6b^3 + 2b^2$ (h) $3w^2 + 6w^4$

B5 (a) $x^2 + 7x - 15$ (b) $a^3 + 5a^2 + 2a$
  (c) $2h^3 - 9h^2 - 4h$

B6 (a) $2d^2 - 1$ (b) $8a + 12$ (c) $2a + 3$
  (d) $4 + 6a^2$

B7 (a) $5d^2 + 10$ (b) $d^4 + d^3$ (c) $16d^5 + 8d^3$

B8 (a) $n + 7$ (b) $2a - 1$

B9 (a) 3 and $2x + 5$ (b) x and $x + 1$ (c) x and $2x + 5$
  (d) $2x$ and $x + 1$ (e) $2x$ and $5x$ (f) x^2 and $2x + 5$
  (g) $5x$ and $2x + 5$ (h) $5x$ and $x + 1$

C Factorising expressions (p 151)

C1 (a) $3(m + 4)$ (b) $2(2n - 3)$ (c) $5(3 - 2p)$
  (d) $4(2q - 1)$ (e) $3(3a^2 - 2)$ (f) $b(b + 3)$
  (g) $c(5 + c)$ (h) $d(d - 7)$ (i) $x(11 - x)$
  (j) $y(y + 1)$ (k) $w(w^2 - 2)$ (l) $h(7h^2 + 1)$

C2 (a) $k + 3$ (b) $p - 2$ (c) $4n + 1$
  (d) $3x + 2$ (e) $h + 2$ (f) $2y + 3$

C3 (a) $3b(b + 2)$ (b) $2a(5 + a)$ (c) $5d(d - 3)$
  (d) $7c(3 + c)$ (e) $2k(3k + 4)$ (f) $3h(3 + 2h)$
  (g) $3x(3x - 1)$ (h) $2y(1 + 5y)$

C4 (a) $7(n + 1)$ $n(2n - 3)$ $3n(n - 1)$
  LARWUS $\rightarrow$ WALRUS
  (b) $7(2n - 3)$ $5(n - 1)$ $5(n + 1)$
  LWESEA $\rightarrow$ WEASEL
  (c) $5(2n + 3)$ $2n(n + 1)$ $n(3n + 2)$
  EBGARD $\rightarrow$ BADGER
  (d) $5(n^2 + 2)$ $5(3n + 2)$ $2n(n^2 + 2)$ $2n(n^2 - 2)$
  EHEDGHGO $\rightarrow$ HEDGEHOG

C5 (a) $n^2(n + 4)$ (b) $n^3(6n^2 - 1)$
  (c) $n^2(5n + 7)$ (d) $2n^2(n + 1)$

C6 (a) $3(n + 2)$ (b) An explanation

C7 (a) $n(n + 1)$
  (b) An explanation such as
  'When n is an integer, $n(n + 1)$ is the product of two
  consecutive integers. One of these integers must be
  even so the product $n(n + 1)$ must be even.'

D Dealing with more than one letter (p 152)

D1 (a) 22 (b) 15 (c) 28 (d) 31 (e) 51
  (f) 100 (g) 20 (h) 50 (i) 13

D2 (a) 1 (b) ⁻12 (c) 0 (d) 11 (e) 30 (f) ⁻2

D3 Puzzle 1
  A 19 B 27 C 47 D 28 E 57 F 75 G 45

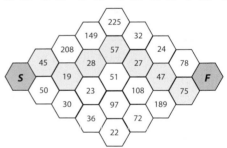

Puzzle 2
A 23 B 8 C 4 D 55 E 35 F 63 G 2 H 25

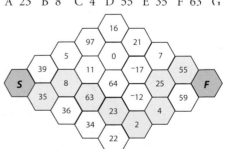

Puzzle 3

A 29 B 10 C 54 D 1 E 0 F 3 G 22 H 18 I 4

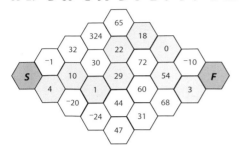

D4 (a) $5a - 4b$ (b) $6ab + 4b^2 + 2$
(c) $a^2 - 3a + 2$ (d) $2a^2 + 10b - 7$

D5 (a) A and D   (b) D and E   (c) A and B
(d) A and C   (e) B and C   (f) C and E

D6 (a) $2ab$ (b) $6xy$ (c) $12pq$
(d) $5cd$ (e) $20mn$ (f) $15vw$

D7 (a) $6a^2b$ (b) $12x^2y$ (c) $6p^2q^2$
(d) $20c^3d$ (e) $14m^3n^4$ (f) $24v^4w^6$

D8 (a) $2q$ (b) $3m$ (c) $3b$
(d) $5x^2$ (e) $5c^2$ (f) $4v^2w$

D9 (a) $2a$ and $3b$ (b) $5ab$ and $2b^2$
(c) $3a^2$ and $5a^2b$ (d) $3b$ and $3a^2$
(e) $2b^2$ and ab^3 (f) $5ab$ and $5a^2b$

D10

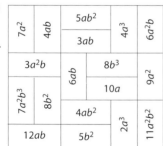

D11 (a) $9x + y$ (b) $12p^3 - 6p^2q + 5pq$
(c) $3m^2n + 10m - n^2$ (d) $9a^4b^2 - 6$

D12 (a) $9p^2q^2$ (b) $8v^3w^3$ (c) $25x^4y^2$
(d) $16a^8b^{12}$ (e) $\dfrac{4p^2}{q^2}$ (f) $\dfrac{9v^2w^2}{25}$
(g) $\dfrac{x^8y^4}{z^{12}}$ (h) $\dfrac{8a^3b^6}{27c^3}$

D13 (a) $5q$ (b) $2x$ (c) $3n$ (d) $4b^2$
(e) $3pq$ (f) $2x$ (g) $4m$ (h) $4a$

D14 (a) $4d$ $4bc$ $3c$ $2b$ $3c$ LEPAP $\rightarrow$ APPLE
(b) $3bd$ $2b^2$ $4bc$ $4d$ cd
ONELM $\rightarrow$ MELON or LEMON

(c) $3c$ $4bc$ $2b$ $2b^2d$ bc^2
PEARG $\rightarrow$ GRAPE
(d) bc^2 $2b^2d$ $2b$ $2b^2$ $3bd$ $4bc$
GRANOE $\rightarrow$ ORANGE

D15 (a) $\dfrac{a}{c}$ (b) $\dfrac{c}{6}$ (c) $\dfrac{6x}{y}$ (d) $\dfrac{2}{n}$
(e) $\dfrac{p^3}{q^2}$ (f) $\dfrac{2b}{3}$ (g) $\dfrac{1}{3ab}$ (h) $\dfrac{1}{2g}$

D16 (a) $4hk^3$ (b) $2n^3$ (c) $2x^2z^3$

D17 $\dfrac{ab^3 + 2a^2b^2}{ab^2} = \dfrac{ab^3}{ab^2} + \dfrac{2a^2b^2}{ab^2} = \boldsymbol{b + 2a}$

D18 (a) $d + c$ (b) $4cd - 3$ (c) $d^2 + 7cd$ (d) $2c - 3d$

D19 (a) $ab + a^2b^2$ (b) $2b + 4a$ (c) $16a + 12b$

D20 (a) $c + \dfrac{2}{c}$ (b) $\dfrac{1}{c} + \dfrac{1}{d}$ (c) $\dfrac{1}{3c} + \dfrac{2}{3d}$
(d) $\dfrac{1}{c^3d^2} + \dfrac{1}{c^2d^3}$

E Expanding and factorising expressions (p 156)

E1 (a) $4a + 4b$ (b) $3x - 3y$ (c) $5m + 10n$
(d) $12a - 20b$ (e) $hk + h$ (f) $p^2 - pq$
(g) $3ab + 5b$ (h) $2cd + 3c^2$

E2 (a) $3(p + q)$ (b) $5(k - h)$ (c) $2(a + 3b)$
(d) $3(2n - 3m)$ (e) $a(b + 1)$ (f) $x(x - y)$
(g) $p(7q + 9)$ (h) $a(4b + 5a)$

E3 (a) $2ab - 2a^2$ (b) $6xy + 15x$ (c) $5mn + 10m^2$
(d) $xy^2 - xy$ (e) $5a^2b + 3ab^2$ (f) $3p^3 - p^2$
(g) $6x^2y + 27xy$ (h) $10y^2x - 2y^2$

E4 (a) $3m(m - n)$ (b) $2x(x + 2y)$ (c) $3p(p - 2q)$
(d) $5m(2n + 3m)$ (e) $ab(b + 3)$ (f) $xy(x - 1)$
(g) $2y^2(3z + 5)$ (h) $5k^2(2h - 1)$ (i) $2xy(x + y)$
(j) $3ab(a - 5)$ (k) $4hk(2 + k)$ (l) $5pq(2p + q)$

E5 (a) $3a(a - 5b)$ $a^2(2a - b)$ $7b(a - 5b)$
PRATOR $\rightarrow$ PARROT
(b) $2a(2a - b)$ $2a(ab + 1)$ $2b(a - 5b)$
HTHUSR $\rightarrow$ THRUSH
(c) $7b(a + b)$ $5(a - 5b)$ $2b(ab + 1)$
OGERSU $\rightarrow$ GROUSE
(d) $2b(2a - b)$ $3b^2(a + b)$ $a^2(a - 5b)$ $ab(2a + 3b)$
STLGARIN $\rightarrow$ STARLING

E6 (a) $a^2b(a + 2b)$ (b) $mn^2(7m + 1)$
(c) $2xy^2(3x - y)$ (d) $3p^2q(p^2 + 4q)$

F Finding and simplifying formulas (p 157)

F1 (a) (i) $P = 4x + 2y$ or $P = 2(2x + y)$
(ii) $P = 4m + 2n + 2k$ or $P = 2(2m + n + k)$
(iii) $P = 18a$

(b) (i) $A = 2xy$

    (ii) $A = mn + 2mk$ or $A = m(n + 2k)$

    (iii) $A = 15a^2 + ac$ or $A = a(15a + c)$

F2 $V = 2x^2y$

    $S = 2x(2x + 3y)$

F3 $V = d(ab + c^2)$ or $V = abd + c^2d$

F4 (a) (i) $V = 2x^2y$

    (ii) $V = bc(2b + a)$ or $V = 2b^2c + abc$

    (b) (i) $S = 5xy + y^2 + 4x^2$

    (ii) $S = 2b^2 + 10bc + 2ac$ or $S = 2(b^2 + 5bc + ac)$

Test yourself (p 158)

T1 (a) $7x - 4xy$ **(b)** $a^2 - a - 3$ **(c)** $15hk$

    (d) $6a^3b^2$ **(e)** $2a$ **(f)** $2x - 3x^2$

T2 (a) $2p + 2q$ **(b)** $x^2 - 2x$

    (c) $3p^3 - p^6$ **(d)** $10h^2 - 5hk$

T3 (a) $13x + 2$ **(b)** $9x + 7$

T4 (a) $3(3y - 2)$ **(b)** $2a(2b - 3a)$ **(c)** $3x^2(2x - 5)$

T5 (a) $10a^4y^6$ **(b)** $7xy(2x - 3y^2)$

T6 $\dfrac{x}{y^3}$

T7 (a) $\dfrac{x^4y}{2}$ **(b)** $\dfrac{2ab^3}{5}$

T8 $V = 3p^2q$

    $S = 6p^2 + 8pq$ or $S = 2p(3p + 4q)$

16 Coordinates in three dimensions

A Identifying points (p 159)

A1 (a) F $(3, 0, 2)$ **(b)** C $(3, 4, 0)$

    (c) E $(0, 0, 2)$ **(d)** H $(3, 4, 2)$

A2 (a) B $(0, 0, 4)$ **(b)** G $(2, 3, 0)$

    (c) E $(2, 3, 4)$ **(d)** A $(0, 3, 4)$

A3 (a) G $(1, 2, 2)$ **(b)** B $(5, 5, 0)$

    (c) F $(5, 5, 2)$ **(d)** H $(1, 5, 2)$

A4 (a) H $(3, 7, 0)$ **(b)** A $(1, 3, 3)$

    (c) D $(1, 7, 3)$ **(d)** G $(3, 7, 3)$

A5 (a) F $(1, 6, 1)$ **(b)** B $(3, 6, 1)$

    (c) G $(1, 2, 4)$ **(d)** A $(3, 6, 4)$

A6 $(0, 0, 4), (4, 4, 0), (4, 0, 4), (0, 4, 4)$ and $(4, 4, 4)$

A7 (a) B

    (b) A $(0, 1, 1)$, C $(1, 2, 2)$, D $(1, 4, 1)$, E $(2, 3, 0)$

A8 (a) 6 units

    (b) (i) $(4, 0, 4)$ **(ii)** $(2, 3, 6)$

A9 (a) A $(0, 1, 0)$ **(b)** B $(0, 1, {}^-2)$ **(c)** C $(2, 3, {}^-2)$

Test yourself (p 161)

T1 B $(0, 1, 2)$, C $(1, 4, 1)$

T2 (a) P $(0, 0, 2)$, Q $(3, 0, 2)$, R $(3, 0, 0)$, S $(0, 4, 0)$,

    T $(0, 4, 2)$, V $(3, 4, 0)$

    (b) (i) On a face

    (ii) Inside the cuboid

    (iii) Outside the cuboid

    (iv) On a face

T3 B $(3, 0, 0)$, C $(6, 6, 6)$, D $(9, 9, 0)$

17 Cubic graphs and equations

A Cubic functions (p 162)

A1 (a) Estimates close to $^-1.7$, 0 and 0.7

    (b) Estimates close to $^-1.5$, $^-0.3$ and 1.9

    (c) $(0, 0)$

A2 (a)

x	$^-2$	$^-1.5$	$^-1$	$^-0.5$	0
$y = x^3 - 2x$	$^-4$	$^-0.375$	1	0.875	0

0.5	1	1.5	2
$^-0.875$	$^-1$	0.375	4

(b)

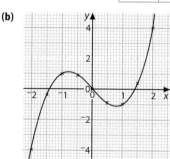

(c) Rotation symmetry order 2, centre $(0, 0)$

(d) Estimates close to $^-1$, $^-0.6$, 1.6

(e) $y = 3$ intersects the graph at only one point so the equation $x^3 - 2x = 3$ has only one solution.

(f) (i) $x = 1.8$ **(ii)** $x = ^-1.4, 0, 1.4$

A3 (a)

x	$^-2$	$^-1.5$	$^-1$	$^-0.5$	0
$y = x^3 + \frac{1}{2}x + 1$	$^-8$	$^-3.125$	$^-0.5$	0.625	1

0.5	1	1.5	2
1.375	2.5	5.125	10

(b)

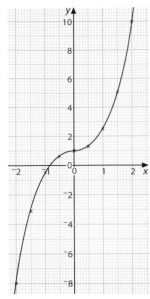

(c) An estimate close to ⁻0.8

B Trial and improvement (p 164)

B1 **(a)**

x	⁻2	⁻1.5	⁻1	⁻0.5	0
$y = x^3 + 2x^2 - 2$	⁻2	**⁻0.875**	**⁻1**	**⁻1.625**	**⁻2**

	0.5	1	1.5	2
	⁻1.375	**1**	**5.875**	**14**

(b)

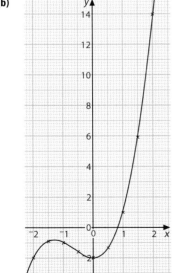

(c) The graph intersects the x-axis between $x = 0$ and $x = 1$ so there is a solution to $x^3 + 2x^2 - 2 = 0$ between 0 and 1.

(d) $x = 0.8$ (to 1 d.p.)

B2 Table leading to $x = 2.4$ (to 1 d.p.)

B3 **(a)** $3^3 + 2 \times 3 = 33$, which is less than 50.
$4^3 + 2 \times 4 = 72$, which is more than 50.
Hence the solution to $x^3 + 2x = 50$ lies between 3 and 4.

(b) $x = 3.5$ (to 1 d.p.)

B4 $x = 3.7$ (to 1 d.p.)

B5 $x = 2.66$ (to 2 d.p.)

B6 **(a)** The volume of the cuboid is the area of base × height $= x^2(x + 1) = x^3 + x^2$
The volume is 230 cm³ and so $x^3 + x^2 = 230$ as required.

(b) $x = 5.8$ (to 1 d.p.)

Test yourself (p 165)

T1 $x = 4.4$ (to 1 d.p.)

T2 **(a)**

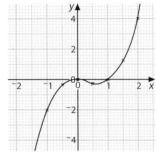

(b) $x = 1.9$ (to 1 d.p.)

T3 $x = 1.67$ (to 2 d.p.)

18 Gradients and rates

A Gradient of a sloping line (p 166)

A1 (a) 3   (b) 1   (c) 0.75   (d) 2
(e) 2.5   (f) 1.25   (g) 0.2

A2 0.6

A3 Ramps A, C and D are suitable.

A4 (a) (i) 0.085   (ii) 0.058   (iii) 0.077
(b) Lydeard Hill

A5 (a) 523 m   (b) 0.50 (to 2 d.p.)

A6 0.24 (to 2 d.p.)

B Positive and negative gradients (p 168)

B1 (a) ⁻3   (b) 2   (c) ⁻1
(d) ⁻1.5   (e) ⁻0.5   (f) ⁻0.25

B2 (a) 1   (b) 2   (c) ⁻1
(d) ⁻0.5   (e) ⁻1.5   (f) 0

B3 Lines with gradient 4 and ⁻4 and comment

B4 Lines with gradient 4 and $-\frac{1}{4}$
The lines are perpendicular.

C Interpreting a gradient as a rate (p 169)

C1 (a) 10 litres per minute   (b) 2 litres per second

C2 (a) 1.75 litres per second   (b) 0.5 litres per minute

C3 (a) 0.5   (b) C

C4 (a) ⁻8
(b) The oil empties from the tank.

C5 (a) (i) 21   (ii) 12
(b) (i) Speed in metres per minute
(ii) Speed in miles per hour

C6 (a) (i) 1.8   (ii) 0.4
(b) (i) Number of pints in one litre (to 1 d.p.)
(ii) Value of a Canadian dollar in £s (to the nearest 10p)

C7 (a) Working from left to right, the gradients are
16 km per hour
0 km per hour
⁻24 km per hour
(b) Descriptions of the stages

C8 (a) Working from left to right, the gradients are
18 litres per minute
4.5 litres per minute
0 litres per minute
⁻45 litres per minute

(b) (i) The rate of flow into the tank decreased.
(ii) The flow of water into the tank was turned off.
(iii) The tank began to be emptied.

C9 The gradients are
3 miles per hour
2 miles per hour
0 miles per hour
⁻4 miles per hour
Descriptions of the stages

C10 (a) 3   (b) Acceleration in m/s^2

D Calculating with rates (p 173)

D1 £5.40 per hour

D2 7.3 hours or 7 hours 16 minutes

D3 37 or 38 seconds (37.5 exactly)

D4 3 litres per second or 3.1 litres per second

D5 10 days

D6 38 250 litres or 38 300 litres

D7 0.4 litre per second or 24 litres per minute

D8 (a) 9.5 litres/100 km
(b) (i) 61.2 litres   (ii) 485 km

Test yourself (p 174)

T1 (a) 0.16   (b) Yes

T2 2

T3 (a) 5.6
(b) The rate of flow of water into the container in litres per second

T4 (a) ⁻33.3
(b) The oil empties from the tank.

T5 (a) (i) 2.3 copies per minute
(ii) 137 or 140 copies per hour
(b) 3 hours 40 minutes

19 Changing the subject

A Simple linear formulas (p 175)

A1 (a) $b = 3w - 5$

(b) (i) 55   (ii) 7   (iii) 100

A2 $Q = 2P + 5$

A3 (a) $w = 3b - 1$ (b) $b = 2w + 3$

(c) $b = 5w - 7$ (d) $w = 7b + 6$

A4 A and D, B and E, C and F

A5 (a) $q = \dfrac{p + 9}{2}$ (b) $q = 8p + 5$

(c) $q = 11p - 1$ (d) $q = \dfrac{p - 10}{3}$

A6 $b = \dfrac{2a + 5}{3}$

A7 (a) $x = \dfrac{3y - 10}{7}$

(b) (i) 2   (ii) 11.5   (iii) 5

A8 (a) $u = \dfrac{w - 5}{5}$ $\left(\text{or } u = \dfrac{w}{5} - 1\right)$

(b) $B = \dfrac{A + 15}{3}$ $\left(\text{or } B = \dfrac{A}{3} + 5\right)$

(c) $x = \dfrac{y - 14}{2}$ $\left(\text{or } x = \dfrac{y}{2} - 7\right)$

A9 $k = \dfrac{h - 4}{8}$

A10 (a) $q = \dfrac{p - 10}{6}$ (b) $w = \dfrac{b + 3}{6}$ (c) $G = \dfrac{F - 12}{28}$

A11 (a) $b = 2(a - 1)$ (b) $E = 7(D + 4)$ (c) $t = 5(s - 9)$

A12 $x = \dfrac{5(y + 7)}{3}$

A13 (a) $G = \dfrac{3(H - 1)}{4}$ (b) $b = \dfrac{8(w + 4)}{3}$ (c) $n = \dfrac{6(m - 1)}{5}$

A14 (a) $h = 3g - 5$ (b) $V = \dfrac{U + 4}{3}$ (c) $p = \dfrac{7q - 1}{2}$

(d) $n = 3(m + 2)$ (e) $x = \dfrac{y - 15}{20}$ (f) $f = \dfrac{C + 6}{6}$

(g) $Z = 4(w - 2)$ (h) $h = \dfrac{3(j - 1)}{2}$ (i) $x = \dfrac{y + 14}{6}$

A15 (a) 8.8 pounds   (b) $k = \dfrac{5p}{11}$ (c) 9.09 kg

A16 (a) 1080°   (b) $n = \dfrac{s + 360}{180}$ $\left(\text{or } n = \dfrac{s}{180} + 2\right)$

(c) 36

(d) Using the formula gives $n = \dfrac{500 + 360}{180} = 4.777\ldots$ which is not a whole number so it is not possible.

A17 (a) $F = \dfrac{9C + 160}{5}$ (b) 86 °F

B Adding and subtracting algebraic expressions (p 178)

B1 (a) $x = 10 - 2y$ (b) $y = \dfrac{10 - x}{2}$

(c) 4   (d) 6

B2 (a) $y = 10 - x$ (b) $b = \dfrac{25 - 2a}{3}$

(c) $p = 2(8 - 5q)$

B3 (a) 10   (b) $x = \dfrac{16 - y}{3}$

(c) $\dfrac{16 - y}{3} = \dfrac{16 - 10}{3} = 2 = x$ so the formula fits.

(d) (i) 5   (ii) 3.5   (iii) 17.5

B4 (a) $r = \dfrac{12 - s}{5}$ (b) $\frac{3}{5}$ or 0.6

B5 (a) $t = \dfrac{8 - s}{7}$ (b) $n = \dfrac{3 - m}{8}$

(c) $h = \dfrac{66 - g}{5}$ (d) $x = \dfrac{12 - y}{3}$

B6 (a) $x = 3(15 - y)$

(b) (i) 6   (ii) 42   (iii) ⁻9

B7 (a) $x = 3(10 - y)$ (b) $x = 5(3 - y)$

(c) $x = 10(10 - y)$ (d) $x = 2(100 - y)$

B8 $3b - 2a = 30$

$3b = 30 + 2a$

$3b - 30 = 2a$

$a = \dfrac{3b - 30}{2}$

B9 (a) $t = 5s - 40$ (b) $j = \dfrac{d - 8}{4}$

(c) $j = \dfrac{6k - 45}{8}$ (d) $b = 4(3a - 20)$

B10 (a) $a = \dfrac{9 - 2b}{5}$ (b) $q = \dfrac{2 - p}{7}$ (c) $m = \dfrac{3 + 5n}{2}$

(d) $k = 5(10 - h)$ (e) $d = 3(4c - 9)$ (f) $g = \dfrac{2(8 - h)}{3}$

(g) $j = \dfrac{20 - k}{5}$ (h) $t = 6 - 3s$ (i) $x = \dfrac{1 - 7y}{3}$

C Formulas connecting more than two letters (p 179)

C1 (a) $m = p - q$ (b) 3

(c) $m + q = 3 + 12 = 15 = p$ so the values fit.

C2 (a) $s = 4m - 6$

$s + 6 = 4m$

$m = \dfrac{s + 6}{4}$

(b) $s = um - w$

$s + w = um$

$m = \dfrac{s + w}{u}$

C3 (a) $a = \dfrac{v - u}{t}$ (b) 14 m/s²

C4 (a) $q = p + r$ (b) $w = \dfrac{b - k}{5}$ (c) $v = \dfrac{l + h}{b}$

(d) $m = \dfrac{y - c}{x}$ (e) $d = \dfrac{f - 8}{n}$ (f) $j = \dfrac{g - lk}{6}$

(g) $c = \dfrac{a + 4f}{d}$ (h) $j = \dfrac{ak + nm}{b}$

C5 (a) $p = \dfrac{q}{2} + 3$

$p - 3 = \dfrac{q}{2}$

$q = 2(p - 3)$

(b) $p = \dfrac{q}{s} + rt$

$p - \boldsymbol{rt} = \dfrac{q}{s}$

$q = s(\boldsymbol{p - rt})$

C6 (a) $q = 3(p - r)$ (b) $w = v(b + k)$ (c) $d = 5f - n$

(d) $h = n(l - km)$ (e) $k = \dfrac{gv + b}{3}$ (f) $c = \dfrac{ad - 5b}{8}$

(g) $x = \dfrac{m(y - 2)}{5}$ (h) $d = \dfrac{an - gf}{c}$

C7 (a) $s = f - kh$

$s + kh = f$

$kh = f - s$

$h = \dfrac{f - s}{k}$

(b) 4

C8 (a) $p = 2q - \dfrac{r}{s}$

$p + \dfrac{r}{s} = 2q$

$\dfrac{r}{s} = 2q - p$

$r = s(2q - p)$

(b) 51

C9 (a) $x = \dfrac{y - z}{2}$ (b) $c = b - a$ (c) $q = \dfrac{p - j}{r}$

(d) $z = w(x - y)$ (e) $q = \dfrac{r(3p - m)}{2}$ (f) $b = u - 5v$

(g) $t = 5s - vw$ (h) $n = \dfrac{3k - p}{m}$ (i) $y = z(x - m)$

(j) $f = \dfrac{2d - an}{7}$ (k) $d = \dfrac{bc - af}{e}$ (l) $r = \dfrac{2q}{2} \dfrac{ps}{}$

C10 (a) $a = \dfrac{T_0 - T}{h}$ (b) 8 degrees per hour

C11 (a) $V_2 = \dfrac{W - aV_1}{b}$ (b) $0.072\,\mathrm{m}^3$

C12 (a) $z = 5x - y$ (b) $b = \dfrac{k - na}{m}$ (c) $t = fs - j$

(d) $g = \dfrac{t - k}{f}$ (e) $m = \dfrac{2a - f}{b}$ (f) $x = \dfrac{K - H}{8}$

(g) $s = \dfrac{r + 5t_0}{5}$ (h) $x = z(y - c)$ (i) $r = t(q - p)$

(j) $c = \dfrac{3(a + d)}{b}$ (k) $y = \dfrac{r^2 - ax}{b}$ (l) $j = \dfrac{A_1k - 45}{A_2}$

(m) $j = \dfrac{cd - 5e}{4}$ (n) $x = \dfrac{hy + 4a}{a}$ (o) $y = \dfrac{5m - xz}{m}$

(p) $y = \dfrac{7(a - z)}{b}$

D Squares and square roots (p 182)

D1 (a) 5.64 cm (b) 1.26 m (c) 0.564 mm (d) 13.8 km

D2 (a) $A = 6b^2$

$\dfrac{A}{6} = b^2$

$b = \sqrt{\dfrac{A}{6}}$

(b) 1.29 cm

D3 (a) $t = \sqrt{\dfrac{D}{4.9}}$ (b) 3.2 seconds (to 1 d.p.)

D4 $a = \sqrt{c^2 - b^2}$

D5 (a) $x = \sqrt{\dfrac{A}{2}}$ (b) $x = \sqrt{\dfrac{A}{5}}$ (c) $x = \sqrt{10A}$

(d) $x = \sqrt{\dfrac{7A}{3}}$ (e) $x = \sqrt{A - 5}$ (f) $x = \sqrt{\dfrac{A + 3}{7}}$

(g) $x = \sqrt{25 - A}$ (h) $x = \sqrt{3(A + 6)}$

D6 A and B, C and E, D and F

D7 (a) $x = (y - 3)^2$ (b) $x = y^2 - 3$

(c) $x = (y + 7)^2$ (d) $x = y^2 + 7$

D8 A and G, B and E, C and H, D and F

D9 (a) $q = \dfrac{h^2}{5}$ (b) $q = \dfrac{(k - 1)^2}{n}$ (c) $q = \dfrac{l^2 - 1}{6}$

(d) $q = 5t^2$ (e) $q = \dfrac{sr^2}{a}$

D10 (a) $x = \pm\sqrt{y - 5}$ (b) $x = \pm\sqrt{\dfrac{y + 1}{2}}$

(c) $x = \pm\sqrt{5(y - 2)}$ (d) $x = 5 \pm \sqrt{y}$

D11 (a) $a = \pm\sqrt{\dfrac{8n}{b}}$ (b) $a = \pm\sqrt{ck + b}$

(c) $a = +\sqrt{1 - h^2}$ (d) $a = \dfrac{b \pm \sqrt{h}}{2}$

D12 $t = \pm\sqrt{\dfrac{2s}{a}}$

D13 (a) $x = \pm\sqrt{\dfrac{y + 1}{4}}$ (b) $\left(\tfrac{1}{2}, 0\right), \left(-\tfrac{1}{2}, 0\right)$

D14 (a) $x = \dfrac{\pm\sqrt{y} - 4}{3}$ (b) $\left(\tfrac{1}{3}, 25\right), (-3, 25)$

Test yourself (p 184)

T1 $t = 3(u - 5)$

T2 (a) $x = 5y + 4$ (b) $V = \dfrac{U - 8}{3}$ (c) $k = \dfrac{9h - 1}{4}$

(d) $f = \dfrac{C + 6}{2}$ (e) $n = 5(m - 3)$ (f) $b = \dfrac{3(a + 5)}{2}$

(g) $q = \dfrac{10 - t}{3}$ (h) $Z = \dfrac{4w}{3}$ (i) $x = 5(6 - y)$

T3 $p = \dfrac{7r - 12}{4}$

T4 $y = \dfrac{40 - x}{8}$

T5 (a) $k = \dfrac{h-s}{a}$ (b) $f = \dfrac{2e-q}{2}$ (c) $d = \dfrac{2r-t}{w}$

   (d) $z = \dfrac{cy-ax}{b}$ (e) $w = \dfrac{e+jt}{j}$ (f) $s = \dfrac{R+fg}{p}$

   (g) $v = \dfrac{bq-u}{a}$ (h) $k = l(h-j)$

T6 $x = \dfrac{3-y}{7}$

T7 (a) $q = \dfrac{p-t}{r}$ (b) $\frac{2}{3}$

T8 (a) $t = \dfrac{v-u}{a}$ (b) 3

T9 (a) $x = \pm\sqrt{y-9}$ (b) $x = \pm\sqrt{5-y}$

   (c) $x = \pm\sqrt{\dfrac{y+6}{3}}$ (d) $x = \pm\sqrt{100-y^2}$

   (e) $x = \pm\sqrt{by+a}$ (f) $x = \pm\sqrt{a^2-100y}$

T10 $x = \pm\sqrt{5y-4}$

T11 $k = \pm\sqrt{\dfrac{4w}{3}}$

T12 $d = t - h^2$

T13 $x = (5y+4)^2$

20 Probability

A Relative frequency (p 185)

A1 (a) $\frac{1}{10}$ $\left(\text{or } \frac{12}{120}\right)$ (b) $\frac{3}{20}$ $\left(\text{or } \frac{18}{120}\right)$

   (c) $\frac{9}{10}$ $\left(\text{or } \frac{108}{120}\right)$ (d) $\frac{17}{20}$ $\left(\text{or } \frac{102}{120}\right)$

A2 (a) The relative frequencies are 0.3, 0.4, 0.4, 0.45, 0.46, 0.45, 0.46 (to 2 d.p.), 0.45, 0.44 (to 2 d.p.), 0.45

   (b)

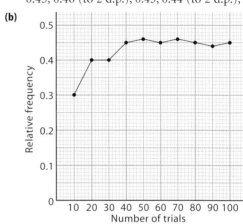

   (c) Jam-down

   (d) Quite good: after about 40 trials the relative frequencies are roughly the same.

   (e) About 0.55

A3 (a) (i) 0.55   (ii) 0.575   (iii) 0.6

   (b) Around 480

   (c) Quite good: her results soon 'settle down'.

A4 0.85

A5 (a) 0.35   (b) 0.65   (c) 70

A6 (a) (i) 0.096   (ii) 0.072

   (b) 1808 (or about 1800)

B Equally likely outcomes (p 187)

B1 A, C

B2 (a) $\frac{1}{3}$ $\left(\text{or } \frac{2}{6}\right)$ (b) $\frac{1}{2}$ $\left(\text{or } \frac{3}{6}\right)$ (c) $\frac{1}{6}$ (d) 0

B3 (a) $\frac{1}{6}$ (b) $\frac{1}{2}$ $\left(\text{or } \frac{3}{6}\right)$ (c) $\frac{1}{3}$ $\left(\text{or } \frac{2}{6}\right)$

B4 (a) $\frac{1}{6}$ (b) $\frac{1}{2}$ $\left(\text{or } \frac{3}{6}\right)$ (c) $\frac{1}{2}$ $\left(\text{or } \frac{3}{6}\right)$ (d) $\frac{1}{3}$ $\left(\text{or } \frac{2}{6}\right)$

B5 (a) $\frac{1}{2}$ $\left(\text{or } \frac{6}{12}\right)$ (b) $\frac{1}{4}$ $\left(\text{or } \frac{3}{12}\right)$ (c) $\frac{5}{12}$

B6 (a) $\frac{1}{2}$ $\left(\text{or } \frac{12}{24}\right)$ (b) $\frac{1}{6}$ $\left(\text{or } \frac{4}{24}\right)$ (c) $\frac{1}{4}$ $\left(\text{or } \frac{6}{24}\right)$ (d) $\frac{5}{24}$

   (e) $\frac{3}{8}$ $\left(\text{or } \frac{9}{24}\right)$ (f) $\frac{5}{8}$ $\left(\text{or } \frac{15}{24}\right)$

B7 (a) 12

   (b) (i) $\frac{1}{4}$ $\left(\text{or } \frac{3}{12}\right)$ (ii) $\frac{5}{12}$ (iii) $\frac{2}{3}$ $\left(\text{or } \frac{8}{12}\right)$

B8 (a) $\frac{8}{25}$ (b) $\frac{19}{25}$

B9 Red: 1 face   White: 2 faces   Blue: 3 faces

B10 Spinner A appears to be fair as the frequencies are roughly the same. Spinner B seems to be biased in favour of the 4.

B11 (a)

	Pink	White
Cherry	7	3
No cherry	4	6

  (b) (i) $\frac{3}{20}$ **(ii)** $\frac{1}{2}\left(\text{or } \frac{10}{20}\right)$ **(iii)** $\frac{11}{20}$

  (c) $\frac{7}{11}$

B12 (a) 30

  (b) (i) $\frac{3}{10}\left(\text{or } \frac{9}{30}\right)$ **(ii)** $\frac{1}{2}\left(\text{or } \frac{15}{30}\right)$

  (c) $\frac{1}{5}\left(\text{or } \frac{3}{15}\right)$

C Listing outcomes (p 190)

C1 (a) $\frac{1}{3}\left(\text{or } \frac{4}{12}\right)$ **(b)** $\frac{1}{4}\left(\text{or } \frac{3}{12}\right)$ **(c)** $\frac{5}{12}$ **(d)** $\frac{1}{2}\left(\text{or } \frac{6}{12}\right)$

C2 (a)

Coin 1	Coin 2	Coin 3
H	H	H
H	H	T
H	T	H
T	H	H
T	T	H
T	H	T
H	T	T
T	T	T

  (b) 8   **(c)** $\frac{1}{8}$ **(d)** $\frac{1}{4}\left(\text{or } \frac{2}{8}\right)$

  (e) $\frac{1}{2}\left(\text{or } \frac{4}{8}\right)$ **(f)** $\frac{1}{2}\left(\text{or } \frac{4}{8}\right)$

C3 (a) TMI, TIM, MTI, MIT, IMT, ITM   **(b)** $\frac{1}{6}$

C4 $\frac{1}{3}\left(\text{or } \frac{2}{6}\right)$: the words are PEA and APE.

C5 (a)

Spinner A	Spinner B	Total score
1	5	6
1	6	7
1	7	8
2	5	7
2	6	8
2	7	9
3	5	8
3	6	9
3	7	10
4	5	9
4	6	10
4	7	11

  (b) $\frac{1}{6}\left(\text{or } \frac{2}{12}\right)$ **(c)** About 10 times

C6 (a)

1679	6179	7169	9167
1697	6197	7196	9176
1769	6719	7619	9617
1796	6791	7691	9671
1967	6917	7916	9716
1976	6971	7961	9761

  (b) $\frac{1}{24}$ **(c)** $\frac{1}{12}$

D Showing outcomes on a grid (p 192)

D1 (a)

  (b) (i) $\frac{1}{36}$ **(ii)** $\frac{5}{18}\left(\text{or } \frac{10}{36}\right)$ **(iii)** $\frac{7}{18}\left(\text{or } \frac{14}{36}\right)$ **(iv)** $\frac{25}{36}$

D2 (a)

+	1	2	3	4	5
1	2	3	4	5	6
2	3	4	5	6	7
3	4	5	6	7	8
4	5	6	7	8	9
5	6	7	8	9	10

  (b) (i) $\frac{1}{25}$ **(ii)** 0   **(iii)** $\frac{1}{5}\left(\text{or } \frac{5}{25}\right)$

D3 (a)

6	5	4	3	2	1	0
5	4	3	2	1	0	1
4	3	2	1	0	1	2
3	2	1	0	1	2	3
2	1	0	1	2	3	4
1	0	1	2	3	4	5
	1	2	3	4	5	6

  (b) (i) $\frac{1}{6}\left(\text{or } \frac{6}{36}\right)$ **(ii)** $\frac{2}{3}\left(\text{or } \frac{24}{36}\right)$ **(iii)** $\frac{5}{9}\left(\text{or } \frac{20}{36}\right)$

D4 (a)

6	6	12	18	24
5	5	10	15	20
4	4	8	12	16
3	3	6	9	12
	1	2	3	4

  (b) (i) $\frac{3}{16}$ **(ii)** $\frac{1}{2}\left(\text{or } \frac{8}{16}\right)$ **(iii)** $\frac{5}{8}\left(\text{or } \frac{10}{16}\right)$

D5 (a) $\frac{1}{5}$ **(b)** $\frac{4}{5}$ **(c)** $\frac{4}{25}$ **(d)** $\frac{9}{25}$ **(e)** $\frac{1}{5}$ **(f)** $\frac{8}{25}$

Test yourself (p 195)

T1 (a) (i) $\frac{1}{9}$ **(ii)** 0   **(iii)** $\frac{2}{9}$

  (b) (i) 1 2 3   1 3 2   2 1 3   2 3 1
      3 1 2   3 2 1

  (ii) $\frac{5}{6}$

T2 (a) $\frac{234}{500} = 0.468$ **(b)** Around 47

T3 (a) 3 2   6 2   8 2   3 4   6 4
      8 4   3 7   6 7   8 7

  (b) $\frac{4}{9}$ **(c)** $\frac{4}{9}$

T4 (a)

	4	5	6	7
0	4	5	6	7
1	3	4	5	6
2	2	3	4	5
3	1	2	3	4

  (b) $\frac{1}{2}\left(\text{or } \frac{8}{16}\right)$

Review 3 (p 196)

1 (a) $P = 6p + 8q$ or $2(3p + 4q)$

  (b) $A = 10pq$

2 (a)

x	-3	-2	-1	0	1	2	3
y	-22	-5	0	-1	-2	3	20

  (b)

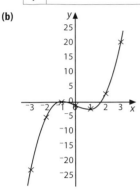

  (c) (i) The graph of $y = x^3 - 2x - 1$ cuts the x-axis between 1 and 2 so the equation $x^3 - 2x - 1 = 0$ has a solution between 1 and 2.

  (ii) Approximately 1.6

3 (a) 0.11   **(b)** Yes

4 (a) $r = \dfrac{s + 12}{3}$ **(b)** $c = \dfrac{3d - 5}{2}$ **(c)** $a = \dfrac{7 - b}{4}$

  (d) $x = 4(y - 10)$ **(e)** $f = \dfrac{g + b}{a}$ **(f)** $b = af - g$

  (g) $p = tr - qs$ **(h)** $s = \dfrac{p - tr}{q}$

5 (a) Rows can be in any order:

H	H	H	H
H	H	H	T
H	H	T	H
H	T	H	H
T	H	H	H
H	H	T	T
H	T	H	T
H	T	T	H
T	H	H	T
T	H	T	H
T	T	H	H
T	T	T	H
T	T	H	T
T	H	T	T
H	T	T	T
T	T	T	T

  (b) $\frac{1}{16}$ **(c)** $\frac{1}{8}$ **(d)** $\frac{5}{16}$ **(e)** $\frac{5}{16}$

6 (a) $10a + 5b$ **(b)** $a^2 - 5ab$

  (c) $2n^3k + n^5$ **(d)** $14h^2 - 8h^3k$

7 24 minutes

8 (a) $r = \dfrac{2p^2 - q}{3}$ **(b)** $p = \pm\sqrt{\dfrac{q + 3r}{2}}$

9 (a) $6p^2q$ **(b)** $9m^2n^5$ **(c)** $6qr^3$

  (d) $\dfrac{w^2}{2k^3}$ or $\dfrac{w^2k^{-3}}{2}$ or $\frac{1}{2}w^2k^{-3}$

10 A $(1, 0, 1)$; B $(3, 1, 0)$; C $(2, 2, 2)$

11 (a) $d^2 + 5$ **(b)** $2 - \dfrac{5x}{2}$

  (c) $1 + pq^2$ **(d)** $\dfrac{2x}{3} - 2x^3y^2$ or $2x\left(\frac{1}{3} - x^2y^2\right)$

12 (a) (i) $V = 3x^2y$ **(ii)** $A = 6x^2 + 8xy$ or $2x(3x + 4y)$

  (b) $550\,\text{cm}^2$

13 (a) $2(4a + 3b)$ **(b)** $x(x - 8)$

  (c) $4k(k - 2)$ **(d)** $4h^2k(2h + 3k)$

14 47.1 hectares (to the nearest 0.1 hectare)

15 (a) $r = \dfrac{s^2}{a}$ **(b)** $r = s^2 - b$ **(c)** $r = \dfrac{s^2 - b}{a}$

  (d) $r = \left(\dfrac{bs}{a}\right)^2$ **(e)** $r = \dfrac{(bs)^2}{a}$ **(f)** $r = \dfrac{bs^2}{a}$

16 2.55

17 (a) $\frac{11}{36}$ **(b)** $\frac{16}{36}$ or $\frac{4}{9}$ **(c)** $\frac{9}{36}$ or $\frac{1}{4}$

18 (a) $a^2 + 2bc$ **(b)** $8x^6y^3$ **(c)** $15y - xz$

21 Large and small numbers

A Powers of ten (p 198)

A1 (a) 10^3 **(b)** 10^5

A2 (a) 100   **(b)** 100 000   **(c)** 10 000

  (d) 100 000 000

A3 A and K, B and L, C and F, D and E, G and J, H and I

A4 (a) 10^5 **(b)** 10^9 **(c)** 10^3 **(d)** 10^6

A5 (a) 120   **(b)** 51 600 000   **(c)** 20 900

  (d) 63 000   **(e)** 294 000 000   **(f)** 7 620 000 000

B Writing large numbers in different ways (p 199)

B1 B, C and D

B2

River	Length (km)
Nile	6670
Yangtze-Kiang	6300
Zaire	4700
Danube	2840
Seine	780

B3 100 000 (billion) or one hundred thousand (billion)

B4 **(a)**

Forest	39 million sq km
Desert	35.3 million sq km
Pasture	34.2 million sq km
Icecap	15 million sq km
Cultivated	14.4 million sq km
Other	11.3 million sq km

    (b) 149.2 million sq km

    (c) **(i)** 26.1%   **(ii)** 9.7%

    (d) 70.7%

B5 **(a)**

Year	Population	Billions
1900	1 630 000 000	1.63
1950	2 520 000 000	2.52
1960	3 000 000 000	3
1970	3 700 000 000	3.7
1980	4 500 000 000	4.5
1990	5 300 000 000	5.3
2000	6 090 000 000	6.09

    (b)

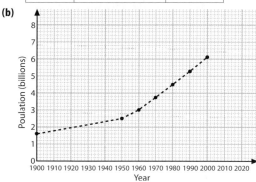

    (c) About 8 billion

C Standard form for large numbers (p 200)

C1 A and D

C2 **(a)** 420 000   **(b)** 810 000 000

    (c) 5 890 000 000   **(d)** 30 000 000 000

    (e) 7 040 000   **(f)** 8 000 000 000 000 000

C3 **(a)** 9×10^4 **(b)** 9.1×10^4 **(c)** 9.1×10^9

    (d) 3.29×10^8 **(e)** 1.078×10^{14} **(f)** 2×10^{22}

    (g) 1.5×10^7 **(h)** 4×10^9

C4 **(a)**

Chinese	1 093 000 000
English	450 000 000
Hindi	367 000 000
Spanish	352 000 000
Russian	204 000 000

    (b) In 1996, the number of Mandarin speakers was about 5 times the number of Russian speakers.

C5

Australia	1.52×10^7
Canada	1.77×10^7
Guyana	9×10^5
Ireland	3.3×10^6
Jamaica	2.4×10^6
New Zealand	3.2×10^6
South Africa	3.6×10^6
Trinidad and Tobago	1.2×10^6
UK	5.68×10^7
USA	2.249×10^8

C6 **(a)** 339 000 000   **(b)** Christianity   **(c)** Baha'ism

C7 4×10^5

D Using a calculator for large numbers in standard form (p 202)

D1 **(a)** 6×10^{13} **(b)** 1.6×10^{13} **(c)** 1.24×10^{10}

    (d) 4.925×10^{15}

D2 **(a)** 2.46×10^7 **(b)** 2.171×10^{15} **(c)** 5×10^{10}

    (d) 5.4×10^6

D3 **(a)** 9.6×10^{11} **(b)** 2.7×10^{12} **(c)** 6.5×10^{13}

    (d) 4.2×10^{18}

D4 **(a)** 3.15×10^9 **(b)** 1.955×10^{18} **(c)** 8.85×10^9

D5 2.97×10^{11}

D6 $5.8\times10^9\,\text{kg}$

D7 20 000 000 kg

D8 **(a)** The mass of **the Earth** is about 18 times the mass of Mercury.

    (b) The mass of Venus is about **372** times the mass of Pluto.

    (c) The mass of Jupiter is about **318** times the mass of Earth.

    (d) The mass of Neptune is about 160 times the mass of **Mars**.

D9 **(a)** An explanation

    (b)

Earth	2.58 m
Jupiter	13.44 m
Mars	3.94 m
Mercury	1.00 m
Neptune	77.65 m
Pluto	102.12 m
Saturn	24.64 m
Uranus	49.58 m
Venus	1.87 m

D10 **(a)**

Earth	$5500\,\text{kg/m}^3$
Jupiter	$1200\,\text{kg/m}^3$
Mars	$3900\,\text{kg/m}^3$
Mercury	$5400\,\text{kg/m}^3$
Neptune	$1500\,\text{kg/m}^3$
Pluto	$2000\,\text{kg/m}^3$
Saturn	$620\,\text{kg/m}^3$
Uranus	$1200\,\text{kg/m}^3$
Venus	$5200\,\text{kg/m}^3$

   (b) Saturn

E Standard form for small numbers (p 204)

E1 **(a)** **(i)** $\frac{1}{10}$ **(ii)** 0.1

   (b) **(i)** $\frac{1}{100\,000}$ **(ii)** 0.00001

   (c) **(i)** $\frac{1}{1000}$ **(ii)** 0.001

   (d) **(i)** $\frac{1}{1\,000\,000}$ **(ii)** 0.000001

E2 **(a)** B, D, E and F **(b)** 4.53×10^{-5}

E3 **(a)** 0.0091 **(b)** 0.0000621

   (c) 0.00000000034 **(d)** 0.0000005

   (e) 0.0000000301 **(f)** 0.000000000000000000001

E4 **(a)** 2.9×10^{-9} **(b)** 4.28×10^{-7} **(c)** 9.234×10^{-2}

   (d) 6×10^{-9} **(e)** 1×10^{-12} **(f)** 8×10^{-20}

E5 **(a)** $0.000014\,\text{kg}$ **(b)** $1.4 \times 10^{-5}\,\text{kg}$

E6 $0.0000067\,\text{g}$

E7 **(a)** $0.00043\,\text{m}$ **(b)** $4.3 \times 10^{-4}\,\text{m}$

E8 **(a)** Blue whale, Giraffe, House mouse, Helena's hummingbird, Kitti's hog-nosed bat, Bee hummingbird, Pygmy shrew, House spider

   (b) **(i)** The mass of a giraffe is **100 000** times the mass of a house mouse.

   (ii) **16** house spiders would weigh the same as a bee hummingbird.

   (iii) A **giraffe** weighs the same as 800 thousand pygmy shrews.

E9 A, B and D

F Using a calculator for small numbers in standard form (p 205)

F1 **(a)** **(i)** 1.66×10^{-8} **(ii)** 0.0000000166

   (b) **(i)** 3.83×10^{-11} **(ii)** 0.0000000000383

   (c) **(i)** 2.09×10^{15} **(ii)** 2 090 000 000 000 000

F2 **(a)** 2.2×10^{-3} **(b)** 2.6×10^{-11} **(c)** 3.0×10^{-6}

   (d) 2.0×10^{-11}

F3 **(a)** 1.67×10^{23} **(b)** 167 000 000 000 000 000 000 000

F4 8000

F5 2000

F6 **(a)** 17 **(b)** 2900 **(c)** 9100

F7 Individual result (10 000 viruses will fit along each mm)

F8 **(a)** The diameter of a 5p coin is **90** times the diameter of the radiolaria.

   (b) The diameter of a 5p coin is **4500** times the length of an ebola virus.

F9 237 000

F10 Scrapie virus

F11 Individual result (each cm would be represented by 2 km)

F12 **(a)** 1800 **(b)** 2×10^{-27} grams

   (c) 6 000 000 000 000 000 000 000

F13 **(a)** 3.27×10^{-22} grams

   (b) 0.000 000 000 000 000 000 000 327 g

F14 $1.1 \times 10^{-22}\,\text{g}$

F15 2×10^{16} newtons

G Standard form without a calculator (p 208)

G1 **(a)** 2.6×10^7 **(b)** 5×10^7 **(c)** 3.4×10^{-3}

   (d) 2×10^{-13}

G2 **(a)** 8×10^{10} **(b)** 2.25×10^{10} **(c)** 4.8×10^8

   (d) 4.9×10^7 **(e)** 9.2×10^{-5} **(f)** 2.7×10^{-3}

G3 **(a)** 2.1×10^8 **(b)** 6.1×10^5 **(c)** 4×10^2

   (d) 2.5×10^5 **(e)** 8×10^{-5} **(f)** 1.5×10^5

G4 **(a)** 80 **(b)** 240 **(c)** 1600 **(d)** 1.26

   (e) 20 **(f)** 0.5 **(g)** 0.000013

G5 **(a)** 4×10^5, 5×10^{-3}

   (b) **(i)** 2000 **(ii)** 8×10^7 **(iii)** 1.25×10^{-8}

G6 **(a)** 2 people per car

   (b) 60 (or 58) people per motorcycle

G7 **(a)** 35 000, 3.5×10^4 **(b)** 840 000, 8.4×10^5

   (c) 493 000, 4.93×10^5 **(d)** 0.082, 8.2×10^{-2}

   (e) 0.0074, 7.4×10^{-3} **(f)** 0.24, 2.4×10^{-1}

Test yourself (p 209)

T1 1.08×10^{12}

T2 0.0000002

T3 **(a)** 1.6×10^8 **(b)** 28 000

T4 4.5×10^6

T5 **(a)** 1.6×10^{-2} **(b)** 1.4×10^{-4} **(c)** 3×10^3

T6 140 000 000 or 1.4×10^8 or 140 million years

T7 4.38×10^5 (to 3 s.f.)

T8 **(a)** **(i)** 2.46906×10^{17}

   (ii) 246 906 000 000 000 000 or rounded equivalents

   (b) 2 200 000 light years or 2.2 million light years

22 The tangent function

A Finding an opposite side (p 210)

A1 (a) 7.7 cm   (b) 9.1 cm   (c) 21 cm   (d) 10.5 cm
(e) 15.4 cm   (f) 28 cm

A2 A drawing

A3 (a) 16.7 cm   (b) 20.3 cm   (c) 21.5 cm   (d) 29.8 cm

A4 adjacent side $\boxed{\times 1.19}\!\!\rightarrow$ = opposite side

or $\dfrac{\text{opposite side}}{\text{adjacent side}} = 1.19$

A5

Angle	Adjacent side	$\boxed{\times ?}\!\!\rightarrow$	Opposite side
10°	10 cm	0.18	1.8 cm
20°	10 cm	0.36	3.6 cm
30°	10 cm	0.58	5.8 cm
40°	10 cm	0.84	8.4 cm
50°	10 cm	1.19	11.9 cm
60°	10 cm	1.73	17.3 cm
70°	10 cm	2.75	27.5 cm

A6 (a) 5.9 cm   (b) 4.6 cm   (c) 24.2 cm   (d) 4.0 cm

A7 $\tan 10° = 0.176$ $\tan 20° = 0.364$ $\tan 30° = 0.577$
$\tan 40° = 0.839$ $\tan 50° = 1.192$ $\tan 60° = 1.732$
$\tan 70° = 2.747$

A8 (a) 2.145   (b) 17.2 cm   (c) 9.01 cm   (d) 472 cm

A9 (a) The adjacent and opposite sides are equal in length.
(b) 45°
(c) Opposite divided by adjacent equals one,
so $\tan 45° = 1$

A10 (a) (i) An estimate   (ii) 1.5 cm
(b) (i) An estimate   (ii) 3.2 cm
(c) (i) An estimate   (ii) 5.8 cm
(d) (i) An estimate   (ii) 3.7 cm
(e) (i) An estimate   (ii) 4.0 cm
(f) (i) An estimate   (ii) 2.3 cm

B Finding an adjacent side (p 213)

B1 (a) 50 cm   (b) 30 cm   (c) 17 cm   (d) 14 cm

B2 (a) 20 cm   (b) 16 cm   (c) 50 cm   (d) 52 cm

B3 (a) (i) An estimate   (ii) 11.5 cm
(b) (i) An estimate   (ii) 8.8 cm
(c) (i) An estimate   (ii) 7.1 cm
(d) (i) An estimate   (ii) 9.1 cm
(e) (i) An estimate   (ii) 6.0 cm
(f) (i) An estimate   (ii) 4.4 cm

B4 (a) 7.6 cm   (b) 20.9 cm   (c) 9.8 cm   (d) 11.5 cm

C Finding an angle (p 214)

C1 (a) 0.42   (b) 38°   (c) 1.28   (d) 76°   (e) 16°
(f) 0.11   (g) 3°   (h) 14.30 (i) 44°   (j) 88°

C2 (a) 1.6   (b) 58°

C3 Tangents get larger very quickly as a approaches 90°.

C4 (a) $\tan a = 0.8, a = 39°$ (b) $\tan a = 0.4, a = 22°$
(c) $\tan a = 2.6, a = 69°$ (d) $\tan a = 0.9, a = 42°$

C5 (a) $\tan x = 0.45, x = 24°$ (b) $\tan x = 0.55, x = 29°$
(c) $\tan x = 4.7, x = 78°$

C6 (From C4:)
(a) 38.66°   (b) 1.80°   (c) 68.96°   (d) 41.99°
(From C5:)
(a) 24.23°   (b) 28.81°   (c) 77.99°

C7 $a = 26.57°$ $b = 18.43°$ $c = 68.20°$ $d = 14.04°$

C8 $a = 36.87°$ $b = 51.34°$ $c = 29.74°$ $d = 50.19°$
$e = 23.96°$ $f = 49.40°$ $g = 68.96°$ $h = 59.04°$
$i = 40.60°$

C9 $a = 55.27°$ $b = 50.50°$ $c = 56.05°$ $d = 37.06°$
$e - 64.54°$ $f = 33.50°$ $g = 62.51°$

D Mixed questions (p 216)

D1 (a) 19.1 cm   (b) 10.9 cm   (c) 35.5°   (d) 15.0 cm
(e) 39.6°   (f) 17.7 cm   (g) 20.3 cm

D2 30°

D3 16°

D4 (a) 51.2°   (b) 231.2°

D5 2.6 m

D6 23 m (to the nearest metre)

D7 (a) 320°   (b) 140°

D8 6.0 cm

D9 115.4° and 64.6°

D10 (a) 8.66 cm   (b) 43.30 cm^2

D11 (a) 45°   (b) 12.07 cm   (c) 482.8 cm^2

D12 The area of each triangle is $\tan 60°$. There are 6 triangles
so the area of the hexagon is $(6 \tan 60°)$ cm^2.

D13 8.2 cm

Test yourself (p 219)

T1 (a) 10.6 cm   (b) 64.5°   (c) 10.7 cm   (d) 34.3°

T2 71 m

T3 75.6°

T4 $x = 66.5°$ $y = 113.5°$

T5 17.3 cm

23 Linear equations 2

A Review: forming and solving equations (p 220)

A1 (a) $x = 3$ (b) $x = 2$ (c) $x = 2.8$ or $2\frac{4}{5}$ or $\frac{14}{5}$

(d) $x = 30$ (e) $x = 1$ (f) $x = 11$

(g) $x = ^-3$ (h) $x = 2\frac{1}{2}$ (i) $x = \frac{^-1}{9}$

A2 $4a + 12 = 180$; $42°, 64°, 74°$

A3 28

A4 (a) $6\frac{1}{2}$ (b) 42

B Forming equations to solve word problems (p 221)

B1 (a) $n - 8$ (b) $2n - 8$

(c) $2n - 8 = 100$, $n = 54$
Alan has 54 DVDs and Beth has 46.

B2 (a) $y - 4$ (b) $2y$ (c) $4y - 4$

(d) $4y - 4 = 24$, $y = 7$
Chloe is 7, Becky is 3 and Emily is 14.

B3 (a) $3x + 2 = 56$ (b) $x = 18$

B4 (a) $y + 5$ (b) $4y + 5$

(c) $4y + 5 = 61$, $y = 14$
The cost of one apple is 14p.

B5 (a) $2x + 13$

(b) (i) $5x + 13 = 163$, $x = 30$ (ii) $60\,$g

B6 (a) $n + 80$

(b) (i) $n + 20$ (ii) $n + 100$

(c) (i) $n + 100 = 3(n + 20)$ (ii) £120

B7 (a) $m + 24$

(b) (i) $m + 6$ (ii) $m + 30$

(c) $m + 30 = 4(m + 6)$, $m = 2$
Mary is 2, her mum is 26.

B8 Alex is 11 and his dad is 41.

B9 Abbas is 4 and Brad is 6.

C Mixed questions (p 223)

C1 (a) (i) $x - 5$ (ii) $3x$

(b) (i) $5x - 5 = 25$; $x = 6$ (ii) 18

C2 $52.5°, 52.5°, 75°$

C3 (a) (i) $10x + 4$ (ii) $2x(3x + 2) = 6x^2 + 4x$

(b) $A = 112$

C4 0.5

C5 (a) $104 - 4n$ (b) 91st term

(c) $104 - 4n = ^-150$ gives $n = 63\frac{1}{2}$, so $^-150$ is not a term

C6 Megan 21, Olivia 26

Test yourself (p 224)

T1 (a) $3x + 16 = 32.5$, $x = 5.5$ (b) $13.5\,$cm each

T2 (a) $60x$ (b) $60x + 30 = 240$, $3.5\,$kg

T3 (a) $8x = 5x + 33$ (b) $x = 11$, $17\,$cm

T4 Bryan 66, Chris 33

24 Loci and constructions

A The locus of points a fixed distance from a point or line (p 225)

A1
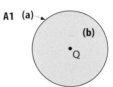

A2
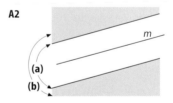

A3
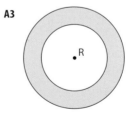

Point X can be marked anywhere in the shaded region.

A4
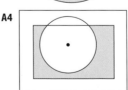

A5
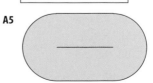

A6

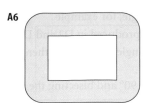

A7

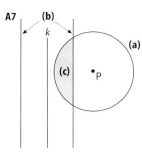

A8

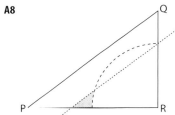

A9 **(a)** The set of points that are more than 2 cm from P and are less than 3 cm from P

(b) The set of points that are less than 3 cm from Q and are less than 2 cm from line *l*

(c) The set of points that are less than 2 cm from R but are more than 1 cm from S

(d) The set of points that are less than 4 cm from T and are less than 4 cm from U

A10

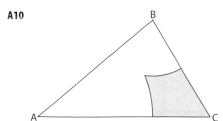

B The locus of points equidistant from two points (p 228)

B1 **(a)** $AP = \sqrt{4^2 + 3^2} = 5$
BP is also 5 units long.

(b) AQ and BQ are both $\sqrt{10}$ units long.

(c) They are both $\sqrt{5}$ units long.

(d) They are both $\sqrt{10}$ units long.

(e) It is the locus of points equidistant from A and B.

B2

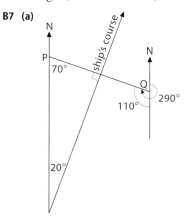

B3 Diagram showing construction of the perpendicular bisector of the line UV. This is the locus of points equidistant from U and V. This locus cuts the circle in two places, which are the required points.

B4

B5 The three perpendicular bisectors should meet at one point.

B6 If the drawing has been done accurately, the circle should go through the other two vertices of the triangle. The point where the perpendicular bisectors meet is called the **circumcentre**, because it is the centre of a circle that goes through all three vertices of the triangle (the **circumcircle**).

B7 **(a)**

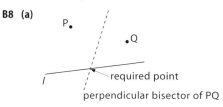

(b) The ship's course is 020°.

B8 **(a)**

(b) The line PQ is perpendicular to *l*.